MARRIAGE AND THE FAMILY IN CANADA TODAY

Edited by

G.N. RAMU

Department of Sociology
University of Manitoba

Prentice-Hall Canada Inc.,
Scarborough, Ontario

Canadian Cataloguing in Publication Data
Main entry under title:
Marriage and the family in Canada today
Bibliography: p.
Includes index.
ISBN 0-13-559196-1
1. Family – Canada.   2. Marriage – Canada.
I. Ramu, G. N., 1937–

HQ559.M37   1988   306.8'0971   C88-093822-6

Quotation on p. 182 reprinted by permission of the publisher from *Ethnic Families in America: Patterns and Varitions*, by Charles H. Mindel and Robert W. Habenstein, p. 428. Copyright © 1976 by Elsevier Science Publishing Co., Inc.

Prentice-Hall, Inc., Englewood Cliffs, New Jersey
Prentice-Hall International, Inc., London
Prentice-Hall of Australia, Pty., Ltd., Sydney
Prentice-Hall of India Pvt., Ltd., New Delhi
Prentice-Hall of Japan, Inc., Tokyo
Prentice-Hall of Southeast Asia (Pte.) Ltd., Singapore
Editora Prentice-Hall do Brasil Ltda., Rio de Janeiro
Prentice-Hall Hispanoamericana, S.A., Mexico

ISBN 0-13-559196-1

Production Editor: Peter Buck
Designer: Denise Marcella
Production Coordinator: Matt Lumsdon
Typesetting: Q Composition

1 2 3 4 5 WC 93 92 91 90 89

Printed and bound in Canada by Webcom Limited

To the memory of my father,
Sri G.B. Nanjappa
—GNR

CONTENTS

PREFACE

This volume is a new version of *Courtship, Marriage, and the Family in Canada*, which appeared in 1979. As with that book, the major purpose of this volume is to present a systematic but cogent summary of significant sociological information on courtship, marriage, family, and related issues in Canada within major theoretical frameworks. Some chapters that appeared in the earlier book have been deleted so as to shift the focus to emerging trends in Canadian marital and family life. However, care has been taken not to neglect any of the substantive issues dealt with in the 1979 version. In fact, this volume includes new chapters on theoretical perspectives, women and work, the family and aging, and family sociology, and features five new contributors who are recognized experts in their area of specialization. It is our collective hope that this volume will provide a comprehensive account of Canadian marital and family patterns.

While the logistics of editing a multi-authored text are complex, and often test one's interpersonal skills, the process certainly tries the limit of the patience of contributors, who are often requested, cajoled, and coerced to revise their chapters many times within short deadlines. My abiding gratitude goes to contributors to this volume, who responded promptly to my numerous requests. I am thankful also to Alan E. Haynes (University of Saskatchewan), Bert Headrick (St. Lawrence College), and David Appavoo (Concordia College), who reviewed the manuscript and provided many useful comments.

It is a great pleasure to work with the editors of Prentice-Hall. Patrick Ferrier, Marta Tomins, David Jolliffe, and Monica Schwalbe efficiently and promptly attended to the intricate pre-publication details. In particular, I am grateful, as are the contributors to be sure, to the excellent editorial skills of Peter Buck. I am certain that this volume has gained in clarity and readability as a result of his patient and careful scrutiny of the manuscript.

Finally, I dedicate this book to the memory of my father, Sri G.B. Nanjappa.

G.N. Ramu
Department of Sociology
University of Manitoba

June 1988

1

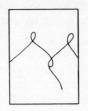

INTRODUCTION

G.N. Ramu

During the past decade, there has been increased concern and debate over the effects of economic, technological, social, legal, and demographic changes on marriage and the family. Although most Canadians will eventually marry in their search for intimacy and stability, the possibilities of alternatives—cohabitation, childlessness, dual-careers, divorce—have altered the grounds of traditional commitments and expectations. Parenthood, the structural core of the family, has also been transformed: couples have fewer children and must socialize them under the increasingly difficult circumstances associated with rapid and widespread social change. All these developments have placed great strains on marriage and the family without fundamentally altering their traditional tasks.

The primary objective of this volume is to account for the changing patterns of marriage and the family in Canada as we approach the end of this century. What are the adaptive capacities of these resilient institutions? Where are we likely to find points of stress and resistance to change? Finally, in order to assess the meaning, rate, and direction of change intelligently, we have to have some understanding of where we stand now. To these ends, each contributor has examined selected empirical materials in the context of major contemporary theoretical perspectives. This approach, we hope, will provide undergraduates (and others interested in these topics) with a broader, more diverse understanding of Canadian marriage and family patterns.

The following assessment of the contributions suggests that, while pockets of resistance to changes in traditional beliefs and values remain, there is a general trend toward change in Canadian marital and family patterns. Part of the tension between stability and change in marital and family life stems from recent changes in both attitudes and behaviour. For example, there has been a sharp decline in the birth rate, resulting in smaller families, as well as an increase in premarital sexual permissiveness and marital dissolution. Moreover, the complex relationship between the family and the maintenance of ethnicity (insofar as the former contributes to the persistence of the latter) has become increasingly tenuous and problematic. The concerted pressure to liberalize divorce laws led to amendments to the Divorce Act in 1986. There are continuing attempts on the part of some who are frustrated with the current marriage and family relationships to engage in "alternative" or "experimental" social arrangements. The net effect of such changes and attempted innovations has been a partial erosion of the stability previously characteristic of Canadian marriage and family patterns.

Although no major empirical study has clearly mapped the direction of such changes, there are numerous suggestions throughout this book that indicate a general convergence toward uniformity in family patterns. For example, in Chapter Four Charles Hobart concludes that, in terms of sexual attitudes and behaviours, marked similarities are evident between francophones and anglophones, on the one hand, and between males and females on the other. Similarly, in Chapter Nine Nicholas Tavuchis argues that the same holds true for family patterns across ethnic lines. In general, although the rates of change may differ among various groups, available evidence suggests increased uniformity. Furthermore, various social policies and legal measures have had the effect, often unintended, of increasing the uniformity of marital and family life. Lacking more reliable data, we can only speculate that the forces of urbanization, industrialization, and secularization have, in fact, not only influenced the direction of change but have also promoted homogeneity rather than diversity.

It is true that the contemporary Canadian family and marital patterns are not as stable as idealists want them to be. The organization of such patterns generally centres around traditional beliefs and values that dictate the type of family that one should form, the nature of marriage, and the manner in which children should be reared. However, adherence to these has historically been uneven. For example, it is questionable whether Canadian families remained intact during the Depression and two World Wars. The problems they faced during such periods of social upheaval necessitated departure from traditional patterns, even if only for short periods of time. This would suggest that families as well as individuals tend to respond both to external pressures and to personal needs. What may be disconcerting to the contemporary observers is the pace and the degree of changes that are occurring in certain aspects of marital and family life.

Despite the rapidity and magnitude of transformations of marriage and the family, there is insufficient evidence to conclude that they are on the verge of dissolution. The obvious instability of marriage as an enduring partnership and the possibility of competing arrangements have not drastically altered the general perception among most Canadians that it is an experience worth trying at least once. Most of those who try remain married to the same person for the rest of their lives. Likewise, the family's importance in performing the taxing but necessary task of reproducing and training successive generations of Canadians is acknowledged by the overwhelming majority of married couples, although the form and content of primary socialization have changed in many ways. This demonstrates that a considerable degree of innovation in these institutions is taking place mainly because most Canadians value them and choose to restructure rather than abandon them. For example, very few of the experimental patterns of the 1960s and 1970s have gained significant ground in Canada. The closest we have come to replacing marriage is cohabitation, or, as it is popularly known, "living together," and even that has in recent years assumed the legal and social characteristics of traditional marriage. Consequently, contemporary efforts to restructure marriage and the family in Canada are directed mainly at making these institutions more efficient and satisfying than they were in the past, and at meeting the personal needs of those who marry and form families.

THEORETICAL APPROACHES

In general, sociological theories offer perspectives or frameworks for understanding social events such as marriage, birth, death, dissolution, and other family matters. From this point of view, theories are ways of cogently and systematically presenting and interpreting social facts by way of abstract propositions. As David Cheal notes in Chapter Two, in the sociology of the family many theoretical frameworks provide different ways of illuminating family structures (forms), processes (change), and relationships.

In reviewing Cheal's discussion, two points should be kept in mind. First, until recently, the sociology of the family in English Canada had not received the same degree of attention as other fields mainly because the family was taken for granted. Family relations were perceived by many scholars as less problematic and interesting subjects than, for example, social inequality, ethnic relations, or criminal behaviour. This is not to suggest that there were no empirical (practical) studies of families in various contexts; there were. However, these were mainly descriptive accounts that lacked a critical application of the major theoretical perspectives that informed the sociological approach to family life in the United States. Second, Cheal's contribution is not intended to provide summaries of major theoretical approaches in the sociology of the family (interested students may consult standard works, for example, Nye and Berardo, 1981; Morgan, 1975; Burr et al., 1979, that are readily available in most libraries), but rather to document past and contemporary theoretical trends reflected specifically in the literature on family life in anglophone Canada.

Cheal identifies two broad and relatively distinctive categories. The first is what he calls "standard sociological theory," including structural functionalism and the developmental cycle approach, that held sway in American family sociology in the 1950s and 1960s. The second and competing set of paradigms (models) consists (either singly or as an amalgam) of feminist, Marxist, and political economy approaches. These paradigms have attempted to place marriage and the family in broader social and historical contexts.

Although structural functionalists have dominated American sociology for several decades, their influence on the study of Canadian family relations was minimal. Structural functionalists view the family as part of a broader social system; the family's main task is to perform certain critical tasks or "functions"—sexuality, reproduction, socialization, and economic activities—necessary not only for the family itself but also for society as a whole. They conceptualize the family as a harmonious and stable institution linked to other social institutions such as the economy, polity, religion, and education. In Canada, Ishwaran (1983) and Schlesinger (1979) have used this perspective in their frequent discussions of the social characteristics of families and their common functions in different social environments and economic conditions. Furthermore, structural functionalism conceptualizes families as systems that protect and support their members in achieving personal and group goals. Consequently, the stress of this approach is on the strengths rather than the weaknesses of the family. The family is held to be an adaptive system creatively responding to individual and social needs. This dimension of the structural functionalist approach has been particularly useful for Canadian social gerontologists in their analysis of the family as a support system and giver of care to its elderly.

The developmental approach analyzes the family in relation to its life cycle, thus introducing a socio-temporal dimension and the idea of family phases. Like the individual, the family goes through a life cycle which begins with the marriage of a man and woman and ends with death or divorce. During this cycle changes occur in the family's composition and in the roles its members perform. There are specific "developmental tasks" or functions that are related to the age and presence of children or others in the home. Lupri and Frideres (1981:283), who have used this approach in their research into marital satisfaction among a sample of couples in Calgary, assert its value in the following terms: "[the findings] demonstrate the usefulness of conceptualizing the family as a unit with a set of developmental task requirements inside and outside the household."

As noted earlier, the standard sociological theory was not systematically employed by researchers, nor did it influence how sociologists interpreted family life in anglophone Canada. As Cheal notes, the introduction of feminist interests, concerns, and orientations in the 1970s and 1980s dramatically changed this situation. The feminist approach considers the nature of family life problematic in both personal and political terms. It raises questions about the influence of wider economic relations on domestic relations, especially the role of women. The intimate interior of the family is not perceived as embodying harmony, interdependence, and stability. Instead, feminists see it as an arena in which inequality and exploitation are institutionally perpetuated.

In his exploration of how feminist writers have influenced the analysis of family in Canada, Cheal discusses three dominant approaches: feminist, Marxist, and political economy. The key element in the feminist approach is the notion of patriarchy, that is, the political and social control of women by men. Patriarchal relations signify an internal stratification of family life in which men exercise power and control over women and derive more benefits than women. While the feminist approach to family has yet to be systematically developed in Canada, it has successfully challenged the functionalist view that the family is an adaptive system. Its proponents argue that family life entails different economic and social interests for men and women which lead to conflict and struggle as well as harmony and integration. They also take the position that, since it has led to the oppression of the female by the male, the gender-based division of labour is neither functional nor conducive to an equitable distribution of power.

There is a historical link between feminist and Marxist approaches. Cheal notes that the Marxist approach to Canadian family life has emphasized the relationship between unpaid work at home (domestic labour by women) and paid work in a capitalist economy. The Marxist approach deals with issues such as the separation of family life from industrial production, the social construction of women's dependence upon men within the family, and the benefits of women's unpaid labour for the owners of capital.

Finally, the political economy or critical approach, drawn mainly from Marxism, is concerned with the relations between the demands for labour in capitalist enterprises and the reproduction of labourers in working-class families. Those committed to this school in their analysis of family life contend that the state serves the interests of capital by encouraging working-class families to reproduce themselves and, in so doing, effectively maintain the dependent status of women within the family.

In brief, studies based on feminist assumptions display a common and recurrent theme: the subordination of women in the contemporary Canadian family. Cheal suggests that the polarization of standard theory and feminist approaches has precluded a constructive debate about the relative strengths and weaknesses different perspectives possess to contribute to a better understanding of marriage and the family in Canada.

COURTSHIP AND MATE SELECTION

In Canada, as in other modern industrial societies, marriage is increasingly perceived as an essentially secular arrangement supported by various legal rights and obligations rather than as a sacred institution. Its basic features ideally include a relatively enduring commitment between two individuals, based on each partner's ability and desire to meet the needs of the other, such as love, affection, communication, companionship, finance, sex, and parenthood. At the same time, implicit but powerful traditional definitions, such as gender-based domestic roles, continue to temper the idea of marriage as a total association in which both partners enjoy equality in all aspects of their lives.

Consistent with the contemporary approach to marriage is the belief that selection of one's marriage partner is primarily an individual matter, although certain structural controls restrict the field of eligible mates in the marriage market. Adolescents are encouraged to come together under various conditions with the ultimate goal of selecting the most suitable person for marriage. The varied and often protracted relationship between an unmarried adult male and female who intend to marry is formally (and technically) referred to as the courtship process. While the main objective of the Canadian courtship process has remained relatively constant for many decades, courtship behaviours have tended to shift in response to the changes in the value systems that govern not only the young but society in general.

Chapter Three notes that Canadian courtship patterns are governed by a complex interplay of subjective considerations and structural, objective conditions. The latter conditions that influence a couple's decision to marry are many and include, among other things, personal attributes, socio-economic status, and area of residence (urban or rural). It is also taken for granted that one chooses a partner following a more or less extended courtship and that relations during this period entail intimate emotional and sexual ties. In some settings courtship may include traditional dating; in others, group encounters or alternative arrangements prevail. Similarly, some individuals may deem it necessary to live with their potential spouse for a certain period of time while some others may follow the traditional pattern of dating, engagement, and marriage.

Nevertheless, there is considerable evidence to show that only after structural determinants, such as residential propinquity, social class, religion, race, and ethnicity, have taken effect do personal and psychological attributes begin to play an important part in the ultimate choice of a person's partner. Chapter Three reminds us that various social controls reflecting endogamous (marriage between numbers of a group) values and norms create generally homogeneous marriage markets: roughly two thirds of Canadians marry persons of their own "kind."

Premarital Sexuality

In recent decades, premarital sexual relationships have become an important component of mate selection in Canada. On the one hand, during the 1960s, 1970s, and 1980s, premarital sexual intimacy, in practice, came to be defined as a recreational activity for partners with no serious intention of marriage. On the other hand, it has been accepted socially as the expression of one's romantic commitment to a potential marriage partner. For whatever reason, Canadian attitudes and behaviour concerning premarital sexuality have undergone substantial changes, as Hobart documents in Chapter Four.

What is the impact of changing sexual standards on the courtship process? To what extent do premarital sexual relationships precipitate or remain independent of the decision to marry? Hobart has attempted to glean some clues to such questions by placing Canadian premarital sexual relationships in a broader historical context and against a background of changing social definitions and mores. Based on his own research and other empirical and theoretical materials, Hobart identifies a general transition in sexual standards from a traditional morality to a new morality. At one end of the spectrum, the old morality advocated abstinence—no sex before marriage—and at the other supported a double standard—premarital sex as a male prerogative denied to females, with the exception of those viewed as being outside the marriage market, such as lower class women and prostitutes. The new morality advocated by many young people sees extramarital sex as an equally legitimate alternative to sex exclusively within the bounds of marriage. For example, the "Love Standard," asserted by the vast majority of university students in the last two decades, represents intercourse as acceptable between *loving* partners, regardless of their marital intentions or status. Mutual love and affection are claimed to be sufficient justifications for sex. A radical extension of this new morality is the "Fun Standard," whose supporters assert that sex is acceptable between willing partners whatever their marital status, the stage of the courtship process, or affectional commitment.

While it is true that the degree of a person's sexual permissiveness depends largely on his or her family, ethnic, religious, social class, and community (rural or urban) backgrounds, there are converging trends in Canada (and in the United States) that cut across regional and cultural boundaries. As Hobart suggests, younger Canadians are becoming increasingly permissive, although the pull is toward the Love Standard rather than the Fun Standard. While the Double Standard persists, at least attitudinally, females seem to be "catching up" with males in their premarital sexual activities in the sense that they are following male sexual patterns.

Finally, Hobart alludes to the moderating effect that the threat of certain sexually transmitted diseases has on premarital sexual permissiveness. While systematic evidence on this point is not yet available, given the serious consequences of such diseases as herpes and AIDS, individuals are likely to be cautious in engaging in what has been termed "recreational sex."

ASPECTS OF MARRIAGE AND THE FAMILY

Family formation is an intricate and protracted process tempered by culture, class, ethnicity, kinship, and religion, among other social determinants. Social concern with the family stems from numerous considerations, but for our purposes, as noted in Chapter Three, two are especially pertinent: reproduction and socialization. Both are essential to the orderly continuity of the population and social organization, and both are, in most societies, the responsibility of the family.

A relatively stable population is critical to the survival and prosperity of institutions such as the economy, polity, and so on. It is not enough, however, that children are born in an identifiable and accountable unit: they also have to be protected, comforted, and trained for a long period of time before they become fully accredited members of society. Children have to be introduced to important elements of social organization such as norms, values, roles, language, and customs in order for them to become fully social beings. This process is known as socialization.

The discussion in Chapter Five should be considered against this background. The socio-demographic profile of marriage and the family in Canada clearly reflects two general trends indicative of the tensions between the commitment to conventional forms of social life and ideas of freedom and individualism widely propagated in our society. On the one hand, the demographic evidence presented in Chapter Five clearly shows that most Canadians are not yet disenchanted with marriage and family, nor have they forsaken them for other arrangements in that the vast majority of them marry, live together as a family, and continue to bear and rear children, although in fewer numbers than in previous decades.

By contrast, a significant minority of Canadians are questioning many of the traditional assumptions. For example, there has been an increase in the proportions of couples who remain voluntarily childless, of individuals remaining single, and of couples living together without formal marriage. In addition, relatively high divorce rates indicate greater reluctance to stay in an unsatisfactory marriage. Finally, the unprecedented entry of married women into the labour force has meant that husbands are no longer sole breadwinners, which in turn suggests eventual changes in the domestic division of labour and a redefinition of marital and familial roles. Such developments reflect the fact that individuals can now tailor the type of marital and family relationships they desire, within certain social and legal constraints, so as to suit their personal goals and preferences.

The availability of family choices has clearly undermined the monolithic "one size fits all" nature of marriage and family patterns in Canada. Nevertheless, the increase and acceptance of the various alternative arrangements have led, in many instances, to uncertainty, confusion, and discrepant expectations. The legitimate coexistence of these arrangements with traditional patterns may eventually force a new synthesis of the old and the new that would warrant new definitions of marriage and family.

Socialization

As noted previously, it is through the complex process of socialization that an infant is trained in those skills that are deemed necessary for full accreditation as a member of society. Socialization entails, among other things, the conferring of initial and consequential identities such as gender, ethnicity, class, and religion, and the provision (or lack thereof) of opportunities for educational and occupational accomplishments.

In virtually all societies the family is entrusted with the critical responsibility of inculcating the significant social heritage among its new members. However, in industrial societies such as Canada the family's responsibility for this task is declining owing to changes within the family and the influence of outside forces, as Marlene Mackie points out in Chapter Six. About two decades ago the nature and purpose of socialization was generally taken for granted since the domestic division of labour in most families was also taken for granted: women stayed home and raised children while their husbands worked. Furthermore, families were less influenced by such powerful forces as mass communication, technology, and the proliferation of "experts" in the matter of raising children. Instead of focusing on conventional theories of socialization, Mackie draws our attention to shifts in contemporary contexts of socialization. The process of socialization has become extremely complex and difficult, especially in the face of powerful countervailing and competing agents such as television, peer groups, and pop culture. As a consequence, parents increasingly experience difficulty in striking a balance between demands for permissiveness and their duties of responsible parenthood. There is little doubt that the family's historical role in bringing up children has been severely challenged and subject to enormous pressures. And it is equally true that this has not necessarily resulted from a lack of parental concern or responsibility.

Marriage, Women, and Work

The emergence of various forms of feminism in the last two decades or so has made an indelible mark on marital and family life in Canada. Not since the Industrial Revolution and, more recently, the Victorian period, has a social movement generated such fundamental alterations in the ways in which marriage and the family have been perceived, defined, and questioned in Western societies. The traditional division of labour based on male dominance in the market place or within the family is under siege, despite the pockets of resistance. The changes have essentially come from women who no longer believe that "biology is destiny" and men who have responded positively, albeit reluctantly, to changes. Although some feminist scholars in Canada have made serious attempts to document the role of women in various sectors of society (see, for example, Armstrong and Armstrong, 1978, 1979; Luxton, 1980; Eichler, 1983), mainstream family sociologists have not yet focused their attention on the impact of feminist ideals on marital and family systems. (For an assessment of the feminist paradigms in Canadian sociology, see Eichler, 1985; also, see Chapter Two.)

In a preliminary attempt to redress this deficiency, Pat Armstrong examines in Chapter Seven the relationships between selected aspects of the formal economy and family structures in Canada. She discusses how the roles Canadian men and women play both in the economy and in the family are affected by considerations such as competing ideologies, educational development, and demographic patterns. Armstrong concludes that one cannot properly understand the marital and family roles without understanding the economic and political forces that determine the positions of men and women in the market place.

Canada's Aging Population

In Chapter Ten, Neena Chappell draws our attention to an area that is becoming increasingly prominent in the study of family life—intergenerational relations. The demographic evidence suggests that by the year 2030 approximately 20 percent of the Canadian population will be defined as "aged" (65 years or over), and of this group about 45 percent will be 75 or older. In effect, the population now defined as elderly is itself aging; the proportions of the "old" old compared to the "young" old is increasing. This growing segment of the Canadian demographic mosaic has serious implications not only for the family in terms of its role and responsibility for its elders, but also for social policies. Chappell outlines how the Canadian family has adapted itself to this changing demographic situation, and also delineates the patterns of response by Canadian health care systems and policy makers.

Contrary to the argument that the nuclear family tends to neglect its needy kin, Chappell provides substantial evidence to support the view that extended kin networks have become an important source of personal care to the aged in contemporary society. Those kin who provide sustained support to the elderly tend to be women, usually wives and daughters.

Nevertheless, non-familial support systems, such as neighbours and friends, also play a crucial role in times of need for the elderly.

While the role of kin in providing informal care to the elderly is crucial, Chappell underscores the importance of formal care systems and the complex problems they face, although they serve only about 20 percent of aged Canadians. She also raises the difficult policy issue concerning our approach to the utilitarian role of the aged in contemporary Canadian society. While our contemporary elderly seem to have established the importance of extended family ties, they are uncertain of their ability to shape future events.

DIVORCE AND REMARRIAGE

As indicated in the preceding discussion on courtship and marriage, the freedom of choice in mate selection and various socio-psychological expectations of marriage have contributed to a shift in the contemporary attitude toward marriage. It has come to be seen as a voluntary association. The sense of permanence which is endemic to any institution is weakened under such an arrangement. The stability of marriage is a function of the stability of mutual and exclusive commitment, love, and the ability to meet the myriad needs of the partners. Divorce often results when there is a serious decline of such a commitment or when people have high or unrealistic expectations that are not fulfilled.

Marriage in our society is viewed ideally as taking precedence over all other relationships—filial, sibling, friendship, and so on. It is the only relationship where we see a convergence of needs—biological, psychological, economic, and social—and a sustained arrangement to meet these needs in a specific dyad (two persons in interaction). The pressures placed on this bond are extremely heavy and intense. Hence, there is a concerted societal effort to preserve the stability of marriage. The legal framework, until recently, has contributed to this conservative effort. Yet, as evident in the divorce statistics presented in Chapter Eleven, a small but increasing proportion of married individuals seem to be unhappy, mainly because their spouses have not been able to deliver what has been anticipated. Thus, divorce is not only indicative of the inability or unwillingness to cope with and adapt to such enormous pressures, but also represents a social mechanism for dealing with unhappy marriages where commitment, communication, and affection no longer exist. From this perspective, divorce serves as an alternative to troubled marriages.

In his chapter on Divorce and Remarriage, John Peters summarizes the changes in divorce laws and places them in broader social contexts. In addition to providing statistical evidence on the incidence of divorce in Canada, he discusses the impact of divorce on children and the emerging family and marital patterns among those who divorce.

The data on the incidence of divorce in Canada presented in Chapter Eleven suggest that although there was a steady increase between 1969 and 1982, since 1983 there has been a gradual decline. Also, while the high incidence of divorce in the 1970s and early 1980s was unprecedented in Canadian history, in comparison with other industrial societies the figures are rather low. For example, among the Western nations, the United States has the highest rate while Canada, Sweden, and Australia have comparably low rates.

Nevertheless, there is a myth perpetuated by some social commentators and mass media to the effect that a significant proportion of marriages are doomed to end in divorce (see, for example, Gordon, 1972, and Lauer and Lauer, 1985). Statements such as "every second or third marriage will end in divorce these days" are commonly heard. There is little empirical support for such declarations. For example, in his preliminary report on the data from the Family History Survey, Burch (1985:10-16) attempts to counter such assertions. Of the 6750 males and 7250 females between the ages of 18 and 64 years interviewed for the survey, only 14 percent and 17.1 percent of ever-married males and females respectively reported divorce or separation (Burch, 1985:12). In sum, if we can extend these findings to the Canadian population, in 1984 about 15 percent of Canadians have either separated or divorced.

The Family History Survey also points out that an analysis of remarriage rates among the respondents indicates that only a fraction of a percent had remarried more than twice (Burch, 1985:11). A significant finding of the survey is the relationship between the incidence of divorce and the period during which the marriages were contracted. For example, of those who married between 1934 and 1944 only eight percent divorced, while 18 percent of those who married during the period from 1960 to 1969 did so (Burch and Madan, 1986:12). These findings suggest that the high degree of public alarm on the rising divorce rate has no empirical support. Important to note also is that declining marriage rates, the rise in the age at marriage, the increasing number of singles and the voluntarily childless, and the increasing number of those who live together without legal marriage may have contributed to smaller marriage cohorts (a group of persons married in a given year) that have led to a slight decline in marriage. This in turn appears to have cumulatively contributed to the recent declines in the divorce rate.

While the divorce rates are stabilizing, issues related to divorce—flexibility in divorce laws, social support for single parents, custody rights—continue to be at the centre of legal and social policy debates in Canada. As part of his discussion of these issues Peters (Chapter Eleven) traces the evolution of divorce laws in Canada with a particular emphasis on changes since 1968. Historically, divorce laws in Canada were aimed at the preservation of the traditional marriage and family, characterized by sexual division of labour, the wife's dependent role, assumptions of the permanence of marriage, and penalties for those who violated these norms and values. Consequently, divorce was granted only upon the establishment of "fault" by either of the spouses; such a procedure was acrimonious and time-consuming. As Peters points out, legal reform in 1968 changed this situation by making it possible for spouses to seek divorce on the grounds of "marital breakdown," which included, among other criteria, a three-year separation. The 1986 amendments to the Divorce Act while retaining the matrimonial offences and marital breakdown clauses, reduced the compulsory three-year separation period to one year. In brief, the fundamental change reflected in the 1986 Divorce Act lies in its recognition of equal rights of spouses in property and children, of the need to minimize adversarial relations generated by divorce proceedings, and of the opportunities for voluntary withdrawal from a contentious marriage.

These reforms clearly broke the historical inflexibility of the Canadian approach to divorce. They were the result of a long and painful public debate and are an acknowledgment of the decline, if not the demise, of the traditional perception of marital relations.

Peters' discussion of divorce and remarriage underscores the implicit tensions between the traditional values that emphasize the continuity of old ways and changes that direct us to new patterns. On the one hand, it is clear that marriage as a social institution continues to thrive in Canada. On the other hand, the increasing divorce rate clearly reflects the relative ease of obtaining legal divorce, individuals' high expectations of marriage and their reluctance to tolerate situations that do not fulfill expectations and perceived needs. In effect, what determines the stability of marriage are not religious bonds or social pressures from kith and kin, but the nature and quality of interpersonal relationships. In this sense, divorce and remarriage patterns signify the changing definition of marriage among some Canadians. Increasingly, divorce is perceived by many not as a negation of the significance or the virtue of marriage but simply as a rejection of an undesirable partner. Since the average Canadian (given contemporary figures of longevity) will be married for more than half a century, and considers marriage the most important relationship in life, it makes little sense to continue a relationship characterized by conflict. Thus, from this point of view, divorce can be seen as a positive solution. This is not to ignore the overwhelming economic, emotional, and social problems created by divorce for the majority of women and children: these can best be addressed by providing equal opportunities to women, and by stricter enforcement of laws pertaining to alimony and child support (see Dulude, 1984).

URBAN FAMILY TIES IN KINSHIP AND ETHNIC CONTEXTS

The relationship between the family and other social institutions and processes is an important area of concern and analysis. Unfortunately our present knowledge is inadequate and superficial. The influence of religion, government, the economy, and the mass media on contemporary Canadian families, and vice versa, is far from clear. Although there have been many theoretical allusions to these relations, we have few empirical insights into them. In Chapter Eight and Chapter Nine, attempts have been made to identify the relationship of the family to two crucial dimensions of Canadian society: kinship networks and ethnic patterns. The linkages between the family and kinship network and ethnicity are well institutionalized; however, as the discussions in Chapter Eight and especially Chapter Nine suggest, gradual changes are underway.

Chapter Eight is an attempt to identify the nature and significance of urban kinship networks in Canadian society and contains the suggestion that most Canadian families are nuclear in structure and autonomous. Kinship networks are maintained not so much on the basis of a binding obligation or as an element of social organization, but on voluntary and selective criteria. People choose certain kin from those available for social and sentimental purposes as well as for pragmatic concerns involving mutual aid. The number of relatives so chosen, the frequency of visits, and the nature of interaction are to a large extent determined by residential proximity, class differences, mutual interests, and genealogical distance. Evident in the literature is a persistence of values that maintains extended-kin contacts and the nuclear family's continuing role as the primary medium through which kin solidarity is expressed. Although there appears to be a general preference to be close to primary kin, especially parents and siblings, geographic mobility is common and there is contradictory evidence as to how this has affected the functioning of kin networks. Available data suggest that the relevance and importance attached to kin varies from one ethnic group to the other: for example, unlike British-Canadians, French- and Italian-Canadians maintain a cohesive kin structure which is reinforced by frequent visits, mutual aid, ritual occasions, and so on. Despite popular notions of the shallow, impersonal, and egocentric nature of urban family bonds, studies cited in Chapter Eight clearly show that one usually turns to relatives in times of personal joy or crisis. Moreover, occasions such as baptism, confirmation, marriage, funerals, and civic and religious holidays act as foci for the cultivation of kinship solidarity. In short, urban kinship networks continue to play an important role in linking individuals and families to wider structures and providing emotional satisfaction and a variety of services including mutual aid.

In Chapter Nine Nicholas Tavuchis attempts to untangle the intricate relationship between ethnicity and family. As he notes, in a society which emphasizes ethnic pluralism the family has a strategic significance. It has the prime responsibility of socializing the next generation to its beliefs and practices which are in turn derived from ethnic culture. Consequently, the family becomes the first line of defence against assimilative influences.

According to Tavuchis, the family as an institution is inextricably linked to the vitality and persistence of ethnicity insofar as it is able and willing to foster allegiance and conformity to traditions. First-generation immigrants and certain persecuted minority groups, such as Anabaptist and Jewish groups, tend to resist acculturation into the larger Canadian society. Until the 1950s the French-Canadians also resisted the influence of modern secular forces, including cultural assimilation by the dominant English-speaking group.

However, the Canadian family as a rampart of ethnicity has lost ground rapidly in recent decades: Tavuchis suggests three reasons for this. First the unavoidable and irresistible forces of industrialization exert pressures toward convergence in all aspects of social life, including the family. Uniformity is reflected in the birth rate, the nature of family life, kinship orientations, and adherence to standardized legal codes pertaining to marriage and divorce. Second, the English language and English-Canadian culture are pervasive. They dominate the media, which press toward homogeneity, ethnicity increasingly being pushed into the background, as the experience of French-Canadian and Polish-Canadian families illustrates. Third, courtship practices, such as dating and premarital sex, interfere with the continuity of particular ethnic differences. Further, ethnic intermarriages over time reduce the prospects of the survival of ethnic differences In sum, Tavuchis argues that despite the pockets of resistance, ethnic family patterns are losing their distinctiveness and converging toward a general Canadian pattern that mirrors urban industrial societies throughout the world.

SOCIAL POLICIES AND THE FAMILY

In recent years, political and legal institutions have come to play a greater role in determining the nature and organization of marital and family life in Canada than they did in the past. Joseph Ryant examines the demographic and the ideological changes that have spurred various social policies and are reflected in myriad rules, regulations, statutes, and codes designed to address the various problems confronting family life in Canada. He also alludes to the limited scope of many of the policies and programs, particularly those related to the economic concerns. Nevertheless, as Ryant acknowledges, although we can unearth some rudiments of a family policy in Canada. we simply do not have a unified approach to marriage and the family. In this regard we are far behind Sweden and other Western countries.

For example, there are no consistent policies on universal daycare for children, facilities for the aged and handicapped, or guaranteed annual income, all of which may be critical to the well-being of the family in Canada.

ALTERNATIVES

The sustained durability of marriage and the family in the face of many challenges and changes raises the question of periodic efforts by individuals and groups to search for alternate social arrangements that reflect their values and desires. Historically, such efforts date back to Plato, who held that marriage and family diminish a person's commitment to the State, and hence should be abolished in favour of the pursuit of excellence and virtue. Following Engels's (1942) discourse on the monogamous family as the first expression of capitalism, Bolsheviks in Soviet Russia between 1918 and 1936 engaged in an abortive effort to reconstruct family patterns. During this century, many Jewish immigrants in areas which are now part of Israel successfully instituted a communal form of family (Spiro, 1956). In the 1960s, numerous communes were established in the United States that attempted to modify or abolish existing family patterns, both on a religious and a secular basis (Kanter, 1977).

In the last two decades several attempts have been made by individuals and groups to institute alternate patterns to contemporary marriage and family forms. Yet one should recognize that the potential impact of these movements or arrangements goes beyond sheer numbers or their more notorious practices. For example, the practice of "living together" before marriage has begun to alter our courtship careers and residential arrangements. Similarly, the drawing up of a contract stipulating details of obligations, rights, and routine chores, if it were to become popular, would change the nature of marital relations.

In Chapter Thirteen, Robert Whitehurst examines the factors that have led to the emergence and decline of the alternative life styles. In general, he notes that the Canadian experiments in the 1960s and 1970s followed the main outlines of these movements in the United States and few major differences exist in these patterns. He attributes the emergence of variant family movement to the rise of liberalism that followed McCarthyism in the United States, to economic inequalities that led to movements against poverty and discrimination, to racism, to the role of mass media (especially television), to liberal educational practices, and to the influence of certain forms of Eastern religions. He further argues that the post-war affluence and excessive materialistic concerns of the parents of the 1950s and 1960s led their children to question the mainstream values concerning the economic success, politics, sexism, sexual mores, marriage, family, and the Vietnam war.

Young people reacted not only by violently opposing war in Vietnam but also by devising different marital and family patterns that were represented by, for example, hippies, communes, and swinging, which lasted only for brief periods of time and failed to leave any major impact on social institutions. As Whitehurst notes, while these movements may not have achieved their goals they did leave a mark at the time. Today vestiges of some of their activities are evident in, for example, contemporary permissive sexual attitudes and behaviour. An important consequence of experiments of the 1960s is greater social tolerance and the accommodation of many patterns of family and marriage, such as single parents, childless couples, cohabiting couples, and dual-earner families, that were once viewed as deviant.

Whitehurst examines why such movements and arrangements failed. Among other developments, he cites changing economic conditions (recession, inflation, impending shortages, unemployment, and the general decline of the economy in the early 1970s), the widespread disillusionment of young people with the outcome of the 1960s movements and with the fact they had aged. He also mentions their fear of sexual diseases, negative public reaction to communes, swinging, and the like, and tolerance to other patterns such as living together, premarital sexuality, and dual-earner families. Since the 1960s, according to Whitehurst, there has also been a shift of attention to other issues such as the environment and poverty.

In brief, Whitehurst points out that in North America, although the nature and form of one's marital and family life are legitimately matters of personal choice (with limits, of course), the widespread tendency of people to conform to mainstream norms will likely result in more stability than change.

CONCLUSION

Our primary task in this volume is to provide an overview of the significant research in the area of courtship, marriage, and the family in Canada. This is a difficult task for two reasons. First and most obvious, research interest in the sociology of marriage and the family is only now beginning to stir. While feminists and others have succeeded in accounting for the relationship between men and women in the wider economic, political, and historical contexts, numerous gaps remain in our knowledge. Even a cursory review of most chapters reveals that the authors have based their analyses on only a handful of research articles and monographs. Second, because of the aforementioned problems, many contributors dwell upon theoretical aspects instead of concrete evidence, while some other topics are treated rather descriptively. Perhaps such problems are endemic to an area which has not attracted a great deal of empirical research. Nevertheless, such an observation should not discourage an analysis of the reasons for these problems, nor should it discourage possible corrective measures for the lethargic pace of research in the areas discussed throughout this volume.

Based on our understanding of the discussions, it appears that research on marriage and family patterns in Canada, with some notable exceptions (for example, women and the family) continues to be fragmented: it lacks direction and fails to meet the standards found in research undertaken in other developed nations, regardless of size. With some exceptions, our overall research efforts do not seem to be related to larger trends or theoretical foci. To be sure, gains have been made by some researchers who have directed their sustained attention to certain specific problems, such as Hobart on premarital sexuality. However, it would take the efforts of a large contingent of researchers to bridge the gaps in our knowledge. We hope that our overview of the field in this volume will serve as a benchmark for what we have accomplished so far, and what needs to be done in the future.

2

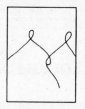

THEORETICAL FRAMEWORKS

David Cheal

*T*he study of family life is a lively area in contemporary social theory. It has been the subject of a vigorous debate over fundamental issues of methods and approaches, and it continues to generate important questions in the social sciences today. In this chapter, we shall examine the major theoretical approaches to family studies in anglophone Canada, emphasizing their differences and the reasons for variations.

Until recently, theorizing about family life was uncommon in Canada. National preoccupations with ethnicity, income inequality, and economic change led social scientists to pay relatively little attention to families, and approaches to the study of family tended to be descriptive rather than theoretical. With the growth of feminism in the late 1960s the nature of family life was seen both as a personal and a political problem and the theory of the family took on a prominent place in feminist scholarship.

At this time Canadian theorists began to develop their own distinctive emphases and concerns in family studies. This does not mean that other theoretical approaches were previously absent from Canadian sociology. On the contrary, all social scientific research is grounded in some theoretical approach, even if it is not explicit. In fact, the theoretical foundations of most Canadian family studies were largely implicit, and they aroused little interest. Scholarly attempts to raise theoretical issues (for example, Ishwaran, 1971) found that the wide audience necessary to sustain a critical debate was lacking. The rise of the feminist movement created that audience, and it encouraged women in sociology to express the causes of their complaints (Mackie, 1983:13-15; Eichler, 1985b). In the following pages we shall describe what feminist sociologists reacted against, and we shall outline the directions they have taken in their attempts to transform the sociology of the family.

STANDARD SOCIOLOGICAL THEORY

According to sociological custom social life consists of individuals who belong to families, which are in turn the building blocks of societies. Concepts such as the individual, the family, and society lie at the heart of the theoretical approach which Mullins (1973) has labeled Standard American Sociology. I shall refer to such an approach here as standard sociological theory.[1]

In the standard theory of family life *the family* is the principal unit of analysis, the unit which has been called "the familial system" (Winch, 1977:2). According to Hill (1971:12), the family is a system because it has the following characteristics:

> 1) family members occupy various positions which are in a state of interdependence, that is, a change in the behavior of one member leads to a change in the behavior of other members; 2) the family is a relatively closed, boundary-maintaining unit; 3) the family is an equilibrium-seeking and adaptive organization; 4) the family is a task performing unit that meets both the requirements of external agencies in the society, and the internal needs and demands of its members.

As Hill acknowledges (1971:15), the use of systems concepts in sociology is rooted in an approach known as structural functionalism, which holds that any major social institution operates to ensure the well-being of individuals and of the society to which those individuals belong. The family is therefore believed to perform such essential functions as socialization and reproduction which are critical for individuals and society. Ishwaran (1983) tends to take this approach: in his frequent discussions of the social characteristics of families he speaks in terms of their common functions in different social environments and economic conditions.

Sociologists who adhere to the structural functional approach believe that each of the various institutions, such as religion, polity, economy, and education, performs in any society specialized tasks which complement the others to produce an integrated social order. They are particularly interested in the family as a primary group that meets a narrow range of emotional needs as a result of its relations with other social groups. Furthermore, they often assert that the family in modern societies is losing many of its traditional functions to formal organizations such as schools, hospitals, and social service agencies. If such an assertion is valid, then it must have considerable relevance for those professions which provide services to families. Schlesinger (1979:170) explicitly addresses these issues in his observations on social change in Canada:

> The family has lost many of its functions or has experienced a reduction of them. In our past, when we lived in small, often isolated communities, the family functioned as a production unit, a consumption unit, a religious unit, an educational unit, a socialization unit, an affectional unit and a protective unit. In Canada today, the family is certainly no longer a production unit, and it is increasingly not a consumption unit. Usually it does not function as a religious unit or as an educational unit. The family is increasingly less important as a unit of socialization. It has less and less impact on the child, as specialized institutions emerge that strongly affect him/her. Moreover, the family in most cases is not a strong affectional unit. It must compete with many other sources of affection. And is it a protective unit? What about the impact of our social services, including medical insurance?

Despite the apparent uncertainty about the future of the family, Schlesinger believes that it will not disappear. Rather, he asserts that the family's new function will be "to provide emotional security to people living in a vast, impersonal society" (Schlesinger, 1979:171). He contends that "no other institutions that can serve this function on a dependable and lasting basis are in sight" (Schlesinger, 1979:171).

Schlesinger's faith in the ability of the family to adapt to changing social conditions is consistent with the principles of standard sociological theory. Standard theorists, structural functionalists in particular, conceptualize the family as a system that enables individuals to adapt to changes in the larger society. This is achieved through an internal specialization of family roles in which the various problems that family members face are resolved. In time, it is thought, successful solutions to problems are stabilized in a common culture of social rules, or norms. Patterns of family interaction are therefore believed to be supported by a general consensus among family members on what is deemed appropriate and useful behaviour.

Standard theorists often think of families as support systems that protect their members and that help them to achieve their goals. As a result, the standard sociological literature emphasizes the family's strengths rather than its weaknesses. The family is described as an adaptive system because its function is to respond creatively to the stresses produced by unfulfilled needs. There has therefore been an enduring interest among scholars in the ways in which families cope with, or adjust to, the periodic crises that affect them. The transition into old age is often thought of as one such period of adjustment. In social gerontology the image of the family as a social support system is firmly established as a major focus for research into the family life of the elderly (McPherson, 1983; Beland, 1984; Norris, 1987; also, Chapter Ten in this volume). Among the relevant theories is Rosenthal's intergenerational solidarity model of family life, in which "the family is viewed as an organization in which people assume responsibility for specialized tasks in order to maintain familial solidarity" (Rosenthal, 1987:311). These tasks include arranging multigenerational ritual occasions by which solidarity between generations is reaffirmed.

The nature of family unity and the ways in which unified families solve their problems have been fundamental issues in standard sociological theory. Those interests have persisted even though in recent years many families have been broken by marital separation and divorce. Nevertheless, Schlesinger (1979:172) believes that, although the family has lost many of its functions, "Canadian families will survive with greater strengths and inner fortitudes." Having this optimistic view of the family, Schlesinger does not associate high divorce rates with the end of family life. Rather, in his own research he has emphasized the prevalence of remarriage. In his view, remarriage is an adaptation that enables families to adjust to the rapid pace of change in a modern society (Schlesinger, 1971:377). As a direct consequence of this approach, Schlesinger became one of the first social scientists to study reconstituted families.

The continuity of family life under changing conditions in the family's life cycle is stressed by the developmental approach. It postulates that the structure of family roles changes in predictable ways as families follow a cycle of birth, growth, and decay. The family life cycle begins when a man and a woman marry and ends when one of them dies. In between, the family expands and contracts as children enter and leave. The developmental approach interprets family development as a series of stages or phases. The passage from one stage to another involves a change in family structure, which in turn has consequences for family functioning. The standard theory of the family life cycle holds that in each stage of the cycle the family faces distinctive tasks which are essential for its further development (Duvall and Miller, 1985). Family life-cycle stages have therefore tended to be defined "in terms of the dominant developmental tasks being faced by individual members in the family and by the family as a system" (Hill and Rodgers, 1964:178). It is generally assumed that the family tackles these tasks, such as preparing children for adult life, as a "well-organized team" (Hill, 1970:11).

The developmental approach has been subject to considerable criticism over the years (Cheal, 1987b). It is often noted that the principal difficulty is the impossibility of incorporating all patterns of family living into a predetermined universal set of stages (Trost, 1977). Cross-cultural differences in the timing and nature of age-graded roles and the enormous variations in individual circumstances within modern societies mean that any model of the family life cycle is likely to be of only limited value. Nevertheless, Lupri and Frideres have followed a developmental approach in their research into marital satisfaction. In their assessment, family life-cycle stages "represent structural transition periods that become potential stress points for the family as a system of interacting individuals" (Lupri and Frideres,

1981:301). Using a modified model of Duvall's family life-cycle stages, they conclude that their findings "demonstrate the usefulness of conceptualizing the family as a unit with a set of developmental task requirements inside and outside the household" (Lupri and Frideres, 1981:283).

The search for universal models of family life has been one of the most distinctive goals in standard sociological theory. It has given rise to a number of characteristic limitations in the work of its practitioners. Perhaps the greatest weakness of standard theory has been its taking for granted a supposedly universal concept of the family, a concept that has not been well suited to the study of conflict and change (Barrett and McIntosh, 1982; Thorne, 1982). Oakley (1974:27) has noted that a theoretical approach is at the same time a way of seeing and a way of not seeing. Standard theory approaches the family as a well organized team that adjusts to the needs of its members. It has recognized the existence of conflict in marriage only in the context of divorce, and it has not seen conflict as an endemic feature of marriage (Laws, 1971:506). Furthermore, standard theorists have not often recognized that some family members adjust to conflict more than others, and that such adjustments are related to gender inequalities. Consequently, feminist theorists have criticized standard sociological theory for its neglect of women's negative experiences in marriage, including domestic violence (Eichler, 1983b:54-57).

FEMINISM

The relationship between men and women in the family is analyzed by a variety of new approaches which have emerged as alternatives to standard sociological theory (Lupri, 1983) Among others, the feminist approach to the family has gained prominence in Canada and elsewhere. It describes the relationships between men and women in the context of a structure of domination conceptualized as patriarchy, the political and social control of women by men. It is suggested that processes of control and domination come into play whenever men and women interact. Consequently, patriarchy includes an internal stratification of family life, in which men have greater power and control and receive more benefits than women.

Feminist theorists have systematically attempted to explore the nature and causes of patriarchy. For example, O'Brien (1981) argues that the origins of patriarchy lie in the sexual process of reproduction. She suggests that the "alienation of the male seed" in sexual intercourse creates for men a deep uncertainty about biological paternity. Since men's biological relationships to the particular children of particular women are unclear, the resulting uncertainty can be removed only by an enforced social agreement. Individual men assert their rights to certain children by claiming to have rights over their mothers. Those claims are supported by an elaborate male culture, including a male philosophy, which, O'Brien (1981:5) states, is "an ideology of male supremacy." "It is the historical movement to provide this support system which transforms the individual uncertainties of paternity into the triumphant universality of patriarchy" (O'Brien, 1981:54).

The feminist approach to the family is still in a formative stage and, therefore, it has yet to produce a unified theoretical framework. Nevertheless, four main arguments can be identified in the literature. First, the view of the modern family as an adaptive system is rejected. Instead, family life is conceptualized as an arena within which individuals who pursue different economic and social interests meet and struggle. Second, relations between women and men within the family are defined as power relations in which men dominate women. Third, the ideological legitimation of patriarchy is held responsible for the acquiescence of women in their own subjection. Fourth, the definition of the family in standard sociological theory is attributed to conventional cultural ideals and, therefore, it is said to promote a selective ideology of familism that legitimates traditional family norms.

Most feminist theorists see the allocation of tasks among family members principally taking the form of the sexual division of labour. Although such a division of labour has the appearance of an equal exchange, it is maintained that women contribute more than what they receive in return. As a result, the gender-based domestic division of labour is defined as a form of oppression. Feminist sociologists stress that oppression within the family is shaped by a complex system of social control that is unified by the collusion of men against women in a variety of social institutions. Canadian feminists have been especially active in analyzing the linkages between gender inequalities and family life that are mediated by the state (Burstyn, 1985; Ursel, 1986). Policies and programs dealing with issues such as social security, family law, and abortion have been examined to delineate the patterns and mechanisms by which they generalize and extend the power men have over women (Gavigan, 1987).

The most subtle form of social control lies in the ideological influence on individuals' perceptions of self. Through childhood socialization into traditional sex roles, men and women acquire different social experiences that are rationalized into sexist ideologies which support the belief that there are natural differences in behaviour between women and men. Feminist theory considers familism as one such ideology. It is characteristic of familism, for example, that heterosexual marriage is believed to be the natural and inevitable basis for family life. Alternatives to such a pattern are seldom tolerated and frequently labeled deviant.

Feminist scholars tend to define the family as an ideological concept (see, for example, Barrett, 1980:199-200). For them, the family is an idea which has been created and expounded by those whose interests it has served and, perhaps, continues to serve. Consequently, the modern concept of the family has been examined as the outcome of a historical process. In

Marxist feminist analysis this process is deemed to have been determined by the growth of the capitalist mode of production.

Feminism and Marxism are closely related approaches in family theory. Beyond the limited affinity created by radical politics, feminism and Marxism are more tightly linked in an analytical interdependence. Feminist sociology has lacked one key ingredient for a systematic account of family life, and that is a theory of how societies work. Therefore, much of the early feminist analysis of the family in Canada was influenced by Marxist feminism, which some observers consider to be a distinct school of thought. The close ties between feminism and Marxism are partly due to their shared interests in the criticism of structures of domination, although their union has not always been a happy one (O'Brien, 1979).

MARXISM

In recent years, Marxist theory has become popular in Canada, as it has elsewhere. The revival of Marxism has both followed from and contributed to the growth of other critical approaches such as feminism. The most distinctive feature of the Marxist critique is its assumption that all major social ills are due to the nature of the economic relations upon which social existence depends. This assumption has led to a method of analyzing social change known as materialism (Armstrong and Armstrong, 1978).

According to the materialist view of social life, human history is determined in the last instance by the production and reproduction of life itself. In order for life to continue it is necessary to produce human beings *and* to produce such material conditions as food and clothing that sustain them. Engels (1942), Marx's collaborator, stated that the nature of social life is determined by both kinds of production. However, most Marxists underscore the significance of the daily reproduction of existence. Consequently, the determining factor in any society is considered to be its mode of production, that is, the system of tools, people, and social organization by which goods and services are produced. In Canada, it is claimed, the capitalist mode of production ensures that all significant social practices serve the interests of those who own capital.

Marxist studies of family life have focused on the relationship between unpaid work that is performed in the home, and the paid work that is performed in capitalist enterprises (Luxton, 1980;1983). Smith argues that the Marxist approach does not begin by analyzing the family as a type of social structure. Rather, it sets out to study a work process that is organized by certain kinds of social relations (Smith, 1985:4-7). Work in the household is referred to as domestic labour, which is performed mainly by women. Marxist theorists trace the origins of such a division of labour to the capitalist mode of production. They hold that the negative social characteristics of domestic labour are caused by the fact that it is not wage labour performed for capitalists. Wives are required to labour for their husbands and children in the household because men are engaged in wage labour in the factory or elsewhere. From this perspective, the issues that have been studied include the separation of family life from industrial production, the social construction of women's dependence upon men within the family, and the benefits of women's unpaid labour for the owners of capital.

From a Marxist perspective, the issue of the benefits of women's unpaid labour for the owners of capital is undoubtedly the most important. Smith (1981:161) has stated that "the general emphasis here is on the significance of the economic relations to which the family is articulated as these organize the inner structure of the family." In her opinion, the nature of contemporary family life must be understood in terms of its uses for capital. Thus, the middle-class family stands in a "sub-contractual relation to corporate capitalism" (Smith, 1973:14). It produces, supports, and molds the kind of person that corporations need for their survival. Smith (1973:21), therefore, believes that the family is "created in the image provided by the corporation."

Marxist analyses of domestic labour provide the most notable contributions to family theory made by Canadian sociology. In particular, the work of Seccombe has had a considerable influence. It has precipitated a series of discussions which are known as the domestic labour debate (Fox, 1980; Armstrong and Armstrong, 1985; Miles, 1985). Seccombe (1974:5) stated that the analysis of domestic labour must begin with a description of the family's relation to the mode of production since "the family is ultimately dependent upon the dominant mode of production for its existence and form." From this perspective, the family in capitalist society is seen to mediate between the commodity market (in which goods are bought and sold) and the labour market (in which workers exchange their labour power for wages). The family consumes the goods that are produced by capitalist manufacturing, and it simultaneously produces the workers that manufacturers employ. The key to this dual process is housework. Commodities must be purchased and prepared before they can be used, and the personal needs of employees must be attended to if they are to be fit to go to work. It is the latter aspect of housework that Seccombe and the other domestic labour theorists consider critical. Seccombe (1974:7) explains that his purpose is "to situate the housewife as a labourer," and so he has concentrated almost entirely upon "the production side of her relation to capital."

According to Marxists, the nuclear family household in Canada is determined by its function of social reproduction, or maintenance, of capitalism (Dickinson and Russell, 1986). Seccombe (1974, 1980, 1986a) believes that the principal function of the working-class family is the reproduction of the capacity to work or, in other words, the reproduction of labour power. On a generational basis the reproduction of labour power is achieved in childbirth and child care, and it is achieved daily in the physical and psychological sustenance of wage workers.

Accordingly, the labour process in capitalist societies is split into two separate units (Seccombe, 1974:6). On the one hand there is the industrial unit (the factory), and on the other hand there is the domestic unit (the family). The labouring population of industrial societies is divided between these two units, with men entering industry and women working at home. The social experiences of housewives are interpreted as direct consequences of this division of labour (Seccombe, 1974:19-21). Whereas men earn wages from their employment, women are not paid for their domestic work. Consequently, women are materially dependent upon men, who exercise authority over them. Furthermore, a woman's work must be justified in non-economic terms. It is a "labour of love" that is performed out of devotion to her family. Finally, domestic labour is privatized in the household, and housewives are socially isolated. In these ways the linkages of the nuclear family to capitalist relations of production are seen as limiting the prospects for women's resistance and liberation (Seccombe, 1974:21-23).

POLITICAL ECONOMY

In Canada, Marxist theory has been a major factor in the development of an interdisciplinary approach to the social sciences known as political economy. According to Marchak (1985), Canadian political economy is concerned with the study of power relations whose origins lie in some system of property rights. Specifically, she observes:

> The property rights of particular importance in an industrial society relate to means of production: the capital, machinery, plant, etc., by which we create goods and services. Standard Marxist theory begins with these rights and obligations, identified as the relations of production. Political economy to the extent that it follows the Marxist paradigm likewise begins there. But where political economy has challenged Marxism is in growing recognition of the existence of other property rights in capitalist systems; as well, of the importance of sources of inequality, subordination, and resistance either unrelated to or not adequately explained within a standard class analysis (Marchak, 1985:673).

It has been suggested that the Canadian political economy tradition should go beyond the analysis of class to include the study of gender inequalities within feminist political economy (Maroney and Luxton, 1987). At least two issues link the feminist and political economy approaches. First, it is now generally recognized that activity in the household (especially women's domestic labour) has a wider economic significance, and that it has a bearing on socio-economic structures such as labour markets (Connelly and MacDonald, 1983; Ursel, 1984). Second, discussions on the role of the state in Canadian social development now include its impact on women's reproductive experiences. The latter issue deserves some comment here.

The political economy of reproduction is an important new topic in the Canadian sociology of the family (Ursel, 1984; Dickinson and Russell, 1986; Seccombe, 1986a). It is concerned with the relations between the demands for labour in capitalist enterprises and the reproduction of labourers in working-class families. Interestingly, it has led to a renewed interest in family life-cycle theory, which has been reconceptualized as the reproductive cycle (Wayne, 1986). The main difference between the developmental approach and the political economy approach is that in the latter the economic difficulties encountered by families are not defined as developmental tasks. Instead, they are treated as budgetary crises that arise from the failure of the capitalist system to provide average wages sufficient for reproduction. Women's responses to these crises include the reduction of fertility and intensified employment for wages outside the household. In turn, these individual responses precipitate a societal crisis of reproduction which requires state intervention.

It is argued that the dominant historical solutions to the crisis of reproduction have been for the state to regulate the wage labour performed by women, and for it to redistribute money in the form of transfer payments that supplement the limited earnings of working-class families with children. The conclusion, then, is that the state serves the interests of capital by encouraging working-class families to reproduce themselves. It is further believed that in this way the state maintains the dependent status of women within the family. According to Ursel (1986), labour laws that were introduced in order to preserve the reproductive capacities of women enforced a distinction between male and female labour. Such a distinction "operated to preserve and solidify the existing sexual segmentation of the labour market. The outcome of this was, in most cases, to maintain women in an economically dependent position compared to men, and hence to preserve the fundamental component of patriarchy—female subordination" (Ursel, 1986:188).

EXPLORATIONS AND ALTERNATIVES

The subordination of women in modern family life has been the principal unifying theme in recent Canadian family theory. As a result, the sociology of the family in Canada today is polarized between the traditional standard sociological theory and the feminist political economy perspective (Baker, 1984). A distinctive characteristic of this polarization is that standard sociological theory and political economy theory have developed in isolation from each other and the result has been little exchange of ideas. It is hoped that future theorizing about family life will include exchanges which lead to constructive debates about the relative advantages of different approaches (see, for example, Seccombe, 1986b). In this chapter an attempt has been made to encourage such a process by delineating important contributions to the theory of family life. It is also necessary to identify some of the limits to the development of family studies in Canada that follow from the narrow terms of theoretical debate. Such limitations are likely to become more serious in the future if they are not addressed in a systematic manner.

Among several negative features of polarization are, first, theoretical problems in political economy that result from its neglect of earlier discussions of standard sociological theory. For example, it appears that the critical literature on models of the family life cycle is not well known among political economists, or at least it has not been heeded. Second, there is the narrowing of perspectives that follows directly from the dominance of two approaches that are opposed in certain respects but similar in others. Here it is important to note that standard sociological theorists and political economists each typically rely upon a conceptualization of the family which is open to a number of objections. Finally, alternative sociological approaches have only been selectively applied, and they have little influence upon theories of family life in Canada. This is notably the case for micro-sociological approaches, such as exchange theory and symbolic interactionism, in which the interactions and transactions that make up family life are investigated.

These three limitations are intertwined in ways which ensure that the pattern of Canadian polarity will not easily be broken. One consequence of the low level of interest in alternative theoretical approaches has been minimal exposure to earlier criticisms of standard sociological theory. In turn, lack of familiarity with earlier critiques of standard sociological theory has made it easy to believe that political economy is the only serious alternative to it. Belief in the inevitable rise of political economy has been further encouraged by the use of a narrow model of family life. That model has come under increasing attack by feminist theorists who are opposed to standard sociological theory, and who are not identified with the political economy approach. In the following discussion this point will be elaborated with special reference to the contribution of Eichler.

Multiple Realities

In Canada the feminist political economy of the family was formed in the "domestic labour debate" of the 1970s. In this debate, the overwhelming emphasis was on the housewife's role as a producer of labour power for capitalism (Eichler, 1985a:68). It has now become increasingly evident that the terms of the 1970s debate were narrow, and that the realities of family economics are more complex than Seccombe's original model allowed. For example, his stress on women as producers of labour power led Seccombe

(1974:4) to dismiss all interest in the consumer behaviour of housewives as the work of "bourgeois economists." Nevertheless, it is now acknowledged that modern families are significant units of consumption as well as units of production (Strong-Boag, 1985:44-47). Similarly, it has been necessary to extend early investigations to account for the fact that many more married women are now engaged in both paid employment and domestic labour (Luxton, 1983).

At present, the range of issues studied in Canadian political economy is steadily expanding. As it does so it increasingly encroaches upon areas that have been investigated by standard sociological theorists. One such area is the family life cycle. We have noted above that the principal difficulty with the concept of the family life cycle is that it sets out a series of stages that are not in fact followed by all families. This state of affairs is due largely to the fact that the model of the family employed in the developmental approach is the nuclear family household, consisting of co-resident husband and wife and their unmarried children. Serious theoretical problems arise when families do not fit this model of the "normal" family—for example, when couples do not have children, or when they join with others to form complex households.

In the Canadian political economy perspective, changing experiences of family life have been explained by introducing the idea of the reproductive cycle (Wayne, 1986). The stages described are:

1) from marriage to birth of the first child;
2) from the birth of first child to employment of a child;
3) from employment of a child to the departure of the last child from home;
4) from the departure of the last child from home to death of a spouse.

Unfortunately, this new concept of the reproductive cycle of the family does not overcome the familiar weaknesses in the developmental cycle approach, since the nuclear family is once again taken to be the unit of analysis (Wayne, 1986:63).

The limited uses of the political economy model of the nuclear family have been recognized by Seccombe (1980:59-62). He observes that:

> In all periods of capitalist development, minority subsistence arrangements have been sustained among the proletarian masses: single parent households (mostly female); single persons living alone or in groups with other single people and doing their own housework; unmarried couples; couples who remain childless by choice; couples who share the domestic labour more or less equally; women who own household property and genuinely control their household's income, etc. In all of these cases the people involved are able to fulfill their proletarian duties, and they remain exploitable by capital. It is not easy to live in these ways. For the majority it is preferable to take the path of least societal resistance, to get married and establish nuclear family households. But one can live as a

proletarian against the grain of its subsistence norms. Nothing in the capitalist mode of production excludes it (Seccombe, 1980:60).

Seccombe (1986a:30; 1986b:193) suggests that, to overcome the narrowness of the nuclear family model, the use of separate concepts of household, family, and kinship, as they have been employed in social anthropology, must be encouraged. Such a step would have the clear advantage of enabling political economy to better describe the multiple realities of family life. Nevertheless, it would also introduce a new level of complexity into political economy. For this reason, perhaps, the distinctions between these three concepts have not yet been systematically employed. As Seccombe (1980:59) notes, if the household is deemed to be "a necessary part of the capitalist mode of production," then the nuclear family is merely "the predominant form for recruitment to and maintenance of private households." If this is the case, then the participation of individuals in family life cannot be determined by the mode of production, but it is presumably due to the pressure of "majority family norms" (Seccombe, 1980:60). Such a position leads political economy back to the descriptions of normative consensus that are favoured in standard sociological theory. It is therefore not obvious at this time what direction the political economy of the family will take, nor how it will differ from standard theory.

A different approach to the multiple realities of family life has been taken by Eichler. She explicitly focuses attention on the theoretical implications of the variety of domestic arrangements found in contemporary family life, and concludes that,

> in general, the image of families that is reflected in much of the sociological literature is clearly inappropriate for today. Blind adherence to the inadequate monolithic model of the family has led to a collective failure on the part of social scientists to investigate those issues which are a lived reality to a majority of people today (Eichler, 1981b:385).

Eichler's views on family life are drawn from a feminist critique of social theory (Eichler, 1973; 1980; 1981a; 1983a; 1983b). They comprise a bold alternative to both standard sociological theory and political economy. According to Eichler (1981b:368), one reason why mainstream sociological theories are unsatisfactory is that they are dominated by "the monolithic model of the family." She argues that conventional concepts of the family are monolithic in the sense that they assume the congruence or correlation of activities such as emotional involvement, procreation, socialization, and economic support. Eichler claims that in reality these activities are often performed in a variety of contexts other than the nuclear family and thus independently of each other. For example, adult emotional bonds between siblings or close friends of the same sex may be as strong as the ties between marriage partners. Eichler therefore recommends that we adopt a dimensional model of family interaction, in which the degree of congruence between the different dimensions is an empirical question open to investigation (Eichler, 1981b; 1983b:2-26). Furthermore, she has shown that each family member's description of who belongs to their family may be different. Eichler (1981b:385) therefore suggests that more attention needs to be paid to members' definitions of families. It remains to be seen whether or not Eichler's reflections will have much influence upon the development of family studies in Canada. However, her approach is an alternative worth exploring (Cheal, 1988).

Interactions and Transactions

Following her open-ended view of family organization, Eichler (1973; 1981a) has repeatedly called for the analysis of families as structures of dependency and interdependency. In her view, families are not closed systems that take only a limited number of forms. It follows that they are most usefully studied as temporary arenas of familial interaction, their members held together by interpersonal bonds of various kinds. Eichler, therefore, has maintained a position independent of both standard sociological theory and political economy from which to analyze the different ways in which men and women are linked in shifting family relations.

Eichler is not the only sociologist who has adopted a relational approach to family life. An earlier, better-known approach is symbolic interactionism (Nett, 1978; Mackie, 1987). In symbolic interactionism special attention is paid to the ways in which individuals' images of themselves are shaped by their interactions with others. Each person's sense of his or her identity as a family member is assumed to be derived from the communications that take place in everyday life (Cheal, 1987a). Those communications include the transactions through which resources are transferred from one individual to another (Cheal, 1984). Identity-defining transactions include unequal exchanges within the family economy, in which women are reminded of their dependence upon the financial generosity of men (Cheal, 1986).

Eichler, too, is interested in the personal dimensions of economic dependency in marriage. She includes among the consequences for housewives of personal dependency a negative self-image created by their constant association with someone who has authority over them (Eichler, 1973:50). According to Eichler (1981a), dependence is a form of powerlessness. Thus she has proposed a dependency model of family power, which moves beyond the analysis of inequalities in resources to consider emotional variables. These variables include feelings that originate in religion, morality and ethics (Eichler, 1981a:208, 214).

CONCLUSION

In this chapter we have noted that in the work of Eichler and others family theory has become established as a distinct subfield of the social sciences in Canada. Only a decade ago it would not have been possible to write a chapter on Canadian family theory, since a coherent body of original work did not exist. Today it is possible to identify several distinct, yet interrelated, streams of theoretical work which sometimes complement each other, sometimes conflict with each other. Either way, their interrelations offer encouraging evidence of the vitality of Canadian social theory.

It is a common experience in the social sciences to find that, after a period of rapid theoretical development, a gap has emerged between theory and research. It is also customary for reviewers to bemoan this state of affairs and issue urgent calls for greater integration. One of the strengths of the new family theory in Canada has been its close connections with empirical investigations, particularly in women's studies and social history. Nevertheless, an increasing separation of theory from research can be found in recent debates. This need not be a cause for concern. It is true, of course, that sociological theories should account for recognized research findings, and that they should provide conceptual frameworks for established research programs. It is also necessary for theorists to raise new questions and propose new solutions that point beyond the present limits of their disciplines. In this respect it can be argued that recent developments in theoretical approaches to family life are essential for future growth. At the same time, it should always be kept in mind that the questions raised must be worth asking, and the solutions proposed must be brought to fruition. How far those goals have been achieved is for the reader to decide.

Note

1. The approach referred to here as standard sociological theory has sometimes been labeled "mainstream sociology" (see, for example, Wilson, 1982:3-4). I have not followed that usage here, since it gives a misleading impression that nothing of real significance has changed in Canadian sociology in the past two decades. It can be argued that standard theory is no longer the dominant approach in sociology in Canada, and that political economy is the current mainstream sociology (see Marchak, 1985).

Suggested Readings

Armstrong, Pat, Hugh Armstrong, Patricia Connelly, and Angela Miles.
 1985   *Feminist Marxism or Marxist Feminism: A Debate*. Toronto: Garamond.

Burr, Wesley, Reuben Hill, F. Ivan Nye, and Ira Reiss, eds.
 1979   *Contemporary Theories About the Family*. 2 vols. New York: Free Press.

Dickinson, James, and Bob Russell, eds.
 1986   *Family, Economy and State*. Toronto: Garamond.

Elliot, Faith Robertson.
 1986   *The Family: Change or Continuity*. Atlantic Highlands, NJ: Humanities Press.

Morgan, D. H. J.
 1985   *The Family, Politics and Social Theory*. London: Routledge and Kegan Paul.

Thorne, Barrie, and Marilyn Yalom, eds.
 1982   *Rethinking the Family: Some Feminist Questions*. New York: Longman.

3

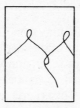

COURTSHIP AND MATE SELECTION

G.N. Ramu

*E*xcept for those who choose to remain single and those who cannot marry, for whatever reasons, the majority of Canadians marry at least once in their lifetime, and most who do so remain married to the same person. Burch (1985:11) recently noted that, of "the vast majority of ever-married Canadian adults, nine out of ten, roughly, have so far realized their traditional ideal of one marital partner." This means that most Canadians remain married to the same person for approximately half a century: therefore the selection of a marital partner is a critical concern. How does one go about choosing a mate? What personal, practical, and ideological concerns govern such a choice? Is the choice of a spouse based merely on individual idiosyncracies, on unstated rules and assumptions, or on a combination of both?

The chapter is divided into four sections. In the first, the main theoretical issues concerning mate selection are discussed. The main argument is that the patterns of mate selection (restricted vs. free choice) are related to the nature of the society (non-Western or Western). It is further argued that, for a variety of reasons, Canadians essentially enjoy "restricted freedom" in the selection of their partners. The second section focuses on changing courtship relations, while the third examines the influence of various social and personal factors in mate selection in Canada. The final section offers a brief concluding comment.

THEORETICAL PERSPECTIVES

Most societies permit their members one approach, or a combination of two or three, to the choice of one's marital partner: arranged marriage, restricted choice, or free choice. In non-Western societies, kin, parents, intermediaries, or professional matchmakers choose one's partner and arrange wedding ceremonies. The criteria of who is eligible to marry whom are generally predetermined, making courtship as we know it irrelevant. In such societies, marriage is considered too important an event to be left to the independent decision of inexperienced youth. The young themselves are often reluctant to assume the burden of making such a critical decision.

The practice of arranged marriage continues to be the primary mode of choice in non-Western societies. For example, in 1979 in Hosur, a village in South India, all of the 25 marriages were arranged by parents or close kin, and little displeasure about the parental choice was expressed (at least in public) by brides and bridegrooms (Ramu, 1977). Likewise, in the Kolar Gold Field, a mining town in South India, the sons of lower-caste Tamil gold miners marry (or have a claim on) their mother's brother's daughter or father's sister's daughter (Ramu, 1977). Such "cross-cousin marriages" are preferred and often encouraged as part of cultural expectations.

The approach directly opposed to arranged marriages is free choice. It should be noted here that, while an individual is theoretically free to choose whomever he or she desires, this freedom is neither total nor unrestricted. In all modern societies there are legal and customary stipulations which exclude certain persons from the "field of eligibles." For example, in Canada there are formal prohibitions with respect to kinship—one cannot marry certain relatives—and other informal ones involving religion, race, and age that effectively exclude categories of persons from the eligible group. The restricted choice option is a compromise between the first and second approaches, and closely approximates free choice. In this case relatives and others play an important role in marriage, but the principals have a say in the proceedings and ultimately can defy their elders.

Since total free choice of marital partners is not a common practice in most contemporary societies, we shall have little to say about it in what follows. Concerning the other two patterns—arranged marriage, and restricted choice—we may ask why some societies insist on arranging the marriage of their younger members while others permit relative freedom? Social beliefs and practices concerning marriage provide a key to our understanding of this difference. Marriage is not just an affair between two individuals. It has wider significance for an orderly replacement of the population as well as the reproduction of political, economic, religious, and other cultural arrangements. Therefore, societies seek to control, by normative and legal stipulations and in varying degrees, the marital process.

The degree of control, however, depends on a society's desire, and the ability of its institutions, to maintain traditional patterns or tolerate flexibility in these matters.

Arranged Marriages and Maintenance of Structural Differences

Although some form of control is evident in virtually all societies, it is more elaborate and overt in those which strive to preserve their distinctive social and cultural attributes such as kinship, caste, social class, race, religion, ideology or ethnicity. In this context, it is not surprising that Stephens (1963:198) notes that in 33 of 39 societies surveyed, extended or kinship groups controlled the marriage market, with elders determining who could marry whom. Goode (1959) identifies several ways in which non-Western societies control or influence the selection of marital partners so as to maintain existing social arrangements. These are child marriage, rules that designate specific marital partners (for example, cross-cousin marriage or a preferential mating system), segregation of potential marital partners so that interaction leading to intimacy can be prevented (an extreme example is *purdah*, a system, common in most Islamic societies and among some groups in India, that sequesters women), and close supervision of eligible females (chaperonage in some European and Latin American societies and in middle-class urban India).

Typically, arranged marriages are endogamous in character. The terms *endogamy* or *homogamy* are from the Greek *endo* (within) and *homo* (same), and *gamo* (marriage), and refer to the tendency of those with similar social characteristics to marry. This pattern is not restricted to arranged marriage systems. It is also evident, though in a less extreme form, in Western societies, where individuals are more likely to marry those with whom they share common cultural traits.

A classic example of a society where endogamy is widespread is Hindu India. Here, caste (the rigid division of society into hierarchical groups) continues to be an important basis for social organization, and informal attempts to preserve it include caste endogamy, intercaste marriages being the exception. When a desired match cannot be arranged within one's kinship or recognized circle of caste members, parents advertise for brides or grooms in newspapers. The most frequently stipulated condition in such classified matrimonial advertisements is the caste or sub-caste of the prospective partners (Wiebe and Ramu, 1971).

Farber stresses the importance of endogamy and arranged marriage in relation to his notion of the *orderly replacement* of family culture. He defines family culture (1964:3-36) as the norms and values that people hold regarding courtship, marriage, divorce, kinship identity and obligation, socialization of children, residence, and household maintenance. He argues that families generally desire to maintain their culture over generations, mate selection being the key. Farber also claims that exogamous rules that encourage individuals to marry someone outside their kinship group open the family to external influences that can prevent an orderly replacement of family culture. Therefore, in those groups or societies where the emphasis is on the maintenance of family culture, the selection of spouses is likely to be made by elders, and kin marriages and endogamy will be the norm (Ramu, 1976;1977). While endogamy is the rule in traditional societies, modern societies, such as Canada, have not totally discarded it.

Restricted Choice and Social Integration

The vast majority of Canadians practise *heterogamy*, that is, they permit their younger members to marry outside their racial, ethnic, or religious group within certain limits. In this system, potential marriage partners go through an extended courtship in which personal rather than group considerations influence the final decision. Ideally, heterogamy prevails in a social milieu which encourages individualism, secularism, and geographic and social mobility. When heterogamy is the dominant pattern in a given society, social and cultural differences tend to disappear, to produce social homogeneity.

The relative freedom that is allowed in the choice of one's mate is consistent with the popular North American principle of individualism. In this respect, Udry (1974:14) notes,

> The philosophy of individualism asserts that the value of the individual is paramount over the value of the social groups. The goals of the individual are given preference and his/her well being and happiness are criteria for social and individual decisions. It is not the duty of the individual to sacrifice his happiness for the well being of other people.

This philosophy leads to a belief that courtship and marriage are means of meeting one's personal needs, and, therefore, people can choose their mates accordingly. Furthermore, in North America there is an overriding cultural imperative that romantic love should be a necessary prelude to marriage. The widely held belief is that it is "mildly shameful to marry without being in love with one's intended spouse" (Goode, 1959:41). Besides love, numerous personal considerations, such as companionship, communication, sexual adjustment, religious and other common values and aspirations, influence one's choice of a marital partner.

Ideally, individualism and love, in conjunction with relative freedom of choice of mates, encourage social and cultural integration of diverse groups. But in practice matters are somewhat more complicated.

The Canadian Approach to Mate Selection

Mate selection in Canada is a system of restricted choice for a variety of historical and cultural reasons. Because of its unique history of immigration, the settlement patterns of various ethnic groups, linguistic differences and a lack of religious homogeneity, Canada has over the years allowed, and often consciously encouraged, "pluralism" as the basis of social organization. The ideology of pluralism, and the institutional support of it, have apparently led to at least two developments which have implications for the mate-selection process.

First, pluralism encourages social groups to maintain their differences with respect to religion, ethnicity, social class, and those characteristics which are specific to one's country of origin—language, literature, arts, food, and so on. Many groups have developed institutionalized means to maintain their distinctive characteristics. One such mechanism is the control of matters related to mate selection and marriage (Ramu, 1983). Not all groups exercise the same degree of control, because some attach more importance to the maintenance of their identities than others. For example, if Catholics or Hutterites are more endogamous than other groups, this may be interpreted as their exercise of greater control than others, for instance, Scandinavians, over mate selection. Therefore, pluralism as a social value has enabled Canadians to maintain social differences with regard to ethnicity, language, and other such factors (although not very successfully, as Tavuchis notes in Chapter Nine).

Second, social and cultural pluralism in Canada encourages tolerance not only of group but also of individual differences. Such tolerance has enabled many individuals to choose alternative courtship and marital patterns to those endorsed by their original subcultural groups. Thus, the children of the recent immigrants from India and Pakistan can reject traditional arranged marriages promulgated by their parents and adopt the dominant courtship practices in Canadian society despite parental disapproval (Wakil et al., 1981).

True, marriages in Canada are not arranged by elders or kinship groups and, therefore, virtually any single person in the marriage market is a potential mate. Nevertheless, the choice is neither as free nor as random as it is believed to be, because the "universe" from which partners are drawn is generally limited to small pools of potential mates from school, church, work, or the neighbourhood. Goode's (1982:54) observation on mate selection in the United States marriage system is applicable to Canada as well:

Since the marriageable population in the United States (and increasingly as well as in other countries) is gradually segregated into pools of eligibles with similar social class backgrounds, even a free dating pattern with some encouragement to fall in love does not threaten the stratification system: That is, people fall in love with the "right" kind of people.

The restriction placed on the choice of partners is not necessarily deliberate (although it may be in certain cases, for instance, Hutterites or orthodox Jews). It is a function of the way in which social and family life are organized in this society. A person is socialized into a family culture that shapes the preferences for the kind of person who will likely be viewed as a desirable and compatible mate. Here, one should not underestimate the role of ethnicity, race, religion, and linguistic preferences. The high degree of Canadians' conformity to norms of endogamy supports this position, a point we will discuss later.

Furthermore, the setting in which individuals routinely interact with potential mates is usually homogeneous. For example, the neighbourhood, school, college, or the workplace where eligible men and women meet, date, and court, are all class-linked. Consequently, in the universe of potential mates, only certain people are eligible to participate. Within this universe, therefore, decisions are made.

Despite such implicit constraints, prospective mates in Canada enjoy a greater degree of freedom than their counterparts in many non-Western societies. While conforming to norms of endogamy in varying degrees, most Canadians retain the freedom to choose the most desirable person from the pool of eligible mates. But the degree to which one conforms to such norms depends on the availability of potentially acceptable mates and the social setting in which selection occurs. For example, other things being equal, individuals living in the metropolitan areas of Southern Canada can be more selective and employ relatively stringent criteria. In contrast, under conditions of scarcity, such as a skewed sex ratio with either not enough males or not enough females, people tend to be flexible and less demanding in their choice. It is likely that in various Northern communities or segregated farm communities, the choices in the marriage market are limited. In such a social environment, courtship tends to be of short duration and practical necessities of life (economy, sex, parenthood), rather than emotional (romantic love) or aesthetic (appearance), determine matrimony.

COURTSHIP PROCESS

In the recent past, courtship in Western societies typically entailed a long and complex process involving two individuals of the opposite sex who develop emotional and sexual intimacies which lead to a more permanent relationship—living together or marriage. Sociologists (Burgess et al., 1963) have identified various phases of traditional dating (casual, steady, engagement) in courtship, although some viewed dating as essentially recreational in its function. While such distinctions may appeal to theorists, in real life they are likely to be less neat and orderly. Less problematic for our purposes is the end product of such heterosexual relationships—a serious commitment leading to an exclusive attachment combined with the idea of permanence and, ultimately, marriage or its equivalent. This process we define as courtship. Obviously, one's position in any particular marriage market will be affected not only by personal traits such as attractiveness but also by objective criteria such as education and economic prospects. In other words, there are many paths that may lead to marriage. Some individuals may only seek casual relationships with no marital or familial objectives, while others may move progressively in the direction of a more permanent association that includes marriage and family.

Historical Origins

In order to understand courtship patterns in Canada it is necessary to consider historical influences. Research indicates that demographic considerations as well as strict cultural norms often dictated the nature of courtship procedures in the colonial period and following Confederation (1867). While considerations of kinship, lineage, and clan played an important role in mate selection among the indigenous populations in the past, these were clearly inapplicable to early settlers. Early immigrants were usually single males, although some may have been accompanied by their wives and children. Later on, the newcomers tended to form enclaves based on nationality, language, and religion. This gave rise to a heavy concentration of certain groups in specific regions of the country (for example, Icelanders in Manitoba, Germans and Ukrainians in the prairies, French in Lower Canada, and English in Upper Canada). Even though small localized kinship groups were eventually formed among these groups, kinship control over courtship was relatively limited. Consequently, individuals had to choose their partners in a demographically-restricted marriage market (see Gee, 1982).

For example, the French migrants to New France (Québec) in their early years of settlement were overwhelmingly male, without access to eligible mates. Some lived with native women while others had to "import" brides from France. In the early periods of colonization, upon the request of his subjects in New France, the King of France persuaded some 1000 women to migrate to New France by offering them lavish gifts and incentives (Elkin, 1964). In a marriage market where demand far exceeded supply, there appeared to be little scope for extended courtship. The question was often not whom one would marry but whether one would marry at all. Quite often marriages between kin took place, a practice that seemed to have continued in the twentieth century among the French Canadians, especially those who lived outside Québec (Piddington, 1971;1973).

In the agrarian and religious society of the early settlers, opportunities for elaborate courtship practices were limited. But "bundling" was a common practice in eighteenth and nineteenth centuries among the West European settlers in North America. The origin of this practice has been traced to North European countries (Doten, 1938; Tomasson, 1970; Stone, 1979; Reiss, 1980) but it seems to have been transplanted to New England by the immigrants. Bundling essentially involved engaged couples sleeping in the same bed, fully clothed, with boards between them to discourage sexual activity. This practice declined by about the end of the nineteenth century and in its place a rudimentary form of "dating" emerged.

It should be noted here that such courtship patterns were not common to all immigrants who followed the English and French settlers. Their customs were diverse and determined by their own traditions and historical circumstances. For example, the Hutterites, who voluntarily chose to live in segregated communities, had, until recently, a system of arranged marriages. Sikh immigrants in British Columbia in the early part of this century were not permitted to bring their wives and children, and the unmarried were unable, for racial reasons, to court white females (see Buchignani et al., 1985). Following the liberalization of immigration laws in the 1950s, many single Sikh men depended on their kin in Punjab to arrange their marriages while others advertised for brides in Indian newspapers, a practice that continues even today.

Rapid urbanization and industrialization of Canada following the Second World War created a demand for an immigrant labour force to work in those sectors of the economy that many members of the charter groups preferred not to enter. This led to the influx of many ethnic groups from East European, Mediterranean, and Asian countries (among them, Poland, Greece, Italy, India, and the Philippines). Such groups tended to gravitate toward urban centres, mainly Toronto, Montreal, or Vancouver. Initially they chose to live in segregated sections of the city, which created homogeneous communities with clear ethnic and cultural boundaries and in turn, facilitated endogamous unions. With the entrance of the second and third generation of immigrants into the marriage market, increasing secularization, and schools and the mass media effectively blurring national and cultural boundaries, especially between the United States and Canada, the traditional forms of courtship are gradually disappearing. This is not to imply that endogamy is on the wane, but rather that the manner in which individuals enter relationships is changing. While the traditional courtship process with predictable stages of dating may exist in some remote regions of Canada, changes are obvious in large cosmopolitan centres, especially on university campuses. What follows is a discussion based on the extant literature, and observations about contemporary youth culture.

Courtship Relations: The Old and the New

Traditionally, middle-class individuals who had the freedom to select their partners within a predetermined marriage market did so by getting to know them in advance, primarily through dating. The term generally referred to specific date, time, and place of meeting for mutually attracted individuals. Gradually, coinciding with the establishment of co-educational institutions, commercial recreational centres, such as theatres, movie houses, ice cream parlours, night clubs, advances in technology (the automobile), and concomitant changes in the norms and values governing heterosexual relations between the unmarried, the nature and functions of dating became more complex and even controversial. With minor exceptions (such as immigrants from East European and non-Western societies who tended to seek mates from their own countries), dating became an essential stage in one's marital career.

Despite these changes, some observers, especially Waller (1937), began to question the putative function of dating—a step toward marriage. In his pioneering analysis of dating patterns on an American college campus during the late 1930s, Waller argued that dating is not part of a courtship pattern because it is concerned mainly with casual fun, excitement, and the honing of social skills. According to him it was a "dalliance" relationship, a recreational activity based on a "rating complex." The personal qualities and possessions rated highly in college settings were campus leadership, money, a car, and expensive clothes. Of course, these qualities and possessions did not necessarily represent characteristics desired in one's future spouse.

Waller and others concluded that dating was nothing but a "fun and thrill seeking" activity and it seldom allowed the participants to assess realistically each other's attributes and qualifications for a successful marriage. Later research (Blood, 1955; Reiss, 1965; Gordon, 1981) challenged those observations and held that, while they may have been true for college students before the Second World War, dating in America became not just a recreational activity but also a necessary and serious endeavour leading to marriage.

Although there are few detailed analyses of dating practices in Canada in the 1970s (Herold, 1984; Ishwaran, 1980; Bibby & Posterski, 1985) we may conclude that dating was a common prelude to marriage during this period and still is among certain groups of young people. A study of a random sample of students in an Ontario university (Whitehurst and Frisch, 1974) found that dating was not only a common activity but, contrary to Waller's contention, it was directed toward the choice of marriage partners. Dating, according to the respondents, was as much an educational activity as it was fun, and great emphasis was placed on candour and honesty. In a study of students at a prairie university, Wakil and Wakil (1975) found that dating was a common activity and that a good many students were dating partners from similar socio-economic backgrounds. This conclusion was consistent with the general findings that individuals seek out partners within their own religious and ethnic groups (Hostetler & Huntington, 1967; Ishwaran, 1980; Anderson and Driedger, 1980; Driedger, 1983). In his recent evaluation of changes among the Hutterites, Peter (1987) suggests that most Hutterite youths now engage in dating, and the stages he identifies are those that were common among the major ethnic groups in the 1940s and 1950s.

The evidence from college campuses on dating practices suggests that the majority of young adults who dated were selective in their choice of partners, according to such criteria as appearance, communication skills, and recreation. Since many of these studies were conducted in the early 1970s, they may not reflect present or future patterns.

Past patterns of dating, understood as an activity with fairly predictable stages—casual, steady, and engagement—with each stage characterized by increased emotional and sexual intimacy and, ultimately, a commitment leading to marriage, are not in vogue in large urban centres. The so-called "dating continuum" appears to be a thing of the past. Even the term "dating" is becoming obsolete among teenagers and adults. Phrases such as "hanging out with," "going out with," or "going around with" are now used to signify certain aspects of traditional dating behaviour. The change is not just in terminology but it is in the nature and quality of relationships as well. In this respect, at least two forms of relationship can be identified.

Getting Together in Groups   The traditional mode, in which the male called the female in advance, picked her up at her home or dormitory, took her to a restaurant, concert, or movie, and then dropped her back at an appointed time, appears to be uncommon among urban youth, although this pattern may be found in remoter parts of Canada. Instead, the general tendency among young people (mostly of high-school age) is to get together casually in groups, to organize parties at home to listen to music, drink, and dance, or to congregate in shopping malls. The relationships between individuals of the opposite sex in these cases are casual and tentative, and less exclusive, predictable, or intense than in cases of traditional dating. Such group encounters in some ways avoid the problems associated with the casual dating of the 1940s and 1950s, such as awkwardness, lack of communication, insecurity, and expectations that the male should initiate matters and bear the expenses, and they diminish heterosexual tensions.

Neverthelss, when such new group relationships fail to progress to a steadier relationship, new problems arise from the point of view of courtship as the formation of close and intimate bonds. For example, the emphasis on casual relations and being "cool," along with the absence of clearly defined steps in courting, may preclude the development of stable and exclusive relationships. That young men and women go out together in groups obviously rules out sexual intimacies. Relationships also taken on a casual and serial character that encourages an exploitative atmosphere between sexes. Although it is difficult to assess whether these arrangements are conducive to less (or more subtle) exploitation between the sexes, they clearly differ from past premarital attitudes and practices as well as from definitions of marriage itself.

"Pairing Off" and Involvement   While some may prefer such group encounters, each participant is likely to develop a special relationship with another and "pair off." When such a pairing takes place, it is often said that "so-and-so is going around with so-and-so." While such an involvement may have all the trappings of the traditional "going steady," there is no expectation that it will necessarily result in marriage, although through many such bonds one's field of eligibles is effectively narrowed. The relationships between those involved may be more exclusive and intense than those in the "going steady" phase of traditional dating continuum but are less enduring since they need not result in engagement and marriage. Consequently, the courtship process among contemporary youth is extended, which may lead to delayed marriages and a lower fertility rate.

While the courting habits of youth have undergone changes, the new patterns continue to exhibit some of the characteristics associated with traditional dating practices. Skipper and Nass (1966) summarized the main functions of dating as recreation, socialization, satisfaction of ego needs, status grading, and marriage. Of these, recreation, socialization, and ego needs have greater relevance for contemporary youth, while others play only a marginal role.

The recreational function depends on whether one's association with his or her partner is casual or more permanent. For those who maintain casual relations either in groups or in pairs, the motive appears to be immediate enjoyment and gratification as Waller (1937) interpreted it. For those who are intimately involved or even living together the relationship signifies much more: it entails economic cooperation and sustained sexuality during the college years and possibly selection of marriage partners. The socialization function is pertinent to those teenagers who get together in groups. It provides an individual with opportunities to build self-confidence as well as to master the necessary social skills to impress and entertain members of the opposite sex. Another function of such courting relationships is the satisfaction of ego needs. Adolescents struggling to emancipate themselves from what they consider parental constraints seek understanding, sympathy, recognition, and respect from persons other than immediate kin.

Implications

In understanding changing courtship relations among young Canadians, it should be noted that, despite the patterns described, most do eventually marry, and the majority of those who do so form families, albeit families

much smaller than those of their parents. In short, they have not fundamentally altered the institution of marriage and the family. Nonetheless, the
apparently nebulous and unstructured character of contemporary courtship
reflects broader social currents. Each generation attempts to modify social
institutions, including courtship and marriage, to suit its own needs and
aspirations. The social, economic, religious, and political developments of
the 1960s led to sustained critiques, of the shortcomings of conventional
dating expectations and arrangements, but what still remains problematic
is the extent to which liberal alternatives provide young people with the
satisfaction and fulfillment they promise. Although the decline in parental
authority is unlikely to be reversed, the fear of AIDS and other sexually
transmitted diseases may very well reverse other permissive trends and lead
to a return to more conservative and traditional sexual patterns.

MATE SELECTION

Two sets of criteria are at work in the process of mate selection in Canada:
structural and interpersonal. First, as we noted in the section on theoretical
perspectives, restricted choice prevails to the extent that the ideology of
pluralism encourages individuals to maintain their cultural and ethnic identity by marrying persons of their own social backgrounds. Thus, even though
their marriages are not arranged by elders or others, Canadians are generally
endogamous. This is not to imply that exogamy (or intermarriage) does not
occur: it does, although in small numbers and in some groups more frequently than others. Numbers of intermarriages are affected by internal and
external demographic considerations. For example, in his discussion of
marriage among Polish-Canadians, Radecki (1980) notes that because of a
sex ratio imbalance during the 1950s and 1960s, Polish men tended to marry
outside their own ethnic group. Campbell and Neice (1979), in their analysis
of patterns of marriage in Nova Scotia, indicated that Blacks, Micmac Indians,
and Jews are highly endogamous, Chinese are moderately endogamous,
while Poles, Italians, and Ukrainians are nearly entirely exogamous (64).
They note that, in the case of the Blacks and Micmac Indians, segregation
was the main reason for the predominance of racial endogamy.

   In other cases, those strongly influenced by individualism, secularism,
and integration into the dominant culture are likely to marry "outsiders."
Also, there are many instances of second- and third-generation East Indians,
especially college educated professionals, courting and marrying persons
of other races and religions. Finally, it has been observed repeatedly that
the smaller the ethnic or religious group *vis-à-vis* majority groups, the higher
their rate of intermarriage unless special measures, such as the importation
of brides and grooms, are taken to ensure cultural integrity.

   The second set of factors that govern mate selection consists of certain personal and interpersonal attributes. These include age, beauty, similar interests, empathy, sexual compatibility, and love. of these, we will consider only the importance of love in marital choice, since most people in North America and other Western societies consider romantic love a necessary prelude to marriage.

Social-Structural Factors

Race   Race is perhaps the most critical factor in one's marital choice: most people prefer to marry a person from their own racial group. Since interracial marriages are relatively infrequent in Canada we know little about their dynamics, strains, and pleasures. The research in the United States suggests that couples who cross racial lines are likely to be older, religiously liberal, college educated professionals. The proportion of non-whites in the Canadian population (including natives) is less than five percent. The general sociological observation, noted earlier, that the smaller the group, the greater the chances of marrying outside of one's group (Heer & Hubey, 1975) does not seem to apply to non-white groups. Historical evidence on the American and Canadian intermarriages may reflect white individuals' reluctance to accept non-whites as marital partners.

The social disapproval of interracial marriages in Canada is perhaps reinforced by the continued salience of race in the American and Canadian societies. Adams (1986:215-218) argues that visibility and salience of race in a society make it difficult for persons to marry across the racial lines. Unlike religion or ethnicity, racial identity is much too conspicuous and thus constrains many persons from choosing their mates from another racial group. Salience, on the other hand, refers to the subjective significance attached to one's racial identity. This would lead to prejudicial attitudes and discriminatory practices, especially by those who deem their racial background superior to others.

Religion   Following race, religion is an important criterion in the selection of one's marriage partner. Although historically all major religions in Canada have opposed intermarriages, the degree of their resistance is associated with the size of the group and its position on an orthodox-liberal continuum. Thus, Jews tend to be more restrictive than Catholics, while Protestants tend to be more permissive than Catholics although their positions are gradually changing as is evident from increasing proportions of intermarriages in these groups. The opposition to inter-religious marriages stems from the assumption that such marriages undermine religious commitment, reduce the size of the group, and are likely to disrupt normal family functions and maintenance of group values, identity, and cohesion.

The 1981 census data on religion indicate that of slightly over 24 million

Canadians, 47.3 percent were Catholics, 41.2 percent were Protestants (nearly 30 different groups), 1.5 percent were Eastern Orthodox, 1.2 percent were Jewish, and 1.3 percent belonged to various other religions. Some 7.4 percent Canadians did not report any religious preference. Heer (1962) and Heer and Hubey (1975) found that the percentage of inter-religious marriages rose from 5.8 in 1927 to 21.5 percent in 1972. They noted some differences in this regard between groups in 1972: 22.7 percent of Protestants, 20.5 percent of Catholics, and 15.4 percent of Jews had married outside their faiths.

Basing their study on the data from the Family File of the 1971 Census for Metropolitan Toronto and Montreal, Campbell and Richard (1979) examined the patterns of inter-religious and inter-ethnic marriages. Their findings reinforce the argument that religious endogamy is still very strong, even in the large metropolitan centres of central Canada. They note that in Toronto over 90 percent of the Protestants, nearly 88 percent of the Catholics, and about 73 percent of those belonging to various other religions had married within their own groups. In Montreal, on the other hand, Catholics tended to be more endogamous than other groups: of Catholics, 97.6 percent, Protestants, 80.8 percent, and those from other religions, 83.9 percent. In short, Campbell and Richard's study suggests that there is high propensity even among urban Canadians to marry within their own religious groups.

The evidence on patterns of intermarriage in Canada permits us to make a few general comments. First, the size of a given religious group relative to others in a particular town or city is a factor which deters or promotes interreligious marriages. For example, the larger the size of a religious group in a city, the lesser the chances of its members seeking partners from other religious backgrounds since the pool of eligible mates will be large enough in their own group (Heer and Hubey, 1975; Latowsky, 1971; Campbell and Richard, 1979). Second, some studies (for example, Frideres, et al., 1971) show that increasing secularization and the perception that inter-marriages will not have any significant effect on the identity of their children encourage a few persons to intermarry. Third, Canadians of second and third generations tend to be more open to inter-religious marriages than more recent immigrants. For example, in a study of Muslims based on 1981 census data, Rashid (1985:57-58) found that, of the 26 235 Muslim families analyzed, only 19 percent of Muslim husbands and eight percent of Muslim wives were married to a spouse of another faith. What is interesting about Rashid's findings is that three out of five such marriages had been contracted by Canadian-born Muslims. But Rashid (1985:60) also suggests that recent increases in Muslim immigration and the establishment of religious and educational centres foster a sense of distinct community that would eventually lower the incidence of intermarriages, an observation shared by Radecki (1980) with regard to Polish-Canadians.

Ethnicity   Canadian society's commitment to ethnic pluralism is best demonstrated in the practice of ethnic endogamy. In 1981, some 35 groups (or 82.4 percent of the total population) reported single ethnic origins with 7.6 stating multiple origins (of which British is a predominant component). If extensive heterogamy were to be the norm, the proportion of those reporting multiple origins would have been significantly higher. The demographic evidence suggests that, although there has been an increase in the rate of ethnic intermarriages, the changes are not dramatic enough to infer that Canadian society is heading toward a "melting pot."

This position is supported by the analyses of the 1971 and 1981 Census data by Kalbach (1983) and Kalbach and Richard (1986).[1] Using the special tabulations provided by Statistics Canada for 1971 Census data, Kalbach (1983) analyzed the propensity among seventeen ethnic groups to intermarry. He calculated an index of the propensity to intermarry by taking actual to expected ratios of families with native-born husbands and wives of a different ethnic origin.[2] Kalbach's analysis showed that certain ethnic groups (Jewish, French, British) demonstrate a higher propensity to marry among themselves than others (Scandinavians). The selected evidence from the 1981 Census does not significantly alter this conclusion. For example, Kalbach and Richard (1986), drawing upon the Census Family Files for Metropolitan Toronto, examined ethnic exogamous and endogamous marriage as a measure of the degree of acculturation that may be taking place in the city of Toronto. The evidence suggested that 75 percent of husband-wife families in their sample were ethnically endogamous (husband and wife of the same ethnic origin) and 22 percent were exogamous (husband and wife were of different ethnic origins). They also noted that the native-born heads of families tend to be more exogamous than those who were born outside Canada. Another significant finding was the range of variation between ethnic groups: for example, the husbands of Chinese origin exhibited the highest proportion of endogamous marriages (93 percent) while the Scandinavians showed the lowest (17 percent).

The studies on patterns of intermarriages by Kalbach (1983) and Kalbach and Richard (1986) underscore the position taken in this chapter that mate selection in Canada is restrictive insofar as it takes place mainly within specific racial, religious, and linguistic groups. As Kalbach and Richard (1986:11) note: "those who enter into ethnically exogamous relationships, by marrying outside their ethnic group, clearly have weaker ties and ethnic commitment than those who enter endogamous unions. They would also be expected to show fewer ethnic related characteristics, and concomitantly, evidence of higher levels of assimilation and economic integration."

Propinquity   Chances are that one will interact with a person who lives close by, who goes to the same school, or who works at the same place.

Physical proximity, or propinquity, however incidental it may appear, is based upon certain structural attributes which facilitate endogamy. For example, residential areas, schools and colleges, and the workplace are all organized around social class and, therefore, bring together persons of similar social class backgrounds. Catton (1964:529), among others, has maintained that, since people with similar social characteristics tend to cluster together residentially, one effect of propinquity is to enhance endogamy. In an earlier study, Shevky and Bell (1955) suggested that the residential arrangements in urban areas reflect social class, and Canadian studies (such as, Porter, 1965; Clement, 1975; Hunter, 1981:129-141) have shown the link between ethnic status and social class. Consequently, residential arrangements, schools, and colleges act as initial filtering devices in the mate selection process.

Interpersonal Factors: Love and Attraction

One of the hallmarks of courtship in North America is the emphasis on romantic love as a prelude to marriage. The emotion of love reinforces companionship, sharing, mutual satisfaction, and commitment through intimacy and self-affirmation (see Casler, 1969). Although romantic attachments do not always lead to marriage, cultural expectations are that individuals should marry only when they are in love with each other. From this point of view, love is not merely an interpersonal phenomenon but also socially structured.

Definitions of love are too numerous and complex to be dealt with in this chapter (see, for example, Goode, 1959; Lee, 1973, 1975). In the context of courtship, however, it may be understood as a complex emotion that is expressed not only in mutual desire and emotional intimacy but in the need for a permanent and exclusive attachment such as marriage or its equivalent. Thus, a powerful sentiment is harnessed and channeled by society through the institutions of marriage and the family (Greenfield, 1965).

Not all societies have institutionalized romantic love as the basis for marriage to the extent the West has. According to Goode (1959), the expression of romantic love and the belief that it is the essential basis for marriage are dependent upon certain structural conditions and social values. For example, in hierarchical societies such as India, in which caste or class barriers are rigid, love is not only considered an inadequate basis for marriage but stringent measures are taken to prevent individuals from marrying because of romantic attraction. It is believed that free choice based on exclusive personal emotional attachments between partners disrupts and threatens existing social arrangements and the power of the elders. Here the stress is on performing one's duties and mutual compromise.

By contrast, a culture that stresses individualism, independence, secularism, and freedom of choice necessarily requires a means for the development of personal and emotional bonds prior to marriage. In the absence of arranged marriages and the related belief that affection between spouses may or may not be developed *after* marriage, the Western "solution" to moving individuals toward marriage is to allow them to have a series of relationships which eventually will lead to their falling in love with an appropriate person. The important function of such a premarital interaction, then, is to create an interpersonal context within which a romantic attachment can develop. Clearly, few Canadians would acknowledge that they married for reasons other than love. Therefore, choice based on emotional bonds prior to marriage has become an inescapable part of Canadian mate selection procedures.

CONCLUSION

A cross-cultural assessment of mate-selection procedures suggests that some form of social control regarding who marries whom exists, although there is variation in the degree of control exercised. In Canada, the historical importance attached to the ideology of pluralism has led to the persistence of social distinctions such as race, religion, and ethnicity. Logically, these distinctions would vanish were endogamy not desired and fostered. Nevertheless, relative to most people in non-Western societies such as India, Canadians do "freely" choose their spouses and "arrange" their own marriages within selected marriage markets. Some form of premarital relationship (dating or its alternative), romantic love, and premarital sex are important determinants of their choices. In short, the freedom of choice one enjoys in the Canadian marriage market exists within certain structural limits.

Notes

1. Kalbach and Richard (1986) qualify their findings in light of the limitations of the 1981 Census data collection procedures and definition of certain categories. Therefore, it is recommended that the interested reader consult this paper for details.
2. A factor that increases the chances of intermarriage is the size of the religious or ethnic group to which the individual belongs relative to the size of the other (combined) ethnic or religious groups. The size factor is controlled by calculating the propensities for intermarriage as ratios of the "actual" to the "expected" proportions of ethnic intermarriage (for details, Kalbach, 1983).

Suggested Readings

Goode, William J.
1959   "The Theoretical Importance of Love." *American Sociological Review* 24.

Gordon, Michael.
1981   "Was Waller Ever Right? The Rating and Dating Complex Reconsidered." *Journal of Marriage and the Family* 43:67-76.

Greenfield, Sydney M.
1965   "Love and Marriage in Modern America: A Functional Analysis." *The Sociological Quarterly* 6:361-377.

Heer, David, and Charles A. Hubey.
1975   "The Trend of Interfaith Marriages in Canada: 1922 to 1972." In S. Parveez Wakil, ed., *Marriage, Family, and Society*. Toronto: Butterworths.

Kalbach, Warren E.
1983   "Propensities for Intermarriage in Canada as Reflected in Ethnic Origins of Husbands and their Wives 1961-1971." In K. Ishwaran, ed., *Marriage and Divorce in Canada*. Toronto: Methuen.

Whitehurst, Robert N., and G. R. Frisch.
1974   "Sex Differences in Dating Orientations: Some Comparisons and Recent Observations." *International Journal of the Sociology of the Family* 4.

4

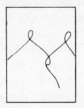

PREMARITAL SEXUALITY

Charles W. Hobart

*T*he past two decades have seen revolutionary change in the sexual mores in North America. In the mass media, sophisticated "skin magazines," such as *Playboy* and *Penthouse* for men, and subsequently *Playgirl* and *Viva* for women, have achieved widespread acceptance and even respectability. In the movies, portrayals of nudity and explicit sexual intimacy have become commonplace, as have references to sexual intercourse in rock music. Nude pictures accompanying advertisements are now found in many magazines. Sex manuals with graphic illustrations have wide circulation. The research on sexual responsiveness by Masters and Johnson (1966, 1970) has given rise to sex therapy, in some instances of which therapists engage in foreplay and intercourse with "patients" who seek to increase their ability to achieve orgasm. For many people the line between earlier conceptions of pornography and what is currently acceptable in advertising, education and science has become increasingly blurred, as has the line between sex therapy and prostitution.

There are indications that many people in North America are responding to this new freedom, and perhaps to basic problems of the family in postindustrial society, in unconventional ways that include premarital sex, living together, and "swinging." The most dramatic evidence reflecting current uncertainty about what is right, proper, and dependable in intimate relationships comes from the United States. Here, perhaps because of the very high divorce rate—about 48 of every 100 marriages since 1976 have ended in divorce (National Center for Health Statistics, 1986; U.S. Bureau of Census, 1984b)—options such as "creative singlehood" (Libby, 1977), are now being considered. In fact, one half of those aged 19 to 39 years—the prime family-forming age—are now unmarried (Libby, 1977). But unmarried cohabitation in the United States has increased in popularity to the point that in 1983 unmarried couples comprised about one in 25 of all couples, married and unmarried (U.S. Bureau of the Census, 1984a).

The Canadian patterns are similar. In 1984, Canada's divorce rate was 35 per 100 marriages (Statistics Canada, 1985), and as many as 12 percent of Canadian women aged 18 to 30 were involved in cohabitation relationships in that same year. Indeed it is estimated that at least 29 percent of the women and 25 percent of the men in this age group had been involved in such relationships by the age of twenty-five (Burch, 1985).

This chapter presents a brief overview of premarital sexual practices, first in pre-literate societies and then in Western societies through history, as a background to understanding recent changes in North America and the theories which have been proposed to explain societal and individual variations. These considerations contribute to a more detailed discussion of premarital sexual attitudes and behaviour in Canada. The chapter concludes with a discussion on the implications of current developments and on future trends.

PREMARITAL SEXUALITY: HISTORICAL AND CROSS-CULTURAL CONTEXTS

A wide variety of sexual practices in general, and of premarital sex in particular, can be found among the pre-literate societies. It ranges from the very restrictive to the very permissive. Restrictions, where found, were based on a number of considerations. Among the Bella Coola Indians of the Pacific Northwest, for example, sexual restraint was believed necessary to achieve individual power and success, while to the African Thonga it was the basis for maintaining orderly relations with nature (Frayser, 1985). One of the most permissive societies was the Marquesan in the South Pacific, where adolescent homosexual or heterosexual relationships were unrestricted, and where, indeed, mothers took pride if daughters had many lovers.

At the other extreme, the Nubians, the Kurds, and the Lebanese killed girls who were found guilty of premarital sexual affairs. In Lebanon, 80 percent of all homicides involved cases of men killing female relatives for violating the sexual code. The Tiwi Kafa killed those men who seduced adolescent girls. In some extremely restrictive societies, such as the Kenuzi Nubians, the clitorises of three- and four-year-old girls were cut out to reduce their sexual responsiveness and their vaginal openings were sewn shut to hinder premarital intercourse. These practices were found in numbers of other societies as well (Frayser, 1985).

Nevertheless, most pre-literate societies were relatively permissive: 64 percent of the societies reviewed by Frayser allowed at least one sex, and commonly both sexes, to have premarital relationships. But this did not indicate complete freedom: there were social and cultural restrictions. Often there was a double standard that allowed premarital sex for men but not women (as was found in 18 percent of the societies studied). There appears to be no society that allowed more freedom of sexual expression to women than to men. Another frequent restriction was acceptance of premarital sex only if pregnancy did not result (Frayser, 1985).

There have been many attempts to explain the wide variations in premarital sexual permissiveness found in pre-literate societies. Frayser's explanation, based on her study of the patterns of sexual relations in pre-literate and peasant societies, relates sexual practices to the structure of society, specifically to descent. She suggests that at the very restrictive extreme are societies which require complete coincidence or "overlap" of a woman's *sexual* and *reproductive* relationships. These tend to be patrilineal societies, where it is important that a woman conceives children only by her legitimate husband so that the children belong to his lineage. This practice is found in hunting and pastoral societies. At the other extreme are the permissive societies in which sexual and reproductive functions are not necessarily linked. These are usually gardening societies which are matrilineal, so the father is unimportant in tracing one's descent. In these societies, a woman may have a succession of sexual and reproductive partners before marriage or through remarriage after a divorce or the death of her husband.

Thus in patrilineal societies, where paternity is important but may be uncertain, the emphasis is on premarital chastity and genetic parenthood, that is, on the biological father. On the other hand, in matrilineal societies, where maternity is important but never in doubt, the emphasis is on premarital permissiveness and social parenthood, that is, on the person who raises the child. This has a bearing on premarital sex because in most societies there is a close association between premarital and post-marital permissiveness: if sexual relations are permitted only between married couples, then there is little scope for premarital sexuality.

European and North American Societies to 1900

The history of Western civilization indicates that sexual standards were as diverse as those found in pre-literate societies. Generally, ancient civilizations were permissive. Early Greek society was tolerant of both homosexual and heterosexual relations, and marital relations in ancient Rome were basically "common-law," thus blurring the distinction between premarital and marital sexual relations. The Old Testament illustrates the permissiveness of the Jews, in that it does not forbid premarital sex.

The history of sex relations in Europe exhibits a cyclical pattern between licence and restriction. The official position of the Roman Catholic Church, which crystalized during the eighth century, showed a fear of sex: the Church held that the ideal was complete celibacy. Even within marriage, sex was forbidden on Sundays, Wednesdays, Fridays, for the entire 40 days before Easter and Christmas, and for three days before attending Mass. However, with the Renaissance came increased permissiveness: women's dress became more provocative and sexual licence again became commonplace, even among the princes of the Church (Taylor, 1959:141).

The birth of Puritanism came with the Reformation, along with its many severe restrictions. What was pleasurable was generally seen as sinful, including all forms of sex, except when performed by married couples for procreation. With the Age of Reason, however, came a period of "astonishing sensuality." There was widespread sexual depravity, and the sale of girls as young as ten years of age into prostitution became commonplace (Taylor, 1959). With the late eighteenth century came the Romantic movement which brought the merging of sexual and romantic love, so important in our own society. Romantic love became the basis for marriage, and with it came the image of free and daring women. Again there followed a reaction during the Victorian period prompted by the puritanical morality of Methodism. Sex was seen as bestial, women were idealized as pure and sexless, and sexual repression led to greater interest in pornographic materials.

Generally, North American societies were subject to these puritanical and Victorian influences, as is clear from historical studies of premarital pregnancy since 1650 in America, England, and France. Fluctuations in premarital pregnancy rates may be taken as indicative of changes in premarital sexual behaviour, and Smith and Hindus' (1975) research has discovered a distinctive pattern characteristic of the three countries. Unwed pregnancy rates, which were low during the middle of the seventeenth century (about 8 percent of total births), rose to a peak between 1761 and 1800 (33 percent). Thereafter they dropped almost to the 1650 rates which prevailed between 1841 and 1880 (13 percent). Then they began to rise again, reaching 24 percent during 1881-1910. (Smith and Hindus, 1975:561).

Smith and Hindus suggest that there was a restrictive sexual ideology throughout this period, but the patterns of enforcement changed. During the Puritan seventeenth century emphasis was on external controls—behaviour was scrutinized by both religious and secular authorities. The nineteenth-century "low" period depended on the internal control or self-repression of sexual impulses characteristic of Victorian morality. The authors argue that "premarital sexual restraint was possible both in the seventeeth-century *community* and in the nineteenth-century *society*, but not during the transition," when unwed pregnancy rates soared (emphasis added, Smith and Hindus, 1975:549). The authors conclude that "discontinuity is the central fact of the premarital pregnancy record. . . . The 18th century upsurge in premarital pregnancy is related to the disintegration of the traditional, well-integrated rural community and to the beginnings of economic and social modernization. Once the crisis of transition to modern society had passed, premarital pregnancy began to decrease." (Smith and Hindus, 1975:559).

The United States in the Twentieth Century

In the context of the analysis by Smith and Hindus, it is appropriate that a review article on premarital sex in America in this century is entitled: "Sex in Transition, 1900-1980" (Darling et al., 1984). In their analysis of 35 studies published between 1903 and 1980, the authors identify two main trends: "a major increase in the proportion of young people reporting intercourse, and the proportion of females reporting coital involvement has increased more rapidly than the proportion of males, though the initial base for males is greater." (385). However, since most of the 35 studies involved university students, the value of the conclusions drawn from this review is limited.

The early studies found that about 35 percent of men and 13 percent of women reported premarital intercourse. These proportions increased slowly until American involvement in the Second World War (1941), when about 45 percent of men and 17 percent of women were reported to have had premarital sexual relations. Thereafter the rates increased to about 53 percent and 30 percent for men and women respectively by the mid-1950s, an increase attributable mainly to the availability of birth control pills. By the late 1970s, some studies reported rates of premarital sex in excess of 80 percent for the samples studied (Darling et al., 1984:Fig 1). This was also the period when women began rapidly to catch up with men in premarital sexual relations. Before 1970 about twice as many college men as college women reported having premarital intercourse; since then, the rates for both sexes have become nearly equal. Moreover, this pattern is not unique to the United States. Similar trends have also been noted in England (Bone, 1986), Scotland (Bone, 1986), Germany, Sweden (Lewin, 1982), and in Canada.

If the sexual revolution was made possible by the birth control pill, its direction was shaped by new, liberal norms governing sexual behaviour. Note that this was an emergence of new standards to specify appropriate and inappropriate behaviour, rather than the mere erosion of old norms. Since the time the Church claimed matrimonial jurisdiction, there have really been two norms: a formal Marital Standard, which prohibits intercourse outside of marriage, and an informal Double Standard, which prohibits premarital intercourse for women, but in effect permits sexual freedom for men. These standards still exist, of course, but as we shall see, they are weakening. Two new standards have crystallized, each from one of the old standards. The Marital Standard approved only of marital sex. Nevertheless, it was a short step for a couple to say, "We are in love; we are going to get married; we are as good as married, so making love is right and beautiful for us." This gave rise to the Love Standard. According to this standard, intercourse is right only for a couple that is in love, whether they are married or not.

The Double Standard says "sauce for the gander, but not for the goose," a form of discrimination that could hardly survive in a time when equal rights for women are a major issue. Double Standard sex was considered right for men, simply because they wanted sex and found it pleasurable. "Egalitarianize" this standard and there emerges the Fun Standard, which holds that a sexual relation is morally right if both parties desire and enjoy it. This is a new morality, rather than an old immorality. According to this standard a sexual relationship is wrong if it is not enjoyable for both participants, even when they are married.

These various standards are predicated upon different values. The Marital Standard is based on the value of procreation: sex is meant for the conception of children. The Double Standard is based on a belief in male superiority: that one purpose for women is to provide men with sexual satisfaction. The Love Standard is based on the value of relationships: sex is for the purpose of expressing and deepening a personal relationship. Finally, the Fun Standard is based on enjoyment and recreation: sex is solely for physical satisfaction. We shall see in a later section how the relative importance of these various values appears to be changing in Canada.

A recent influence on sexual behaviour is the threat of sexually transmitted diseases, the most lethal being AIDS, which will be discussed later in this chapter.

PREMARITAL SEX:
SELECTED THEORETICAL PERSPECTIVES

Psychological Theories

Explanations of variations in sexual attitudes and behaviour range from psychological theories of sexual drive and motivations to the analyses of sexual norms in terms of how they contribute to other aspects in the society. Generally, psychologists explain human sexual behaviour in terms of "drive reduction." Their theories posit a sex "drive" which, like the hunger drive, builds up with deprivation and is satisfied or reduced by coition or masturbation. Alternatively, Hardy (1964) has proposed a cognitive-affective model of sexual motivation which seeks to understand it as a developed appetite that is heavily influenced by social interaction and other experience. This theory can account not only for coitus but also for hand-holding, fetishism, sexual masochism, and "kinky" sexual behaviour.

On the borderline between psychology and social psychology are those accounts of variations in attitude and behaviour in terms of "personal characteristics" such as gender and age (Reiss, 1967, Middendorp et al., 1970 and, indeed most studies), attractiveness (Kaats and Davis, 1970; Lindemann, 1974; Collins, 1975; Furstenberg, 1975), "interpersonal psychological variables" such as responsibility, firmness, skepticism, and conformity (Keller, Elliott, and Gunberg, 1982), religiosity (most studies, including, recently, Davidson and Leslie, 1977; Hornick, 1978; De Lamater and MacCorquodale, 1979), liberalism or conservatism (studied more by earlier researchers, including Reiss, 1967; Middendorp et al., 1970; Maranell et al., 1970), and self-esteem (Stratton and Spitzer, 1967; Perlman, 1974). These "characteristics" are analytically diverse. Sexual identity, attractiveness, and self-esteem relate largely to a labelling process, with the associated meanings and expectations attached to particular physical features. Interpersonal psychological characteristics, such as activity or passivity, are the result of social learning experiences perhaps with some element of innate predisposition. The religiosity and liberalism-conservatism characteristics refer to the strength and consistency of attitude-learning in the home and to the associated norms governing behaviour. Research shows that sexual attitudes and behaviour are related to these characteristics, but they provide little basis for a comprehensive theory.

Social Psychological Theories

Of the many social psychological theories, interaction, reference group, and exchange theories are relevant to our purpose. Many interaction theories are inductively based, such as the often demonstrated hypotheses that premarital sexual activity varies inversely with age for a first date (Bell and Chaskes, 1970), and for steady dating (Hobart, 1972b), and directly with age for love relationships (Eastman, 1972; Christensen and Gregg, 1970), with number of persons dated and steady dated (Hobart, 1972b), and with engagement experience (Hobart, 1972b). Kirkendall has argued that sexual relations, like other interpersonal relations, may increase cooperative attitudes, self-respect, faith and confidence in people, fulfillment of individual potentialities, and may dissolve the barriers that separate people (1961). As such, they are socially reinforcing. On the other hand, sexual relationships that are exploitative and brutal may be destructive as well, and have consequences quite the opposite to those Kirkendall describes.

Reference Group Theory

Reference group theorists explore ways in which the attitudes and behaviour of an individual are shaped by the expectations of his or her normative reference groups. They tend to see parents as a conservative reference group that loses influence during a child's adolescence, and other adolescents as a liberal reference group which gains influence. This explains the tendency for adolescents to become more sexually permissive and the continued unpermissiveness of young people with strong conservative church-based reference groups. Support for hypotheses based on reference group theory concerning premarital sex has often been reported (Teevan, 1972; Davidson and Leslie, 1977).

Exchange Theory

Exchange theorists understand all continuing social relationships as exchange processes, in which each person tries to maximize his or her benefits and minimize his or her costs. This approach was implicit in Waller's discussions of "rating and dating" and "dalliance" relationships reported to have prevailed decades ago (1938): the "big men on campus" attempt to date the most popular "campus queen," and such interest is returned because each benefits from the high rating of the other. In dating, women will seek to exchange a minimum of sexual favors for a maximum of entertainment or affection. Such conceptions are yet relevant to understanding differences in sexual experience and sexual attitudes today. Support for this approach is found in research by Lindemann (1974), Furstenberg (1975), and Davidson and Leslie (1977).

Structural Functional Theory

Structural functional theorists study the functions some practices (structures) of a society perform for other aspects of the system, either the societal system as a whole, or a sub-system such as the family. Thus structural functional discussions, such as Frayser's (1985), have emphasized the importance of premarital virginity and marital chastity for unambiguous recognition of kinship affiliations. This point has current relevance: as the value of large families declines and as childless marriages increase, the emphasis on sexual exclusiveness would also be expected to decline, according to Frayser's theory. This, in fact, is happening.

The structural functional approach contributes to an understanding of current changes in sexual mores, as may be seen in Reiss's work. Based on findings from surveys of students' sexual attitudes and experience, Reiss's theory states that sexual permissiveness varies directly with the freedom from family influences of the courtship couple and the sexual permissiveness in the social setting (1967). His conclusions are rooted in structural functionalism since he relates the freedom of the courtship couple to a lack of family responsibilities. Tests have failed to produce strong or consistent confirmations of this theory (Middendorp et al., 1970; Maranell et al., 1970; Bayer, 1977), but Reiss has argued that these studies were not valid tests.

Recently there have been tests of comprehensive models for predicting sexual intimacy that incorporate a variety of influences identified in the literature. For instance, Hornick's approach includes four broad categories of influences: background variables (rural-urban residence, traditional religious membership, age and grade in school), reference group variables (perceived permissiveness of the father, the mother, and the peer group), individual psychological orientation variables (the religiosity, openness to change, and self-esteem of the respondent), and individual attitude variables (sexual permissiveness and frequency of dating). Hornick tested his model using survey data obtained from 800 high school and university students in Ontario and found a complex pattern of significant relationships between the influences he studied and the sexual intimacies of these students. This theoretical model did achieve some predictive accuracy since it was able to explain 56 percent of the variation in intimacy of sexual behaviour for male respondents, and 52 percent of the variation for females.

Generally, the research identifies the major sources of variation in the premarital sexual activity of young people today in the influences of societies, groups, and individuals, in the interaction or bargaining processes between members of a couple, and in the opportunities offered by the physical settings in which they find themselves. Many influences not yet identified may affect the sexual interest and compliance of a man and a woman in particular circumstances. Nevertheless, the preceding review of theories helps to explain increased premarital sexuality in Canada today.

PREMARITAL SEX IN CANADA

General Trends

Serious research interest in premarital sexual attitudes and behaviour in Canada began to develop during the mid-1960s, about the time that general availability of the birth control pill reduced the risk of unwanted conceptions. Since then the results of at least 28 studies have been published. Two thirds of these studies have been based on samples from Ontario. Of the rest, four have been from Québec, four from the Prairies and two from data in two or more regions of Canada. Most of the respondents were students: in universities or technical schools in 17 of the studies, and in high schools in five. Only six studies were based on data from non-student samples. Accordingly, no single study can claim to be representative of Canadian youth. However, the number of recent studies and the consistency of their findings permit valid generalizations.

As in the case of research in the United States, these studies show a trend toward increasing rates of premarital sex and a convergence of rates with

Table 4-1   Sexual Experience of University of Toronto Students for Selected Years, by Gender of Respondent, in Percentages

Year	Number of Respondents	Response rate	SEXUALLY EXPERIENCED UNMARRIED RESPONDENTS		"OCCASIONAL" OR "OFTEN" SEXUAL EXPERIENCE (UNMARRIED RESPONDENTS)	
			Males	Females	Males	Females
		%	%	%	%	%
1968	1200	44	40	32	24	20
1971	1300	59	55	37	36	29
1974	2950	52	59	56	43	46
1978	2985	53	62	58	48	50

Source: Adapted from Barrett, 1980:369-371.

women "catching up" with men, in terms of sexual experience. Thus a study conducted among University of Western Ontario students in 1965 found 35 percent for the men and 15 percent for the women had experienced pre-marital sex (Mann, 1967). The most recent, conducted among Guelph University students in 1982, found rates of 60 and 52 percent for men and women respectively (Herold, 1984).

A more detailed picture emerges from Barrett's analysis of mail questionnaire data collected at the University of Toronto in 1968, 1971, 1974, and 1978 (1980). The samples were drawn from the student directory, and the numbers of respondents obtained are large—1200, 1300, 2950, and 2985 respectively—but the response rates are low, ranging from 44 to 59 percent as the data in Table 4-1 show. Barrett found a converging pattern of increasing sexual experience rates among male and female respondents, the same pattern found by studies in the United States. The proportions of sexually experienced unmarried women students increased from 32 percent in 1968 to 58 percent in 1978, while the figures for males were 40 percent and 62 percent. The number of women and men reporting intercourse "occasionally" or "often" increased during these years as well, from 20 percent for women and 24 percent for men in 1968 to 50 percent for women and 48 percent for men in 1978. Note the recent tendency for sexually active women to report greater frequency of intercourse than men. Moreover, when Barrett's 1974 and 1978 surveys asked about intercourse experiences during the three months prior to the survey, six or more episodes were reported by 58 percent of the women in 1974, and by 61 percent in 1978, while these proportions for male respondents were substantially less, 49 percent and 48 percent respectively (Barrett, 1980).

Little difference was found between the number of intercourse partners reported by male and female samples: six or more partners were cited by about 17 percent of the women and men in both 1974 and 1978. There is no clear evidence of declining age at first intercourse. The proportions of those who were sexually active and had their first experience by age 17 included 30 percent of the women and 44 percent of the men in 1974, and 35 and 40 percent respectively in 1978, differences which are not significant (Barrett, 1980).

Few researchers have asked young people about oral sexual contacts, but Herold and Way did obtain this information from 200 women at the University of Guelph in 1982 (1983). Sixty-one percent reported performing oral sex on a male, and 68 percent said they had received oral sex from a male. The fact that women had been the receiver at least as often as the giver of this form of sexual attention points to the demise of the Double Standard in this as in other areas of sexual behaviour. A further point of interest is that, while 97 percent of women with coital experience had engaged in oral sex, no less than one third of the women who were virgins had oral sex experience, 35 percent having received and 26 percent having given oral stimulation. Half of each group had achieved orgasm or had brought their partners to orgasm in this way (Herold, 1984). The fact that so many women had this experience suggests that many see this as less intimate than full intercourse; in contrast Kinsey found that during the 1930s and 1940s, oral sex was usually experienced only after intercourse, if at all (Kinsey et al., 1953).

Inter-Regional Studies in Canada

A comprehensive picture of the changing involvement in premarital sex emerges from the work of Hobart, who conducted comparative studies in several regions of Canada in 1968 and 1977, focusing both on attitudes toward premarital intercourse and on actual sexual experience. These data provide a picture of changing attitudes and behaviour and of discrepancies between the standards young people profess and the behaviours they practice.

Hobart collected data from students enrolled in a number of universities and technical schools across Canada in 1968 (Hobart, 1972b), and again in 1977, using essentially the same questionnaire. The 1968 student samples were drawn from universities in Alberta, Ontario, and Québec, one school in each province, and from technical schools in Alberta and Québec. The 1977 data were collected again from the same schools as the 1968 data, as well as from a university and a technical school in Nova Scotia, British Columbia and Ontario.

In the 1968 study, a total of 1104 responses were obtained from randomly drawn samples at the five schools. About 90 percent of those contacted responded in the Alberta and the Ontario schools. However, the rate from the Québec university students was only 44 percent, in part because the data collection was interrupted by the mail strike of 1968. Owing to this limitation in the 1968 francophone data, the contrasts between the 1968 anglophone and francophone students and between the 1968 and 1977 francophone data are merely suggestive.

The sample design for the 1977 study called for random selection of 100 white male and female students aged between 18 and 25, and not members of a religious order, from each of 10 schools. The final sample consisted of 2062 students, including 414 francophones and 1848 anglophones. Over 75 percent of the students contacted completed questionnaires in eight of the ten schools surveyed in 1976 and 1977. The two exceptions were in British Columbia where the response rate for technical school students was 56 percent and for university students, 61 percent.

Attitudes Toward Premarital Sex

A comparison of the attitudes of the 1968 and 1977 anglophone and francophone samples toward premarital intercourse under various relationship conditions is seen in Table 4-2. Generally, the data show three important trends: an increase in permissive attitudes to sexuality in all samples, a decline of the Double Standard with a resulting convergence of the attitudes and practices of male and female respondents with respect to premarital sex, and a convergence of the attitudes of francophone and anglophone students. In terms of the four sexual standards previously discussed, there was a decline in support of the Marital Standard, among anglophone respondents from 41 percent to 18 percent, and even more dramatically from 46 percent to only nine percent among francophone sample members. The decline in support for this standard was substantial for both sexes, but was greater for females in every school in the study. The decline was smallest (22 percent) among the anglophone males advocating the Abstinence Standard for females, and it was greatest (49 percent) among the francophone women advocating this standard for themselves.

Support for the Love Standard increased by 24 percent among men and by 34 percent among women. The data show stronger shifts toward the Love Standard by female than by male respondents, for female than for male behaviour, and by francophones than by anglophones. Support for the Fun Standard also increased, though to a more modest extent. The increase amounted to seven percent for anglophone students and to 18 percent for francophone students. Again, the shift toward this standard was stronger by female than by male respondents, for female than for male behaviour, and by francophones than by anglophones.

Table 4-2 Attitudes of Anglophone and Francophone Respondents Toward Sexual Intercourse in 1968 and 1977, by Sex of Respondent, in Percentages

ISSUE		1968 SAMPLE		1977 SAMPLE	
Sexual Intercourse Is:	*Respondent*	*For Males* %	*For Females* %	*For Males* %	*For Females* %
Never	Anglophone Males	33[2]	36[2]	13[2]	14[2]
acceptable	Females	48	53	23	24
	Total	41	44	18	19
	Francophone Males	40	40[2]	9	8
	Females	53	58	9	9
	Total	46	49	9	9
Acceptable	Anglophone Males	67[2]	66[2]	87[2]	86[2]
if the couple	Females	52	47	77	76
is engaged	*Total*	59	56	82	81
	Francophone Males	60	60	91	92
	Females	47	42	91	91
	Total	54	51	91	91
Acceptable	Anglophone Males	64[2]	61[2]	85	83
if the couple	Females	50	42	77	76
is in love	*Total*	57	51	81	80
	Francophone Males	56	52	84	86
	Females	42	40	84	83
	Total	50	46	84	84
Acceptable	Anglophone Males	38[1]	24[1]	46[1]	39[1]
if the couple	Females	13	4	18	16
feels no	*Total*	25	13	32	27
affection	Francophone Males	22[2]	13	39	34
	Females	6	1	27	22
	Total	14	7	32	27
Numbers of	Anglophone Males	329	329	796	795
respondents	Females	352	352	832	832
	Total	681	681	1628	1627
	Francophone Males	190	203	189	189
	Females	187	196	222	222
	Total	377	399	411	411

1. Signifies differences between same sample males and females: significant at .01 level.
2. Signifies differences between same sample males and females: significant at .05 level.

There may be a Double Standard approach to any of the other three sexual standards: respondents may more frequently prescribe the Marital Standard for women than for men, or may advocate a more liberal standard for men than for women. Comparison of the "for males" and "for females" columns in Table 4-1 provides information on the advocacy of the Double Standard by male and female respondents under various relationship conditions. By 1977 a Double Standard approach was no longer significant with respect to the Fun Standard. It was advocated most strongly by anglophone males who gave males a seven percent advantage in respect to this standard. Francophone males and females followed with five percent each, while anglophone women showed the least difference—two percent—in favoring the Fun Standard for men and women.

These data clearly show widespread support for premarital sexual relationships among the samples of Canadian students in 1977, with fewer than one in five young anglophones and fewer than one in ten francophone respondents opposing it. The shift in attitudes of young francophones is particularly remarkable, especially among women, whose opposition to premarital sex dropped from 53 percent to nine percent. Among both groups of respondents the change in support was greatest toward the Love Standard, though support for the Fun Standard also increased, particularly among francophone respondents, and especially francophone women. Thus the greatest liberalization in attitudes in 1977 occurred among those elements of the student population which were most conservative in 1968.

Premarital Sexual Experience

To what extent have these shifts in attitude been reflected in behaviour? The data in Table 4-3 provide the answer. Considering petting experience first, the data show no change in the incidence of petting experience among either anglophone men or women but, generally, a significant increase in such experience among francophones, particularly women. The data also show an increase in premarital sexual intercourse experience between 1968 and 1977 among anglophones, slightly greater in the case of the women than men (19 and 17 percent). Francophone women reported a very large increase—35 percent—in intercourse experience while, surprisingly, francophone men reported no increase.

An indication of the extent of actual conformity to the Love Standard is found in Table 4-3 in the proportions reporting they were in love with all intercourse partners. A convergence of male and female patterns is seen for anglophone respondents, with 11 percent more men reporting an increase and ten percent more women reporting a decrease in intercourse only with loved partners in 1977 as compared with 1968. Francophone men and women show a weaker pattern of convergence: both reported higher

Table 4-3 Incidence of Various Sexual Experiences among 1968 and 1977 Anglophone[1] and Francophone Sample Members, by Sex of Respondent, in Percentages

Sexual Experience	Sample	1968 SAMPLE			1977 SAMPLE		
		Total %	Males %	Females %	Total %	Males %	Females %
Has never petted	Anglophone	8	9	8	10	10	11
	Francophone	33	20	47	14	17	12
In love with all petting partners	Anglophone	25	10[1]	38	21	17	25
	Francophone	NOT AVAILABLE			40	35	44
Has experienced intercourse	Anglophone	50	56[2]	44[1]	68	73	63
	Francophone	47	63[1]	30	62	59	65
Engaged to all intercourse partners	Anglophone	20	14[2]	29	11	9	13
	Francophone	NOT AVAILABLE			5	6	5
In love with all intercourse partners	Anglophone	50	34[1]	70	53	45[2]	60
	Francophone	46	38[1]	56	64	62	66
Sexual experience conformed to							
The Marital Standard	Anglophone	50	44	56	32	27	38
	Francophone	NOT AVAILABLE			38	41	35
The Double Standard	Anglophone	1	2	0[3]	0.3	1	0[3]
	Francophone	NOT AVAILABLE			0	0	0[3]
The Love Standard	Anglophone	24	19	28	47	48	47
	Francophone	NOT AVAILABLE			50	48	52
The Fun Standard	Anglophone	26	37	16	20	26	14
	Francophone	NOT AVAILABLE			12	11	13
Number of respondents	Anglophone	699	336	363	1560	765	795
	Francophone	369	194	177	398	184	214

1. Signifies differences between same sample males and females: significant at .01 level.
2. Signifies differences between same sample males and females: significant at .05 level.
3. Women professing the Double Standard in effect practise the Marital Standard.

incidences of intercourse only with loved partners, with this increase greater in the case of men than of women (14 and ten percent). Generally, the data in Table 4-3 show that the trends in attitude changes among anglophone and francophone respondents during the 1968 to 1977 period are apparent in their reported sexual behaviour as well.

It is possible to determine the proportions of respondents conforming *behaviourally* to the various sexual standards previously described, for anglophones in 1968 and 1977 and for francophones in 1977, as seen in Table 4-3. The pattern for the anglophones is generally similar to that found for changes in professed standards: there is a decline in practice of the Abstinence Standard among both men and women, but the decline is greater in the case of the women. For men, practice of the Double Standard declined virtually to zero—note that women who behaviourally conform to the Double Standard practise abstinence. Very large increases in the practice of the Love Standard were found in respondents of both sexes, and both also showed declines in practice of the Fun Standard. Thus, these data show that the pattern of changes in students' reported behaviour is parallel to changes in the standards they profess, the Fun Standard being an exception.

If 1977 behavioural patterns of anglophone and francophone students are compared (Table 4-3) we find that among the men, more francophones practised the Marital Standard and fewer practised the Fun Standard relative to the anglophones. Only insignificant differences are found between anglophone and francophone women. The most important point here is that the anglophone data clearly suggest increasing acceptance of the Love Standard, in terms of both profession and practice. The data for francophone respondents also show increasing profession of the Love Standard, but also a rather strong shift toward the Fun Standard as well, more so than among the Anglophone respondents.

It is possible with the anglophone students, to determine how much consistency there is between the sexual standards that respondents professed and those that they practised. Many respondents of course practise what they profess. Among the rest there may be two broad patterns of inconsistency: students may practise a more liberal standard than they profess, or they may profess a more liberal standard than they have (yet) had opportunity to practise. The data in Table 4-4 show that seven patterns may be identified, in addition to a residual category. Four of these are consistent patterns, in response to the Marital, Double, Love, and Fun Standards. Almost half (48 percent) of all anglophone respondents reported consistent patterns in 1968, and somewhat less, 44 percent, did so in 1977. The declines were similar for both male and female respondents. Within these consistent types there were shifts, however, with large declines in consistent Marital Standard adherents, and equally large increases in consistent Love Standard adherents. Men and women showed no changes in the proportions adhering consistently to the Double or the Fun Standards.

Table 4-4 Professed-Behavioural Standard Types for Anglophone Respondent in 1968 and 1977, by Sex of Respondent, in Percentages

Standard Type	MALE			FEMALE			TOTAL			MALE-FEMALE DIFFERENCES	
	1968 %	1977 %	Difference %	1968 %	1977 %	Difference %	1968 %	1977 %	Difference %	1968 %	1977 %
Consistent Marital	20.9	6.9	− 14.0	41.6	13.2	− 28.4	31.7	9.8	− 21.9	20.7	6.3
Consistent Double	1.8	1.1	− 0.7	0.0	0.0	0.0	0.8	0.6	− 0.2	*****[3]	*****[3]
Consistent Engaged	2.4	1.1	− 1.3	2.5	1.3	− 1.2	2.4	1.2	− 1.2	0.1	0.2
Consistent Love	3.3	16.5	+ 13.2[1]	6.9	30.8	+ 23.9[1]	5.2	23.1	+ 17.9[1]	3.6	14.3
Consistent Fun	14.6	13.3	− 1.3	2.5	3.8	+ 1.3	8.3	8.9	− 0.6	12.1[1]	9.5
Dissatisfied Chaste	21.5	18.1	− 3.4	14.4	13.8	− 0.6	16.4	16.1	− 0.3	7.1[2]	4.3
Regretful Non-virgin	6.6	3.7	− 2.9	10.3	6.3	− 4.0	8.5	4.9	− 3.6[2]	3.7	2.6
Other	31.9	39.4	+ 7.5[1]	21.7	30.8	+ 9.1[2]	26.6	35.4	+ 8.8[2]	10.2[1]	8.6
Number of Respondents	335	188		360	159		695	347		57.5	45.8
Total consistent in profession in practice	43.0	38.9	− 4.1[1]	53.5	49.1	− 3.6	48.4	43.5	− 4.9		
Total inconsistent: practised standards were less stringent than professed	56.5	45.2	− 10.3[1]	52.7	44.4	− 8.3[2]	44.8	26.0	− 18.8[1]		
Total of sexually experienced consistent in profession and practice	22.1	32.0	+ 9.9[1]	11.9	35.9	+ 24.0[1]	16.8	33.7	+ 18.9[1]		

1. Significant at .01 level
2. Significant at .05 level.
3. Women professing the Double Standard practise abstinence: thus, a male-female comparison on this standard is not possible.

Two inconsistent types are of particular interest: those professing a non-Marital Standard who lack sexual experience (the 'dissatisfied chaste") and those professing the Marital Standard who are sexually experienced (the "regretful non-virgins"). The data in Table 4-4 show that, in terms of total numbers, the former outnumbered the latter by more than three to one in both 1968 and 1977. Men predominate among the dissatisfied chaste and most regretful non-virgins are women, although more women are among the dissatisfied chaste than among the regretful. Note that among those who were sexually experienced the proportion consistent in profession and practice increased by ten percent (from 22 to 32 percent) between 1968 and 1977 among men, and by 24 percent (from 12 to 36 percent) among women. In both cases the increase was primarily the result of increases in consistent Love Standard adherents in 1977 at the expense of other types, and particularly the Abstinence Standard.

We saw early in this chapter that there have been strong tendencies in the Western cultural heritage to define premarital sex as sexual immorality and that, since early Victorian times, enforcement of these norms has depended on internalized controls inflicting guilt, rather than on externalized controls imposing shame. How many young Canadians suffer from guilt in recent years as a result of violating the traditional Abstinence Standard? The data in Table 4-5 show that in 1968 among the anglophones about half the women, and larger proportions of the men, said they experienced no regret following their first intercourse experience, and that they did not need to justify it or justified it very well. Nevertheless, about 80 percent of the women and 60 percent of the men said they experienced some guilt following their first experience. Nine years later there were significant increases in the number of respondents, larger among women than men, who said they experienced no regret and justified their first intercourse experience well. Yet over half of the men (53 percent) and about three quarters of the women (74 percent) reported experiencing some guilt. During these nine years the "guilt gap" between men and women shrank very slightly, by three percent, but the continued vitality of Double Standard morality among anglophones is yet seen in the fact that about 50 percent more women than men experienced guilty reactions to their sexual initiation.

Figures are not available for francophones in 1968, but their 1977 responses present some interesting contrasts with the anglophones. In the francophone sample, 95 percent of the men and 88 percent of the women said they experienced no regret, and only about 40 percent of the men and 53 percent of the women reported feeling guilt. These figures suggest that by 1977 a permissive, single standard with respect to premarital intercourse was more deeply rooted in francophone than in anglophone Canadian society.

There has been a number of more recent surveys of sexual experience among young Canadians, none of which have reported intercourse rates

Table 4-5 Reactions to First Intercourse Experience among Anglophone and Francophone Respondents in 1968 and 1977, by Sex of Respondent, in Percentages

Reaction	Respondents	1968 SAMPLE			1977 SAMPLE			1968-1977 DIFFERENCES	
		Total %	Males %	Females %	Total %	Males %	Females %	Males %	Females %
Justified it very well, or no need to justify it	Anglophone	49	54	43	54	58	50	+ 4	+ 7
	Francophone	NOT	AVAILABLE		63	61	67	—	—
Definitely no regret following this experience	Anglophone	62	71²	50	75	69	+10	+19	—
	Francophone	NOT	AVAILABLE		9195	88	—	—	—
No guilt at all following this experience	Anglophone	32	40²	22	37	47¹	26	+ 7	+ 4
	Francophone	NOT	AVAILABLE		53	61	47	—	—
Number of Cases	Anglophone	343	186	157	1081	569	512		
	Francophone	NOT	AVAILABLE		258	115	143		

1. Signifies that differences between males and females in the same sample are significant at .01 level.
2. Signifies that differences between males and females in the same sample are significant at .05 level.

greater than 62 percent for males and 58 percent for females (Hobart, 1979). This might seem to suggest that the sexual revolution has passed its peak. Nevertheless, the more likely explanation is that in every case the mean age of the more recent survey respondents was lower, indicating that they were less sexually experienced than those in Hobart's sample (Barrett, 1980; Frappier, 1983; Herold, 1984). Since each of these studies was based on a sample from a single school and since all but one was made in Ontario or Québec, they provide little additional basis for projecting Canadian trends.

In any case, the growing public awareness of the threat posed by AIDS during the second half of the 1980s would certainly invalidate any discussion, based on earlier data, of current Canadian trends with respect to casual sex. The January 12, 1987, issue of *Maclean's* magazine published the results of a nationwide telephone survey that indicated increased cautiousness, because of the risk of AIDS, among those involved in unmarried sexual relationships (Barber, 1987). In early summer 1987 the federal government began a widespread media campaign to increase public awareness of the seriousness of this risk and to urge the practice of "safe sex." A special report on "AIDS and Sex" published in the August 31, 1987, issue of *Maclean's* carried the lead statement: "the deadly plague of AIDS is spreading with frightening swiftness. The panic level is rising, and more and more people are asking: when is sex safe. Their lives depend on the answer" (Corelli, 1987, cover page). Thus it seems inevitable that the incidence of extramarital sex, and particularly of casual sex, will decline substantially as awareness of the risks and of the death toll caused by AIDS continues to grow.

CONCLUSIONS

The brief review of the history of sexual mores at the beginning of this chapter shows that a variety of meanings may be imposed on sexual behaviour and that such meanings and their associated norms have varied considerably, even during the Christian era. During the past quarter century or more, Canada, along with the rest of the Western world, has experienced dramatic changes in sexual standards that are particularly visible in premarital sexual attitudes and practices. The old Double Standard is virtually defunct, and the proportion of young people advocating the Marital Standard is in decline. In the place of these "old moralities" the Love Standard has emerged as the strongest "new morality," claiming support from about half of both the anglophone and the francophone respondents in 1977, while the Fun Standard was professed by about one quarter. While a major feature of the last 25 years has been the erosion of the Double Standard in all its forms, significant differences in the sexual attitudes of men and women are yet apparent. Thus, among both anglophone and francophone respondents, support for the Love Standard was around 25 percent stronger among women than men, while three times as many anglophone men and one-and-a-half times as many francophone men advocated the Fun Standard as did women in these language groups.

Despite these differences, the effects of the "sexual revolution" have been more dramatically apparent among women than among men; indeed, they are well on their way toward eliminating differences between themselves and men in the sexual standards they profess and practise. The most dramatic example of this is seen in the case of francophone women who, in 1968, were the most conservative in their profession of the Marital Standard, more so than anglophone men and women, as well as than francophone men. By 1977 they had overtaken anglophones of both sexes and, while they professed the Marital Standard in the same low proportion as francophone men (about eight percent), they were second only to anglophone men in proportions having premarital experience. Thus francophone women provide a dramatic illustration of the speed with which the acceptable sexual attitude may change in a whole segment of society, and their example raises intriguing questions about the causes of this change.

Undoubtedly there are many contributive factors, one of the most important being the increased availability and acceptability not only of contraception, especially the birth control pill, but of abortion, and of unwed pregnancy and motherhood as well. Both the risk and the stigma of unwed pregnancy have been substantially reduced. The increased employment of women, particularly in French Canada, which gives them an alternative to the exclusive wife and mother role and tends to make them economically independent of and more equal to men, certainly reduces their need to guard their virginity as a prerequisite to a respectable marriage. At the same time, religious definitions of sexual morality have either been liberalized, as the in the cases of the United and the Anglican Churches, or have experienced significant losses in credibility, as in the case of Catholic teachings for many of its adherents. Generally it appears that most, if not all, of these influences have worked more strongly in Québec than in the rest of Canada.

In addition to these, however, there appear to be other, more profound influences at work in the form of value changes. Three may be noted. There is a shift from familistic to more individualistic values, most clearly seen in Québec in the current rapid disappearance of the large family form, but apparent also in the steep slide in the birth rate in Canada generally since the mid-1960s. There is an increased emphasis on egalitarian relationships, which is difficult to document but is certainly illustrated by the pre-eminent position of the egalitarian Love Standard. Finally, there is increased valuation of hedonistic gratification, physical pleasure for its own sake, seen in the Fun Standard, and also in the sizable and equal proportions of men and women reporting oral sexual experiences.

There is no reason to suspect that the support for any of these three

values—individualism, egalitarian relationships, and physical gratification—
is only short term. Certainly the world population situation and the secularization of modern urban society seem to preclude any speedy return to
more traditional values of procreation, family, male dominance, and spir-
ituality. Does this imply, however, the continued liberalization of the sexual
scene, with premarital experience becoming increasingly commonplace for
consenting couples at progressively earlier ages, and with frequent changes
in partners? Certainly it may; we have seen that such practices have been
common in a number of simple societies.

But there are important counter-influences operative in the world today.
The most significant may be the health threat which promiscuous sexual
relations pose—the herpes risk was seen by many as somewhat daunting,
and a deep fear of AIDS is becoming widespread. While AIDS was initially
most commonly spread through homosexual contacts, it has now become
established among heterosexuals and is spreading rapidly among them. In
time, a form of innoculation against AIDS, and perhaps treatment for this
disease, may be found. In the meantime the threat of AIDS is beginning to
induce more cautiousness about sexual relationships among young people,
though many seem to feel there is yet little risk among their associates
(Barber, 1987). Most at risk, of course, are Fun Standard adherents, so that
increased cautiousness may become more apparent among them. The effect
of the AIDS threat on practice of the Love Standard will likely be less, since
many may feel that to be in love with someone involves knowing enough
about the person to be able to judge whether he or she had been exposed
to AIDS or not. There will doubtless be increased practice of the Marital
Standard among those most fearful of the disease.

In sum, with the rapid change period of the sexual revolution past, with
women well on their way to catching up with men in incidence of sexual
experience, and with the fear of AIDS to discourage growth of the Fun
Standard, it seems unlikely that the next five or ten years will witness any
significant new trends in premarital sexuality among Canadian young people. Support for the Love Standard may continue to grow at the expense of
the Fun Standard, and the Marital Standard will probably experience some
increased support as well. As of 1987, support for the Double Standard has
virtually disappeared, and there is no reason now to expect a reversal of
this development.

Suggested Readings

Barrett, F.M.
1980   "Sexual Experience, Birth Control Use and Sex Education of Unmarried Canadian University Students." *Archives of Sexual Behavior* 9:367-390.

DeLamater, J., and P. MacCorquodale.
1979   *Premarital Sexuality*. Madison, WI: University of Wisconsin Press.

Frayser, Suzanne G.
1985   *Varieties of Sexual Experience*. New Haven, CT: HRAF Press.

Herold, Edward S.
1984   *Sexual Behavior of Canadian Young People*. Markham: Fitzhenry & Whiteside.

Hobart, Charles.
1984   "Changing Profession and Practice of Sexual Standards: A Study of Young Anglophone and Francophone Canadians." *Journal of Comparative Family Studies* 15:231-256.

Masters, W., V. Johnson, and R.C. Kolodny
1985   *Sex and Human Loving*. Boston: Little, Brown.

Rodman, Hyman, Susan A. Lewis, and Baralyn B. Griffith.
1984   *The Sexual Rights of Adolescents*. New York: Columbia University Press.

Wilson, G., and M. Cook, eds.
1979   *Love and Attraction*. New York: Pergamon Press.

5

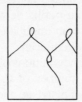

PROFILES OF MARRIAGE AND THE FAMILY

G.N. Ramu

For most Canadians marriage and the formation of a family are intricate, protracted, and, to a large extent, problematic processes. They are subtly tempered by cultural definitions such as social class, ethnicity, religion, and other social determinants. Societal interest in marriage and the family stems from the traditional functions they perform—reproduction and the primary socialization of children. Canada, like other nations, is concerned with the maintenance of its population in order to ensure social stability and continuity as well as the survival of such social institutions as the economy, the state, and religion. When population growth declines beyond the point of replacement, serious doubts arise about the ability of a society to maintain and perpetuate itself, as is clearly indicated in the case of Québec. For example, the current fertility rate is no longer sufficient to ensure the renewal of generations which, in turn, has had an impact on Québec's demographic position within Canada and on its unique cultural and linguistic heritage and identity (Lachapelle and Henripin, 1982; Romaniuc, 1984:14-18).

Traditionally, the family has been the most dependable and efficient organization to perform legitimate reproduction and rearing of children. All societies have evolved ways to motivate individuals to marry and form families. Furthermore, given the importance attached to reproduction and training of the young, it is not surprising that varying degrees of legal and social controls are exercised in these areas, the primary emphasis falling on the distinction between legitimate and illegitimate union and offspring. These controls are expressed in matters pertaining to social definitions of maturity, age at first marriage, mate selection, premarital and extramarital sexual relationships, to cite a few. In most societies marriage, as a ritual, public ceremony, or legal contract, is required prior to the birth of a legitimate child. A wedding is a public demonstration of a couple's commitment to each other and also an implicit expression of its goals—reproduction and the socialization of children.

Nonetheless, moral and legal definitions of marriage and family are being questioned by an increasing number of Canadians who have chosen to reject traditional expectations of marriage and family patterns. For example, some couples (about 10 to 15 percent) may decide deliberately to remain childless (Veevers, 1980; Ramu, 1984, 1985), although in other instances, couples who desire children may not be able to have them because of infertility (Matthews and Matthews, 1986). There are others who either remain unmarried or live together without a formal marriage contract. There is also greater freedom and legal accommodation now to terminate unsatisfactory and stressful marriages than there was, for instance, in the 1960s.

There have also been changes in the traditional structure and functions of the family. The unprecedented entry of married women into the labour force has eroded the role of husbands as sole breadwinners and, in turn, will eventually bring about changes in the domestic division of labour and a redefinition of marital roles. While the nuclear family (husband, wife, and their children) continues to be the predominant pattern, alternatives such as single-parent and reconstituted families may also perform most of the traditional functions of the family.

These changing trends suggest that there are now choices in marriage and family relationships in Canada. Individuals can, within certain social and legal limits, freely construct the patterns of marriage and family which suit their personal goals and preferences. It should also be noted that, while not all of these emerging patterns have received unconditional and universal support, there is an increasing tolerance and even accommodation of such developments.

The main objective of this chapter is to outline the nature of marriage and family in Canada in relation to their traditional and changing patterns. The discussion is based primarily on demographic trends recorded by the Census and on related data. (Note that empirical and statistical information on aging and family, divorce, and remarriage are not included in this chapter: they are dealt with in detail elsewhere in this book.)

MARITAL PATTERNS

Demographic data on marriage rates, age at marriage, proportion of singles, those who cohabit without legal marriage contract, divorce, and remarriage serve as a barometer of the status of marriage and the family in Canada. In general, the findings suggest that, although marriage remains a popular personal and social undertaking for most Canadians, there is a slight tendency today either to delay or forego legal marriage, and to divorce more frequently than ever before. These demographic trends reflect the tensions between the freedom and individualism widely propagated in our society and the commitment to conventional forms of social life.

Marriage Rates

There are several ways of ascertaining the marital state of the population in Canada. One is to count the number of marriages contracted in a given year. Thus we can say that in Canada in 1984 some 185 597 marriages were contracted, slightly more than the 185 096 contracted a year later. Although such figures would tell us the number of marriages increased or decreased relative to past years, they would not provide us with an accurate statistical or demographic profile.

Consequently, demographers (those concerned with the characteristics of populations) generally use what is known as the marriage rate, which involves counting the number of marriages per 100 000 total population in a given year. Although this approach has some deficiencies because it includes those who are highly unlikely to marry, it does serve as a useful indicator for comparative purposes. In Table 5-1, the numbers and rates of marriage for selected years are given.

The data in Table 5-1 indicate that Canadian marriage rates have fluctuated over time. These fluctuations are attributable to major political events such as wars, and to economic crises such as depression, recession, or inflation. For example, the major economic event of this century, the Great Depression of the 1930s, was accompanied by a steep decline in the marriage rate. Before and after the Second World War and during the period of economic recovery from the Depression, the rate rose to 1090—the highest ever in Canadian history—and this resulted not only in a post-war "marriage boom" but also in a "baby boom." An offshoot of this baby boom was an increase in the marriage rate during the 1970s (Romaniuc, 1984).

In brief, although the demographic evidence on the marriage rate shows a slight decline in marriage, it by no means indicates that Canadians have become disenchanted with marriage or forsaken it for other arrangements.

Age at First Marriage

A consideration of age at marriage is sociologically important because it gives us clues regarding certain structural and personal aspects of marriage in a given society. For example, where an individual (especially the male) is expected to complete his educational or occupational training and to acquire a job prior to marriage, the age at marriage tends to be relatively

Table 5-1 Number of Marriages and Marriage Rates for Canada, 1921–1985

	MARRIAGES	
Year	Number	Rate*
1921	71 254	790
1931	68 239	640
1941	124 644	1060
1946	137 398	1090
1951	128 408	920
1956	132 713	830
1961	128 475	700
1968	167 538	790
1969	179 413	920
1971	191 324	890
1976	193 343	840
1980	191 069	800
1981	190 082	780
1984	185 597	740
1985	185 096	730

* Rate is marriages per 100 000 population.

SOURCE: *Canada Year Books, 1941–1981, Vital Statistics,* vol. II, 1981–1986. Reproduced with permission of the Minister of Supply and Services Canada.

high. Consequently, the age difference between the bride and bridegroom is likely to be fairly large. In fact, a few studies in other countries indicate that the difference could be ten years or more (see Ramu, 1977:51-54). In cases of an age discrepancy, interpersonal relations may be affected, resulting in a lower probability of egalitarianism and in the greater authority of the husband.

Demographic materials indicate that there have been fluctuations in age at first marriage during the last half century or so. Prior to the 1900s, Canadians tended to marry later in their lives than they do now. For example, Gee (1982) has estimated that in the late 1800s, the average age at first marriage in Canada was about 29 years for men and 26 for women. She also found that the averages increased over the period 1851 to 1891, which coincided with the decline of fertility rates.

An analysis of the statistical data on the age at marriage for the last half century reveals three trends, as seen in Table 5-2. First, there was a gradual but sustained decrease in age at marriage of both males and females until 1979. Second, there has been a gradual increase in the age at first marriage in recent years. Third, age differences between brides and the bridegrooms

Table 5-2   Mean and Median Ages at First Marriage of Brides and Grooms

	MEAN AGE		MEDIAN AGE	
Year	Grooms	Brides	Grooms	Brides
1921	29.9	25.5*	—	—
1931	29.2	24.9*	—	—
1941	27.6	24.4	26.3	23.0
1946	27.1	24.1	25.4	22.5
1951	26.6	23.8	24.8	22.0
1956	26.1	23.4	24.5	21.6
1961	25.8	22.9	24.0	21.1
1966	25.2	22.6	23.7	21.2
1971	25.2	22.6	23.5	21.3
1976	25.0	22.7	23.7	21.6
1980	25.5	23.3	24.3	22.3
1981	25.7	23.5	24.6	22.5
1982	25.9	23.7	24.8	22.8
1983	26.2	24.0	25.1	23.1
1984	26.5	24.3	25.4	23.4
1985	26.7	24.6	25.6	23.7

SOURCE: *Vital Statistics, 1941–1985.* Ottawa: Statistics Canada. Reproduced with permission of the Minister of Supply and Services Canada.

* Dominion Bureau of Statistics, *Nuptiality* (Ottawa: The Queen's Printer, 1967). Tables 4 & 5.

have decreased. For example, in 1921, the average difference was 4.4 years and in 1985 it stood at 2.1.

Statistics Canada reports indicate that approximately 30 percent of first-time brides were under 20 years of age in 1971. Nevertheless, in the following decade the trend reversed. In 1985 the mean age at first marriage for brides was 24.6 years, and for grooms 26.7 years while in 1980 it was 23.3 and 25.5 respectively, an increase of one year for both sexes. A similar comparison for the fourteen-year period from 1971 to 1985 indicates an increase of about two years for both partners.

Why do contemporary Canadians tend to delay marriage? In the absence of empirical studies we can only speculate about the causes. It is quite likely that an increasing number of individuals are delaying their marriages until they complete schooling and become settled in occupations. These are constraining imperatives, given the high rate of unemployment and recessionary trends in recent years. Furthermore, for many Canadians legal marriage entails too many encumbrances; consequently, they tend to resort to casual liaisons to meet their immediate sexual and emotional needs. Those who seek a relatively permanent relationship have chosen simply to live together.

These observations indicate that for a significant minority alternative marital patterns are relevant, at least during some periods of their lives. They also point to the flexibility and accommodation in social attitudes and norms concerning marriage and the family in the face of structural changes in Canadian society. In this regard, in a recent analysis of changing marriage rates among the Canadian women, Trovato (1986) has argued that the emphasis on individualism in Western societies (including Canada) has resulted in the decline of the centrality of marriage in people's lives. From the point of view of present demographic trends, the declining rates of marriage, and rising ages of brides and grooms at first marriage may influence the fertility rates, a point to which we shall return later in this chapter.

Living Together

Students of the family are not sure whether living together (or non-marital cohabitation) is a contemporary alternative to the steady dating and engagement stages of the traditional courting continuum, or simply an alternative to marriage. Reiss (1980:106-107) defines these alternatives as "courtship cohabitation," and "non-legal marital cohabitation," respectively. The courtship cohabitation is generally a temporary alliance serving as either an alternative or an adjunct to steady dating and engagement. The changing sexual norms, availability of contraceptives, peer-group support, decline in parental authority, and reformed legal codes permit young men and women to live together without being socially stigmatized. Although in the 1970s living together was seen as common among the middle-class college-age youth, in the 1980s it appears to have spread among other sections of the population. Non-legal marital cohabitation is hardly a novel phenomenon and historically has always existed, primarily among the lower classes or other marginal groups, as well as among upper-class men who had mistresses.

In Canada, although the proportion of those who are reported to be living together is on the increase, it still constitutes only a small minority. The 1981 census found that couples living together as common-law partners represented six percent of all couples, or 352 000, twice as many as in 1971. Their numbers further rose in 1986 to 487 000 (or eight percent of all families) which constitutes a 38 percent increase from 1981 (Statistics Canada, *The Daily*, July 9, 1987). In sum, one in 12 couples in 1986 was living together.

Furthermore, the proportion of those living under common law differed from one region of the country to the other. The highest proportion of non-legal unions was found in Yukon (20 percent), followed by Northwest Territories (17 percent). Among the provinces, 13 percent of all couples in

Québec were not formally married while less than five percent of all couples in Newfoundland and Prince Edward Island fell into this category. The high proportion of non-legal unions in Québec is indicative of the rapid changes in traditional French-Canadian marriage and family patterns.

Burch (1985:13-15) found in his study only 5.2 percent of all male respondents, and 6.5 percent of all female respondents reported living together. The survey also found that the percentage of those living together is highest in the age group from 19 to 29. The Canadian Fertility Survey, conducted among women across Canada at the University of Western Ontario (see Balakrishnan, 1986), found a higher proportion of those interviewed were cohabiting: 25 percent of single women in the age group from 18 to 29.

Burch (1985:15) notes that common-law relations in Canada reflect neither instability nor promiscuity, and in most cases they are as much a prelude to marriage as substitute for it. For example, there is no evidence that those who live together do so with numerous consecutive partners: fewer than two percent of the respondents reported two or more persons as their partners and virtually none reported three or more. Also, about eight percent of ever-married males and females reported having legally married their common-law partners. Of those ever in a common-law union, 46 percent of males and about 43 percent of females had married their formerly common-law partner.

In a subsequent study, Burch and Madan report that among the respondents of the Family History Survey the tendency to live together is relatively high (about 30 percent) among those who are in the age group from 20 to 29, followed by 8 percent among the age group from 30 to 39 (Burch and Madan, 1986:11). These researchers suggest that living together as an alternative to marriage is a relatively unstable arrangement; over four fifths of common-law unions terminate within ten years, the median survival time being about three years (Burch and Madan, 1986:19). The authors claim that most Canadian common-law couples either marry or separate fairly quickly. Common-law union does not appear to have become a substitute for marriage but rather serves as a prelude to a potential marriage (a trial marriage) or as a co-residential love affair (Burch and Madan, 1986:19-20). Finally, there is no evidence that those who live together fare any better or worse with respect to subsequent marital adjustments than do their conventional counterparts (Watson, 1981).

Close scrutiny of the literature shows that although living together may be held by many as an extension of the traditional courtship process or an alternative to legal marriage, its features are strikingly similar to those of monogamous marriages: common residence, a negotiated economic relationship, sexual division of labour, intimate sexual and emotional ties, and occasionally even parenthood. What non-marital cohabitation lacks is a formal legal contract. In the past, living together was perceived as a common-law arrangement that could be terminated without penalty if problems occurred in the relationship. This has changed because many recent legal decisions, both in Canada and the United States, have supported the woman's claim to certain portion of property accrued during the period of living together. Furthermore, provinces such as Manitoba, New Brunswick, and Ontario have passed legislation protecting the rights of couples who live together, and their children, in matters of property and child support. However, since non-marital unions are governed by provincial laws, there are differences across provinces in matters of the rights and obligations of those who live together and their children (for a detailed discussion, see Fels, 1981).

Singles

In 1981, 1.6 million (or nine adults in every 100) lived alone, twice the number of those who had done so a decade earlier. There are five categories of singles, taken to mean here as those who are living alone at the time of the census-taking: never married, separated, divorced, widowed, and married. In Table 5-3 data on only three categories (never married, divorced, and widowed) are given and therefore percentage in each column will not add up to 100.

Never-Married Singles   Historically, as Bernard (1982:108-110) notes, marriage was not for everyone. It was forbidden for selected groups, such as the lower class, clerics, slaves and thus was deemed a privilege rather than a right in many European societies. As in other aspects of life in Western societies, certain fundamental changes occurred in this regard and marriage became popular. It came to be viewed as a natural state and was accompanied by the idea that one should marry at an appropriate age, except for those

Table 5-3   Persons Living Alone as a Percentage of the Population 15 Years and Over by Sex and Selected Marital Status, Canada, 1971 and 1981

	TOTAL		MEN		WOMEN	
Categories	*1971*	*1981*	*1971*	*1981*	*1971*	*1981*
Single (never-married)	7.8	14.2	7.6	13.6	8.2	14.9
Divorced	25.7	36.9	30.5	46.1	22.2	30.7
Widowed	35.1	48.0	31.5	43.8	36.0	48.9

SOURCE: Statistics Canada; *Living Alone*, Ottawa, 1984. Reproduced with permission of the Minister of Supply and Services Canada.

who for physical or religious reasons could not or would not marry. Given this context, to remain single in Canada or other Western societies was to go against the demographic and social trends and to risk being stigmatized.

Some changes have occurred with regard to being single. While remaining single may be perceived as a rejection of marriage and the family, it also may represent an extreme expression of individualism or, in less charitable terms, selfishness. In recent decades, the proportion of those over 15 years of age who remain single in Canada has nearly doubled: from 7.8 percent in 1971 to 14.2 percent in 1981 (Statistics Canada, *Living Alone*, 1984). Most of those who have remained single are part of the baby-boom generation who reached their twenties in the 1970s. The number of singles aged from 20 to 29 increased by 633 000 between 1971 and 1981 with more women remaining single than men. In 1971, the percentages of single men and women aged 15 years and over were 7.6 and 8.2 respectively and in 1981 they stood at 8.2 and 14.9. Those who remain single tend to have higher than average levels of education, and more single women than single men have university degrees.

In terms of demographic trends, the slightly increasing proportion of singles obviously contributes to the declining marital and fertility rates. Although there is little research on those who have made a conscious choice to remain single in Canada, Bernard's work in the United States suggests that remaining single is more beneficial to women than to men. Single women tend to enjoy higher educational and occupational success, personal satisfaction, and mental health (see also Libby, 1977). In contrast, single men tend to be less successful, they experience emotional and personal distress, and have higher mortality rates than married men.

Divorced Singles In 1981, of the singles 15 years of age and over, 46.1 percent of men had been married at least once, this number having increased by nearly 15 percent from 1971. The proportion of divorced single men in the population aged 15 years and over is considerably higher than that of women in the same category. The proportion of previously married single women rose from 22.2 percent of the population aged 15 years and over in 1971 to 30.7 percent in 1981. At least two explanations may be offered for this difference. First, following a divorce, it is common for women to gain custody of children and thus form single-parent families. In 1981, about half of the divorced women headed lone-parent families while only a ninth of divorced men did so. Second, although a return to being single is not a smooth and emotionally easy transition for either men or women, it is quite likely that an increasing number of men are either delaying their remarriage or getting readjusted to being single again. Furthermore, their economic circumstances, such as the burdens of divorce settlements in terms of child support and alimony, may restrain men from entering new relationships immediately after divorce.

Widowed Singles   A significant number of single people over 15 years of age in Canada is widowed: 48 percent in 1981 (35.1 percent in 1971). The proportion of women in this category is slightly higher than the proportion of men (48.9 percent women and 43.8 percent men in 1981). The explanations for this trend are both demographic and cultural. It is common for men to marry women who are younger than themselves. This practice, in conjunction with women's longevity (77.5 years compared to men's 70.2 years), results in a shortage of men in their age-group which in turn restricts their remarriage prospects.

Married Women in Paid Employment

There is considerable attitudinal and behavioural evidence that suggests that the idealized traditional conceptions of the marital roles—husband as breadwinner and wife as homemaker—have been challenged for some time now. Following an analysis of five Gallup polls taken between 1960 and 1982, Boyd (1984:11-12), observes that "Canadians increasingly believed that married women should take a job outside the home, although the magnitude of acceptance is conditioned by the presence or absence of children." While a significant majority of Canadians continue to believe that women's economic role is incompatible with their maternal role, there has been a gradual change in attitude. As Boyd (1984:12) notes, "whereas in 1960, only one out of 20 Canadians indicated that married women with young children should take a job outside the home, by 1982, 38 percent held similar views."

Married women have entered the non-agricultural labour force at an unprecedented rate since the Second World War (Statistics Canada, *Women in the Labour Force*, 1975, 1985). For example, in 1931 only 3.5 percent of married women in Canada were employed. This figure rose to 4.5 percent a decade later. Since 1961, the increase has been phenomenal: in 1961, 22 percent, and in 1981, 50.5 percent. In the last four years, it has grown steadily: from 60.8 percent in 1982 to 65.1 percent in 1984. The dramatic increase from 1931 to 1984 closely parallels the rapid expansion of the service sector of the economy.

Clearly, personal, economic, and ideological conditions have stimulated the rate of married women participating in the labour force. Although many contemporary Canadian women see marriage or maternity as reasons either for not entering the labour force or for interrupting their jobs or careers, their numbers are decreasing. For example, in 1971 just over a quarter of married women with preschool children were employed but this rose to about 76 percent in 1981. It is important to recognize that women participate in the labour force not merely to achieve personal satisfaction but also to contribute financially to the well-being of their families. According to Boulet and Lavalle (1984:5), the earnings of married women constitute about 30 percent of the combined income of spouses in Canada and without their contribution a significant proportion of Canadian families would have incomes below the poverty line.

Despite the economic value of married women's employment, traditional expectations concerning their domestic roles and natural constraints continue to prevail. Between 1978 and 1981, an average of 140 000 Canadian women per year quit their jobs because of pregnancy. Many studies have pointed out that, in general, women with young children at home are less likely to be employed, and more likely to leave their jobs than men are in a similar domestic situation (Boulet and Lavalle, 1984). In her analyses of data from the 1984 Family History Survey, Robinson (1987) found that 58 percent of women who have ever worked outside the home had interrupted work for a year or more. The vast majority of them were forced by family considerations such as marriage, pregnancy, childcare, or a move to be with their husbands. These findings confirm Boyd's interpretations in her review of Gallup poll data mentioned previously. The presence of preschool children at home determines the extent to which women can seek employment. For example, in 1981, the highest labour force participation rates were found among women aged between 20 and 44 who had no children at home. However, the rates dropped significantly for women under age 45 with children at home (see Statistics Canada, *Women in the Work World*, 1984; Robinson, 1987).

The difficulty that many working mothers and wives face is balancing the competing demands at home and at the workplace. In the domestic sphere, support systems are inadequate. For example, there is ample evidence that most employed women continue to work longer hours than their husbands and experience physical and psychological stress as a consequence (Meissner, et al., 1975). There is little or no evidence to suggest that modern household appliances or the increasing needs of the family for the additional income of women have substantially altered the amount of domestic work performed by women. As Boyd (1984:9) points out, although there is some change in the contribution of husbands to domestic work, it is relatively insignificant.

Another dilemma facing Canadian couples in which both members work outside the home concerns child care. Although most of them are as committed to responsible parenthood as they are to their occupational goals, there is little institutional support in the form of quality daycare. The political priorities of this society will sooner or later have to include universal daycare. The economic and psychological hardships experienced by working parents with preschool children have reached a desperate point and need immediate attention in order to redress the difficulties that men and women in dual-earner families are experiencing.

Marital Interaction

Sociological understanding is sketchy about how, among Canadians, the changing economic role of married women has influenced marital inter-action in areas such as power and authority, decision-making, and satis-faction. There are some attitudinal data indicating that Canadian marriages may be more egalitarian today than they were some two decades ago. The assumption that the husband, by virtue of his breadwinner's role, or simply because he is male, ought to be the "boss" of the household is increasingly being challenged. Instead, as Boyd (1984:5-7) documents, the tendency among contemporary Canadians is to profess equality between spouses. The extent to which such attitudinal shifts have been translated into behavioural patterns has not yet been determined.

On the quality of marriage and distribution of power, the Canadian evidence is restricted to a handful of publications, the most prominent being based on the Calgary survey conducted by Merlin Brinkerhoff, James Fri-deres, Eugen Lupri, Marlene Mackie, and Donald Mills. While their findings are complex and require more space than is available here even for a summary, two major conclusions of their report should be noted. First, Lupri and Frideres (1981:302) found that, among their respondents, "wives who work outside the home show significantly lower levels of marital sat-isfaction than do their husbands. Employed wives experience greater role strains than non-employed wives because of the cumulative effect of em-ployment *and* and the presence of teenagers in the home." In contrast, the authors note, "husbands whose wives are employed are much more likely than the husbands whose wives are not employed to report very satisfying marriages, with the greatest difference in midlife." The overall findings on marital satisfaction among the Calgary couples suggest that there is a steady decline in the level of satisfaction from the time the marriages begin to the period when children leave home. Following this phase the couple expe-riences significant improvement in the quality of the marital relationship.

Based on data from the same study, Brinkerhoff and Lupri point out that the employment of the wife does not necessarily lead to an increase in her role in decision-making. "Findings indicate that wives who work for pay actually have less power than do those who are not in the labour force" (1983:219). The authors conclude that, "according to decision-making scales, wives may appear to be equal to, or even more powerful than, their hus-bands. But, in reality, wives only make decisions in areas in which it has been traditionally expected—areas of lesser importance."

Although these findings need to be compared with studies in other settings, some preliminary observations are in order. While males generally recognize, and appreciate, the monetary significance of their wives' em-ployment outside the home and espouse egalitarian views, they balk at making necessary adjustments in their domestic behaviour—adjustments that reduce the physical fatigue and emotional strain women experience from excessive and competing demands in different spheres ("role overload").

FAMILY PATTERNS

In sociology, family is understood as a basic kinship unit consisting of a husband, wife, and their own or adopted children. The members are economically interdependent, and maintain a common residence. Such a definition, although it includes a majority of families in most societies, is not comprehensive because it fails to include many other forms: for example, dual-career couples who live apart, single-parent families, or even couples who by choice have no children. In a free society, individuals construct different family structures (parts that constitute a family, interrelationships between parts, and norms and values that govern relationships) according to their personal circumstances and preferences. Consequently, there are many family structures in Canada, including nuclear, extended, single-parent, and reconstituted families. These families differ in their social and economic characteristics as well as in their membership.

For example, a nuclear family is composed of a married couple and their own or adopted children while an extended family includes one or more relatives of either or both spouses. Although most Canadians are members of either their own or their parents' nuclear family, there are those who live alone or independently (the aged, singles, and so on). In some communities, especially those of Inuit, Cree, Hutterites, and Amish, extended family units (three or more generations) still prevail. A single-parent family refers to a mother or a father living with one or more unmarried children in a home. Single-parent families are the second largest family structure in Canada, next to nuclear families. A reconstituted family (also referred to as step-family) is composed of a husband and wife, at least one of whom has been married before, and one or more children from a previous marriage. With the increase in remarriages in Canada, the numbers of reconstituted families is gradually increasing (for more on this point, see Chapter Eleven). The existence of all these patterns suggests that the composition of families in Canada is diverse. It is necessary to recognize these distinctions since they have implications not only for the way we live but also for government social policies.

Major Types of Families in Canada

The data on family types collected by Canadian census are not totally according to sociological categories of the family noted above. The Canadian "census family" refers to a husband and wife (with children who have never

Table 5-4   The Number and Percentage of Husband-Wife, Single-
Parent Families, 1931–1981

| | FAMILIES | |
Year	Husband-Wife	Single-parent
1931	1 857 105 (86.4)	291 943 (13.6)
1941	2 202 707 (87.8)	306 957 (12.2)
1951	2 961 685 (90.1)	325 699 (9.9)
1961	3 800 026 (91.6)	347 418 (8.4)
1966	4 154 381 (91.8)	371 885 (8.2)
1971	4 591 940 (90.6)	478 740 (9.4)
1976	5 168 560 (90.2)	559 335 (9.8)
1981	5 610 970 (88.7)	714 010 (11.3)
1986	5 881 335 (87.3)	853 645 (12.7)*

SOURCE: *Canada's Lone-Parent Families.* Ottawa: Statistics Canada, 1981. Reproduced
with permission of the Minister of Supply and Services Canada.
* Statistics Canada, *The Daily,* July 9, 1987.

married, regardless of age, or no children at all), or a lone parent of any
marital status, with one or more children who have never married, regardless of age, living in the same dwelling (Census Canada, *Summary Tabulations,* 1987:ix). A census family now includes even those who live together
(common law). Accordingly, the Canadian census family structure includes
only two broad categories: the husband-wife family, which includes "common-law couples" and "now-married couples" (with or without children),
and the lone-parent family, classified according to the sex of the parent.
The husband-wife family in Canada would normally include not only nuclear
but also reconstituted family and couples without children. These considerations have led us to examine only two major family types in Canada on
which census data are easily accessible: husband-wife families and single-
parent families.

Table 5-4 provides a summary of the number and proportion of two
major types of families in Canada for a period of fifty years. As the data
show, in the last fifty years the number of husband-wife families has almost
tripled, mirroring the growth of the total population. One can also detect
slight fluctuations in the percentages for each census year, which may be
attributed to economic, social and ideological changes that Canadian society
has experienced in the last half century. In 1986, roughly four out of five
Canadians (or 84 percent of the population) lived in various types of families:
husband-wife, nuclear (parents with their own or adopted children) and
single-parent families. In 1986, there were 6 734 980 families in Canada of
which 5 881 335 (87.3 percent) were husband-wife families (with or without
children) and 853 645 (12.7 percent) were single-parent families (151 740

or 2.2 percent headed by male parents while 701 900 or 10.5 percent headed by female parents).

Although the proportion of Canadians living in families of various kinds is gradually declining, the number of families has increased since 1971. Between 1971 and 1976, the number of families increased by 13 percent and between 1976 and 1981 by ten percent. At the same time, compared to such increases, the 1986 Census statistics indicate only a moderate growth of six percent from 1981. The declining rate of family formation may be due to delayed marriages among those between the ages of 21 and 31, and also to the aging population that has moved beyond the prime family formation phase (Statistics Canada, *The Daily*, July 9, 1987).

The fact that approximately 84 percent of the population in 1986 was living in some form of family is indicative of the continuing popularity of the family in Canada on the one hand, and the absence of *satisfying* alternatives on the other. This is particularly significant given the fact that in the last two decades a variety of options has been available to those who found it difficult to adjust to or rejected traditional arrangements. It should also be noted that despite the profound changes during the last two decades (such as the greater economic status of married women, rising divorce rates, and the increase in the proportion of single-parent families, people living together or not marrying), individuals have not fundamentally changed their level of commitment to the nuclear family. This conclusion is supported by a recent public opinion poll. In its year-end poll of Canadians on various issues, *Maclean's* (January 5, 1987:71-72) found overwhelming support for the family from all age groups. Over 90 percent of the respondents with children at home acknowledged the increasing importance of family in their lives, as did some 73 percent of those whose children had left home. By contrast, less than eight percent of the respondents did not consider the family an important institution in their lives.

Single-Parent Families An important recent trend evident in Table 5-4 is the increase in the percentage as well as in the number of single-parent families in Canada. In the years from 1966 to 1986, while the pecentage of husband-wife families gradually declined, there was a corresponding increase in single-parent families. In 1986, lone-parent families constituted 12.7 percent of all families, an increase from 11.3 percent in 1981.

Although the majority of single-parent families historically were headed by widowed parents, this is no longer so. In 1931, nearly three out of four lone-parent families were headed by a widowed parent; fifty years later only a third were. Therefore, a majority of single-parent families in the 1980s are headed by divorced or separated parents. The results of the Family History Survey shed more light on the demographic and marital characteristics of the lone-parent families among those studied (see Pool and Moore,

1986). Lone parents, who are mostly women, tend to enter some form of marital union at younger ages, and are likely to have their first child before they are twenty years of age. They tend also to be pregnant at the time of their marital union (for details, see Pool and Moore, 1986).

Of 714 000 single parents in 1981, nearly 83 percent were women (about 80 percent in 1986). One reason for this disparity is that men generally do not receive custody of children even when they seek it. For example, McKie, et al. (1983:219-225) point out that only one of seven husbands who seek custody of their children succeed. Consequently, in a vast majority of cases, divorced or separated women shoulder family responsibilities.

Most single mothers with preschool children live in economically deprived circumstances. A 1979 Survey of Consumer Finances suggests that in 44 percent of the cases the income of single-parent families placed them close to the poverty line (Boulet and Lavalle, 1984:39). "Child support is awarded to only about one-third of divorced or separated women with children. Moreover, less than half of debtor ex-husbands live up to their financial obligations, and many of those who do pay, pay less than the full amount ordered by the courts" (Boulet and Lavalle, 1984:39; see also Dulude, 1983). Female-headed single-parent families confront not only the financial difficulties but also hardships of coping with their personal and social lives and of child-rearing (for further details, see the Chapters on Socialization, and Divorce and Remarriage).

Some changes are taking place in this pattern which may eventually reduce the stress female single parents have experienced in the past. An increasing number of men are seeking sole or joint custody of children upon separation or divorce. Between 1976 and 1981, the proportion of single-parent families headed by men increased by 31 percent followed by a 22 percent increase between 1981 and 1986 (Statistics Canada, *The Daily*, July 9, 1987).

Single-Person Households   There has been a dramatic increase in the numbers of single-person households in Canada in the last 25 years. In 1956, only eight percent of the 3 923 600 households were single-person households, but it rose to over 20 percent of the 8 281 500 households in 1981. This trend continued well into 1986 and the proportion of single-person households rose to 21 percent of 8.9 million (Statistics Canada, *Living Alone*, 1984). This means that roughly ten out of every 100 Canadians were living alone and these were mostly those who have never been married (see the previous discussion of singles in the section on marital patterns), or widowed persons. "The results of the 1981 Census seem to indicate a growing inclination for the young and old to live alone. Since both groups are expected to increase in size, one-person households will likely multiply as well" (Statistics Canada, *Living Alone*,1984).

FERTILITY PATTERNS

Social demographers periodically measure rates of reproduction by using the crude birth rate, total fertility rate, and cohort-completed fertility rate, each of which represents different degrees of statistical refinement. The least refined is the crude birth rate, which is the number of births per 1000 members of the total population, and includes those who do not or cannot reproduce, such as children, men, and the elderly.

The total fertility rate refers to the average number of children that would be born to women if they were to live through their reproductive period and bear children according to age-specific fertility rates recorded in a given year (Romaniuc, 1984:12). For example, "the total fertility rate observed in 1982 is 1.7, this number refers to the average number of children that would be born to a hypothetical cohort of women, if they were to experience at various ages the fertility observed in Canada during that year" (Romanuic, 1984:12).

Although there are practical difficulties of measurement, the cohort-completed fertility rate gives a reliable picture of fertility. It records the actual number of children born to a cohort of women during their reproductive period. "One can thus study the fertility of women born, say, in 1940, and follow them along as they age, right up to the end of their reproductive life" (Romanuic, 1984:12).

Table 5-5 gives these three types of fertility rates and Table 5-6 provides age-specific fertility rates.

The data given in Table 5-5 chart changes beginning from the base year of 1921. Following the Second World War (1945 onwards), the rates consistently rose until 1956 when they began a downward trend that has continued to the present. The rates of recent years are even lower than those of the Great Depression and two World Wars. In a short span of about twenty years (1946-1986), we have experienced both "baby boom" and "baby bust."

Another way of understanding fertility patterns is to consider the number of children that women bear during their lifetime, or the completed fertility rate. For example, at the turn of the century women bore, on the average, six children; today they bear fewer than two (the average in 1985 was 1.3). This low fertility rate has serious implications for the demographic structure of Canada because it would take an average of 2.1 children per female to replace the present generation. If the current trend continues, replacement may no longer be certain unless extra fertility considerations come into play, such as an increase in immigrants. It is apparent that Canadian social policy makers have yet to address the potential severity of the country's demographic situation.

The implications of falling rates of fertility are more obvious in the case of Québec. Historically, the Québécois had the highest birth rate in Canada.

Table 5-5 Fertility Rates for Selected Years, 1921–1985*

Year	Crude birth rate	Total fertility rate	Cohort-completed fertility rate
1921	29.3	3 536	3 714
1926	24.7	3 357	3 444
1931	23.2	3 200	3 138
1936	20.3	2 696	2 725
1941	22.4	2 832	2 867
1946	27.2	3 374	2 890
1947	28.9	3 595	3 229
1951	27.2	3 503	3 260
1954	28.5	3 828	3 244
1955	28.2	3 831	3 294
1956	28.0	3 858	3 266
1961	26.1	3 840	3 152
1966	19.4	2 812	2 810
1971	16.8	2 187	2 285
1976	15.7	1 825	2 015
1980	15.5	1 746	1 838
1981	15.3	1 704	—
1982	15.1	1 694	—
1984	15.0	1 686	—
1985	14.8	1 669	—

SOURCE: Statistics Canada, *Vital Statistics, Births and Deaths*, Annual Catalogues; Romanuic (1984); *Canada Year Books*, 1980–84. Reproduced with permission of the Minister of Supply and Services Canada.

* Data for Newfoundland and the Yukon and Northwest Territories are either not available or excluded prior to 1951.

It was often said that women in New France bore as many children as, for example, women in many developing nations (Kalbach and McVey, 1979:10-30). Even as late as 1956, the average number of children born to Québécois women was 4.0 which fell sharply to 1.5 by 1983 (see Romanuic, 1984; Lachapelle and Henripin, 1982). A consequence of such recent low birth rates in Québec is a linguistic and demographic imbalance. Romanuic (1984:18) points out the number of French-speaking Canadians is dwindling rather steadily: In 1951, francophones constituted 29 percent of the Canadian population and in 1981 this figure stood at 26.7 percent. The demographic projections suggest that it will shrink further to about 25 percent by the year 2000. With their declining population growth the francophones in Québec will find it more difficult to maintain their unique linguistic, cultural, and political status within the Canadian confederation.

The data in Table 5-6, while they confirm declining fertility trends, further suggest that from 1981 to 1985 the fertility rate among those in the age

Table 5-6 Age-Specific Fertility Rate per 1000 Women, 1926–1985

Year	15–19	20–24	25–29	30–34	35–39	40–44	45–49
1926	29.0	139.9	177.4	153.8	114.6	50.7	6.0
1931	29.9	137.1	175.1	145.3	103.1	44.0	5.5
1936	25.7	112.1	144.3	126.5	90.0	36.3	4.4
1941	30.7	138.4	159.8	122.3	80.0	31.6	3.7
1946	36.5	169.6	191.4	146.0	93.1	34.5	3.8
1947	42.6	189.1	206.4	150.5	93.1	34.1	3.3
1951	48.1	188.7	198.8	144.5	86.5	30.9	3.1
1954	54.3	217.4	213.2	156.6	88.5	32.4	3.2
1955	54.2	218.3	215.1	153.8	89.8	32.3	2.9
1956	55.9	222.2	220.1	150.3	89.6	30.8	2.9
1961	58.2	233.6	219.2	144.9	81.1	28.5	2.4
1966	48.2	169.1	163.5	103.3	57.5	19.1	1.7
1971	40.1	134.4	142.0	77.3	33.6	9.4	0.6
1976	33.4	110.3	129.9	65.6	21.1	4.3	0.3
1980	27.6	100.1	129.4	69.3	19.4	3.1	0.2
1981	26.4	96.7	126.9	68.0	19.4	3.2	0.2
1982	26.5	95.4	124.7	68.6	20.2	3.1	0.2
1983	24.9	92.4	124.6	70.5	20.5	3.0	0.2
1984	24.4	88.8	126.0	73.3	21.5	3.0	0.1
1985	23.7	85.3	125.3	74.6	21.8	3.0	0.1

SOURCE: Statistics Canada, *Vital Statistics, Births and Deaths*, Annual Catalogues. Reproduced with permission of the Minister of Supply and Services Canada.

group 24 years or below has gradually declined, it has remained relatively stable in the 25-29 age group and it has increased among those in 30-34 age group. This trend reflects the fact that many women are postponing their decision to bear children for educational and occupational reasons.

Couples now tend to have fewer than two children, to bear children later in life, and to space them apart much more than did the previous generation. Furthermore, there also appears to be a slightly increased tendency among some contemporary couples either to postpone parenthood or not to become parents at all. The causes for this variety of shifts cannot easily be established. The following account suggests factors that may have contributed to the declining reproductive function of the family.

First, there is little evidence to suggest that the positive emphasis on parenthood or children has declined in Canadian society (see Ramu and Tavuchis, 1986). Children today continue to have emotional, personal, and genealogical significance for parents and kin. Nevertheless, the practice of having large families as an expression of one's familial commitment to parenthood has not prevailed. Undesired pregnancies can be avoided with inexpensive and readily available contraceptives. Second, a later age at first marriage, delayed parenthood, and increased spacing between children (see Romanuic, 1984; Beaujot, 1986, Balakrishnan, 1986) may also have contributed to low birth rates.

Third, although a causal connection is difficult to establish, it is now believed that there is a negative relationship between women's participation in post-secondary education and entry into the labour force, and fertility. As Romanuic (1984:68) points out, "working and mothering compete for women's time and energy. Career building takes place over the same years that families are usually formed and children are raised." In the absence of institutional support, and with significant changes in husband's domestic role, decisions to have smaller families are made by an increasing number of employed women and their husbands.

Fourth, as Armstrong and Ryant point out elsewhere in this volume (Chapter Seven and Chapter Twelve), the absence of support systems in the domestic and economic environment involves serious compromises and hardships for those who want to become parents. Such things as equitable division of labour between husbands and wives in the home, universal daycare, pensions for homemakers, equal pay for equal work by men and women, and so on, could all potentially ameliorate this situation.

Fifth, although accurate figures are difficult to obtain, there is some indirect evidence that the proportion of voluntarily childless couples may be on the increase (Veevers, 1980). Demographers have documented the trends of intentional childlessness by examining the age cohorts of married women. For example, Romanuic (1984:32) notes that "the proportion of ever-married women aged 20-24 who have not yet had any children rose from 26% in 1961 to 42% in 1971, then to 54% in 1981. Similarly, for women aged 25-29 years, the proportion rose from 14% to 21% and to 30% for the same years. Among the 30-34 year olds, 14% were childless in 1981 as against 9% in 1971." It is quite possible that many have just postponed motherhood, but even postponement contributes to reduction in fertility.

Sixth, as we already noted in the section on marital patterns, there has been a significant increase in the proportion of singles, especially women, and this in conjunction with aforementioned demographic shifts would influence the fertility rate.

In sum, although there is evidence that most Canadians marry, it is clear that an increasing number of couples are remaining childless, postponing parenthood, or opting for small families. This suggests that the days of large families and even of orderly demographic replacement are over, at least for now.

Births Outside Legal Marriage

Historically, "illegitimate births" included births to single women and those that occurred outside legal marriage. Census Canada used this definition until 1974, and in subsequent years this term includes births not just to

Table 5-7[1]   Births to Unmarried Women in Canada for Selected Years, 1951–85

	NUMBER OF BIRTHS TO UNMARRIED WOMEN	
Year	All ages	15–19 years
1951	13 931	4 548
1956	16 839	5 544
1961	19 581	7 731
1966	28 343	11 601
1971	31 177	14 074
1976[2]	30 234	15 658[3]
1981	45 501	17 354
1982	56 286	18 045
1983[4]	52 929	—
1984	55 794	—
1985	59 604	—

SOURCE: Adapted from Romanuic, 1984:36.

1. Newfoundland has been excluded from the calculation of the fertility rate for Canada. The non-stated births have been prorated. Since in the case of the Yukon and Northwest Territories no data were available for women aged 15–44, an estimate of their fertility rate was obtained using the data for total births. No data were available from which a similar estimate for the 15–19 age group could be derived.
2. Due to the large number of non-stated births in Québec, data for this year are not reliable.
3. From 1974 onwards fertility rates for the 15–19 year group have been calculated for births to single women only.
4. Data for 1983 to 1985 are from *Vital Statistics*, 1983–85.

never-married single women, but to divorced and widowed women as well (Romanuic, 1984:35). In Table 5-7, data on births to unmarried women in Canada for selected years have been presented.

Since 1971, the number of children born outside marriage has increased phenomenally despite the number of therapeutic abortions, which almost doubled during a period of seven years (from 23 468 in 1974 to 41 890 in 1981). The magnitude of the increase has perplexed many analysts, especially in the context of the easy access to contraceptives and a generally liberal approach to their use in Canada.

The tendency to risk pregnancy appears to be most common among teenagers. For example, the number of out-of-wedlock births to single women 15-19 years old has increased almost four times from about 4500 in 1951 to over 17 000 in 1981" (Romanuic, 1984:38). Permissive sexual mores, early sexual initiation, extended courtship, and delayed marriages have all had some influence on the increased rates of birth outside marriage. Also not to be ignored is the movement of a baby-boom generation into childbearing years which may account for increase in the number of young women at risk of bearing children outside marriage (Romanuic, 1984:37-38).

CONCLUSION

The brief review of marital and family patterns in Canada suggests two general and secure conclusions. First, demographic data detailed in this chapter point clearly to significant shifts in various aspects of marriage and the family and indicate fundamental changes in the structure of the ideal family in Canada. While Canadians still attach importance to marriage, family, and socialization of children, the "marriage rush" (Beaujot, 1986) of the 1950s and 1960s and the post-war "baby boom" are unlikely to be repeated in the immediate future.

Second, the contemporary marital and family systems in Canada can at best be described as being in a state of flux. There is a slow but steady increase in the variety of marital and family patterns that suggests a growing social acceptance of arrangements alternative to the traditional if not dominant forms.

While there are some social policies and programs that recognize new arrangements, the policy makers are slow to come to grips with changing realities and attitudes. Marriage and the family (whether they are traditional or alternatives) have not received the institutional support they merit, despite their fundamental importance for the survival of economic and political stability of Canadian society.

Suggested Readings

Beaujot, Roderic.
  1986 "Dwindling Families: Making the Case for Policies to Sustain or Raise the Birth Rate in Canada." *Policy Options 7.*

Boulet, Jac-Andre, and Laval Lavalle.
  1984 *The Changing Economic Status of Women.* Ottawa: Economic Council of Canada.

Burch, T.K.
  1985 *Family History Survey—Preliminary Findings.* Ottawa: Minister of Supply and Services, 39.

Burch, Thomas K. and Ashok K. Madan.
  1986 *Union Formation and Dissolution: Results from the 1984 Family History Survey.* Ottawa: Minister of Supply and Services.

Pool, Ian, and Maureen Moore.
  1986   *Lone Parenthood: Characteristics and Determinants.* Ottawa: Minister of
         Supply and Services.

Romanuic, A.
  1984   *Current Demographic Analysis. Fertility in Canada: From Baby Boom to
         Baby Bust.* Ottawa: Minister of Supply and Services. (Cat. no. 91-524E).

Statistics Canada.
  1984   *Canada's Lone-Parent Families.* Ottawa: Minister of Supply and Services.

Statistics Canada.
  1984   *Women in the Work World.* Ottawa: Minister of Supply and Services.

Statistics Canada.
  1984   *Living Alone.* Ottawa: Minister of Supply and Services.

Statistics Canada.
  1985   *Women in Canada: A Statistical Report.* Ottawa: Minister of Supply and
         Services.

6

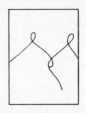

PRIMARY SOCIALIZATION

Marlene Mackie

Socialization refers to the learning process through which persons acquire the knowledge, skills, and dispositions that render them more or less effective members of society (Brim, 1966). Although socialization necessarily occurs throughout life, this chapter focuses upon the transformation of a helpless infant into a responsible adult, a process that has always been one of the major functions of the family. Sociologists apply the label "primary socialization" to this basic learning which takes place in childhood and adolescence.

Socialization, which links individual and society, is absolutely essential to both. From the point of view of the individual, interaction with other people is the means by which human potentialities are actualized. Loving attention from reasonably intelligent adults is required for both the newborn infant's survival as a physical being and its development as a social being.

Effective socialization of the newly born is equally vital for the continuity of society. The failure of this task could threaten social order. If the approximately 376 600 Canadian babies born in 1986 (Statistics Canada, 1987:2) are not properly raised they could threaten the social order. Here is one sociologist's tongue-in-cheek description of unsocialized children:

> They are barbaric. They do not love democracy and suspect communism. They hold no brief for the Judeo-Christian tradition. . . . They have no manners, no respect for others, no respect for tradition. They have not learned to keep up appearances, to knock before entering, to be silent in church, or to worry about bad breath and underarm stains (Campbell, 1975:1).

The continuity of Canadian society requires these neophytes to learn self-discipline, develop an ability to think, believe, and behave as Canadians.

Nevertheless, it is important not to overstate the efficiency of the socialization process or the conformity which results. Socialization begins with the individual "taking over" the world as it has been constituted by others. However, people rebel and innovate so that "the world, once 'taken over,' *may* be creatively modified or . . . even re-created" (Berger and Luckmann, 1966:130). Therefore, each generation seldom duplicates the one it succeeds. Moreover, socialization is a two-way process. Just as parents socialize the child, the child socializes the parents.

This chapter places the topic of primary socialization in a socio-historical context. Its major thesis is that the modern Canadian family faces a serious dilemma in rearing its younger members. On the one hand, the family bears the major responsibility for the child's future because modern Western society assumes, in the words of Jerome Kagan (1984:242), that if the child develops undesirable qualities, "the practices of the family during the early years—especially parental neglect, indifference, restriction, and absence of joyful and playful interaction—are the major culprits." After all, the family has had jurisdiction over the child during its most malleable years and the strongest of emotional bonds are forged among family members. Therefore, if the child ends up hating school, becomes a drug addict, or robs a corner store, parents, especially the mother, are blamed.

Furthermore, today's parents are judged by their children, themselves and various professional experts according to higher standards than ever before. To wit, journalist Lynne Caine (1985:12) writes: "ever since my children were babies . . ., I've always been afraid of damaging them, of not knowing enough as a mother, of not being good enough, not patient enough, unselfish enough. . . ."

On the other hand, an increasing number of obstacles complicate and interfere with the family's traditional socialization function. These impediments originate in the larger socio-historical context as well as in the structure of the family. This complex problem has stimulated considerable speculation. Some writers argue that the modern family has neither the power nor the capacity to socialize its younger members effectively (see Nelsen, 1985). However, more optimistic sociologists remind us of the historical record which shows the family to be a resilient institution. Himelfarb and Richardson (1982:381), for example, observe that "change is built into the family, more than in other institutions" of society. They go on to say that "the family is both a *dependent* and an *independent* variable, having things happen to it, certainly, but also creating and amplifying changes in the wider society" (382).

Against this background the present chapter examines both the challenges facing contemporary Canadian families in their task of socialization and the strategies that have emerged to meet such challenges. At this writing, the empirical data provide a detailed, elaborate picture of the challenges confronting the family while research on the internal dynamics of familial strategy has only just begun. Therefore, the discussion in this chapter reflects this imbalance.

THE NATURE OF CANADIAN SOCIETY

It is the responsibility of the family to prepare its children to be successful adult members of society. Ideally, the social order is thereby perpetuated and the offspring provided with a reasonable measure of life satisfaction. The socialization process involves more than the unfolding of innate potentialities during biological maturation, more than child-rearing techniques, more than face-to-face interaction between the child and its parents (or other socialization agents). At every step in the process, society intervenes since it has a stake in this process. As Inkeles (1968:75) observes,

> In their efforts to socialize the child, parents are guided, however fallibly, by their awareness of such social expectation and their image of what the child must become if he is to live successfully in the world as the parents envision it will be at the time the child becomes an adult.

As Zureik and Pike (1975:ix) point out, certain major characteristics of Canadian society present difficulties to parents attempting to convey to their offspring a sense of society—its values, norms, patterns of behaviour. A sparse and unevenly distributed population in a vast territory, repeated waves of immigrants of diverse ethnic composition, and British and American influences have all placed Canada's internal coherence under continual pressure (Hiller, 1986:3). At the present time, foreign control of the Canadian economy and cultural penetration by American television, books, music and entertainment heroes are of particular concern.

An interpretation of Canadian society meaningful to the next generation is further complicated by regional, linguistic, ethnic, and religious distinctions within our borders (Peters, 1984). Native peoples, French-speaking Canadians, Canadians whose origin is neither British nor French, people living in the various regions of Canada—all have at one time or another felt alienated from the rest of Canada. Québec francophones, for example, felt intensely "that Canadian society was not their society, its institutions not their institutions, its meanings and symbols, not their meanings and symbols" (Breton, 1984:129). Though a common core of values and experiences are shared by Canadians, primary socialization also reflects subcultural differences. Youngsters must be prepared to take up adult roles in Newfoundland fishing outports (Firestone, 1978), Northern resource communities (McLaren, 1983), Manitoba mining towns (Luxton, 1980), or in French Canada (Lambert, 1981). Although no ethnic group can maintain its culture intact in the face of powerful pressures for assimilation to the "Anglo-dominant" culture (Zureik and Pike, 1975:ix), Canada's various minorities have managed, in varying degrees, to maintain their ethnic identity and have selected cultural patterns as symbolic expressions of identity (Burnet, 1984). In summary, socializing children into socio-cultural and political reality is more problematic for parents in a society such as Canada which is diverse, and lacks a homogeneous cultural heritage and a distinct national identity.

Primary socialization is especially difficult for recent immigrant families. A study (Wakil et al., 1981) of the socialization of the children of immigrant Indian and Pakistani children in a western Canadian city illustrates conflicting expectations and practices among parents and children in adjusting to a social milieu that encourages homogeneity. While parents were willing to tolerate their children's enthusiasm for Western food, music, and festivals such as Christmas and Halloween, the generations clashed over critical matters such as dating and arranged marriage. These immigrant parents perceived that Canadian practices such as dating and courtship weakened their authority and threatened basic values of their ethnic group.

Finally, social class divisions in Canadian society, often related to ethnicity, critically influence socialization. Public education and government-sponsored student loans are intended to equalize opportunities for Canadian youngsters. However, research shows that the child's class origins continue significantly to influence his or her educational attainment and subsequent occupational success (McRoberts, 1985).

In brief, the heterogeneity of Canadian society complicates the family's socialization task. After all, the family is *of* society; its environment and standards for socialization derive *from* society (Inkeles, 1968:75). In the next section, we shall consider the impact upon the family of a variety of socio-cultural trends which transcend Canadian society.

THE SOCIAL CONTEXT OF CONTEMPORARY SOCIALIZATION

The fact that the family is embedded in specific historical periods and cultures has profound implications for its socialization function. Although the Western family should not be dismissed as a passive recipient of modernization, it has been changed significantly by the influence of industrialization, separation of home and work, urbanization, and secularization.

Certain socialization requirements are universal. In order to survive and thrive, children have always needed nurturance, protection, and instruction in cultural values and norms. However, young people born into the contemporary Canadian family place additional socialization requirements upon their caregivers. The experiences of this generation differ in many ways from those of their predecessors.

What follows is a brief overview of the major socio-historical factors which impinge upon socialization. Before we begin, two caveats are in order. First, we must be careful not to romanticize the historical family, to posit what Goode (1963) called the "classical family of Western nostalgia." Second, though the various social forces are discussed one after the other, social change results from the *interaction* of cultural *and* social structural variables.

Changing Values

Culture—the sum total of our social inheritance of language, values, beliefs, knowledge, arts, literature, material artifacts—provides the foundation of group life. The family, including its child-rearing practices, is affected by and, in turn, influences all such dimensions of culture. We will confine our analysis to the overarching category of values. Central to our discussion is the general shift of emphasis from the family unit to individuals, which began in the nineteenth century. The collective interests of the family no longer take precedence over individual desires for autonomy, self-realization, and the accumulation of material goods. The changing aspirations of women and men have serious implications for socialization.

Childhood   Childhood is a social construct, not an invariant, natural category. Conceptions of childhood vary from epoch to epoch and from culture to culture (Aries, 1962) and are based on gender and class (Suransky, 1982:7). With the industrialization of the economy, children lost much of their utility as contributors to family income, while becoming more rewarding emotionally for parents (Zelizer, 1981). Beginning with the bourgeoisie, "there appeared a new tenderness toward children, an interest in their development, and a prolongation of the period considered proper to childhood" (Berger and Berger, 1984:92). Eventually, children's education was taken over by the state, and their rights were protected by law. Since the turn of the twentieth century, a variety of childcare professionals have emerged (Strong-Boag, 1982). While all these developments were felicitous for children, they nonetheless weakened the family's control over them.

As Synnott (1983:91) observes, our current ideas about children and childhood are rather confused. Publicly and officially, children are held in high regard. An expectation that all married couples want to and should reproduce still exists. Despite the phenomenon of "baby craving" in the 1980s—the passionate, frequently desperate desire to have children (Quindlen, 1987)—many people are privately ambivalent, even hostile towards children. Some potential parents view them as expensive luxuries, hindrances to their personal growth or career advancement (Lasch, 1979). An environment hostile to children, where youngsters are as welcome in many restaurants as flies in the soup, and banned altogether from some stores and housing developments, suggests that childhood has become unfashionable among some sections of our society. Adults tend to be especially negative about teenagers, who are "criticized as people whose chief delights are sexual immorality and attendance at rock concerts, smoking drugs and listening to shocking music" (Friesen, 1986:11).

Women   As Armstrong discusses at length in Chapter Seven, the women's liberation movement, women's increased participation in the labour force, along with other factors, have been responsible for the gradual shift in Canadians' evaluation of the sexes. However, society remains as ambivalent about women's changing status as about its children. Boyd (1984:23) writes, "data collected from the Gallup polls during the past 30 years are a testimony of the enormous change which has occurred during the period with respect to women and women's issues. Yet, they also reveal a residue of earlier norms and practices." For example, 81 percent of a national Canadian sample agreed in 1976 that "when children are young, a mother's place is in the home." (Gibbins, Ponting and Symons, 1978). A decade later, 64 percent agreed with this statement (Ponting, 1986).

Personal Freedom   Closely associated with Canadians' changing views of children and women has been a greater emphasis on personal autonomy and a decline in the importance of the parental role as a central focus of identity (McLanahan and Adams, 1987:240). Perception of the child as "a beautiful young bird to be cared for until it is ready to fly free in the forest" (Kagan, 1984:244) follows logically from acknowledgment of children's self-hood. Moreover, as women experience increasing independence from their husbands, they seem reluctant to demand subservience and restriction from their children (Winn, 1983). Ironically, the family remains responsible for its children, yet urges them to be free.

Once again, a certain amount of ambivalence seems inevitable. Many parents, reluctant to be overprotective, worry about the dangers threatening their children:

> "People keep telling you to let go of your kids, let them be independent. I allow my 10-year-old daughter to ride her bike to school, because everyone said I'd be overprotective if I didn't. Then I was driving to work and saw her riding down the middle of the road and through a stop sign" (Landsberg, 1982:182).

The family is expected to encourage its children to be independent and to accept the blame when such independence leads to trouble.

Technological Change

Scientific and technological innovations have transformed family life in general and the socialization process in particular. For example, young people are surrounded by television sets, computers, video arcades, and equipped with Walkman cassette players and portable stereos. Interpretation of society, as well as socialization goals, are now provided by the media, not the family. Television bypasses parents and directs its programming and advertising to children. As Singer (1986:80) notes, Canadian children from two to 11 years of age are reached more often by advertisers than are children from any other age group. Television programming discloses adult secrets to children. When a commercial break was about to intrude, a talk show host said, "Don't go away. We'll be back with a marvelous new diet and, then, a quick look at incest" (Postman, 1982:81). While many authorities acknowledge the educational value of television programs such as "Sesame Street," they are appalled by the pervasive violence and sexism of the medium.

When children reach adolescence, music, especially rock music, replaces television as their top leisure activity (Bibby and Posterski, 1985:36). Many parents find rock music's "knee-jerk misogyny" (Harding and Nett, 1984) and rebellious messages worrisome, and the anti-religious, satanic content of the heavy-metal subculture particularly offensive.

Moreover, computers, "the most powerful yet of the artifacts of this inventive century" (Condry and Keith, 1983:88), are fundamentally altering work, education, and recreation. The intensity of children's engagement with video games and computers often intimidates parents. "It's eerie when their playmates are machines" (Turkle, 1984:14).

> Television is something you watch. Video games are something you do, something you do in your head, a world that you enter, ... and, to a certain extent, they are something you "become" (Turkle, 1984:67).

Technological knowledge youngsters gain elsewhere appears to contribute to a shift in the family's traditional power structure. The bored child condescending to help his bumbling father struggle with his home computer has become a stock plot in the comic strips. As we mentioned earlier, socialization is inherently a two-way process involving mutual influence between child and caretaker. However, contemporary youngsters command especially valuable knowledge.

An equally important concomitant of technological development is the challenge to parental authority presented by rival socialization agencies. The knowledge and skills required to function effectively in an urbanized, industrialized society such as Canada are too complex and extensive for parents alone to transmit to their children. Therefore, a significant proportion of the socialization function must be delegated to educational institutions. At school, the child encounters the ideas of teachers, textbooks, and especially other pupils, which often contradict the notions espoused in the home.

Recent Economic Trends

Closely related to technology, the economy is another significant component of the context in which young Canadians are socialized. Among economic developments that have an impact on socialization include the involvement of both parents in work outside the home, recession and unemployment, and changes in projected job opportunities.

The rapid expansion of the economy following the Second World War (especially the availability of service and clerical jobs), along with the ideology of the women's movement and improved contraception, was responsible for a dramatic increase in women's participation in the labour force (Armstrong and Armstrong, 1984). National economic circumstances during the past 15 years or so—inflation, recession, rising levels of expectations— made it necessary for many wives and mothers to seek outside employment. By 1984, more than half of Canadian mothers of preschoolers were in the labour force (Labour Canada, 1986:22). As other chapters in this volume make clear, these considerations have profoundly affected the Canadian family. Their impact on socialization is discussed in the latter part of this chapter.

Various difficulties in the Canadian economy over the past decade have also affected primary socialization. In the late 1980s, some regions of Canada, such as the Maritimes and the West, continued to experience economic hardship. In a national poll reported in *Maclean's* (January 5, 1987), 27 percent of the sample rated unemployment as the most important issue in this country. Nearly 12 percent singled out youth unemployment as the key concern (27). Unemployed and discouraged parents, physical privation, and family moves from one end of the country to the other in search of employment have influenced the socialization of many Canadian children.

Economic trends have a severe impact upon adolescents. As economic opportunities for young adults have become scarce, older children, instead of becoming independent, are returning to the parental home (Schnaiberg and Goldenberg, 1986). This "crowded nest" phenomenon produces difficulties for both generations. Also, because the work ethic has long been a central motivation for Canadians' lives (Burstein et al., 1984), youth unemployment and the prospect of permanent unavailability of preferred jobs is a serious concern to both adults and young people. Professional status and material success are increasingly emphasized.

> The economic forecasts for the next 10 years indicate that low-paying service-sector jobs are what will be predominantly available—indeed, already are in major cities. Meanwhile, television and the other media tell the young that to truly succeed they should become doctors or lawyers (Gerner, 1987:37).

Fewer than one in four of the 18 to 24 age group gain full-time enrollment in universities or community colleges. Surveys show that Canadian young people are becoming increasingly pessimistic about their own prospects of succeeding (*Maclean's*, September 7, 1987). Instead of blaming the abstract, imperfectly understood economic forces that are responsible for their plight, these youngsters (and their parents) tend to personalize failure (Brake, 1985).

Demographic Changes

Socialization in Canadian society is influenced by demographic trends, which in turn are affected by the technological and economic forces noted earlier. Because these matters are treated at length elsewhere in this text, only brief mention need be made here.

In recent years, Canada's birth rate has dramatically declined as the result of a variety of factors, including later marriages, postponement of parenthood to later years, a greater proportion of people who never marry, voluntary childlessness and, perhaps most important of all, married women's increasing participation in the labour force. Obviously, the nature of primary socialization is different in the 1980s family of one or two children from what it was in the larger families of previous decades.

Divorce is another major contributor to changing socialization patterns. More than half of the divorces involve dependent children (Statistics Canada, 1985:3). Moreover, women retain custody of over three quarters of the children involved in such marital dissolution (Statistics Canada, 1985:3). Since three quarters of the divorced eventually remarry (McKie et al., 1983:233), socialization occurs in the context of reconstituted families, as well as single-parent families.

One in ten Canadian single parents has never been married (Davids, 1985:3). Despite the decline in teenage pregnancy and the increase in the number of therapeutic abortions, an estimated 80 to 90 percent of all single teenage mothers are keeping their children (Schlesinger, 1985:35).

Declining death rates also affect socialization in various ways. The probability of a child being orphaned or growing up without grandparents has diminished (Sullivan, 1983). Indeed, these grandparents have fewer grandchildren among them than ever before (Eichler, 1983:35). Since Canada is an "aging society," contemporary children are becoming increasingly familiar with the elderly. Indeed, improved life expectancy contributes to the complexity of modern families with which children must deal. "The family of four and five generations may become more frequent in spite of trends toward later marriage and childbearing" (Settles, 1987:160).

Population migration, into Canada and within Canada, represents a final important contextual aspect of socialization. In the 1960s and 1970s, large numbers of people arrived from Asian, Latin American, and Caribbean countries. These newcomers face the dual challenge of conveying something of their culture of origin to their children, while they and their offspring learn to fit into their new society. Often, the new immigrant family protects its members from stress by a "creative schizophrenia," that allows its members to be "modern" at work and "traditional" at home (Berger and Berger, 1984:88). As mentioned above, the mobility between and within Canadian cities experienced by many Canadian families for economic reasons, for example, involves psychic and social costs.

In sum, the contemporary Canadian family is subjected to the influence of a complex set of socio-cultural forces and this has serious implications for primary socialization. In the next section, these implications are examined at length.

CHANGING FAMILY STRUCTURE

Our main thesis is that the family's task of socialization is becoming increasingly complicated, both by global influences and special characteristics of Canadian society. Sociologists have recently attempted to interpret the relative importance for the family of two trends. On the one hand, there is the ethnic, regional, and social class heterogeneity of Canadian society described earlier in this chapter. On the other hand, the family is subject to homogenizing trends such as industrialization, urbanization, and the takeover of mass industry and mass communications, outlined in the section immediately preceding. After reviewing the evidence on these divergent and convergent trends, Ramu and Tavuchis (1983:64) conclude that "the family in Canada continues to perpetuate certain aspects of social structure such as ethnicity and class, but that this function is being gradually eroded by the forces of modernization. . . ." We turn now to a more detailed consideration of family structure which is at once effect and cause of these forces.

Non-traditional Family Forms

A "Herman" cartoon depicts a "smart-alecky" child holding out his report card to his teacher and asking, "Which parents do you want to sign it: my natural father, my stepfather, my mother's third husband, my real mother or my natural father's fourth wife who lives with us?" Despite the humour, this cartoon poignantly reminds us of the complex family types that have recently emerged as a result of the socio-cultural forces reviewed in the previous section. Single-child families, single-parent families, blended families, and dual-earner families are to a greater or lesser extent, novel developments that have wide-ranging influences upon primary socialization.

Two aspects of single-parent and reconstituted families particularly capture sociologists' attention: their emergent social organization and socio-economic status. First, novel circumstances not covered by traditional societal scripts demand role shifts ("How is one parent to handle responsibilities society assigns to two parents?"), role making ("How does a stepmother prove herself as a parent to a 15-year-old boy?"), and negotiation of relationships ("How do divorced parents with joint custody relate to the child and to one another?").

Second, social class is a key factor affecting socialization in single-parent families (Ambert, 1985). As noted earlier, single parenthood typically means single motherhood. The end of a marriage frequently spells downward economic mobility, even poverty, for the woman involved (Boyd, 1977). Amount of money available, together with values associated with social class, affect parent-child interaction, children's diet, housing, physical health, and educational opportunities. Single mothers from lower socio-economic levels are especially vulnerable.

Divorce Separation and divorce produce intense emotional reactions from most children at the time of the family breakup, and lingering negative effects for a sizable minority (Bumpass, 1984). The child's developmental stage when parents separate is one of the many variables which affect children's reactions. Preschool children do not understand divorce and often blame themselves for their parents' separation. As Nelson (1985:121) points out, "school-aged children experienced mixed feelings of sadness, anxiety, and anger. Many of these children had conflicts of divided loyalty, wished for their parents to reconcile, and openly expressed anger towards their parents." While younger children often react with disruptive behaviour, older children tend to do so with depression (Nelsen, 1985:125). According to Ambert (1985), custodial mothers in lower socio-economic ranks experience particular difficulty in disciplining their children. The fathers, as males, seem to command authority and respect from their children. By contrast, women of lower socio-economic status, unable to provide a decent standard of living, become scapegoats for their children's frustration.

Divorce brings inevitable social and economic changes in children's lives. For example, many learn that, when marriages break, "money is tight for winter coats, babysitters, running shoes and penicillin . . . " (Maynard, 1984:65). Moves to new neighbourhoods or communities which often occur result in the loss of friendships and the challenge of establishing new ones. Relationships with both custodial and non-resident parents deviate from traditional nuclear-family scripts. Children are likely to find these changes stressful, at least initially. One beloved parent may now be labeled a villain and enemy by the other. A small proportion of fathers become "Mr. Moms" in custodial-father households (a popular topic for movies and television sitcoms). Many more join the legion of indulgent "Uncle Dads" (Smith, 1985) with a limited meaningful role in their children's lives beyond visiting privileges. Many non-custodial parents eventually disappear altogether. Parents' boyfriends or girlfriends who come and go may exercise temporary authority over children of divorced parents. A large-scale study of a national sample of American children of divorced parents arrived at this conclusion:

> Marital dissolution typically involves either a complete cessation of contact between the nonresidential parent and child or a relationship that is tantamount to a ritual form of parenthood. We have seen that the predominant pattern... involves the replacement of the biological parent with a sociological or stepparent. Little is known about how this transition is accomplished and even less about the consequences for the well-being of the children (Furstenberg et al., 1983:667).

The lone parent available to carry out the family's socialization tasks faces many difficulties. The custodial parent is frequently overwhelmed with the responsibilities for earning a living, child care, and housework (Michelson, 1985:90). The lone parent, burdened with new responsibility, may treat the child as a pseudo-adult, equal out of sheer necessity. Toronto children in single-parent homes cited many functions of the missing parent which they had assumed, such as serving as a listening post for the parent, discussing sex, cooking, cleaning, caring for younger siblings (Schlesinger, 1983). While such experience may operate as anticipatory socialization for future adult roles, it may also force youngsters to grow up too quickly. The effect of a parent's absence upon children is a complex and controversial research topic. However, there is wisdom in Green's (1976) observation that "two adults involved in the upbringing can counteract each other's more bizarre tendencies and complement each other's talents and blind spots."

Nevertheless, it is important to acknowledge that divorce frequently has positive results for children as well. Many children benefit by escaping the stressful family environment produced by a conflict-ridden marriage, and by establishing closer relations with their custodial parents. Though divorce can make children cynical about marriage, they do develop a broader vision of "normal" social arrangements (Whitehurst, 1984:225). Children's response depends on such considerations as their age at the time of divorce, and pre-existing conflict in the home.

Unmarried Mothers   The circumstances of never-married mothers vary with the age and resources of their parents. Children of unmarried teenage mothers are usually disadvantaged in a variety of ways (Schlesinger, 1985). For one thing, there are high risks to the health of children born to young unmarried mothers. According to a London, Ontario, study (Grindstaff, 1983), because of deficiencies in the mothers' nutrition and prenatal care, their children are more likely to be born prematurely and to die in infancy. Babies of young mothers are especially prone to respiratory illness and feeding problems. Moreover, adolescent single mothers are ill-equipped to socialize their offspring. "Children" themselves, they lack wisdom and experience. They also lack financial resources. Many drop out of high school and are without job training. The poverty, social isolation, and other social problems, such as depression and alcoholism, which characterize the lives of young single mothers, have serious implications for their children. Quite different is the little-studied situation of mature women who choose to be unmarried mothers (Zwarun, 1985). The fact that many of these older women have successful careers and supportive social networks suggests a more promising future for their offspring.

Blended Families   Many children of divorced and never-married parents eventually find themselves part of a reconstituted family of parents, siblings, step-parents, step-siblings, half-siblings, and extended kin. Unfortunately, relatively little is known about socialization in blended families. However, a few tentative generalizations can be made.

On the positive side, the support system of the child is expanded, and his or her life enriched by many new relationships. Money may be more plentiful in blended families than in single-parent families. Nevertheless, a certain degree of role confusion and ambiguity seems inevitable when relationships must be negotiated with a new cast of characters as confusing as those in a Russian novel (Jarmulowski, 1985:33).

There are numerous questions for which answers are not immediately forthcoming. Who has authority to discipline children? What kinship terms are to be used (If a child calls her mother "mom," what should she call her stepmother)? Does the erstwhile eldest child who has acquired older siblings lose privileges as he descends the pecking order? When children are exposed to conflicting norms and values, the family's influence on the socialization process may be attenuated.

Siblings   The size of a group is an important factor in our understanding of social patterns (Simmel, 1950) and this is critical for socialization. Socialization is influenced by the number of children in a family, as well as the number of parents. Despite the increase in the proportion of reconstituted families, the demographic trends (discussed in the previous section) suggest that, on the average, Canadian youngsters now have fewer siblings or none at all.

What are the consequences for socialization of shrinking family size? Larger families offer each child more autonomy and independence from adult supervision. "The greater numbers give a certain amount of protection from parental despotism and emotional absorption by spreading parental attention over more children, thereby diminishing the influence on any one child" (Gecas, 1981:171). With fewer children, the increased potential exists for intense parent-child relationships. In middle-class families, pressure to succeed in school, in sports—indeed, in life—is concentrated on one or two children. In such a situation, the possibility of coalitions of siblings against parents becomes more limited because of their numbers, and consequently children's familial power declines.

Siblings have traditionally served as major agents of socialization for one another. For example, both older same-sex and opposite-sex siblings provide gender models. In this regard Goffman (1977:314) observes that "it is as if society planted a brother with sisters so women could from the beginning learn their place, and a sister with brothers so men could learn their place." With the decline of siblings' participation in socialization, the role of other socialization agents, such as parents, playmates, and the mass media, has become decisive. Although children in small families are spared the pain of sibling rivalry, they are also deprived of lifelong friends who share the same family history (Bank and Kahn, 1982). Fewer children per household mean more space, more privacy (and probably more isolation), more material possessions, and more educational opportunities for children in Canada, especially for middle-class children (Eichler, 1983:38). Finally, the stereotype of the only child who is self-centred, spoiled, and anxious is not supported by empirical evidence. Compared to children in two-child families, only children "have better cognitive performance and are more mature, socially sensitive, and tidy." No difference exists between these children and those from larger families with regard to "calmness, self-confidence, drive, vigor, leadership" (Hernandez, 1986:173).

Employed Mothers

What are the implications for socialization of the ever-increasing numbers of Canadian mothers of preschool- and school-aged children who enter and stay in the labour force? Here, we consider two: alternate childcare arrangements and non-traditional gender models.

Non-familial Child Care   It is now clear that the majority of Canadian preschool children are regularly cared for by someone other than a parent (Eichler, 1983:249). Therefore, according to the Federal Task Force on Child Care (1986), chaired by Katie Cooke, the availability of quality daycare has become an urgent national issue. This task force concluded that "Canada's childcare and parental leave programs lag behind systems operating in most western industrialized countries" (277). This finding raises the issues of cost and who should bear it, and the ideological and political considerations. Good daycare is expensive (up to $6000 per year per child) and scarce. In fact, the number of children in need of daycare outnumbers spaces available in licensed centres by more than ten to one (*Maclean's*, November 10, 1986:48).

It is extremely difficult to generalize about the socialization consequences of non-familial childcare facilities which range from nannies in residence, to mothers' babysitting cooperatives, from licensed childcare centres run by highly trained personnel, to unlicensed arrangements in church basements, to the neighbours babysitting in their homes to make a few dollars. Obviously, social class and income influence the type and quality of non-familial child care experienced by a child.

Research shows that children are not adversely affected by a mother's decision to work outside the home or to stay at home, provided she is comfortable with her decision and the alternative childcare arrangements are nurturing, stimulating, and safe (Task Force on Child Care, 1986:209). Moreover studies of the development of bonding between mother and child find little difference between children at home with their mothers, daycare children, and youngsters cared for by babysitters (Gerson et al., 1984:447). Positive effects accrue from *good* child care, especially to children from disadvantaged homes (Task Force on Child Care, 1986:209). Unfortunately, quality childcare is in short supply in this country.

Experts on child development (Suransky, 1982:200) caution that effective socialization requires that one or more adults be unconditionally involved with the child. Effective socialization also requires consistency and predictability in the child's relations with significant others (Berger and Berger, 1984:152). The shortage of quality childcare facilities in this country does create serious problems.

> Locating adequate care arrangements is becoming increasingly difficult for parents, most of whom must repeat the process many times until their children are old enough to care for themselves. Indeed, many parents, frustrated by the lack of available alternatives, leave children alone at a very young age. All of these problems—affordability, accessibility, quality—are exacerbated for families to whom any special circumstance applies: low income, shift work, a handicapped child, multiple birth, or residence in a rural area, to name just a few (Task Force on Child Care, 1986:208).

In any case, children socialized by babysitters or daycare centres are necessarily exposed to other people's norms and values. Children whose parents oppose war toys and violent television shows may spend their day playing with "Rambo" action figures or watching "Autobots" blasting their way through "Decepticons."

Gender Socialization   In general, the division of labour children experience in their homes is a critical determinant of their understanding of femininity and masculinity. Children who grow up in households where the "father brings home the bacon and the mother cooks it" develop traditional notions about gender. On the other hand, "if sex is unimportant as a basis of role assignment in the family, then children will think in 'modern' or non-differentiated ways" (Lambert, 1971:31).

Children with employed mothers (and single mothers) experience domestic social organization which is, of necessity, less sex-typed than that of families which continue traditional patterns. Nevertheless, despite predictions of "symmetrical families" that share household tasks (Young and Willmott, 1975) and "androgynous fathers" anxious for involvement in their children's lives, several Canadian studies (Lupri and Mills, 1987; Meissner et al., 1975) conclude that when wives go out to work, husbands do *not* substantially increase their share of housework or child care. Although child care is shared by couples more than are domestic tasks, the father still plays a "minor part" in child care, even when the mother is employed full time (Horna and Lupri, 1987). For example, whether she works full or part time, it is still usually the mother who stays home with her sick child (Northcott, 1983).

Consequently, it is hardly surprising that Canadian youngsters continue to be quite sex-typed in their thinking. A recent study by Labour Canada (1986) of career aspirations of elementary-school children found that children now understand that women may participate in traditionally masculine occupations. However, the girls did not apply to themselves their belief in gender equality:

> Many of them seemed to be saying, "Yes, women can become doctors, but I expect to be a nurse," "Bank managers can be women as well as men, but I am going to be a teller... " (Labour Canada, 1986:55).

Canadian adolescents continue to regard housework as women's work (Baker, 1985:152). Although the children of professional and divorced mothers entertained more egalitarian ideas about their future occupations, "both sexes seemed to be bound by traditional stereotypes of gender and work" (160). Essentially, children learn that although women are now active in public as well as domestic arenas, females must still depend on and manipulate the males who control the power and resources.

A final comment: the trends analyzed in this chapter have provoked a right-wing, authoritarian reaction calling for the return of the traditional patriarchal family. The fundamentalist Christian churches spearheading the movement seek to restore to the family the religious authority lost through secularization. The organization R.E.A.L. Women accuses feminists of destroying marriage and motherhood (Dubinsky, 1985). The long-term impact of this reactionary countermovement upon the socialization process remains to be seen.

CONCLUSIONS

Primary socialization may be likened to putting on a play (Inkeles, 1969:616-617). Under the simplest of circumstances, such as those which obtain in stable, isolated, "primitive" societies before they encounter modern "civilization," the play proceeds smoothly along well-practised lines. The script is fixed and has been handed down unchanged for generations. The parts are few and well-known. The director's authority is accepted without question. Props and costumes are in ample supply. Since the actors are well-acquainted with one another and know exactly what is expected of them, the interaction among them is orderly and satisfying.

To continue the analogy, the socialization process in modern industrialized Canada resembles improvisational theatre more than the fixed, frozen drama of traditional socialization. The play has never been put on before in exactly this form. A host of would-be directors, many shouting advice from the audience, vie for control. There is no specification of how many actors are involved; their parts are only vaguely defined; indeed, there is no fixed script at all. New parts are continually added, while others suddenly disappear. The players switch roles and improvise their lines. The interaction among directors, actors, and audience members is confusing and difficult. Nevertheless, since anything is possible and no one can predict exactly what might happen, "improv" theatre can be very exciting.

Reverting once again to the language of the sociologist, socialization is "the transmission of social knowledge considered essential for the occupancy of social statuses and the implementation of corresponding roles" (DiRenzo, 1977:264). As a result of this learning process, the infant becomes "humanized," thus realizing its potential; the continuity of the society also becomes assured. However, in societies like Canada in the late twentieth century, future roles and statuses can no longer be predicted with confidence. The family shares intellectual and moral authority with other socialization agencies. Rivals intrude upon the emotional bond between parent and child that is absolutely essential for primary socialization to occur.

Throughout this chapter, we have argued that, although the family continues to be responsible for primary socialization and judged according to ever-rising standards, modern developments impede and complicate its performance. In the Age of the Expert and Big Government, educators, psychologists, and pediatricians help, advise, and bully parents in order to protect children from putative parental ignorance. Changes in the sociocultural context and family structure have served to enhance the influence of competing socialization agencies. Parental authority is shared with the mass media, the peer group, babysitters, teachers. The quality of the teaching provided by these alternate socialization agencies, compared with that which was once offered by the family, is sometimes questionable. Large parts of childhood and youth are being lived outside the familial home in daycare centres, shopping malls, and schools.

Considerable justification exists for viewing structural changes in the family, in response to the developments enumerated above, as evidence of that institution's continuing resilience. Nevertheless, as we have tried to show in this chapter, the adaptations themselves further complicate the socialization function.

Because the contemporary family lacks institutionalized solutions to many of the complex situations it faces, socialization tasks are often handled on an *ad hoc*, emergent norm basis (Cherlin, 1978). Delegation of responsibility to other agencies is the most obvious example. However, other strategies should be mentioned. Adults improvise ways of juggling multiple role obligations to children, fellow workers, and aging parents. For example, women in the labour force eliminate housekeeping "frills" and recruit assistance from unorthodox sources. Consciously-constructed networks shore up family resources (Whitehurst, 1984). Friends are transformed into "fictive kin" to replace missing or non-functioning relatives. Single mothers pair up to share homes, living expenses, and child care. Parents form babysitting cooperatives and car pools. Groups are developed for emotional support after divorce (Minus One), for self-help for child abusers (Parents Anonymous), and for child protection (Neighborhood Watch). "Bibliotherapy" helps families to deal with children (Lynn Caine, *What Did I Do Wrong: Mothers, Children, Guilt*, 1985) and children to cope with families (Jean Little, *Mama's Going to Buy You a Mockingbird*, 1984). Since institutionalized solutions emerge through time and practice, an optimist might argue that the family will eventually "get it right." Certainly, social scientists need to pay more attention to these emerging strategies.

Judging whether the Canadian family's socialization function has been seriously compromised is a matter for cautious inference. Canadian data bearing directly on the question are scarce; disentangling the influence of the various socialization agents would be a difficult task in any case. However, the extent information suggests that the family has not lost control of its children. Canadian society does not seem threatened by delinquent or psychopathic youngsters. The continuing impact of social class and traditional gender norms upon children may also be interpreted as indications of direct or indirect familial influence (Nett, 1986:362). Furthermore, parents remain more influential than peers when the issues are teenagers' future goals and educational aspirations than when they are fashion and music (Davies and Kandel, 1981). Children's religious and political views correspond closely to those of their parents (Glass et al., 1986). The recent resurgence of loyalty to the family described elsewhere in this volume is another hopeful sign.

Suggested Readings

Bibby, Reginald W., and Donald C. Posterski.
1985 *The Emerging Generation: An Inside Look at Canada's Teenagers.* Toronto: Irwin.

Brim, Orville G., Jr., and Jerome Kagan, eds.
1980 *Constancy and Change in Human Development.* Cambridge, MA: Harvard University Press.

Elkin, Frederick, and Gerald Handel.
1984 *The Child and Society: The Process of Socialization.* Fourth ed. New York: Random House.

Mackie, Marlene.
1987 *Constructing Women and Men: Gender Socialization.* Toronto: Holt, Rinehart and Winston.

Postman, Neil.
1982 *The Disappearance of Childhood.* New York: Dell.

Turkle, Sherry.
1984 *The Second Self: Computers and the Human Spirit.* New York: Simon and Schuster.

Williams, Tannis MacBeth, ed.
1986 *The Impact of Television: A Natural Experiment in Three Communities.* Orlando, FL: Academic Press.

Winn, Marie
1983 *Children Without Childhood.* Markham: Penguin.

7

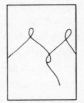

WORK AND FAMILY LIFE: CHANGING PATTERNS

Pat Armstrong

Our ideas about appropriate female and male behaviour, and family life, are in some ways fundamentally different from those of our grandparents. So are our family structures. Although many of these emerging ideas and developing structures have been attributed to the rebirth of feminism, they reflect a complex interaction of a variety of factors. This chapter begins with an outline of the overall trends in education, labour force participation, fertility rates, and domestic work which influence and are influenced by attitudes and family forms. In the following sections we analyze the reasons for the development of these patterns and their consequences for family lives of the women and men. In the final pages, this analysis becomes the basis for some speculations about the future of men, women, and families.

PATTERNS IN THE FORMAL ECONOMY

Over the last thirty years, the patterns of male and female participation in the formal economy have been changing. While more women have sought and many have found paid work, more men have remained out of the labour force. The patterns for men are somewhat erratic but, in general, the proportion of married men in paid employment has been declining and the proportion of unemployed men is on the increase. Older men in particular have withdrawn from the labour market. Of course, the overwhelming majority of married men under 65 years of age—more than 80 percent of them—have or are seeking paid work, and men continue to constitute the majority of the employed (Statistics Canada, 1983: Series D146–174).

In contrast, the employment of married women has grown dramatically, although their unemployment rates have been steadily rising and are now above those of men. In the early 1950s, only ten percent of married women were in the labour force; by the 1980s, 50 percent were (Armstrong and Armstrong, 1984:160). Not all of them had jobs, however, given that more than one in ten of those counted as members of the labour force were unemployed (Statistics Canada, 1985a:59). Even women with very young children are staying in the job market. While less than a third of those with children under three years of age were in the labour force in the mid-1970s, a mere ten years later nearly half of them were employed or looking for paid work (Riddell, 1985:56). Unlike older men and younger women, women over 55 have had relatively steady participation rates during the last ten years (Statistics Canada, 1985a:48). Primarily as a result of the movement of younger women into the job market, then, women now account for more than 40 percent of the labour force.

Patterns of female and male participation in education have also been shifting during this period. Both women and men are staying in school longer, but here too changes have been more dramatic for women. By the 1980s, more women than men had completed high school, post-secondary certificates or diplomas (Statistics Canada, 1985a:36). While more men than women have university degrees, women are rapidly catching up. In the mid-1960s, women received one third of the bachelor's and first professional degrees, nearly four in ten of the master's, and one in four of the doctorates (Nakamura and Nakamura, 1985:200). "In 1982, women received 51% of bachelor's degrees, 40% of master's degrees, and 25% of doctorates" (Statistics Canada, 1985a:24).

Changes in attitudes have accompanied the developments in labour force participation and education. "Canadians increasingly believed that married women should take a job outside the home, although the magnitude of acceptance is conditioned by the presence or absence of young children" (Boyd, 1984:11). In 1960, just under two thirds of those responding to Gallup polls thought married women without children should work outside the home if they wanted such employment. By 1982, nearly 90 percent of Canadians thought married women should take paid work but only 38 percent thought they should do so when there were young children at home (Boyd, 1984:12). While an increasing number believed women can perform as well as men, a decreasing number believed that women have an equal opportunity to succeed in the business world (Boyd, 1984:19). Nevertheless, views of women and men frequently differ on such issues. For example, women are more likely than men to support the principle of equal pay for equal work.

Women now constitute more than two out of every five persons in the labour force. The number of years women spend in formal education compare favourably with those of men and most people of both sexes acknowledge a woman's right to paid work. Despite these developments, however, women remain segregated in a limited number of jobs. "In 1983, 77% of all female employees worked in just five occupational groups—clerical, service, sales, medicine and health, and teaching. This was only a three percentage point drop from what the proportion had been in 1975" (Statistics Canada, 1985a:43). The slight decline of female concentration in women's traditional occupations means that few women have moved into more prestigious and better paying jobs. Certainly there are more female doctors, lawyers, dentists, architects, miners, and construction workers than ever before. Yet in the last 40 years, there has been an increase of only 1.4 percent in the proportion of women employed in professional and technical jobs, and most of these have gone into lower level technical rather than the more prestigious professions. Indeed, if the many technologists, technicians, and employees in other categories related to the professions are excluded from this broad category—the category which is so often cited as an indication of women's advancement—the concentration of women in the professions actually declined between 1971 and 1981.

For men, the reverse was true. The male concentration in the professions increased between 1971 and 1981, and at a faster rate than that in technical jobs (Armstrong and Armstrong, 1984:41). In fact, more men have moved into traditional female jobs in teaching than have women into the traditional male areas of medicine, law, architecture, and engineering combined. Furthermore, the few women who have managed to capture jobs in construction, mining, quarrying, or oil drilling are increasingly facing unemployment as these sectors reduce their labour force in many regions and as women, the last hired, are the first to be fired.

The continuing segregation of women into clerical, sales, service, and factory jobs helps to explain why women receive lower wages than men and why legislation that demands equal pay for the same work has had little effect (Ornstein, 1983). On average, women employed full-year full-time in the early 1980s were paid more than a third less than their male counterparts-64 cents on the male dollar (Riddell, 1985:61). Moreover, such comparisons underestimate the actual differences in pay between women and men because they fail to take into account the fringe benefits which have been growing faster than wages. If fringe benefits are included, the total wage difference between women and men is increasing, not decreasing, as more women enter the labour force (Dulude, 1985).

Moreover, the differences are even larger when the wages of the many women who work part-time are included. While 64 percent of all men had full-time jobs in 1984, only 35 percent of all women had full-time paid employment (calculated from Statistics Canada, 1985c). According to official statistics, more than a quarter of employed single and married women had part-time jobs: they account for more than 70 percent of those working part-time. In contrast, most men who work part-time are single. More than 97 percent of the married men with employment work full-time. When the wages of all workers are considered, women are paid on average only 55 percent of what men are paid.

In education, as in employment, the segregation remains. While women account for rapidly increasing proportions of those enrolled in university law, medicine and business programs, the numbers of women entering technical courses have increased to a much lesser extent. Moreover, the proportion of women studying fine and applied arts—where the overwhelming majority of women are found—is still growing. In 1981, while almost 90 percent of those in engineering and applied sciences and over over 60 percent of those in law, medicine and commerce were male, over 60 percent of those in arts were female (Nakamura and Nakamura, 1985:201).

Similar patterns appear in community colleges. Between 1976 and 1982, the largest relative increase for women was in arts. The number of women graduating from engineering did grow but they accounted for less than two percent of all graduating women. In contrast, a quarter of the male graduates were in engineering. About half of the women completing community college were in secretarial, nursing, or community and social service programs; since 1976 only in nursing has the proportion declined (Statistics Canada, 1985a:35).

Furthermore, as is the case with the labour force, women are much more likely than are men to be part-time students. During the 1970s, only a quarter of the increase in male undergraduate enrollment, compared to more than half of the female increase, was in part-time studies (Statistics Canada, 1985a:23).

In education and the labour force there are still male and female streams. Women and men do different work for different wages and their education continues to prepare them for different types of careers.

PATTERNS IN THE HOME

Work in the home has been changing for both women and men as new equipment, services, and products make work easier and often faster to do. Washers, dryers, dishwashers, frozen foods, cake mixes, and power lawn mowers are all postwar developments which have transformed domestic labour. In many cases, however, new products have locked tasks more firmly into individual households. For example, the production of washing machines designed for private use rather than the development of cheap, efficient market laundry services ensures that most clothes are cleaned at home. Indeed, while few visible goods are now made at home and appliances have lightened the load in a majority of Canadian households, the less visible personal service work has expanded. As Strasser (1982:8) explains in her exploration of American domestic technology, the introduction of these commodities has "left the cooking, cleaning and nuturing to the housewife."

Recent changes of fertility patterns are also altering domestic work. Women now have fewer children, delay the birth of their first child, have children at shorter intervals, or remain childless (see Chapter Five). In the words of a Statistics Canada study (Romaniuc, 1984:11), we have moved "from baby boom to baby bust." The number of births per woman has fallen from close to four to less than two in a mere 20 years. Because children not only require care but also increase the volume of other household chores, fewer children often mean less domestic work as well as more years without children at home.

There have also been new developments, however, which have served to counteract this potential reduction in childcare work. With fewer children born at closer intervals, there are fewer older children to help. Commuting fathers spend less time at home and therefore are around less often to help. Moreover, here, too, work has been transformed without being eliminated and technology has done little to lighten the childcare workload. Mothers in particular are advised by experts on the crucial and extensive nature of their parenting tasks (see Strong-Boag, 1982). Consequently, the nature of childcare work has changed and the time spent on each child expanded. Women spend more time keeping children's teeth, hands, and clothes clean, driving their children around, making their beds and lunches, and worrying about the consequences of toilet-training techniques, reward systems, or salt intake (see Armstrong and Armstrong, 1984:89–100 and Luxton, 1980).

As the fertility rate is decreasing, life expectancy is increasing for both sexes. Women, however, tend to outlive men by an average of seven-and-a-half years (Wilkins and Adams, 1983:12). Moreover, many elderly women married men significantly older than themselves. The years by which such women outlive their husbands, and their husbands' pensions, are even greater. Women's increasing longevity, the age difference between them and their husbands, along with women's lack of employment-related pensions, largely account for the fact that over half of all elderly unattached women live below the Low Income Cut-Off (Statistics Canada, 1985a:66).

Many of the growing number of elderly cannot survive independently or be accommodated in state facilities. Consequently, a large proportion are cared for at home by their children. While some childcare demands may be declining, demands for the care of parents are rising.

Although the amount and kind of work done in the home vary with social class, region, ethnicity, the number and ages of children and adults, as well as the labour force participation of women, almost all women bear the major responsibility for organizing the work and providing the personal services. Canadian research suggests that domestic tasks, and care of the children and the elderly, are left to women, whether or not they work exclusively in the home (see Chapter Ten).

In Flin Flon, Manitoba, women who hold paid jobs and who believe husbands should help with household chores still do an average of 73.9 hours of work a week, 31.4 of them spent in housework (Luxton, 1983:33–34). In Vancouver, when women in childless households enter the labour force, their husbands do on average an extra six minutes of regular housework a week. If there are children, husbands contribute an additional hour a week to regular tasks when their wives take on paid work. "Most married women do the regular, necessary, and most time-consuming work in the household every day" (Meissner et al., 1975:431). In Halifax, when women enter the labour force, "the wife does most of the adapting; she reduces her household work and leisure hours quite significantly and is more likely than her husband to hold a part-time job" (Clark and Harvey, 1976:64).

According to a study by the Canadian Advisory Council on the Status of Women, 79 percent of women in Canada who do part-time paid work and 73 percent of those in full-time paid employment are mainly responsible for family health care (Heller, 1986:12). Many of those who have assistance receive it from other women. Even when women have highly paid careers or when, like their partners, they are graduate students, it is women who adjust their work to fit household and childcare responsibilities (McFarlane, 1975; Hitchman and Symons, 1976). Paid domestic workers often reduce the workload of women in high-income households, but the task of arranging this assistance usually belongs to women. Moreover, hired helpers seldom do all the necessary tasks in the home.

Meg Luxton's (1983) study of Flin Flon families indicates that when husbands take over tasks in the home, they tend to do those with clearly defined boundaries or those which are the least boring and monotonous. Moreover, the increasing number of men who participate in household chores does not seem to reduce the amount of time women devote to household labour (Luxton, 1983:36). The decreasing hours of paid work performed by 'men and the rising labour force participation of women make it both possible and necessary for men to help more with the care of children. However, the man frequently "plays with them and tells them stories and other nice things" while the mother does most of the personal service work and other domestic tasks which accompany children (Luxton, 1983:37). While some men babysit, barbecue, occasionally change diapers, or take their parents for a drive, in most households, women iron, clean the toilet bowls, plan the meals, and care for the sick and elderly. At home, too, there is men's work and women's work.

While ideas concerning women's paid work have been changing along with their rising labour force participation, attitudes about the legitimacy of male assistance with housework have changed only slightly over the last two decades. Almost two thirds of those polled by Gallup in 1981 thought men should help, and nine out of ten married men said they did. However, only eight out of ten wives thought their husbands did housework and half of the men who helped did not do so on a regular basis (Boyd, 1984:7–9).

In the labour market, changes for men have been gradual. Men now spend less of their day, week, year, and life in paid jobs, but almost all, especially married men, still leave home five days a week to work at their paid jobs until they retire. More are moving into white-collar rather than blue-collar jobs. An increasing number of men do professional work and experience periods of unemployment.

On the other hand, changes for women, especially married women, have been rapid. Now, most younger women are in the labour force. The majority of these, however, do not have full-time jobs and almost half drop out to stay home with their very young children. And while more and more women are permanently in the labour force, their unemployment rates are higher than those of men and three quarters of those with paid jobs do women's work at women's wages.

As men's hours in paid work decrease and women's hours increase, men tend to assume only a slightly greater share of domestic chores. Paid work, declining fertility rates and new domestic technology have not significantly reduced women's housework hours. Instead, most women have taken on a double day, working many more hours than men.

UNDERSTANDING CHANGE AND CONTINUITY: WOMEN AND MEN IN FAMILIES

What accounts for the combination of relative stability and dramatic change in family? The explanations are complex, but they are found primarily in the interrelationship between formal economy and household, and between conditions and ideas. They may also be found in the actions women and men take, collectively and individually, to alter their lives. There are, of course, many reasons for change, or lack of change, in general patterns and in individual actions. There are also many variations according to social class, ethnicity, race, region, age, and marital status. The concern here, however, is with the most significant causes for the largest group of people. Nevertheless, it should always be remembered that there are important differences among women as well as between women and men, and that there are rarely single causes for any trend. Moreover, effects are frequently contradictory, both improving and hindering conditions for any specific group at a particular time.

A significant factor in changing male and female participation patterns is the rapid restructuring of labour force jobs since the Second World War. New technologies and new methods of organizing work have contributed to higher productivity and lower demand for workers in the traditionally male areas of agriculture, primary resource extraction, and processing. In the other industrial sectors dominated by men, such as construction and manufacturing, demand remained relatively constant until the recent recession, when jobs began to disappear and male unemployment rates rose. Collective bargaining, however, helped to reduce hours and extend vacations, which in turn limited overall job loss. Men's time at paid work was also reduced by the introduction of the forty-hour week, of compulsory retirement in many jurisdictions and of government-supported universal pension plans. Moreover, more years in school mean fewer years in the labour force (Armstrong, 1984; Armstrong and Armstrong, 1986).

During the same period, the service, finance, and trade industries expanded rapdily with the development of new services and with the enormous increase in managerial and clerical work. The dramatic extension of hospital, education, welfare, and other services, which reflected a response to postwar demand for compensation, the baby boom, and a new philosophy of state intervention to ensure economic stability, contributed heavily to this expansion (see Armstrong and Armstrong, 1986). Consequently, the demand for workers grew quickly in traditional female areas. While the managerial and much of the professional work went to men, for a variety of reasons large numbers of women were hired, mainly at other levels. Women were not only available but their labour was cheaper than that of their male counterparts. Initially at least, there was plenty of other work for men to do and women had, or were thought to have, the skills required for the work (see Armstrong, 1984, ch.3; and Lowe, 1986).

The growth of the sales and service sectors as well as the fragmentation of more jobs into discrete tasks also increased the demand for part-time workers. Women were hired as part-time employees in grocery and department stores, in hospitals and schools, in restaurants and hotels (see Armstrong and Armstrong, 1986).

Because many of the employers in the service sector used years of formal education as a basis for selecting employees, both females and males were encouraged to stay longer in school. The creation of new post-secondary educational institutions across the country, the expansion of older ones, and the increasing availability of financial aid also supported this trend. Parents traditionally gave priority to the education of their sons; additional funds for student aid meant fewer parents had to choose between children and many more daughters stayed in school. In recent years, the rising youth unemployment rate has also encouraged males and females to extend their education, both because more education is considered to provide better access to the limited number of jobs available and because there are fewer alternatives.

The expansion of the service sector helps to explain the growth in demand for women workers and for the increased number of years women spend in school. It does little to explain, however, why so many married women have been willing to take low-level clerical, sales and service jobs. The research on this issue clearly demonstrates that, while general and regional economic conditions, earning potential, social values, ethnicity, and age all influence the participation of women in the labour force, the most significant factors are years of formal education, the presence of young children in the home and husband's income (Armstrong and Armstrong, 1984:168). All have change dramatically over the last 30 years.

Higher education improves women's access to good jobs. Better jobs and better pay mean that women are also better able to hire substitutes to perform the child care and domestic tasks. Not surprisingly, then, the higher a woman's level of education, the more likely she is to be in the labour force. However, the increasing educational accomplishment of women accounts for only a small part of the increase in labour force participation. Less than one third of the women over 25 years of age have completed post-secondary education and more than a quarter of them are not in the labour force (Statistics Canada, 1985a:37, 38).

While more education encourages women to stay in the market, young children encourage women to stay at home. Licensed child care "is available to fewer than nine percent of the core population group needing it" (Status of Women Canada, 1986:72). Good child care is not only difficult to find it is also expensive, often doubling the cost of raising children (Status of Women Canada, 1986:15). Consequently, the families most likely to enjoy access to such care have "either an income high enough to pay for the service or an income low enough to quality for subsidy" (Status of Women Canada, 1986:72). In families that cannot afford or find child care, women's lower wages mean that it is economically sensible for mothers to stay home with the children, whether or not they prefer to do so. This is particularly the case for single mothers because they do not have spouses helping with child care or financial support. Women, not men, interrupt their labour force participation in order to care for children (Burch, 1985:25).

Although alternative care is difficult to afford or find, more women with children are staying in the labour market. They leave their children with their spouse, with other relatives or with another woman who provides unlicensed and uncounted paid care. For more than one third of mothers, the solution to these conflicting demands is part-time work (Statistics Canada, 1985a:55). For others, shift work permits them to be home with their children while the children are awake and allows their spouse to babysit at night or on weekends. Maternity leave, introduced in response to demands from women who needed paid employment but who also wanted to have children, helped women combine two jobs. There are few other forms of assistance, however, for these mothers once they return to their work in the labour force.

Care for others may also be a factor in older women's lower labour force participation rates. Their limited formal education and job experience give them few employment prospects. However, they may also be restricted by demands for the care of elderly parents. Moreover, many of these women are married to men several years older than themselves: these aging husbands often require nursing. Home care for the elderly is also expensive, difficult to find and frequently beyond the means of older women.

Why, then, are so many of the women with such extra responsibilities and without the advantages of higher education taking on paid work? A crucial factor in women's movement into the labour force market is economic need. Women have fewer ways of working in the home either to reduce expenses or to earn an income. Men's wages have not kept up with the cost of living and child rearing has become increasingly expensive. As one woman we interviewed explained,

> "All of a sudden . . . you find out your husband's pay cheque wasn't adequate. Expecialy when the family was younger, there was always so many things they needed. When the necessities became hard to come by, then you knew that you had to go out to help" (Armstrong and Armstrong, 1985a:36–37).

Furthermore, an increasing number of women do not live with an employed man.

In the past, many women were able to cook, sew, grow and preserve vegetables, in order to keep domestic expenditures low. Many took in boarders, sewing or laundry, or sold produce as a means of bringing money into the home. Today, new technology and state legislation have eliminated most of these possibilities. It is cheaper to buy goods such as sweaters and chocolate-chip cookies in the market than it is to make them at home. Repairs, such as darning socks, are increasingly difficult on new fabrics. Apartment buildings, washing machines, frozen foods, fast-food restaurants, laundromats and inexpensive, permanent-press clothing have all reduced the demand for places to board, for home laundry and for sewing services. Regulations, for example, on selling, on raising livestock and on installing bathrooms limit opportunities for women to earn extra money at home at the same time as they increase the need for income. Not all means of earning money at home have been eliminated of course. Women still sew for factories, and now they type, babysit, sell Tupperware and clean other people's houses. That more women are doing such homework, however, is a further indication of their economic need.

In addition, many of what were once considered luxuries have become necessities. For example, people who live in apartments and areas where it is illegal to hang clothes out to dry have little choice but to use clothes dryers. In any case, once clothes dryers have been developed they become necessities in households which have to survive through Canadian winters. Moreover, those costs which have been rising most rapidly—mortgages, taxes, and fuel for instance—cannot be readily reduced by women working harder at home, nor can they be easily abandoned. New technology and other developments in the market, in the state, and in health care have raised standards and created some new work in the home. They have also reduced domestic work enough to make a labour-market job possible while increasing the need for money enough to make it necessary.

Another factor contributing to growing family expenditure is the increasing cost of raising children. Here, too, what were once considered luxuries have become necessities. Children often need to be driven to and from school, to doctor's appointments, and various lessons. The numerous extra-curricular activities which are thought to be, and often are, required to improve future employment possibilities are expensive and time-consuming. Although health and education services are provided by the state, increasingly there are additional costs for such things as vitamins, dental bills, school trips, and sports equipment. Rising unemployment rates among youth and post-secondary school attendance serve to increase the number of years children are dependent on their families. Furthermore, university educations and special training constitute a large and direct expense for parents. Children, once economic assets, are now economic liabilities.

In the 1960s, the income of married women helped to sustain family living standards and even added a little extra to the household budget, reinforcing the myth that women worked for luxuries, for pin money. Between 1971 and 1981, however, the income of wives "was the significant factor in preventing family income from declining in real dollars." "By 1979–81, increases in wives' income were no longer able to offset the decline in husbands' average income" (Pryor, 1984:102). Most women, then, work for bread, not for pins.

Furthermore, rising male unemployment means that households cannot always count on male income even if it is usually adequate for family needs. Although many men receive unemployment insurance, benefits are rarely sufficient to cover the continuing payments on houses and car—costs which cannot easily be eliminated, reduced or delayed (Johnson and Abramovitch, 1986).

For the increasing number of women who parent families alone, economic need is even greater than it is for women married to men whose real wages are falling. While women heading lone-parent families are the women least likely to have full-time employment while their children are very young, they are the most likely to have full-time work as their children grow older (Status of Women Canada, 1986:10). Whether or not they have been married, these single parents get little financial support from their children's fathers. Monica Boyd's (1977:56) research indicates that their own employment was the major source of income for nearly three quarters of the divorced and for half of the separated women.

Economic need is a less significant motivation for the growing labour force participation of women married to men whose income remains high, although as Gunderson (1976:102) points out, economic factors cannot be ruled out even in the case of these women. Many such women have qualifications and education or access to economic resources, which open up good opportunities for them in the labour market. Many place a high value on economic independence; few have domestic chores which they cannot pay substitutes to perform. In any case, these women, and unmarried career women constitute only a small minority of all employed women.

Women's economic need has also increased with their longevity. Women live longer not only because of improved sanitation, nutrition and housing, and because of more effective, accessible medical care, but also because of declining fertility rates which mean that women face the risks of pregnancy and childbirth less often. Living longer and bearing fewer children, women have more years free of the heavy child care responsibilities that restrict labour force participation. As a growing number of women live well into old age and well beyond their husband and their husband's pensions, many have been encouraged to take paid work in order to ensure an income in their old age.

In sum, women are entering or staying in the labour force for a variety of reasons related to changes in the formal economy and in the household as well as in ideas about women's place. The demand for female workers has grown while male employment has declined along with the value of their wages. At the same time, technology has reduced both the need for household labour and the possibility of earning money at home, while it has increased both women's control over birth and their economic need, making it both possible and necessary for women to take on paid work.

Just as the explanations for changes must be sought in the home as well as in the market, so too must the relative stability of other patterns be understood in terms of developments in both spheres. Responsibility for mothering continues to limit women's full and equal participation in the labour market while poor pay and limited job opportunities in the market encourage women's responsibility for domestic work.

Although new reproductive technology may eventually make women's unique childbearing capacities irrelevant, for now at least they provide a basis for inequality in and out of the home. The introduction of surrogate mothering and the growth of childcare services mean that some aspects of both the biological and social reproduction of children take place under market conditions, but the reproduction of children still happens primarily outside the market. Given that only women have babies, it is women who are separated, for a limited period at least, from continuing participation in the labour force (Armstrong and Armstrong, 1983). This separation is socially rather than biologically constructed, although it is often justified in biological terms. It is reinforced by the lack of paid leave for childbirth and of parental leave for fathers (Townson, 1983) as well as by the scarcity and high costs of child care and by women's low wages.

The segregation is also supported by ideas about the value of maternal care. Although more men than women think women should stay home with the children, more than half of both sexes still think married women should not take paid work when their children are young (Boyd, 1984:49). Women's continuing responsibility for child care in turn supports the belief that women have more child-rearing skills. A Statistics Canada study found that the "exigencies of marriage, pregnancy and child care had a major impact on the continuity of work for a majority of women, but almost no impact for men" (Burch, 1985:26).

When women stay at home with the children, they usually take over responsibility for other domestic tasks as well, even if these had been more equally shared before the children arrived. For many women who try to combine jobs by working for pay part time, most household chores become or remain theirs because these women are employed for fewer hours per week than their husbands. Women who take only the unpaid maternity leave required by law are still usually the ones who interrupt their work to care for sick children or to respond to other household emergencies. If elderly relatives need home care, it is also usually women who make the compromises in their market work (Rogers, 1986:7).

Only a tiny minority of men are eligible for leave when babies are born and the time allowed for paternity leave or other family responsibilities is very minimal (Johnson and Abramovitch, 1986:iii). "The link between 'family' and 'motherhood' remains implicitly or explicitly intact as employers describe their opinions and personnel policies" for alternative working arrangements which accommodate demands for care of children and the elderly (Rogers, 1986:6). Similarly, women may be constrained by these responsibilities as well as by the priority given to their husband's higher paying job to refuse overtime or transfers or promotions or union executive positions that could lead to better conditions or pay (White, 1980). With women working shorter hours for less pay at what are often considered less demanding jobs than those performed by men, it is easy to rationalize women's heavier responsibility for domestic work.

These interruptions in employment and the other constraints placed on women by their domestic responsibilities are also often used to explain women's segregation in the job market and for women's part-time work. Obviously they do play some part in the structure of women's jobs and pay. But these constraints do not explain why married women in public sector jobs have better pay and job security, more flexible working conditions (Johnson and Abramovitch, 1986:iii), and more opportunities for promotion than do those in the private sector. Nor do they explain why "marital status turns out to be in itself an inconsequential determinant of earnings for women" (Denton and Hunter, 1982:32). Nor why "women who work part-time because they cannot find other work accounted for 51% of the growth in part-time work among women between 1975 and 1983" (Statistics Canada, 1985a:45).

Explanations for these patterns must be sought in the labour market as much as in the home. "By far the largest factor in explaining women's low wages is their concentration in low-wage occupations" (Ornstein, 1983:46). The segregation of women into female dominated occupations makes it possible to pay them all the same low wages, especially when there is a large supply of married women seeking paid work because their economic needs are growing. As Denton and Hunter (1982:44) suggest in their study of wage inequality, the search for profit means that it is "in the interest of and within the power of employers to discriminate against women in the private sectors" while the motivation is less strong in the non-profit making public sector. Strong unions made possible by the earlier scarcity of qualified workers and the inability of the state to relocate in order to resist union demands also contributed to better public sector conditions (Armstrong and Armstrong, 1986). In the private sector, women have been systematically excluded from highly paid male occupations. But men too may suffer from these wage differentials, because "women's relatively low wages exert a downward competitive pressure on men's wages as well (Fox and Fox, 1986:15). Moreover, there is little to suggest that employers have expanded their part-time jobs as a means of attracting more female employees. Rather, they have hired more part-time workers because few of them receive fringe benefits, most can work harder than their full-time counterparts and none are paid when demand is low (Armstrong and Armstrong, 1986).

Furthermore, job turnover is itself encouraged by the conditions and pay women face in the labour market. The least continuous jobs for both sexes are those in sales and service occupations where women are more highly concentrated. Many of these jobs are dull, monotonous and closely supervised in addition to being poorly paid (Armstrong and Armstrong, 1983:63–67). Not surprisingly, women often leave such jobs and stay home with the children whenever they have the opportunity. But staying home also means taking responsibility for domestic work.

Thus, while women's domestic responsibilities limit their ability to participate in the labour market on the same basis as men, it is also the case that the structure of paid jobs for women also limits their ability to participate equally and encourages their responsibility for domestic work.

CONSEQUENCES

What has been the impact of these developments in ideas, in education, in domestic and wage labour for the family life of women and men? Causes and consequences are difficult to establish. The aforementioned patterns are interactive and thus may serve both as cause and consequence. Moreover, history does not unfold in a linear fashion and change is continuous. When considering feminist research and action, these analytical problems become more obvious. The ideas about and evidence on the subordination of women have provided a basis for feminist demands. In addition, such demands are at the same time a result of changes in women's lives. Gains women make are frequently turned into losses or yield mixed benefits, and thus are subjected to constant re-evaluation. Nevertheless, it is possible to note the major and often contradictory effects of these trends. While the impact of these trends on women has been more obvious and dramatic, men's lives have necessarily been altered as well.

Women's growing and more continuous participation in formal education shapes and reflects ideas about their place in society. Brought together in educational institutions which were promoted as providing equal opportunity, but which in fact remained segregated, women developed a vocal and militant movement in response to their ghettoization. Participants in this movement documented the discrimination, successfully demanded better access to male-dominated programs, and demonstrated that women were as competent as men in a wide range of fields. These moves, in turn, contributed to changes in the traditional notions about women's capacities.

The rising participation of women in education and in the women's movement which accompanied this trend, are factors also in the increasing number of couples living together without marrying and in the growing demands by women for greater control over their bodies. Not in a position to marry, many couples decide to "pair up to share rent and household expenses; they see living together as a solution to their financial problems and lack of family support" (Fels, 1981:34; see also Burch, 1985). These practices both indicate changing ideas about women's sexuality and alter traditional ideas. Similarly, female students' demands for better birth control information and for improved access to birth control methods reflect both their need to postpone pregnancy and changing perceptions of their sexuality. At the same time, these organizing efforts themselves, as well as the greater rights that result, help to change their attitudes and values. Furthermore, men and women who share the experiences of education are also more likely to share views about women's place and family life.

Nevertheless, these changes were not entirely beneficial. The removal of some formal barriers and the entry of some women into all programs seems to imply that continuing segregation results not from continuing structured inequality but from individual choice or lack of effort. Furthermore, the persistent streaming of women into certain disciplines in schools and colleges and the high proportion of female part-time students suggest that women, not men, make most of the compromises. Many obvious formal restrictions on birth control were removed and improved techniques were made more accessible. Safe, effective methods are still unavailable, however (Montreal Health Press, 1980), and the consequences of poor birth control methods mainly affect women. Better access to birth control often puts pressure on women to engage more frequently in sexual relationships but it does not ensure that they can participate on the same basis as men, especially in light of untoward consequences of most contraceptives.

Women's increasing participation in the labour force reflects and shapes ideas not only about paid work but also about family life. Employment of women enable them to share many experiences, pressures and responsibilities which were historically in the male domain. With a paycheque, women gain some power and independence in the home, especially as their financial contribution has become more obviously necessary for the economic stability of the family. Furthermore, economic independence allows women greater freedom to terminate unsatisfactory marriages. This implies that women are in a better position to develop a more egalitarian relationship, one in which their preferences are taken into account.

The emergence of women's rights, combined with the sheer exhaustion and the logistical problems created by women taking on two jobs, puts pressure on many husbands to do more household chores. The demands of a double workload, in addition, encourage women to redefine their standards of household care. As one clerical worker we (Armstrong and Armstrong, 1983:206) interviewed explained, "When I went to work, I felt sort of guilty about being out of the house five days a week. That gradually disappeared. What was happening, we knew that two wages were necessary. You lost your sense of guilt."

Opinion polls indicate that a growing number of women and men think that the husband's domination is declining, that this is good for the family, and that men should help more with the housework (Boyd, 1984:Tables 1 and 3). Taking on paid work seems to have benefited women in other ways as well. Many research studies on the impact of employment on married women suggest that "in terms of mental health, self-esteem, and marital happiness wives with paying jobs fare better than housewives" (Eichler, 1983:188).

Feminist research and action has been both cause and consequence of these changes in the home. While an increasing number of women stayed in school and entered the labour force, feminists convincingly argued that women need not be mothers and that children need not be cared for by their mothers. They pointed out the biological similarities between the sexes existed. They established that there was no scientific basis for maternal instinct and they highlighted the advantages of daycare centres. Theoretical and empirical studies contradicted the traditional claims that maternal instinct and children's dependency inextricably tied women and children to each other within a heterosexual monogamous marriage. They also challenged the notion that innate female characteristics provide a decisive basis for placing women into certain jobs and excluding them from others.

Besides demonstrating that women's childbearing capacities need not relegate them to household and child care, feminist research also convincingly established that domestic labour deserves to be recognized as necessary work. Moreover, it is work that requires a considerable amount of both effort and skill; work which makes an important contribution to the economy in general (this point is discussed in detail in Chapter Two). Based on such arguments and on women's growing economic strength, feminists' collective efforts have succeeded in obtaining more equitable property rights (Dulude, 1984) and in persuading political parties to consider pensions for housewives.

Feminist research, combined with women's growing economic strength, has also led to the increasing public exposure of violence against women, so long hidden in the household (see, for example, MacLeod, 1980). Women's demands have resulted in the introduction of programs to assist battered wives and to punish offenders. These developments do more than help some women. They also alter beliefs about homes as havens for women, revealing and rejecting as they do women's subordination and dependency.

Exposed as not so exclusively havens, homes have also been revealed as not so separate after all. The overlap between what are often referred to as public and private spheres has become increasingly obvious with the massive entry of women into the labour force and with feminist research demonstrating the interconnections between domestic and wage work. Child care, for instance, has become a public issue, as have birth control, abortion, divorce, pensions, and property rights. At the same time, unemployment and job-related tensions have been linked to violence in the home (see, for example, Luxton, 1980:67–68). Consequently, the personal has become political, and domestic matters are more clearly part of the public agenda.

The increasing participation of married women in the labour force and the value of their earnings for domestic economy have eroded the traditional position that women should stay at home, dependent on a male breadwinner, taking care of children. By 1982, seven out of ten males and females thought that women should have opportunities equal to those of men in the labour market. This represents an enormous change from the one in four who favoured equal opportunity 20 years earlier, when only one fifth of married women were in the labour force (Boyd, 1984:Table 11). Furthermore, as some women have demonstrated their ability to perform jobs traditionally reserved for men, it has become increasingly difficult to maintain that women are incapable of assuming positions of responsibility.

With the more permanent movement of women into the labour force have come more militant collective actions as well. By 1984, 32 percent of all paid female workers were unionized, compared to 22 percent in 1970 (Labour Canada, 1986:87 and Statistics Canada, 1985a:Table 8), and many others belong to a variety of groups dedicated to changing conditions of work for women. The pay inequity, the discrimination in hiring and promotion, the sexual harassment, and the continuing segregation were exposed and changes demanded. Collective efforts led in many areas to equal-pay legislation, affirmative-action programs, legislation on sexual harassment and maternity-leave provisions. These successes improved women's access to better work and pay, increased their strength and altered ideas about women's place in the labour market and in the home.

However, rising labour force participation rates should not be taken simply as a sign of progress, equality, or changing values. Here too the removal of many formal barriers and the entry of some women into traditional male areas implies that the remaining segregation results from choice, lack of effort or perhaps of skills. Yet family responsibilities still interfere more with women's than men's labour force participation, given the lack of assistance at home and lack of support in the market. Reducing the number of children, delaying childbirth, hiring substitutes, or rejecting childbearing altogether permit women to participate more like men in the labour market. However, these strategies also mean that women have to forego many of the pleasures and rewards of caring for their own children or they have to care for their children under severe time restraints when they have little energy. The conflicts between the demands of household responsibilities and job requirements put enormous pressure on women and on marriages. As one telephone operator explained to us, "If you keep one up, you fall down on the other. You have to be a pretty super lady to keep both of them going" (Armstrong and Armstrong, 1983a:202).

The double load also means that fewer women have the energy or patience to handle the tensions at home. To the extent that families provide "havens in a heartless world," they are maintained largely by women who smooth out the quarrels, watch for signs of stress, attend to the routine needs of children, take part in parent-teacher meetings, and offer support to children and husbands. As more women enter the labour market, they have fewer resources to draw on in order to do this kind of work.

While a paycheque helps many women gain some power in the household, the size of the paycheque usually ensures that they remain subordinate. Even when a woman is employed full time, male-female wage differentials indicate that she contributes the smaller portion—about 40 percent in 1980. Not surprisingly, the more than one in four married women who work part time contribute much less—about 23 percent of family income (Status of Women Canada, 1986:13). When choices have to be made, the preferences of the person with the higher paycheque usually prevail. Asked if her husband helped with the housework, a dry cleaner employed full-time responded: "He'd just tell me to do it myself. Why should he do it? He's bringing the most money into the house and he's doing the most work" (Armstrong and Armstrong, 1983a:207).

Lower wages for women have also meant that those without husbands are much more likely than men to be poor. Half the lone-parent households headed by women live in poverty and more than half of the elderly women living alone are subsisting on incomes that fall below Statistics Canada's poverty line (Statistics Canada, 1985b). Many social assistance programs have prevented the position of elderly women from deteriorating further, but such is not the case for female single parents. In 1982, "the real incomes of families with female heads fell by 5% while those of families headed by men declined by only 2%" (Statistics Canada, 1985a:64). Various studies suggest that "while marriage breakdown usually means financial disaster for women, it almost invariably entails a substantial *increase* in the standard of living for men" (Dulude, 1984:70). Consequently, women, especially women with children or elderly women, are more economically dependent than men on their families, and greater dependency usually means less power.

Continuing high levels of male unemployment, however, increase the dependency of some men. Although the economic consequences of unemployment seem to be more severe for women (Burke, cited in Johnson and Abramovitch, 1986:6), unemployment is "a major shock to the self-esteem of fathers" (Johnson and Abramovitch, 1986:12). It creates boredom, depression and anxiety. Given higher male incomes, families suffer significant reductions in economic resources when men lose their jobs. Benefits such as dental care that are often part of a male's employment package are likely to be lost. The financial, physical, and psychological stresses on the man lead to stresses in family relationships as well and also undermine the man's authority. Since unemployed men have more time, many look after the children, thus enabling their wives to seek employment. However, a Toronto study found that the longer the period of unemployment, "the more likely they were to describe their children in negative terms" (Johnson and Abramovitch, 1986:11).

At the same time, the increase in longevity is extending the years of marriage. Married in their twenties, couples can expect to live well into their seventies, long after their children have grown, long after the men have retired from paid work and, far too often, long after their health has gone. Tensions can increase with the years, as household membership, household tasks and household incomes change. Women in particular are likely to spend their last years alone, poor, and unhealthy.

The developments in labour force participation, education, and domestic work have been accompanied by changes in attitudes, practices, and family structures. However, while much has changed, much has remained the same.

FUTURE POSSIBILITIES

There are many indications that women's economic need, as well as the length of their stay in formal education institutions and the labour force, will continue to grow. Such trends may gradually lead to pay equity, equality both at home and in the market, and shared domestic responsibility for child rearing and housework. The beliefs in and demands for equality are deeply entrenched and cannot easily be neglected or altered.

On the other hand, new micro-electronic technology may eliminate many of women's paid jobs and transform many of those that remain, creating work that is less skilled, lower paid, more harmful to health and more closely monitored (Armstrong, 1984). This technology may also transfer more paid work to the home, a process which would reinforce women's responsibility for domestic work and limit their social contacts, their possibilities for collective action and training (see Armstrong, 1984; ch. 7). Furthermore, technology makes it easier to employ women part time, a trend that in turn reinforces women's responsibility for domestic work. Free trade too may reduce women's possibilities for employment, because many jobs in sectors such as the garment industry, where a large number of women work, are likely to disappear (Cohen, 1987). Rising female unemployment would then threaten the fragile basis of women's growing strength.

Policies of restraint and reductions in the public sector are threats to women because they could eliminate some of women's best jobs. At the same time, cutbacks could reduce the support for women in their old age, during their parenting years, when they separate, divorce or are subjected to domestic violence. Restraint programs also could mean that the care for the sick, the elderly, the disabled, the depressed, and the young would have to be provided by unpaid women working at home. If tuition fees for higher education are raised, it would be difficult for women to continue their education, because families would be more likely to give preference once again to their male children, and because women would have fewer opportunities than men to earn their tuition fees through summer or after-school employment. In addition, the quotas now being discussed on the numbers of students entering medical school would put restrictions on women in one of the few areas where they have recently made significant gains. And current controversies over the right to have an abortion may well lead to further restrictions or fertility control.

If male unemployment remains high, then men may take on more of the domestic responsibilities and give up some of their power. However, unemployment may also destroy their health and break up their families, making women not only less powerful but poor.

None of these more depressing possibilities are inevitable. The future of families will depend on economic and political conditions as well as on ideas about the work of women and men. The future will also depend on the choices we make collectively and individually in all these areas.

CONCLUSION

The ideas and actions related to feminism are as much a consequence as they are a cause of major changes in women's work and family life. As Edward Pryor (1984:96) makes clear in his Statistics Canada study, "current family change in Canada is not merely a matter of enlightened values or an egalitarian ideology but also a response to mounting economic pressures on the family system." At the same time, as the demand for female workers in the labour force is growing, women's economic needs are increasing. Male wages have not kept up with the rising cost of those goods and services that women cannot easily produce at home, and more men have experienced unemployment. Children have become more expensive to raise and a growing number of women have been forced to survive with little, if any, financial support from men.

The more permanent attachment of women to the labour force and their declining fertility rates have both reflected and served to increase their demands for equality in and out of the home. Their segregation into low paid jobs in the market, as well as their continuing responsibility for personal service and caring work in the home, have, however, ensured that women remain subordinate and "that women need men more than the other way around" (Ehrenreich, 1984:2).

Attitudes women and men have about themselves and each other are changing, bringing about the emergence of new patterns and responsibilities. Furthermore, as the participation of women in wage labour and in household tasks become more similar to those of men, so too do their perceptions of themselves. Nevertheless, women's different and often inferior jobs in the market, the personal services they perform for others in the home, and their childbearing work contribute to their separate experiences and attitudes.

Suggested Readings

Armstrong, Pat, and Hugh Armstrong.
   1984 *The Double Ghetto: Canadian Women and their Segregated Work*. Toronto: McClelland and Stewart.
Eichler, Margrit.
   1987 *Families in Canada Today*. Second ed. Toronto: Gage
Maroney, Heather Jon, and Meg Luxton, eds.
   1987 *Feminism and Political Economy*. Agincourt: Methuen.
White, Julie.
   1983 *Women and Unions*. Ottawa: Minister of Supply and Services for the Canadian Advisory Council on the Status of Women.

8

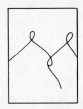

URBAN KIN NETWORKS

G.N. Ramu and Nicholas Tavuchis

*T*he organization and functions of kinship systems differ according to the nature of the society involved. In preliterate societies, kinship is the core of social organization, corporate groups being the focal point of individuals. Members usually live in close proximity and collectively control the means of livelihood (for instance, land, fishing and hunting rights). Kin-based systems consist mainly of those related by blood (consanguines) and, occasionally, those related by marriage (affines). Members perform tasks critical to the survival of the individuals and groups. In the majority of societies in which kinship is the organizing principle, descent and authority are traced either through males (patrilineal) or through females (matrilineal). This is important because membership in either the father's or the mother's group is essential for a person to inherit property, to enjoy fishing and hunting rights, and to be protected from hostile outsiders. Because of interlocking relationships and proximity between individuals, one's kin are often one's neighbours and friends. As Schneider (1969:v) points out,

> In many primitive and peasant societies a large number of kinds of institutions are organized and built as parts of kinship system itself. Thus the major social units of the society may be kinship groups—lineages perhaps. These same kin groups may be property owning units, the political units, the religious units, and so on.

On the other hand, in urban industrial societies many social and economic conditions are not conducive to the functioning of well-structured kinship systems. Modern ideologies of individualism, secularism, rationality, and social mobility based upon personal efforts militate against the pre-dominance of collectivities beyond the immediate family predicated on kinship. Many of the tasks of traditional kinship systems, such as finances, education, and religion, are assumed by specialized institutions in modern societies. As a result, kinship systems are replaced by a loose network of relatives, what anthropologists call a "kindred." Schneider (1969:27–28) suggests that such a network of kin is made up of kin linked by blood (father, mother, brother, sister, son, daughter, uncle, aunt, etc.), nature (natural child, natural father and mother), and law (husband, wife, in-laws). While relatives by blood and nature share heredity, those by law are brought together by marriage based on customary and judicial codes.

Given the functional irrelevance of kinship systems in modern industrial societies, kin relations are seldom dictated by normative considerations and sanctions but rather by personal likes and dislikes. Contemporary kin networks are best considered as mainly informal ties among such relatives as parents, their adult children, siblings, grandparents, uncles and aunts, to name a few. They consist of interlocking nuclear families bound together by affectional ties and choice. For the most part, participation is voluntary rather than obligatory. Members perform supportive rather than coercive roles (Sussman and Burchinal, 1962:320) and depend on mutual interest, affection, concern, and often aid.

In this chapter, we shall first outline the main theoretical issues of the relationship between urbanization and kinship. The main question here concerns the existence and functions of kinship networks in industrialized societies. Second, we shall consider the major findings about kinship ties in urban Canada. The concluding section summarizes the main points and offers a set of open questions about research on urban kinship patterns in Canada.

A THEORETICAL OVERVIEW

Historically, the analysis of kinship systems was confined to anthropologists who attempted to examine them as a means of understanding the basic principles of social organization of pre-literate or peasant societies. Until the 1950s, sociologists generally neglected this important aspect of social life because they assumed that urbanization and industrialization minimize the social and personal significance of kinship. To be successful in an urban milieu, it was considered imperative that one cultivate certain characteristics, such as individualism, aspirations for achievement and social mobility, and ties with non-kin. Over half-a-century ago, Park (1928) noted that, in cities, old clan and kinship groups are broken up and replaced by social organizations based on rational interests and personal choice. Wirth (1938:12), agreeing with Park, stated that

The bonds of kinship . . . and sentiments arising out of living together for generations under common folk-tradition are likely to be absent, or at best, relatively weak. . . . The family as a unit of social life is emancipated from the larger kinship group characteristic of the country and individual members pursue their own diverging interests in their vocational, educational, religious, recreational, and political life.

Consequently, the nuclear family, and *not* the extended family and lineage, was held to be the most important kinship unit in urban areas. This distinguished urban from pre-literate, or peasant, kinship systems. In this regard, Farber (1964:188) noted that the reduction in the importance of extended kinship structures in contemporary societies implied that they continue to exist mainly for "emotional and sentimental reasons."

With the publication of Talcott Parsons' controversial evaluation of contemporary kinship systems in the United States in 1943, sociologists began to focus their attention on the nature and functions of kinship networks in urban societies[1]. Parsons (1943) argued that extended kinship elements do not form firmly structured units of the urban social system. Indeed, the basic unit of kinship, especially among the middle class, is the nuclear family, consisting of husband, wife, and their unmarried children, living separate from and independent of extended kin. Such an isolated nuclear family is structurally suitable for meeting the demands of an urban industrial society. Parsons argued further that any significant deviation from such a nuclear unit would result in a "reduction in the productivity of our economy and drastic limitation of the realizability of our democratic values (cited in Irving, 1972:5). Thus, for Parsons, the kinship system in modern societies such as Canada and the United States is an open, multilineal system (equal recognition of both lines) in which the isolated nuclear family is the primary kinship unit with a corresponding stress on relations between husbands and wives (conjugality).

It should be pointed out that Parsons' analysis was comparative: it attempted to describe how the kinship systems in the United States and pre-literate societies differed. Furthermore, his evaluation of the structural isolation of the nuclear family was not based on concrete observations but was part of a general theoretical framework. One aspect of this framework, structural differentiation, underscored a tendency among the modern industrial societies to develop specialized social institutions to perform the tasks that in traditional societies were performed by kin groups. Thus, although the family gives up many of its traditional activities, it concentrates on certain critical tasks, such as reproduction, socialization, and sexual and emotional gratification, which other structures cannot accomplish. These tasks can best be performed if the nuclear family is economically independent, unburdened by obligations to extended kin, and physically mobile and neo-local, that is, residentially separated. As such, "structural isolation" implies not the absence of social interaction and affective ties among relatives but the primacy of the nuclear family, not the extended family, among the middle classes (see Morgan, 1976:60–86).

In the late 1950s, research in England and the United States generated evidence that challenged many of the assertions made by Park, Wirth, and Parsons. For example, Firth (1956), Bott (1957), and Young and Willmott (1957) found extended-family ties in England that involved frequent visits, mutual aid, and affection. Young and Willmott's study of working-class families in England suggested that these people were reluctant to move to new and better homes built by the city of London in other neighbourhoods, mainly because of their close ties to their kin. The researchers noted that the persistence of traditional working-class extended-kin solidarity was established and maintained mainly by women.

This is not to suggest that urban extended-kin networks were only manifested in the working-class groups. Young and Willmott, and Firth and his colleagues noted that extended-kin networks were prevalent even among the middle classes. Their respondents not only recognized a variety of relatives but also ranked them in order of importance. Some relatives were "pivotal" for maintaining interaction by way of correspondence, mutual exchange of aid, and gatherings on special occasions. These people, most of them women, were defined as "kin keepers." The kinship universe, that is, the circle of known relatives, was usually organized in terms of degree of knowledge about particular relatives (named and unnamed), mutual influence (effective and non-effective), and intimacy (intimate and peripheral). Most respondents reported a loose but open network of relatives, and the freedom to interact only with those who would please them and be helpful to them in their daily lives.

Numerous studies in the United States identified similar patterns. Sussman (1953, 1959, 1965), Litwak (1960abc), and Adams (1968), to cite a few, carrying out their studies in different urban settings, attempted to test empirically Parsons' notion of the structural isolation of the nuclear family. The studies by Sussman revealed that there were extensive patterns of mutual aid among various kin, especially among parents and their adult children. Such aid ranged from large gifts such as furniture and financial aid toward the down payment on a house to such day-to-day assistance as lawn care (if proximity permitted) while the children were on vacation, babysitting, and so on. The aid was given very frequently by parents during the early years of their children's marriages, when the young couples had limited resources and growing expenditures. The parents, in turn, expected their children to show a certain degree of affection and concern, attention, and to include them in some of their activities. Sussman and Burchinal (1962:332) concluded that parental aid was for the most part:

    (a) given voluntarily and based on feelings and sentiments between parents and children rather than on legal or cultural norms of obligation;

(b) intended to assist rather than to direct the achievement of occupational goals of family members receiving aid;

(c) a means to weaken the financial autonomy norms of the nuclear family unit without replacing it;

(d) available for an increasing number of families because of higher incomes, retirement programs, the increasing number of middle-aged women returning to the labour market, and the emergence of new grandparent roles.

In an effort to understand the nature of modern urban kinship systems, Litwak (1960abc) argued that the nuclear family was not necessarily isolated from the rest of the kinship network. Instead, urban families often represented a modified version of the extended family of an earlier era and could be located somewhere between the classical corporate family found in traditional societies such as India and pre-modern Japan, and the isolated nuclear family which Wirth, Parsons, and others proposed. Litwak argued that the modified extended family was suited to modern industrial society because it did not depend on geographical proximity or restrictive rights and obligations. Through reciprocal aid, communication, and identification among its members, the modified extended family could enhance social mobility and, therefore, could function as a positive force in the rapid industrialization and urbanization process.

Undoubtedly, the discussions of Sussman, Litwak, and others in the 1950s and 1960s required a re-evaluation of previous assumptions about the structural isolation of the nuclear family. Such a reconsideration led to general agreement that extended-family networks and urbanization were not mutually antithetical. As Goode (1963:75) points out in a cross-cultural analysis of family patterns:

> no matter what index is used, the family in most industrialized nations has not taken on the supposed characteristics of an isolated nuclear family system. The extended kin network continues to function and to include a wide range of kin who share with one another, see one another frequently, and know each other.

Based on such assertions and on his own findings, Sussman concluded that "the isolated nuclear family is a myth. It does not merit any further attention of the field, and I, for one, refuse to waste any more time even discussing it" (quoted by Rosow, in Shanas and Streib, 1965). Such a categorical assertion by Sussman does not seem to have affected the persistent controversial character of kinship research. For example, Litwak's views have been questioned by Reiss (1962), who maintains that geographical propinquity is an important factor in maintaining intimate relations. Tavuchis (1972:40) casts further doubt when he notes that "Litwak's data do not refer specifically to the effects of mobility on extended kin ties but rather suggest that individuals with strong extended kin ties are not necessarily hampered with respect to geographical or occupational mobility. This is an analytically and empirically different question, we would argue, from the effects of mobility on family relationships although certainly pertinent in other contexts."

Gibson (1972) has offered an excellent critical commentary on the theoretical formulations of Sussman and others. Gibson's main argument is that the conclusions drawn by Sussman (and others) are not valid because these scholars have not adequately delineated the nature and patterns of urban kinship networks, the sampling procedures are not scientific enough to permit generalizations, and, finally, because there is a certain amount of exaggeration of the significance of kin in urban settings in their writings. Gibson, on the basis of his study of 486 disabled men and their families, in which there was a need for aid from kin, argued that the Parsonian notion of the structural isolation of the nuclear family was still valid. Adams (1968) also suggests that the emphasis should be placed on "relative" rather than "isolated."

It is evident that most studies of urban kinship patterns focused on the issue of structural isolation of the nuclear family and neglected the basic argument of Parsons that kinship is not central to the social organization of advanced societies. They emphasized the role of kinship not in terms of an organizing principle of social systems but as a network of relations among selected relatives, particularly between parents and adult children or siblings. As Morgan (1975) has observed, most of the sociological studies of kinship merely examined "generational relationships," that is, interactional and mutual aid patterns between parents and adult children, and occasionally between adult siblings and other relatives.

With these theoretical perspectives in mind, our next task is to ascertain what is known about kin networks in Canada today.

STUDIES OF URBAN KIN NETWORKS

The nature of kinship ties in Canada has been and continues to be influenced by immigration patterns, the demographic distribution of population, and ethnic, cultural, and linguistic enclaves. There is a concentration of a small but diverse indigenous population, mainly in the remote parts of Northern Canada, and many of these groups continue to maintain certain elements of traditional kinship systems and practices (see Cruikshank, 1971; Damas, 1971; Dunning, 1971; Valle, 1971; Acheson, 1980; Matthiasson, 1980). The early immigrants, mainly from Britain and France, came either alone or with their immediate family members and settled in the Atlantic region, Ontario, and Québec. As historical analyses have shown, strong kinship ties emerged, over time, among these settlers, although the family unit was essentially nuclear. Both environmental and economic conditions predisposed interrelated families to be interdependent and to live in close proximity. During a period when farming and fishing were not mechanized, it was common for members of such families to engage collectively in productive activities while women tended to share the domestic responsibilities (see Queen and Habenstein, 1974:376–422; Parr, 1982; Donnelly, 1986). This resulted in patrilineal kin residing in the same community, engaging in collective economic endeavours, and sharing common names, in such places as New Brunswick, Newfoundland, and Québec (Queen and Habenstein, 1974:376–422; Donnelly, 1986). Later, industrialization and urbanization, the mechanization of agricultural and fishing activities, and the migration of younger generations seeking educational and occupational success led to the dispersal of individuals and the consequent weakening of community-based kinship ties.

Nevertheless, the kinship ties among those Canadians who have resided here for generations are relatively easy to maintain since their relatives likely live in Canada. Among recent immigrants, however, one can observe at least two patterns. Many European immigrants continue to maintain close ties with their kin in their country of origin (Sturino, 1980; Chimbos, 1980) while attempting to establish new relationships with available kin in Canada. For those immigrants who do not have relatives living in Canada, establishing kinship-like bonds among friends, especially those from one's own ethnic group, is common. This phenomenon is called "ascriptive friendship" by Goode (1963:76) or "fictive kinship" by anthropologists. The solidarity and interdependence of such ascriptive friends have enabled many new immigrant families to adjust to the complexities of an urban industrial society.

Most studies of kinship patterns in urban Canada have taken into account neither the respondents' period of residence in Canada nor the presence of surrogate kin. Instead, they have dealt with the issues that were raised in the United States and Britain in the 1950s, as noted earlier in this chapter. In what follows we shall consider the nature of kinship ties among selected ethnic groups.

British-Canadians

Although British-Canadians are demographically the dominant group, there are only three major studies of their kinship patterns. Using historical documents and census materials, Donnelly (1986) examined the kinship patterns among the residents of West Isles Parish in New Brunswick around 1871. Nearly 76 percent of the 299 households examined were of British origin. The small size of the village and the occupational homogeneity of its residents (mainly farming and fishing) enabled these people to maintain a high level of kin solidarity. The evidence suggests that some 225 of the 299 households examined were connected by one or more family ties resulting in a web of kinship bonds: parent-child, in-laws, sibling, grandparent-grandchild, and cousins. This study provides us with a brief account of the nature of kinship relations among the pioneers and serves as a benchmark for charting changes in contemporary patterns.

Osterreich (1976) conducted genealogical research on the extended kin relations among forty-five British-Canadians in Montreal. It may be recalled that one of the assumptions in Parsons' hypothesis of the structural isolation of nuclear family was that occupational and physical mobility were likely to weaken kinship bonds between parents and their adult children. Osterreich's study focused on the relationship between geographic mobility and kinship interaction. The respondents in this study were of lower-class and middle-class origin. The major findings were that

(a) geographic mobility did not have a significant influence on either the respondents' knowledge of kin or the frequency of contact;

(b) although major forms of mutual aid were not dependent upon geographic proximity, day-to-day household services were;

(c) intimate ties and a commitment to maintain them were not dependent upon geographic proximity but rather on genealogical closeness;

(d) the kinship networks were closer to Litwak's conceptualization of the modified extended family than to Parsons' isolated nuclear family.

Irving (1972) studied kinship patterns among fifty-four Canadian-born, lower middle-class couples of British origin. The respondents were chosen from the list of clients who used Metropolitan Toronto Family Service Agencies and the study focused on patterns of interactions and mutual aid among the couples and their parents and parents-in-law. The results indicated that over 86 percent of the couples had parents and parents-in-law living in the Metropolitan Toronto area. Based on the high frequency of interaction in such things as visits and telephone conversations between the couples and their parents, and of financial support parents provided for their children, Irving (1972:91–93) claimed that, contrary to the suggestion that extended-family solidarity is weak among British-Canadians, and contrary to the hypothesis of structural isolation of the nuclear family, intergenerational ties were extremely important to the couples and their parents. He also noted that despite a structural predisposition for strain between certain relatives (such as married women and their mothers, according to Irving's study), parents and parents-in-law played a salient role in the life of their married children.

French-Canadians

Numerous studies of the French-Canadians claim the existence of strong family and kinship solidarity. Two important studies were conducted by Garigue (1956), and Piddington (1973).

Garigue explored the association between urbanization and kinship structure in Montreal by interviewing 52 persons in 43 households between 1954 and 1955. Garigue posited that kinship solidarity and cohesion were likely to dissipate not because a society undergoes urbanization but because of changing values that undermine the significance of the French linguistic and cultural identities. However, the major findings were that the French-Canadians studied by Garigue maintained very close ties with their immediate relatives, visited them frequently, and exchanged goods and services, Garigue (1956:272) concluded that there was

> no trend toward transformation of the present French-Canadian urban kinship system into the more restricted system reported for the United States.... Far from being incompatible, kinship and urbanism among French-Canadians seem to have become functionally related. Each urban domestic family, each household, each person, is normally part of a system of obligations arising from the recognition of kinship ties.

Garigue explained the strength of kinship solidarity among the Montreal French-Canadians in terms of the historical continuity of familistic values and ideals buttressed by religion.

Garigue's study is clearly dated: more than a generation has since passed. Various social, economic, demographic, and political changes in the last two decades have undoubtedly affected French-Canadian kinship networks, although no major studies have been conducted to indicate to what extent.

Piddington (1973) collected sixteen genealogies from French-Canadians in St. Boniface, a suburb of Winnipeg. The ancestors of the informants had originally migrated from Québec and other kin had migrated to other parts of Canada. Such patterns of migration allowed Piddington to examine the impact of geographic mobility on kinship ties. He found that kinship networks, in terms of visiting and emotional ties, were maintained not necessarily because of geographical proximity but rather from a strong sense of linguistic and cultural solidarity. At the same time, he noted that the kinship knowledge of his St. Boniface informants was not as extensive as his rural French-Canadian sample in the nearby township St. Jean Baptiste. Piddington suggested that family gatherings, correspondence, and knowledge of kin residing in other parts of Canada and the United States contributed to the maintenance of intimate kinship ties among his subjects. Another important factor contributing to kinship solidarity was the frequency of marriages between relatives which effectively facilitated the continuity of the French-Canadian culture.

Greek-Canadians

In his analysis of family and kinship patterns among Greek immigrants in Ontario, Chimbos (1980) observed at least two patterns of kinship solidarity.

First, they tended to maintain close ties with their relatives in Greece. This they did by regular remittances, the sponsoring of relatives, frequent visits in connection with various ceremonies and festive occasions, and gift-giving. Consequently, their migration to Canada did not fundamentally alter the emotional and social links with relatives in the home country.

Second, the kinship ties among the Greeks in Toronto and Northern Ontario were intense, reinforced by cultural, linguistic, and ethnic homogeneity. It was not uncommon for a new Greek immigrant to seek financial assistance from his Canadian kin to start a business of his own. As Chimbos observed, the Greek immigrants came to Canada to improve not only their own fortunes but also those of their relatives. This they did through remittances and through helping immigrants to resettle comfortably.

Furthermore, Chimbos suggested that among Greek-Canadians spiritual kinship, that is, the institution of godparenthood, cemented the ties among distant and intimate relatives as well as outsiders. The spiritual relations refer to reciprocal relationships between individuals and families established through religious sacraments such as marriage and baptism. Such a relationship entails moral obligations and responsibilities between individuals and groups and thus contributes to the maintenance of family and ethnic solidarity. Chimbos (1980:33) noted, "An essential characteristic of the spiritual kinship system is that it provides spiritual kinsmen with socioeconomic support and cooperation when the need arises. During the earlier periods of immigration, many immigrants who came to Canada were sponsored by the spiritual kinsmen who had already established themselves in Canada."

Close relationships between relatives and friends, coupled with adherence to the norms of endogamy, have enabled the Greek-Canadians to maintain their distinct identity. Whether these survive beyond the first and second generations remains to be seen.

Italian-Canadians

Italians in Canada, like Greek-Canadians, have maintained kinship solidarity not only with those relatives here but those in their country of origin. Let us consider here two studies of family and kinship patterns among Italian-Canadians.

In his Montreal study of Italian-Canadians of Southern Italian origin Boissevain (1976) pointed out that a strong commitment to kindred, friends, and neighbours was their source of community solidarity. Between 1964 and 1965, Boissevain observed the family and kinship patterns among 261 Italian-Canadians. The study revealed that:

(a) the nuclear family characterized by neolocal residence (a customary practice of newly married couples establishing their own residence) and a bilateral kinship system (descent or inheritance patterns are determined equally by mother's and the father's line) were central to their social structure;

(b) the majority of nuclear families resided very close to other kin;

(c) Italian-Canadians and their relatives not only saw each other a great deal but neighborhood and friendship groups were also often part of a vast kinship network;

(d) the kinship networks played an important role in marital arrangements.

In his study of family and ethnicity among 92 immigrants to Toronto from southern Italy Sturino (1980) suggested that emigration to Canada brought with it a certain degree of elasticity in kinship ties. He argued that although chain migration along kinship lines resulted in a concentration of relatives in Toronto or nearby towns, these immigrants enjoyed some freedom with regard to their kinship obligations. In their native villages the immigrants were bound by an intricate set of rights and obligations to close and distant relatives. Upon migration, such bonds were loosened in that migrants could choose more freely the associations they would cultivate and the kinds of assistance they would render to their kin. "The point is that though the kinship field is large, meaningful relationships are only entered into with some of the kin. . . . In short, just as the kinship tie *per se* is flexible, so are the interpersonal relationships between them due to their multi-stranded nature and kinship flexibility of rights and obligations" (Sturino, 1980:88).

Sturino notes that the tendency among new Italian immigrants to settle near the core of pre-war immigrants in Toronto has given rise to a "colony of kin and paesani." Such a colony has served essentially as a receiving point for new immigrants. It is common for Italians to assist the migration of their kin from Italy, helping to secure documentation, travel money, a job upon arrival, and housing.

The experience of the Italian migrants suggests that the three levels of Italian kinship structure—nuclear family, family circle, and kindred—have been successfully adapted to the new urban environment of Canada without the abandonment of traditional patterns.

Other Studies

In the summer of 1962, 327 heads of households in a working-class area of Hamilton, Ontario, were interviewed for a kinship study by Pineo (1976). The respondents were of British, Sicilian, Italian, and East European origins. The major findings were that

(a) extended-family bonds among the respondents were the norm rather than the exception;

(b) there were frequent visits between kin;

(c) although the overall relationships were bilateral in character, it is fairly common to attach greater importance to the relationships with patrilineal kin.

In his discussion of family life among Polish-Canadians, Radecki (1980) suggested that kinship ties involve primarily three generations of one's family: parents, children, and grandchildren. Religious and social occasions, such as Christmas, Easter, and weddings, provided opportunities for relatives to reunite, exchange information and gifts, and observe family and ethnic customs. Nevertheless, Radecki cautioned that Polish families were undergoing changes. These were reflected in changing attitudes toward elders, who were no longer cared for exclusively by their children but were increasingly encouraged to move into nursing homes. Such a shift was due mainly to the increasing number of employed wives among the Polish-Canadians, the lack of space adequate for proper care of the aged, and integenerational conflicts. These all point to the integrative process, namely the acculturation that the Polish-Canadian family had experienced by the middle of the 1970s.

In sum, empirical evidence from the studies outlined above indicates that in urban Canada there is a widespread persistence of kinship networks. This is consistent with the findings of Sussman and others in the United States and Great Britain. Canadian kinship continues to be primarily bilateral, both parental lines receiving equal recognition with regard to descent, interaction and material aid. One's kinship universe is composed of relatives by blood and relatives by marriage. Furthermore, kinship networks of varying degrees of group significance were found in other studies as well (For details, see essays in Ishwaran, 1980).

SOME ASPECTS OF URBAN KINSHIP PATTERNS

Based on our discussion of various studies of kinship in Canada, Britain, and the United States, the following theoretical suggestions are offered to contribute to an understanding of Canadian urban kin networks. First, although interrelated nuclear families with common ethnic origins tend to live in close proximity, they can hardly be considered what anthropologists characterize as localized corporate or descent groups. Second, kinship relations are primarily voluntary, which means that many families enjoy the freedom to choose whether or not to have close relationships with their relatives, although in practice most do. Third, although many recognize and maintain formal relationships with a wide range of relatives, they are also fairly selective in developing and sustaining close ties. Fourth, kinship ties are stronger among some ethnic groups than others: French-Canadians in Québec, for instance, tend to maintain more extensive and intimate ties than, say, Polish-Canadians. Fifth, interaction and mutual aid among kin are common, although these depend on residential proximity and the social class of the families. The possible ramifications of some of these attributes of Canadian urban kin networks are discussed in the following section.

Types of Kin

At the beginning of this chapter, it was stated that kinship is defined in terms of nature (blood) and culture (law or custom). The fact that an individual is related to others in these ways does not necessarily mean that all relatives are treated or viewed equally. People tend to maintain active ties with kin they get along with or to whom they feel a deep obligation. For practical purposes, three types of kinsmen and kinswomen may be distinguished according to the following criteria: the amount of knowledge one has about them, patterns of interaction, and emotional closeness. These can be broadly categorized as nominal, effective, and intimate kin (Firth, 1956). Nominal kin are those whose names and whereabouts one knows but with whom one has little formal or informal contact. Effective kin are those with whom one maintains certain ritual ties, such as the exchange of greetings on holidays or attendance of weddings and funerals. Intimate or core kin are those with whom one maintains a close and continuous relationship, such as those found in the studies by Garigue, Irving, Sturino, and others.

In studies of urban kinship, the information obtained on the size of an individual's kinship universe is usually taken as an indicator of the significance of kinship. Although the size of a person's kin group is only a crude measure of the social significance of kinship, the studies reviewed above indicate that kin recognition is extensive even in Western societies (Firth, 1956; Young and Willmott, 1957). While most Canadian studies attempt to determine the size of respondents' kinship universes, they do not systematically classify the kin in terms of the degree of interrelationship (intimate or peripheral, effective or non-effective).

In Montreal during the 1950s, Garigue found that the average number of kin his French-Canadian respondents could identify was 215 persons (Garigue, 1956:264). Presumably, these included all relatives irrespective of genealogical or emotional closeness. "The most extensive knowledge was usually concentrated into the generations of ego and his parents, which together included from one-half to two-thirds of the persons known (Garigue, 1956)." By contrast, Piddington in his St. Boniface study (1973:124) found the average number to be 142 while in the neighbouring rural French-Canadian settlement (St. Jean Baptiste) the number was 256. The relatively young age of the St. Boniface informants and their urban backgrounds might account for the lower average of recognized kin. Among Montreal Italian-Canadians, effective recognition for the purpose of mutual aid and friendship went only as far as first cousins. This meant that the kinship universe among the Italian-Canadians was effectively limited to intimate kin (Boissevain,

1976:287). Perhaps the recency of migration may account for the vast difference between the French-Canadians and Italian-Canadians.

Patterns of Interaction

In considering the nature and frequency of interaction among relatives in Canada, it should be kept in mind that most Canadians also maintain social relations with non-kin, such as friends, neighbours, and colleagues. Quite often these persons are considered by many to be as important as close relatives because of sustained interaction and emotional ties. The influence of close ties with non-kin on one's pattern of interaction with relatives is not yet systematically understood. Nevertheless, studies show that people tend to choose certain relatives for intimate and frequent exchanges. The quality and degree of such exchanges are often determined by geographic distance, gender, and social class.

Visits, Telephone Contacts, and Correspondence As Barr (1976:77) notes, researchers measure kinship ties mainly in quantitative terms of correspondence, telephone conversations, and visits, but rarely, if ever, do they assess the content and quality of these forms of interaction. For example, one might visit an aging relative in a nursing home just as a formality, and the nature of interaction may be very superficial. By contrast, one person may be in regular contact with a parent in the same nursing home and may supervise her or his care without frequent visits. Therefore, one must weigh the relative significance of each method of interaction in terms of its quality and its result.

The inner core of the intimate kin group consists of parents, parents-in-law, siblings, and, occasionally, first cousins. Relationships with brothers and sisters are based upon blood ties, friendship, affection, and mutual compassion. Ties with more distant relatives tend to be formal and ritualistic.

The frequency of contacts, according to most studies, is a function of physical and kinship proximity and personal preference. Among Montreal anglophones, "biological and geographic distance of relatives were found to affect the contact ratio. [Those studied] were in touch with parents and grandparents and almost all siblings. . . . The contact ratio was higher for relatives who lived in Montreal or within 200 miles of the city than for others. . . . Face-to-face contact occurred with much greater frequency among people who had relatives in Montreal" (Osterreich, 1976:536). In Hamilton, 68 percent of the respondents had close contact with at least one relative (Pineo, 1976).

In Toronto, it was common among the young married couples to drop in unannounced on their parents and parents-in-law, but the older generation usually gave prior notice. Such visits took place at least once a week, depending on whether these kin lived in the same neighbourhood or within the metropolitan area (Irving, 1972:42–51). French-Canadians in Montreal and St. Boniface not only visited their intimate kin frequently but tended to use such occasions to reinforce their emotional ties (Garigue, 1956; Piddington, 1973). Among Italian-Canadians, different family ceremonies and arrivals of new immigrants provided an opportunity for the meeting of various kin and for the exchange of information about other relatives (Boissevain, 1976; Sturino, 1980).

Most Canadian data suggest that, when the degree of kinship is distant, respondents tend to attribute their infrequent contacts to geographical distance. Telephone calls and letter-writing have also become means of "keeping in touch" with kin who are geographically dispersed. Most of those who are visited, regardless of geographic distance, include such intimate kin as parents, parents-in-law, and siblings.

In sum, most studies conclude that, although there is considerable interaction among kin in urban contexts, it is confined to a small group of preferred consanguinal and affinal relatives.

Initiation and Management of Kinship Ties It is often suggested that in urban kinship relations, effective ties are initiated and maintained by females. For example, it has been repeatedly demonstrated that mother-daughter bonds are especially strong (Young and Willmott, 1957; Adams, 1968). Among the French-Canadians, for example:

> Women are more active within the kinship system than men, and this fact combined with their primary role as wives and mothers gives them a great deal of influence and supplies the continuity of the kin group. . . . Urban French-Canadian men and women not only give different stress to kinship, but also have different roles. Men, for instance, reported that they usually thought of their kin group in terms of their male relatives; their knowledge of their female relatives was more restricted. Women seemed to have greater awareness of the kin group as composed of both sexes. Not only was their knowledge of the total kin group greater, so that in a number of instances wives knew more of their husbands' kin than the husbands themselves did, but they also had much greater knowledge of the affairs of the kin group (Garigue, 1956:263, 266).

Females not only maintained close relationships with their mothers but also demonstrated a knowledge and capacity to maintain extensive kinship relationships. The mother-daughter relationship was, perhaps, the closest, both affectively and interactionally and this was true regardless of their relative socio-economic status (Adams, 1968:308).

In Hamilton, however, a different type of relationship was noted. "The first indication that matrifocality is not the pattern . . . is that proportions reported [of] at least weekly contact with kin were virtually identical for men and women" (Pineo, 1976:549). Moreover, the Hamilton respondents maintained contact outside the household more frequently with the husband's parents than with the wife's (Pineo, 1976:550). Among British-Canadians in Toronto, a similar equivalence of kin lines was observed:

> Contrary to the findings of other studies there was no significant difference between husbands and wives in the frequency of face-to-face contacts with parents. . . . Perhaps the main reason for the rather unusual finding of minimal differences between husbands and wives with regard to the frequency of visiting was that . . . [the] societal ideal of bilateral symmetry was realized in this sample in relation to proximity of parents (Irving, 1972:54–55).

A recent study in Hamilton found patterns different from those Pineo noted a decade or so earlier in the same city. Rosenthal's (1985) study indicated that nearly 56 percent of 458 Hamilton respondents aged 40 and over reported the presence of a "kin keeper" in their families: 74 percent of these were women, most of them older women. Rosenthal defines kin-keeping activities as part of the domestic division of labour or, as she puts it, "work positions" in a family which are normally occupied by women. By virtue of their age, knowledge, and interest, kin keepers tended to promote solidarity by keeping in touch through telephone calls, visits, letters, and by organizing periodic family gatherings. Although women, more than men, carried the burdens of kin keeping, according to the study they derived much pleasure in fostering extended family solidarity.

The different patterns noted above demonstrate the flexible nature of urban networks with regard to the choice of kin as well as the fact that older women are more likely than men to assume the role of "kin keepers," even though both familial lines tend to receive equal attention. They also indicate that women are more likely to be strongly involved in kin-related activities. This latter finding needs to be interpreted cautiously. On the one hand, to the extent that women do not have alternative outlets, such as jobs and occupations, for their time and energy, kinship is a convenient source of self-esteem and satisfaction. On the other hand, it should be noted that many studies do not adequately tap the subjective and symbolic salience of kin for males or explore the possibility that what appears to be a lack of interest reflects a lack of opportunity and availability. We would predict, therefore, that women will continue to play central roles as kin keepers; however, as they become more fully integrated into the work force, kinship will play a smaller role in their daily lives. Similarly, unemployment, earlier retirements, and the desire for a better balance between work and family are factors that will predispose men to interact more with relatives than was the case in the past.

Mutual Aid

The structural isolation hypothesis is based on the assumption that urban societies emphasize individualism, autonomy, and self-reliance and that all these are antithetical to the development of ties beyond the nuclear unit. This suggests that kinship has little objective significance or subjective relevance. In addition, the emergence of daycare and health-care centres, commercial banks with liberal lending policies, instant credit, an array of recreational activities, and voluntary associations are further considered to undermine the role of kinship. This may be true for some first generation immigrants or those whose parents and other significant kin are not affluent enough to give support in times of need. However, among those who have the resources and inclination, the exchange of goods, services, and money is hardly an isolated or uncommon practice. Less obvious is the patterned flow of mutual aid between kin at different points in the family cycle, its meaning to the participants, and the forms it takes.

For example, parents or adult children show varying degrees of discretion in extending a helping hand lest this be seen as an infringement on the financial autonomy and self-reliance of the recipient. Consequently, aid is often disguised in the form of gifts offered on ceremonial or festive occasions such as birthdays, graduations, anniversaries, or Christmas. What is important here is that "the vast majority of these acts of filial and kin responsibility are carried out voluntarily or on the basis of affection rather than because of a compulsion to do so emanating from the legal system" (Nye and Berardo, 1973:416).

The significance and continuity of urban kinship networks can partially be explained by the fact that mutual aid (whether disguised or direct) continues to be an important value and function. In the words of Sussman and Burchinal (1962:321), "the lifelines of the network are help and services exchanged among members of nuclear families related by blood and affinal ties. Help, services, and social interaction characterize the activities of this independent kin family network."

In Canada, there is considerable evidence to suggest the prevalence of mutual monetary assistance and the exchange of various forms of service. Osterreich (1976) and Irving (1972) found that among British-Canadians an exchange of goods and services was common. In many cases, when a young couple planned to buy a new home or furnishings, the parents provided either the full cost or the downpayment. Such assistance was usually given to newly married couples who did not have savings of their own. After five or more years of marriage such help was seldom sought or given, with the exception of gifts to grandchildren (Irving, 1972:79).

In a recent study in Edmonton, Kennedy and Stokes (1982) examined how much financial support the extended family provides to families who confront high costs of housing in that city. Their findings indicated that although various forms of kin support were common, the most crucial was the financial assistance given by parents to their children, especially those who were in the early stages of their family life cycle and social class appeared to have had little relevance. Furthermore, they pointed out that, in Edmonton, the ratio between housing cost and income (the ratio is an indicator of the financial burden caused by shelter costs) was related to the financial assistance extended by relatives of homeowners but not by relatives of renters. This implies that kin tend to assist when such an assistance is used as an investment for capital goods.

The exchange of gifts among relatives on important occasions such as births, weddings, and holidays has always been an important custom in most societies, including Canada. There is some question as to whether gifts can be considered part of the mutual aid among kin because the monetary (not necessarily the symbolic) value of gifts exchanged is usually not high (see Cheal, 1984; 1986). However, the patterns of exchanging gifts during Christmas do shed some light on kinship bonds. In an interesting analysis of the exchange of gifts by a sample of 573 adults in Winnipeg in 1984, Cheal (1986) noted that the average worth of the most valuable gifts exchanged during Christmas was about $200. While exchange of gifts was common among close relatives (spouses and their parents, husbands and wives, parents and children), only husbands and wives gave or received the most expensive gifts. This latter observation does not refute the general point of mutual aid but suggests that large gifts in the form of money, a downpayment, and so on, are likely to be exchanged as needed rather than on special occasions. Moreover, Christmas is generally not deemed an appropriate occasion to give (or receive) gifts that are clearly instrumental in nature: to do so would undermine the symbolic significance of this holiday if not border on being interpreted as outright charity.

Relatives who live in the same neighbourhood or city frequently extend each other non-monetary assistance which includes baby-sitting, advice on major decisions, care during illness, the repair of cars and appliances, and the upkeeping of homes or apartments. Although in the past the direction of such help was from parents to their married children. (Irving, 1972:62–79), in recent years there has been a shift in this pattern: married children in increasing numbers have begun providing care for their aging parents, especially if they are in nursing homes (for details, see Chapter Ten).

Mobility and Kin Network

Sociological analyses of the relationship between mobility and kin networks have generally addressed two questions. First, what is the impact of geographic and social mobility on the extended-kin network? Does the combined impact of such experiences weaken kinship relations? Second, how do extended-family ties affect mobility patterns? Does commitment to one's kin reduce the prospects of geographic or social mobility? In this section, we shall briefly address these issues.

Geographic Mobility and Kinship Ties The evolution of Canadian society during the last 100 years or so into a modern, urban industrial system necessitated massive internal migration—movement of groups of people from one city, province, or region to another. Economic considerations have motivated families or individuals to shift their residences on short notice. The impact of such uprootings on kinship solidarity is not as negative as the theory of structural isolation of the nuclear family hypothesizes. A study that deals primarily with this issue was conducted by Osterreich (1976) in Montreal. She found that geographic mobility did not have a significant influence on the overall kinship networks and that the families involved conformed to Litwak's notion of the modified extended family. In fact, Osterreich found that the mobile respondents knew more relatives than the non-mobile. At the same time, patterns of interaction depended upon geographic proximity, with non-mobile respondents demonstrating a significantly higher frequency than mobile ones. Osterreich also noted that "dependence on relatives for help was not general among these respondents; some forms of help were much more common than others, and, moreover, geographic mobility reduced the dependence on relatives for aid." In short, "the respondents in this study whether mobile or non-mobile reported essentially the same kind of relationships with kin" (Osterreich, 1976:543).

Studies of family life among Greek-Canadians (Chimbos, 1980), Polish-Canadians (Radecki, 1980), and Italian-Canadians (Sturino, 1980) suggest that, even after migration to Canada, most members of these ethnic groups maintained very close links with their kin in their countries of origin and accepted the obligations to provide regular financial aid and other forms of assistance.

Social Mobility and Kinship Ties Individuals seeking increased economic and occupational opportunities tend to move where they are available. Cities are the centres of modern industrial and bureaucratic establishments. With their pervasive ideology of equal opportunity cities are magnetic forces for qualified, competent, and achievement-oriented persons. Having close or distant relatives in these places further enhances the decision to make the move. Until recently the flow of internal migration has been in the direction of urban centres from rural areas. This is evident from Canadian census data which show that in 1871 roughly 82 percent of the population was rural, but in 1981 it had dwindled to about 24 percent, and less than five percent of the total population was classified as exclusively rural farm population. In 1871, there were no large cities (cities with a population of 100 000 or more) in Canada. In 1981, there were 24. Such growth of urban centres not only represents a high degree of urbanization but also enhances their social and economic importance. Historically, in-dividuals and families have tended to move from one city or region to another in order to find better economic opportunities. It has been asserted that such mobility would result in the erosion of extended-kin ties over time.

A common assumption in the 1960s was that upward mobility required individuals and families to change their values, attitudes, and roles radically. Specifically, this meant a significant decrease in kinship solidarity and in feelings of obligation toward one's extended family. It was thought that migrants subscribe to values and norms associated with modern industrial systems—individualism, secularism, and rationalism. Consequently, it was postulated that extended-kin solidarity would become more an impediment than a support to one's aspirations. However, as Goode (1966) and Tavuchis (1972) argue, the relationship was far from clear and such premises were based on inadequate data. Many studies suggest that extended-family net-works and occupational mobility are not intrinsically incompatible. On the contrary, extended kin, depending on their ethnic and social class status and the degree of kinship solidarity, may effectively contribute to the upward mobility of individuals (Litwak, 1960; Adams, 1968; Tavuchis, 1972).

Kinship and Ethnicity

There are indications that in Canada many groups, such as Italian-Canadians, Dutch-Canadians, Greek-Canadians and French-Canadians, along with the Hutterites and some native groups, to name a few, depend on kinship networks, ceremonies, and rituals to foster their cultural identities (Bois-sevain, 1976; Ishwaran, 1977; Piddington, 1973, 1976; Chimbos, 1980; Ra-decki, 1980; Sturino, 1980). For instance, among Italian-Canadians, kinship ceremonies and rituals reinforce their Italian identity and as Boissevain (1976:290) puts it, "kin relations are almost couched in the idiom of Italian culture."

Both Garigue and Piddington consider that kinship is also central to the cultural identity of French-Canadians. "The[se] ideals about family and kin-ship were not isolated but were part of a cultural complex system of edu-cation, membership in the Catholic Church, and various political theories about the status of French-Canadians in Canada. To be a member of a French-Canadian kinship group implied attitudes and beliefs about some or all of these" (Garigue, 1956:273). Piddington notes that kinship among Franco-Manitobans plays an important integrative function:

The French-Canadian culture continues to survive, though in a variety of new forms which are themselves constantly changing. In this process of survival, kinship plays an important part. It serves to integrate the local community by providing a complex set of interlocking kinship relationships. These provide channels through which significant social activities can be organized.... [The data] suggests that over the whole of Canada ... there spreads a network of recognized kinship relationships which helps to keep French-Canadians aware, despite their geographical dispersion, of their identity as a distinct ethnic group and of the advantages of belonging to such a group (1976:571).

Thus kinship among some groups serves as a source of cultural identity and stability. By providing structured opportunities for sustained interaction, ethnicity is reinforced. However, we do not know whether this interrelationship is commonly found among ethnic groups other than those mentioned.

CONCLUSIONS

Sociological research of urban kinship networks in Canada is not extensive or systematic. The present state of our knowledge on this issue is confined to less than a dozen studies that deal directly or indirectly with the major theoretical issues generated in Britain and the United States. What is known and what is problematic about this area may be summarized as follows.

What is Known

First, urban kinship networks consist of interpersonal ties between an individual and his or her blood kin and affines, and between nuclear families. The neo-local nuclear family is the basic unit of kinship.

Second, the nuclear family is *not* as structurally isolated as posited by Wirth and Parsons. Close ties exist between intimate kin and most studies reveal that a high degree of kinship solidarity is common among Canadians. The Canadian data lend support to Litwak's (1960) contention that a modified form of extended family is the norm even in urban centres.

Third, urban families maintain contacts with kin through frequent mutual visiting, telephoning, writing, and helping. The frequency, effectiveness, and subjective salience of such contacts are not contingent on geographic proximity but on the degree of genealogical relatedness. Further, although females typically serve as the focus and point of articulation of the web of kin ties, the cultural ideal of bilaterality is realized by the equal recognition of both maternal and paternal consanguines and affines.

Fourth, a strong sense of mutual concern and welfare among intimate kin is evident from the reciprocal aid and services that are voluntarily given.

Issues That Need Further Exploration

First, there is lack of clear evidence on the relationships between social and geographical mobility and kin networks. The only study available focuses mainly on the impact of geographic mobility on extended-family ties. We do not know the role of class and occupational mobility in the maintenance or attrition of kinship ties. What is the initial state of contact between geographically dispersed, occupationally and socially diverse but interrelated nuclear families?

Second, although there are scattered findings on mutual aid, we lack information on the details and specifics. What is the nature of financial aid? How frequently does one give or receive aid? Is the extent of aid a function of one's social class? Do children reciprocate when the parents are in need of such aid in their old age? While there is some evidence on gift-giving, the Canadian data on reciprocal financial aid do not address these issues.

Third, the role of kinship networks in the maintenance of ethnicity is unclear. There is limited evidence suggesting that kinship serves as a source of integration among some minorities, but comparative data are needed before valid generalizations can be made.

Fourth, in recent years new forms of family patterns have emerged in Canada. These include single-parent families and families that result from remarriages or the adoption of children (Kirk, 1985). There is little information on kinship ties among these families. Particularly interesting would be an assessment of whether kinship ties are strengthened or weakened by divorce and remarriage.

In conclusion, while there are gaps in our understanding of kinship networks, the available evidence suggests that for most Canadians kin networks remain salient because of their economic, emotional, and interactional functions.

Note

1. The interested student is referred to Morgan (1975, Chapter 2) for a detailed overview of sociological literature on kinship.

Suggested Readings

Boissevain, J.
1976   "Family and Kinship among Italians of Montreal." In K. Ishwaran, ed., *The Canadian Family*. Revised ed. Toronto: Holt, Rinehart and Winston.

Firth, Raymond.
1956   *Two Studies of Kinship in London*. London: Athlone Press.

Garigue, Philippe.
1956   "French Canadian Kinship and Urban Life." *American Anthropologist* 58 (December 1956): 1090–1100.

Irving, Howard.
1972   *The Family Myth: A Study of Relationships between Married Couples and their Parents*. Toronto: Copp Clark.

Kennedy, Leslie, W., and Dennis Stokes.
1982   "Extended Family Support and the High Cost of Housing." *Journal of Marriage and the Family* 44.

Litwak, Eugene.
1960   "Occupational Mobility and Extended Family Cohesion." *American Sociological Review* 29.

———.
1960   "Geographic Mobility and Extended Family Cohesion." *American Sociological Review* 30.

Morgan, D.H.J.
1975   *Social Theory and the Family* (Chapter Two). London: Routledge and Kegan Paul.

Osterreich, Helgi.
1976   "Geographic Mobility and Kinship: A Canadian Example." In K. Ishwaran, ed., *The Canadian Family*. Revised ed. Toronto: Holt, Rinehart and Winston.

Parsons, Talcott.
1943   "The Kinship System of Contemporary United States." *American Anthropologist* 45.

Piddington, Ralph.
1973   "The Kinship Networks among French-Canadians." In G. L. Gold and Marc Adelard Tremblay, eds., *Communities and Culture in French-Canada*. Toronto: Holt, Rinehart and Winston.

Pineo, Peter C.
1976   "The Extended Family in a Working-class Area of Hamilton." In K. Ishwaran, ed., *The Canadian Family*. Revised ed. Toronto: Holt, Rinehart and Winston.

Sussman, Marvin B.
1965   "Relationships of Adult Children with their Parents in the United States." In E. Shanas and Gordon Streib, eds. *Social Structure and the Family*. Englewood Cliffs, NJ: Prentice-Hall.

9

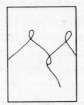

ETHNICITY AND THE FAMILY

Nicholas Tavuchis

More than two decades have passed since the publication of Elkin's *The Family in Canada*. In this invaluable compendium the author charted trends of research on the family, took inventory of extant sources and studies, and indicated the gaps in our knowledge of this institution. After surveying empirical studies of a variety of ethnic groups, Elkin came to the following conclusion:

> It is apparent that valid information on ethnic and immigrant groups is meager. For most groups, the authors have been primarily interested in historical studies and secondarily in folklore and demography. Relatively little has been written on family patterns, family variations or family problems. Undoubtedly, considerable changes have taken place, but what they are and how they have affected family relations, we do not know. (1964:64).

Given the centrality of ethnicity in Canadian history, this is, to say the least, a curious state of affairs. For as Kralt (1977:1) reminds us, "with the exception of some 300 000 of Canada's Native Peoples, today's entire Canadian population consists of immigrants and their descendants." No doubt, many individuals are only dimly aware of their ethnic roots or choose to retain only selected and superficial vestiges of this once prominent aspect of social identity. For others, however, salient or latent influences of ethnicity continue to shape their lives from birth to death. Whatever the contemporary meaning and relevance of ethnicity—and there is much disagreement on this issue, with some observers proclaiming its decline and others its resurgence—any failure to consider ethnicity as it relates to the family impoverishes our understanding of both.

Our primary purpose in what follows is to see how far we have come since Elkin's evaluation. This will entail an exploration, based mainly on selected sociological and anthropological materials, of what is known and what is unknown or problematic about ethnic families in Canada. Our point of departure will be a brief discussion of the socio-psychological concept of "ethnic group" and the relationships between the family and ethnicity.

ETHNIC GROUPS AND ETHNICITY

The term "ethnic group," as it is conventionally defined and used here, refers to those who conceive of themselves, and are so viewed by others, as sharing a distinctive social and cultural heritage that is passed on from generation to generation. This sense of a unique identity may be based upon the criteria of racial, religious, or national origin, or some combination of these social categories (Gordon, 1964:27; Shibutani and Kwan, 1965:47; Mindel and Habenstein, 1964:4). The extent to which individuals identify with and participate in socially significant activities of the ethnic community is influenced by a host of psychological, sociological, and historical variables. (The same may be said for differences between ethnic groups in their members' sense of identity.) Our guiding premise is that the family setting is a major sociological determinant in patterning attitudes and behaviours, and it is a primary institutional bridge between individuals, ethnic groups, and the wider society.

Although the range of ethnic groups in Canada is as varied as its geography, certain dimensions of ethnicity have historically been more conspicuous than others. In order to keep this discussion within a manageable scope we have focused upon European national ethnic groups for which data are available. An obvious omission is the rich but often inaccessible literature on Native Peoples. Students interested in the family patterns of these groups, past and present, are directed to the following sources: on the Inuit or Eskimo, Briggs (1970), Damas (1971), and Matthiasson (1980); on other indigenous peoples, Dunning (1971), Valle (1971), Cruikshank (1971), Acheson (1980), Price (1983) and Shkilnyk (1985). Needless to say, our decision to be restrictive is not to deny the importance of smaller ethnic groups, but to have included all would require a volume in itself.

THE FAMILY AND ETHNICITY

Any group bent on preserving the integrity of a distinctive cultural legacy is faced with the crucial and perplexing problem of effectively socializing a next generation to its beliefs and practices. This sociological truism underscores the strategic significance of the family—whatever its form or structure—for it is this institution that is inextricably linked to the vitality and persistence of ethnicity, insofar as it is able and willing to foster allegiance and conformity to traditions.

In this respect, the family is the first line of defence against potentially erosive and competing assimilative pressures. As Kalbach (1974:2) suggests, such influences are especially pervasive in urban industrial societies, which stress rationality and impersonality:

> Developments in modern society have made it difficult for groups to remain regionally and culturally isolated. Increased mobility, rapid growth, and social change in general, have brought diverse cultural groups into increasing contact with the larger regional and national system. Under modern conditions, it becomes increasingly difficult to maintain strong ethnic identities arising from different cultural experiences. Educational opportunities and experience have become increasingly standardized throughout the country, and the effects of mass production and distribution, as well as the mass media, have contributed to an increasing similarity of life styles from one end of the country to the other.

A similar thesis stressing convergence is advanced by Goode, with specific reference to the family (1963:1):

> For the first time in world history a common set of influences—the social forces of industrialization and urbanization—is affecting every known society.... The alteration seems to be in the direction of some type of *conjugal* family pattern—that is toward fewer kinship ties with distant relatives and a greater emphasis on the "nuclear" family unit of couple and children.... We are witnessing a remarkable phenomenon: the development of similar family behaviour and values among much of the world's population. [Emphasis in original.]

In addition to the twin factors of industrialization and urbanization, another element that cannt be ignored in the Canadian context is linguistic homogeneity. Although there are variations between older and more recent ethnic groups in retention of their mother tongues, the increased dominance of English is clear: "By far the major language transfer in Canada has been from all languages (including French mother tongue) to English home language" (Kralt, 1977:37). Similar trends were found in a study of the ten largest non-official language groups in five metropolitan areas (O'Bryan, Reitz, and Kuplowska, 1976). If we accept the axiom that language is the lifeblood of ethnicity and is nourished within the family, these patterns have profound implications for the future of ethnicity.

Each ethnic group evolves different sets of responses to alien influences which are filtered through the family. As Mindel and Habenstein (1976:7) put it, "one of the most significant ways in which an ethnic culture is expressed is through those activities that we identify as family activities.... If traditional ethnic values are to be found anywhere, they will be found in the family."

Having set down some of the general issues, let us try, before proceeding to specific studies, to locate some of the broad contours of ethnicity in

Table 9-1 Population by Selected Ethnic Origins: Canada, 1981

Ethnic Origin	Population	Percent
SINGLE ORIGINS		
British	9 674 245	40.2
French	6 439 100	26.7
German	1 142 365	4.7
Italian	747 970	3.1
Ukrainian	529 615	2.2
Native Peoples	413 380	1.7
Dutch	408 240	1.7
Chinese	289 245	1.2
Scandinavian	282 795	1.2
Jewish	264 025	1.1
Polish	254 485	1.1
Portuguese	188 105	.8
Indo-Pakistani	196 390	.8
Greek	154 365	.6
Other single origins	1 260 560	5.2
MULTIPLE ORIGINS		
British and French	430 255	1.8
British and other	859 800	3.6
French and other	124 940	.5
Other multiple origins	423 620	1.8
TOTAL POPULATION	24 083 500	

SOURCE: Derived from *Canada Update, 1981 Census*. Ottawa: Statistics Canada, April 26, 1983, 2. Reproduced with permission of the Minister of Supply and Services Canada.

Canada by examining some demographic trends. This account will necessarily be abbreviated. Those interested in more detailed expositions are referred to several reports that draw upon the census materials and vital statistics (Statistics Canada, *Canada's Immigrants*, 1984; Kalbach and McVey, 1979; Kralt, 1977).

ETHNIC DISTRIBUTION

The population of Canada rose from approximately 3.7 million in 1871 to 24.1 million in 1981. The proportions of various ethnic groups in 1981 are shown in Table 9-1. The ethnic distribution has been relatively stable over this period, with immigration peaking between 1900 and the First World

War, slowing down until the end of the Second World War, rising dramatically between 1945 and 1961, and levelling off to about 141 000 immigrants per annum during the 1960s and 1970s. In the last two decades, migrants have increasingly come from Asian and Caribbean countries. Although the proportion of persons identifying themselves as British (English, Irish, Scots, and Welsh) has declined from a high of 60 percent in 1871 to 40 percent in 1981, this group is dominant in all regions except Québec and the prairie provinces and continues to be the single largest source of migrants to Canada.

Despite recent decreases in fertility and the absence of any significant immigration, Canadians of French origin are concentrated in Québec (80 percent) and account for about 27 percent of the population—the position they have historically maintained. The largest European ethnic groups in 1981, after British and French, were Germans (4.7 percent), Italians (3.1 percent), Ukrainians (2.2 percent), Dutch (1.7 percent), Scandinavians (1.2 percent), Jews (1.1 percent), and Poles (1.1 percent). Thus, the ethnic origins of the population are divided between the French and all others (excluding British), each having about 30 percent of the total population, with the remaining 40 percent being of British origin.

At first glance, these figures support the image of Canada as a multiethnic society. What they do not reveal, however, is that the influence of the British extends far beyond their numerical superiority into every major institution (Porter, 1965; Forcese, 1975). This fact, along with their linguistic hegemony, raises two important questions that are related closely to the notions of convergence and homogeneity. To what degree do the family patterns of this dominant group serve as models for other ethnic groups to emulate? Second, is there anything distinctively "British" or "Anglo" about such configurations or do they represent the Canadian version of the global trend toward a conjugal form of family organization? Obviously, we cannot begin to address these issues without first looking at specific studies of family patterns among various ethnic groups.

ETHNIC FAMILY PATTERNS

British-Canadians

We are virtually ignorant of British-Canadian family patterns. Because of the lack of studies at the time, Elkin did not include those of British origin in his survey of ethnic groups and even a cursory examination of the literature indicates that the situation has not changed significantly since then.

One of the earliest and most frequently cited studies on British-Canadians, *Crestwood Heights* (Seeley et al., 1956), was based on research conducted after the Second World War. The authors of this detailed analysis, which spans five years of interviews and observations, describe and dissect the social life of an affluent, upper middle-class Toronto suburb which was predominantly English, but had a substantial Jewish minority. A picture emerges of the stereotypical isolated nuclear family, based on romantic love betwen spouses and minimal ties with other kin, in a socially mobile community. Within the small family unit the husband's primary function was to earn an income, and the wife's to express the family's social position by keeping the home running smoothly through her roles as social director, child raiser, and consumer. Ideally, an egalitarian atmosphere prevailed, and there was an emphasis on the development of individuality, autonomy, respectability, and achievement. Children were an important focus during their tenure in the household and the philosophy guiding their nurture was sensible and balanced—neither over-solicitous nor over-protective. Fathers were mildly patriarchal by the standards of previous generations, and mothers the emotional hub of the family and marriages. Daily routines and tasks in the home reflected the economic division of labour and were divided into masculine and feminine spheres.

All this is not to suggest that there were no strains in these families. For example, women tended to rely heavily on a variety of "experts," whose approaches were viewed with skepticism by men, for guidance in such matters as child rearing, education, and so on. This is indicative of numerous other cleavages between the belief systems of men and women. Although feminist ideals were not articulated until many years after this study, the seeds of the ideology and the "problem" are clearly delineated by the authors.

Although published almost 35 years ago, *Crestwood Heights* has become a minor classic and illuminates two issues that continue to concern family sociologists. First, Seeley et al. found no consistent differences between the family relations of Jews and Anglos. This suggests that at a particular class level ethnicity is neither salient nor consequential. Second, Larson (1976:59–60) and others postulate that the family described in this report represents the ideal-typical Canadian family that later generations of various ethnic groups would attempt to approximate. As we shall see, existing studies support this position. We would stress, however, that there does not appear to be anything specifically "Canadian" about this model: its essentials conform to the global conjugal form that transcends national boundaries. Although lack of comparative materials at the time the study was done made it difficult to substantiate the impression of apparent convergence, the same point is cogently made by David Riesman in his introduction to the book: "In fact, there is almost nothing in the book which strikes me as peculiarly Canadian, although when I visited Crestwood Heights during the course of this research I felt I was in the presence of three provincialisms: towards London, towards Hollywood-New York, and towards Tel Aviv" (1956:xi).

No comparable work has appeared since *Crestwood Heights* was published. Instead, the literature on British-Canadians consists of a handful of studies dealing with specific aspects of family and kinship (for example, Osterreich, 1965; Pineo, 1968; Irving, 1972. For detailed discussions of these and other works see Chapter Eight). These investigations reveal that urban British-Canadians of all classes, like their counterparts in the United States and Western Europe, participate in extensive-kin networks involving mutual aid, affection, and frequent contact, despite geographical and social mobility. If these ties are not as elaborate as those found in pre-industrial societies, they are still more prevalent and socially significant than those in *Crestwood Heights*.

Larson has summarized a number of surveys on college students' attitudes toward courtship, marital roles, sex, children, divorce, the employment of women, and so on. The most striking differences were between the sexes, women being significantly more egalitarian and less conservative in their views than men—a pattern adumbrated, as we have seen, in *Crestwood Heights*. Larson cautiously concludes that, "collectively, these papers appear to document both the persistence of middle-class Anglo-Saxon traditions and the emergence of considerably more liberal attitudes and behaviours" (1976:61). Precisely what these traditions are, however, remains unclear since we lack both a firm empirical base and studies of the trends over time on British-Canadian families.

French-Canadians

As compared with that on British-Canadians, the corpus of works on French-Canadians is richer, though not as substantial as we would desire. A major impetus for the studies that have appeared over the past two decades has been the seminal research of Garigue (1962, 1968, 1976), which focused on the effects of urbanization on the kinship patterns of the French in Montreal. In addressing this question, Garigue's accounts of urban French-Canadian families have become the standard references for an understanding of this ethnic group.

In contrast to the atomistic portrait of British-Canadians painted in *Crestwood Heights*, Garigue's first work stressed the resilience, salience, and adaptability of family and kin ties among French-Canadians. The unique social and demographic contexts of socialization within the family also diverge from the British model (1976:229):

> The fact that a French Canadian is normally socialized in a large household conditions him at an early age to multiple kinship obligations. The socialization is carried out in a world in which authority is male and narrowly defined and emotional needs are satisfied through sibling, cousin, mother-child, grandmother, and aunt relationships. The pattern is continued in adult life, but with greater freedom since each person can have a wider range of personal preference.

These patterns, together with the stress on premarital female chastity, maternity, a marked division of marital roles and authority, and the structural importance of women's maintaining and managing relations with kin, comprise a set of family ideals defined as peculiarly French-Canadian. Garigue also notes the interlocking nature of family and ethnicity (1976:299):

> These ideals about family and kinship were not isolated but were part of a culture complex which included the French language as spoken in Québec, a specific system of education, membership in the Catholic Church, and various political theories about the status of French Canadians in Canada. To be a member of a French Canadian kinship group implied attitudes and beliefs about some or all of these.

Subsequent investigations have challenged (Rioux, 1959), confirmed (Carisse, 1964; Tremblay and Laplante, 1971; Moreux, 1973; Piddington, 1976), and modified (Hobart, 1972; Tremblay, 1973; Carisse, 1976a) various facets of this view of French-Canadian family patterns. Rioux argued that Garigue had underestimated the effects of urbanization on kinship because its impact had just begun to be felt. His critique, however, is not especially convincing. Although his discussion of French-speaking Acadians, whose genealogical knowledge was staggering compared to that of Garigue's informants, is fascinating, it does not, as he contends, invalidate the latter's findings concerning the strength of kinship in an urban context.

Both Piddington's study of a small French-Canadian community in Manitoba and the work of Tremblay and Laplante on Acadians in Nova Scotia indicated that the patterns outlined by Garigue were also evident in rural settings. Piddington's data on kinship recognition, intermarriage of relatives, mutual aid, and so on, again highlight the interconnections between the family and ethnicity (1976:574):

> The material from St. Jean Baptiste suggests that over the whole of Canada and large areas of the U.S.A. there spreads a network of recognized kinship relationships which helps to keep French Canadians aware, despite geographical dispersion of their identity as a distinct ethnic group and the advantage of belonging to such a group.

In his theoretical assessment of traditional and contemporary authority models in French-Canadian families, Tremblay (1973) corroborates and extends the observations of Garigue and others. He finds evidence of a subtle but definite shift toward a conjugal form of family, with an emphasis on individualism, behavioural and ideological autonomy from the wider kin group of the nuclear-unit form, expansion of feminine roles, and the democratization of marital and parent-child relationships.

Moreux's study of a Montreal suburb and Carisse's report on working-class families indicate that the pace of change, especially with respect to the traditional status of women, has been slow and that these families generally conform to the patterns found by Garigue.

What conclusions, however tentative, may be derived from these and other inquiries? First, it appears that the family structures and processes recognized as distinctly French-Canadian continue to shape and dominate the lives of members of this large group and are resistant, if not totally immune, to novel influences and ideas. Nevertheless, there is increasing evidence of change and strain at various points in the traditional system and particularly among the educated, the middle classes, and women. The pivotal role of women in effecting social change is also suggested by Carisse's study of innovative women in Québec (1976a) and Hobart's findings that French-Canadian females were more egalitarian and permissive in their attitudes toward marriage (but not premarital intercourse) than were English-Canadian males and females and French-Canadian male students (1972:192). Moreux also alerts us to strains that are likely to accompany changes:

> Among the low-income families where the father is absent most of the time and less sensitive to the attacks on his pride or less aware of modern themes, one finds a better equilibrium. He will be more willing to take a back seat or will not be aware that he plays a secondary role. Generally speaking family conflicts are at their highest in bourgeois environments where links with relatives are weak, and where the father has more difficulty relinquishing his ideal role (1973:76).

Second, Garigue has pointed to the importance of large families in the perpetuation of family ideals. What effects the decreased birth rate will have, or to what extent this and other social trends will be affected by a resurgence of ethnicity in Québec, remain to be seen.

Finally, there are signs that family relationships once viewed as deviant and "un-French," such as small families and divorce, are beginning to be accepted as legitimate variants. In discussing such alternatives, Larson (1976:64) writes, "There is evidence of a professional family with democratic and egalitarian intra-family relations. . . . If such a family exists, it is clearly distinct from the matricentric family and might be thought of as marriage-centric. It is closer in many respects to the emergent English Canadian family than to the common ideal-typical middle-class family system."

German-Canadians

Persons of German origin are a large and heterogeneous population concentrated mainly in the less urbanized areas of Ontario and the prairies. Although there has not been a comprehensive sociological study of this group, there are numerous reports on German-speaking subgroups such as the Hutterites (Hostetler and Huntington, 1967; Hostetler, 1974; Peter,

1987) and to a lesser extent on Mennonites (Francis, 1955; Anderson and Driedger, 1980).

Hutterites have been the focus of considerable interest because of their extraordinarily high birth rate, distinctive communal social organization, economic success, and ability to flourish in a society that clashes sharply with their beliefs and practices. Hutterite colonies are located primarily in isolated rural areas in the prairie provinces, the Dakotas, Montana, and Washington. In 1985, the group numbered about 28 000 according to Peter (1987:62). Traditional Hutterite family patterns are finely attuned to fundamentalist and ascetic Christianity, which stresses reconciliation with God through the merging and subordination of individuals to the community. Such commitment entails strict sex and age distinctions expressed in the authority of males and elders as is demonstrated in the family. Socialization is strictly controlled with clearly marked stages geared explicitly to progressive de-individuation and the inculcating of appropriate sex- and age-linked attitudes and conduct. The efficacy of this process is aided by isolation from alien influences during the formative years, by distinctive language and dress, and by an uncompromising belief in the rectitude and desirability of the Hutterite way of life.

In the past, their family patterns deviated from those of wider Canadian society at virtually every point. For example, Hutterite kinship is formally patrilineal (descent is traced through males exclusively), patrilocal (the wife usually moves to her husband's community or colony), colony-exogamous (individuals from the same colony marry those from other colonies), and endogamous within the three historical branches (*Leut*) that divide the total population along doctrinal lines and some social customs. Courtship was formally free but clearly restricted by communal norms and limited opportunities. The primary purpose of marriage was procreation and the channelling of sexuality. Romantic and affectional ties between spouses were weak and their potentially disruptive force was deflected to other communal and kinship relations, such as male sibling groups. Finally, "Hutterites have maintained the extended family. Three, sometimes four generations live in the same community although the members of an extended family might not necessarily live under the same roof" (Peter, 1987:62).

The most recent study of this group, by Peter (1987), documents a number of changes that have occurred since the mid-1960s that challenge conventional views about the Hutterite society's stasis. Among these, the author cites the erosion of the traditional collectivist orientation and a shift to individualism in both secular and religious spheres, a breakdown in customary social controls, competition from other fundamentalist sects, and the social impact of changing technologies and economic imperatives. With respect to courtship, marriage, and the family, dating and going steady have become more common, individuals are increasingly remaining single or marrying at later ages, children are kept at home longer, traditional female occupations have declined, and there is relatively greater emphasis on affectional ties between husbands and wives. Finally, there has been a significant drop in the birth rate. How the Hutterites will respond to such changes remains to be seen.

The sources cited affirm the crucial role of the family in the perpetuation of a distinct religio-ethnic culture among the Hutterites. Similar claims about the approximately 175 000 Mennonites in Canada have more often been asserted than demonstrated. Studies by Maykovich (née Kurokawa) on socialization (1971) and mental health (1976) in three Ontario Mennonite Orders of varying orthodoxy raise some questions about the stereotype of a solitary, culturally unique, and harmonious family system. Maykovich found clear variations between the groups in the adherence to and effectiveness of different modes of induction procedures, such as consistency of discipline and authoritarianism. In addition, there were patterned variations in the psychological adjustment, value conflicts, and degree of self-esteem among Mennonite children. In a related study (1975), the author compared the success values of Japanese, Italians, and Mennonites with respect to educational and occupational aspirations. Unlike their orthodox counterparts, progressive Mennonites resembled the other two ethnic groups in having high aspirations for their children, pressuring them to achieve, placing a high value on education, and so on.

Italian-Canadians

The overwhelming majority of Italian-Canadians are found in the urban centres of Québec and Ontario and most are recent immigrants—persons who came to Canada after the Second World War (Kralt, 1977:16, 19). General descriptions of this group have been provided by Hobart (1966), Richmond (1967), Jansen (1971), and Sturino (1980).

The small number of works on Italian-Canadian families are contradictory and equivocal. On the one hand, Jansen found that first-generation immigrants in Toronto were occupationally, residentially, and linguistically segregated and had minimal contacts beyond primary groups based on kinship, village, or regional affiliations. Similar patterns were reported by Boissevain (1976) for Italians in Montreal. The maintenance and commitment to traditional Italian family values, predicated on strict rules of inclusion and exclusion with regard to obligations and loyalties, shield the individual and family from the strains of acculturation. At the same time, they also retard the rate of absorption into the larger Canadian society.

On the other hand, this socio-cultural insularity is not manifest with respect to the intermarriage of males or in the socialization of later generations. Despite the ambiguities in interpreting the sociological meaning of ethnic intermarriages,[1] a high incidence among Italian males has been noted (Hobart, 1966; Kalbach, 1974; Boissevain, 1976) and attributed, in part, to the differential rearing and treatment of the sexes, that is, stricter and more protective attitudes and practices toward females. Detailed analyses of socialization (Danziger, 1971, 1976ab; Maykovich, 1975) have compared Italians who were more or less acculturated (as measured by language competence and length of residence in Canada) with native-born Canadians and non-Canadian-born members of other ethnic groups. The findings indicated that a large proportion of immigrant parents, acculturated and unacculturated, had high (if unrealistic) aspirations for their children, were as supporting of them as were other groups, and were more conservative in the rearing of females than of males. There is little question that, like other ethnic groups, Italians will experience a blending of old and new family patterns until the younger generation finds its own way. As Sturino (1980:102) concludes:

> At three kinship levels of nuclear family, family circle, and kindred, elements from a peasant past were merged with an urban present. The kinship patterns that emerged can neither be referred to as Canadian nor as Italian, but as uniquely "Italo-Canadian." Evidence suggests that this emergent entity is sufficiently consonant with the culture of the host society that it will prove to be tenacious, though only with time and the birth of new generations will its durability be confirmed.

Although admittedly exploratory, these words provide a firm point of departure for understanding change and stability, relative to other ethnic groups in the family patterns of Italian-Canadians.

Ukrainian-Canadians

To date, there is only one study (Hobart, 1976) of any sociological import on Ukrainian-Canadian family patterns, and these data were collected over twenty years ago. Hobart examined attitudes toward family size, marital roles, and childbearing among a sample of three generations in Edmonton and surrounding rural communities. In summarizing the results, Larson (1976:352) observes that:

> The patterns of the first generation closely reflect those of their native country. Those of the third generation, in contrast, closely approximate those of the ideal-typical English Canadian family: small families, maternal employment, egalitarianism in marital and parent-child relationships, values supportive of divorce and intermarriage, and weaker kin orientations.

He further notes that, because there are no comparisons with other ethnic groups, it is difficult to point to any unique characteristics of Ukrainian families. This appears reasonable. Nevertheless, two futher comments may be added. First, since we do not have reliable information on the family patterns of the first generation in Canada *or* in the Ukraine, integenerational comparisons are, at best, problematic and speculative. Second, despite the absence of comparable studies, it is apparent that the direction of changes parallel those referred to earlier by Tremblay in his discussion of emergent French-Canadian patterns. Thus, Hobart's study, with all its methodological problems, provides further evidence for the thesis of convergence.

Dutch-Canadians

The Dutch live primarily in Ontario and the prairie provinces and are less urbanized (65 percent) than the national average (76 percent). Compared with all other European ethnic groups (except the Hutterites), they have the highest fertility rate, as measured by the average number of children born to ever-married women (Kralt, 1977:15, 19, 56). Our knowledge of this group is limited to a single monograph based on field work conducted between 1965 and 1971 on a small, self-contained farming community in rural Ontario (Ishwaran, 1977).

A singular feature of this ethnography is the author's consideration of the historical roots of the migration, including conditions in the Netherlands and the development of the community in Canada over time. Ishwaran discerns several configurations that set these Dutch apart from their neighbours and wider Canadian society. Although the effective social unit is the nuclear family, ties between families and more distant kin in Canada and the Netherlands are strong and active. The close institutional ties between the family and religion are expressed in ideals and practices that accentuate male authority, maternal and domestic roles of women, rigid socialization based on sex, the structural importance of the eldest child as a parental surrogate, extended-kin ties, and extremely conservative attitudes toward intermarriage, sex, contraception, and divorce. To the extent that this combination of values is realized in conjunction with the Dutch language and other customs, the community's concept of "Dutchness" is reinforced and maintained.

Ishwaran indicates that the families of Holland Marsh had, at the conclusion of his research, been successful in implementing their ideals. Nevertheless, he also detected internal and external sources of potential conflict and strain that the community would have to confront in maintaining its cultural coherence and uniqueness. These included internal divisions related to communal norms between generations, the increased use of English, the diffusion of competing values through the mass media, and economic problems arising from an increase in population and a decrease in arable lands.

Jewish-Canadians

The Census data show that Jewish-Canadians are concentrated in Montreal, Toronto, and Winnipeg. They have the lowest fertility and highest incomes of any group we have considered, are highly educated, and are primarily in professional, managerial, and technical occupations (Kralt, 1977:14, 55, 66, 67). There is no reason to believe that these patterns have changed since the 1981 census.

Apart from demographic profiles and historical descriptions of pre-migratory *shtetls* (small towns in Eastern Europe), accounts of Jewish family patterns in Canada are limited to excellent, but fictional, literary works of Mordecai Richler (*St. Urbain's Horseman, The Apprenticeship of Duddy Kravitz*), and unpublished theses and dissertations. One of the few published empirical studies available is by Kallen (1976) on a second-generation sample of adults in Toronto. She oberves that the family in Canada carries on many of the same activities it did in the *shtetl* and serves as the focal point for more extended kinship relations and Jewish communal identity. The author goes on to explore the ways in which the family inculcates ethnic consciousness and the ideal of secular achievement through its stress on learning and formal education. The dominant familial motifs include an egalitarian marital ideology superimposed upon a sexual division of labour in domestic and occupational spheres, permissive and love-based child-rearing practices aimed at inculcating a high need to achieve, and concentration on the immediate family at the expense of more distant kin ties.

The relatively large family size and preferences (an average of 4.5 children) of this group are anomalies and probably reflect the high socio-economic status and religious commitment of the sample Kallen studied (1976:153). Patterns conducive to preserving ethnic identity reported in other studies were also found in this community: these included residential segregation and low rates of intermarriage (Kalbach, 1974). Finally, Kallen noted a shift in the basis of ethnic consciousness from religion to various cultural aspects of Judaism and a strong identification, especially among the younger generation, with Israel (Kallen, 1976:161). In sum, she views the family patterns of Toronto Jews as a mixture of traditional and modern influences which have been instrumental in the survival and success of this group in Canadian society. This research was conducted from 1967 to 1968, hence it is difficult to say how valid these generalizations are today.

Polish-Canadians

Canadians of Polish descent reside mainly in Ontario and the prairie provinces and numbered about 255 000 in 1981. One of the few studies of this ethnic group (Radecki and Heydenkorn, 1976:128) found that, "The family . . . has been almost totally neglected or ignored by writings dealing with the Polish group in Canada. Only one novel, based on research, deals extensively with Polish families in Canada (Wańkowicz, *Three Generations*, 1973)."

In evaluating the changes that have taken place over time, the authors trace the evolution of traditional extended-family patterns in Poland to the predominantly conjugal system characteristic of contemporary Canada. In Canada, traditional values, such as undisputed male authority, arranged marriage, large families, stern child-rearing practices, and care of the aged, were undermined and altered by the absence of supporting institutions such as the Church, by geographical dispersion and isolation, and by the exposure of the young to the Canadian educational system.

In a study of postwar immigrant families in Toronto (Radecki, 1970; 1980), it was found that the historical trend toward conjugality and the nuclear family had accelerated. This was indicated by preferences for smaller families by the decreased salience of kinship ties, by the younger generation's rejection of traditional values, by working wives and their increased participation in decision-making, by marriage based on personal preference, and by the placing of the aged in homes.

The general trends noted by Radecki and Heydenkorn are summarized as follows:

> New patterns of family interaction and new attitudes and beliefs are plainly discernible not only among the post-war immigrants but also among the whole Polish aggregate in Canada. Nuclear family orientations are slowly replacing the traditional extended family values. There is a generally greater permissiveness and very little authoritarianism on the part of the father; equally noticeable is the abandonment of previously rigidly held attitudes and values. It is likely that the Polish family in Canada is fast becoming indistinguishable from the Anglo-Saxon urban Canadian family, sharing many of its values and attitudes in parent-child and husband-wife relationships. The changes have taken place here while much traditionalism still seems to remain in Poland (1976:137).

CONCLUSION

This all too brief sketch of ethnic families leads to a number of conclusions, some of which are more secure than others. First, it is amply clear that adequate and systematic data, historical and contemporary, are scarce: there is little indication that researchers have given high priority to this area. To say that we know little is not to admit total ignorance but rather to remind us that caution should be exercised in interpreting current patterns or predicting future trends.

Second, the thesis of convergence advanced by Goode and others is, with certain qualifications, applicable to a large if unspecified proportion of Canadian families and, with other changes in Canadian society, suggests the waning importance of ethnicity. An extreme formulation of this position is exemplified by Kralt's (1977:81–82) conclusion to his careful examination of census materials on a variety of social and demographic characteristics of ethnic groups:

> Although there are exceptions to the rule, it seems to the author that Canadian society is not the multi-ethnic society it is often conceived to be.... It would appear that the differences between ethnic groups are as much due to the time the individual has been exposed to Canadian society as to ethnic origin in and of itself.... With the almost universal adoption of the English or French language by nearly the entire population, it seems likely that Canadian society will effectively consist of two dominant groups with generally similar values, i.e., those values associated with urban, industrial societies. The impact of ethnic origin, as it has been characteristically understood and examined seems to be at an end. The only major exception to this generalization being the Native Peoples of Canada.

Our own reading of the fragmentary research available presses toward a similar judgment but with reservations stemming, paradoxically, from the very deficiencies of the materials themselves. Aggregate demographic data, such as fertility and language loyalty, are generated by complex family structures and processes that we are only beginning to explore, let alone comprehend. Moreover, a crucial part of Goode's argument that has not been sufficiently appreciated emphasizes that even if all family systems are moving toward some form of the conjugal pattern, the trend is not necessarily uniform, continuous, or simply a function of industrialization and urbanization. Changes in values and ideologies, as well as commitments to existing family arrangements also affect the rate of change independently. With respect to the groups we have considered, signs of convergence are manifest in instances like the British and the French, and questionable in others, such as the Dutch, the Italians, and the Hutterites. If those who predict the impending demise of ethnicity are even partially correct, then the latter groups represent isolated, rearguard pockets of ethnicity destined for cultural envelopment (or decimation) by the larger society. This may be so, but until we have more detailed and reliable reports over time, such pronouncements must be treated as hypotheses, not as accomplished facts.

Finally, there are sufficient traces of resistance to the pervasive forces of standardization and rationality in urban industrial societies to give us some reason to believe that obituaries attesting the death of ethnicity may be premature. As Mindel and Habenstein (1976:428) concluded after evaluating the status of ethnic families in the United States:

> Somewhere between these great grindstones that would pulverize traditional family organization, a type of family, once consigned to oblivion—being ground or melted down—persists: protean, adaptive, conservatizing, generating mean-

ings, and forming a sense of identity partly from the realities of an earlier time, partly from the exigencies of the present. The bonds of ethnicity are reminiscent of the life forces of those desert creatures that, buried in the earth for years, come "alive" when it rains.

Precisely how closely this vision pertains to Canadian society will remain an open question until scholars from all disciplines (including writers and poets) begin to consider this subject worthy of their attention.

Note

1. See Chapter Three for discussions of the significance of intermarriage.

In a recent study based on census data of ethnic intermarriages in Toronto, Kalbach and Richard (1986) found that the incidence of ethnic intermarriage, although still relatively low, about 25 percent of the husband-wife families in their sample, generally rose among the native-born ethnics (second and later generations of children born to immigrants in Canada). On the basis of these and other data, such as language use, fertility, education, and occupational status, the authors cautiously conclude that intermarraige is becoming an increasingly important means of acculturation and assimilation for families with heads of non-British origin. These findings generally reiterate those of an earlier study on the internal dynamics of intermarriage between British- and French-Canadians. Carisse (1976b) reported that the cultural orientations of spouses—for instance, choice of community, relevant social networks, language, exposure to mass media—tended to mirror British dominance in the wider society, and that this skewing was especially marked when the husband was British.

We would interpret these conclusions, along with those of other works cited, as supporting the convergence hypothesis advanced in this essay. Moreover, Kalbach and Richard highlight the pivotal position of native-born children of immigrants in the integration of ethnic groups in Canada with respect to one indicator—intermarriage. When other factors are taken into account, such as language maintenance and identification with and participation in ethnic-related activities, which are not easily documented, the extent of convergence is, as Elkin's (1985) recent overview of families in English-speaking Canada suggests, likely to be even greater than existing sources indicate.

Suggested Readings

Canadian Ethnic Studies.
   Bulletin of the Research Centre for Canadian Ethnic Studies. Calgary: University of Calgary, n.d.

Goode, William J.
1963 *World Revolution and Family Patterns*. Glencoe, IL: Free Press.

Gordon, Milton M.
1964 *Assimilation in American Life*. New York: Oxford University Press.

Gregorvich, Andrew, ed.
1972 *Canadian Ethnic Groups Bibliography*. Toronto: Ontario Department of the Provincial Secretary and Citizenship.

Ishwaran, K., ed.
1980 *Canadian Families: Ethnic Variations*. Toronto: McGraw-Hill Ryerson.

Kalbach, Warren E.
1970 *The Impact of Immigration on Canada's Population*. Ottawa: Dominion Bureau of Statistics.

Kralt, John.
1977 *Ethnic Origins of Canadians*. Ottawa: Census Canada, Profile Studies, Demographic Characteristics. Bulletin 5. Catalogue 99–790:1–9.

Larson, Lyle E.
1976 *The Canadian Family in Comparative Perspective*. Scarborough: Prentice-Hall.

Mindel, Charles H., and Robert W. Habenstein, eds.
1976 *Ethnic Families in America: Patterns and Variations*, New York: Elsevier.

10

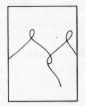

AGING AND THE FAMILY

Neena Chappell

Although research into aging was conducted in the United States and Europe during the 1950s and 1960s, similar research has been conducted only relatively recently in Canada. Prompted by the aging population and by developments in Canadian sociology, many scholars in the 1970s focused their attention on the sociology of aging, making it an important and growing area in Canadian social sciences.

While the general theoretical and conceptual frameworks used in the analysis of aging are drawn primarily from the disciplines of the researchers, there are some exceptions. For example, the activity theory and the disengagement theory, neither of which has been confirmed by subsequent work, are specific to the substantive area of aging and are not deemed part of general sociological theories. Advocates of activity theory claim that high social involvement and activity are keys to successful aging (Havighurst and Albrecht, 1953). In response, Cumming and Henry (1961), with the disengagement theory of aging argue that society and the elderly mutually and willingly withdraw: as people age they disengage from roles they played in their younger adult lives and emotionally divest themselves of their network of friends and relatives. This process accompanies an increased preoccupation with the self.

In social gerontology, an area devoted to the study of the aged and the aging process, theories derived from sociology include the view of the aged as a sub-cultural group (Rose, 1968), a version of labeling theory in which the elderly view themselves negatively because society values neither the aged nor the aging (Kuypers and Bengtson, 1973), and an exchange theory that views the elderly as having little to exchange in their interactions with others (Dowd, 1980). Besides the sociological theories used in the analysis of aging, social gerontology also uses theories drawn from other disciplines such as psychology and anthropology. This has led many gerontologists to claim that the study of aging is a multidisciplinary endeavour, rather than a discrete discipline.

The roles of elders in the intricate patterns of family interaction, and in the mutual aid between generations, link the substantive study areas of the family and social gerontology. Evidence of kin support for the aged has refuted the assumptions inherent in the notion of "the isolated nuclear family" (see Chapter Eight for a detailed discussion of this concept). Likewise, the modernization theory of aging (Cowgill and Holmes, 1972), which was popular in the 1970s, contended that modernization leads to a decline in the status and social integration of the aged. Specifically, it was argued that scientific technology, urbanization, literacy and mass education, and health technology lead to a lower status of the aged in society, a decline in their leadership roles, a reduction of their power and influence, and an increase in their disengagement from community life. That is, the negative status of the elderly in the family in particular, and in society in general, was a function of modernization. However, the modernization theory of aging was not supported by empirical evidence (Palmore and Manton, 1973; Bengtson et al., 1975).

Research on aging and the family has confirmed Litwak's (1960) suggestion that the modified extended family, with its emphasis on mutual aid and close interpersonal ties among kin, is an important social institution in contemporary industrial societies (see Chapter Eight). Recently, Brody (1981) summarized the findings on this issue, noting the strength of intergenerational ties and the extended family, the continuity of responsible familial behaviour, and the frequency of contact between the generations. Nevertheless, research on informal support systems has neglected to examine the role of non-familial networks, including friends, neighbours, and the community at large, in the life of the aged, making it impossible to describe kin interactions in comparison with non-kin exchanges.

In light of these introductory comments, we shall examine selected demographic trends of the elderly in Canada, the nature and functions of support systems, which include informal networks of relatives and friends, as well as the more organized and publicly funded agencies, such as community services and institutions, and social policies related to aging.

SOCIAL AND DEMOGRAPHIC CHARACTERISTICS

An old person has generally been defined in our society as 65 years of age and over. This practice will be followed here, but it should be recognized that this numerical demarcation is a social definition based primarily on retirement norms and legislation related to old-age-security payments. Some scholars object to this arbitrary shorthand because they believe that it reinforces prevailing negative attitudes concerning age. In reality, old age varies considerably from individual to individual (and from culture to culture). It is signified by declines in health and effective functioning which, in turn, restrict one's independence. Furthermore, even when one's health begins to decline, one may not perceive oneself as old.

The social definition of aging is different from the physiological process of aging which begins much earlier than age 65. For example, greying hair and deterioration of eyesight are indications of aging which occur before one reaches 65 years. Similarly, menopause and changes to the skin begin before the age of 65. The primary distinguishing event which occurs around the age of 65 is retirement, currently the subject of intense debate. With the introduction of human rights legislation, many provinces have now removed the provision of mandatory retirement at 65 years for certain occupations.

Numbers of the Elderly

Table 10-1 shows that the proportion of Canadians in the age group of 65 and over has increased in recent decades. It will continue to increase until approximately 2031 when the baby-boom generation enters this age group. By then, 20 percent of the Canadian population will be 65 years of age or over. Furthermore, the percentage of the elderly who are themselves older is increasing (see Table 10-2). By the year 2031, when many of the baby-boom generation reach old age, approximately 45 percent of the elderly will be age 75 or older. In other words, the population we now consider elderly is itself aging; the proportions of the "old" old compared to the "young" old is increasing.

The percentage of elderly females has been increasing and has stabilized at around 57 percent (see Table 10-3). In the first half of this century, slightly more than half of the elderly were male. However, this proportion had reversed by 1961. Demographic projections suggest that the proportion of female elderly will continue to outnumber the proportion of male elderly and that the gap between them will stabilize, not increase, when the baby-boom reaches old age.

Social and Economic Conditions

Approximately half of the elderly are married, a condition that has remained more or less stable throughout the century (see Table 10-4). This percentage is expected to decline slightly when the baby-boom generation reaches old age. In addition, roughly one third of those who are over 65 years of age

Table 10-1 Number and Percentage Aged 65 + in Canada, 1891–2031

Year	Number	%
1891	218 790	4.5
1901	271 201	5.0
1911	335 315	4.7
1921	420 244	4.8
1931	576 076	5.6
1941	767 815	6.7
1951	1 086 273	7.8
1961	1 391 154	7.6
1971	1 744 410	8.1
1981	2 360 975	9.7
1986	2 697 575	10.7
2001 (projection)	3 425 000	11.9
2031 (projection)	6 240 000	20.2

SOURCES: 1890–91 Census of Canada (vol. II, Table I, 5); 1961 Census of Canada, Catalogue 92-542, Table 20, 20-1, 20-2; 1971 Census of Canada, Catalogue 92-715, Table 7, 7-1, 7-2; 1981 Census of Canada, Catalogue 92-901, Table 1, 1-1, 1-2, Powell and Martin, 1980, Table 1, 205; 1986 Census of Canada, summary tabulations, Table DM86A01, July, 1987. Reproduced with permission of the Minister of Supply and Services Canada.

are widowed. Widowhood, a state that usually occurs in old age in our society, causes many personal, emotional, and economic problems for those who experience it. However, marital status varies considerably with gender (see Table 10-5). Women are more likely to be widowed than are men (48 percent compared to 14 percent in 1986). On the other hand, elderly men are much more likely to be married than are women (75 percent compared to 40 percent in 1986).

The variation in marital status according to gender is reflected in the living arrangements of men and women (see Table 10-6). In 1981, 77 percent of elderly men were living either with a spouse or with unmarried children, while only 47 percent of elderly women did so. By contrast, women were more likely to be living alone (36 percent of elderly women lived alone in 1981 but only 14 percent of elderly men lived alone in that same year). The differential position of women relative to men in old age is confirmed when age specific income of men and women is compared (see Table 10-7). For each age group, for each of the years from 1971 through to 1985 for which census data were reported, in old age women have a lower average income than men. This is not surprising. It is a continuation of the disadvantaged economic position women experience throughout their lives. Since women

Table 10-2   Percentage of Population 65+ by Age, for Canada, 1891–2031

Year	65–69	70–74	75+	Total
1891	38.8	28.7	32.5	100.0
1901	39.2	28.4	32.4	100.0
1911	39.3	28.2	32.5	100.0
1921	41.0	28.0	30.9	99.9
1931	40.1	29.8	30.0	99.9
1941	40.1	28.3	31.6	100.0
1951	39.9	29.0	31.1	100.0
1961	35.0	28.9	36.1	100.0
1971	35.5	26.2	38.2	99.9
1981	35.8	26.8	37.4	100.0
1986	33.8	27.4	38.8	100.0
2001 (projection)	28.6	25.8	45.6	100.0
2031 (projection)	28.8	26.1	45.1	100.0

Sources: 1890–91 Census of Canada, Vol II, Table I, 5; 1921 Census of Canada, Vol. 2, Table 4, 6-7; 1931 Census of Canada, Vol. 3, Table 1, 2-3; 1961 Census of Canada, Catalogue 92-542, Table 20, 20-1, 20-2; 1971 Census of Canada, Catalogue 92-715, Table 7, 7-1, 7-2; 1981 Census of Canada, Catalogue 92-901, Table 1, 1-1, 1-2; Statistics Canada, Population Projections for Canada, Provinces and Territories, 1984–2006, Catalogue 91-520, Table D.3, 140-1, 186-7, 232-3, 278-9, 324-5, Table D.4, 338-42; 1986 Census of Canada, summary tabulations, Table DM86A01, July, 1987. Reproduced with permission of the Minister of Supply and Services Canada.

tend to outlive their husbands, they will more likely live in a disadvantaged economic situation. As will become clear later in this chapter, women are the primary providers of care to men as they age and as their health deteriorates, but when women experience deteriorating health other women, not men, step in to provide care.

Health   A major concern of old age, apparent at both the individual and societal levels, centres around decreasing health, characteristic of this phase in one's life cycle. For the individual, deteriorating health is associated to a large extent with one's increased dependency and decreased autonomy. At the societal level, policy makers and government officials are concerned about increasing demands on the health care system. The status of the health of the elderly has generally focused on the presence or absence of disease, or on the degree of functional capacity or disability.

Aging is associated with increases in both chronic conditions and functional disability. Over 80 percent of the elderly report at least one physical health problem (Chappell et al., 1986). Importantly, however, chronic con-

Table 10-3   Percentage of Population 65+ by Gender in Canada, 1891–2031

Year	Male	Female
1891	52.3	47.7
1901	51.2	48.8
1911	50.8	49.2
1921	51.1	48.9
1931	51.1	48.9
1941	50.9	49.1
1951	50.8	49.2
1961	48.5	51.5
1971	44.8	55.2
1981	42.8	57.2
1986	42.0	58.0
2001 (projection)	43.0	57.0
2031 (projection)	43.6	56.4

SOURCES: 1890–91 Census of Canada, Vol. 2, Table I, 5; 1921 Census of Canada, Vol. 2, Table 4, 6-7; 1961 Census of Canada, Catalogue 92-542, Table 20, 20-1, 20-2; 1971 Census of Canada, Catalogue 92-715, Table 7, 7-1, 7-2; 1981 Census of Canada, Catalogue 92-901, Table 1, 1-1, 1-2; Statistics Canada, Population Projections for Canada, Provinces and Territories, 1984–2006, Catalogue 91-520, Table D.3, 140-1, 186-7, 232-3, 278-9, 324-5, Table D.4, 338-342; 1986 Census of Canada, summary tabulations, Table DM86A01, July, 1987. Reproduced with permission of the Minister of Supply and Services Canada.

ditions need not lead to functional disability or limitations on activity. Approximately half the elderly studied reported some limitations to their activities (Chappell et al., 1986). However, functional disability can refer to instrumental or basic activities of daily living. The former include such activities as housework, preparing meals, household maintenance, transportation, shopping, and banking. The latter refer to activities more essential to survival: the ability to walk, feed oneself, wash and bathe, and use the toilet. In distinguishing betwen functional disability with basic activities of daily living or severe limitations and those referring to instrumental activities of daily living, Branch and Jette (1981) report approximately 20 percent of the elderly experience severe limitations. In other words, while both chronic conditions and functional disability increase with age, chronic conditions do not always result in functional disability among the elderly; only a minority of elders (about one fifth) are severely limited in their activities.

Leisure   Life during old age, then, entails various physiological changes and some deterioration in health. However, for most, old age is not devastating. Life for the elderly means much more than adjusting to the usually

Table 10-4   Percentage of 65+ by Marital Status for Canada, 1921–2001

Year	Single	Married	Widowed	Divorced	Totals
1921	9.4	53.9	36.5	.1	100.0
1931	10.7	53.0	36.2	.1	100.0
1941	11.5	52.9	35.4	.1	99.9
1951	11.1	53.8	34.9	.2	100.0
1961	10.5	54.5	34.8	.3	100.1
1971	10.6	53.8	34.7	.8	99.9
1981	9.1	55.2	34.1	1.6	100.0
1986	8.2	56.0	33.6	2.2	100.0
2001 (projection)	10.2	47.1	(42.7)		100.0

SOURCES: 1921 Census of Canada, Vol. II, Table 19, 115, Table 20; 1931 Census of Canada, Vol. III, Table 12, 94; 1941 Census of Canada, Vol. III, Table 7, 94-95; 1951 Census of Canada, Vol. II, Table 1, 1-1, 1-2; 1961 Census of Canada, Catalogue 92-552, Table 78, 78-1, 78-2; 1971 Census of Canada, Catalogue 92-730, Table 1, 1-1, 1-2; 1981 Census of Canada, unpublished data, Winnipeg Regional Office; Statistics Canada, household and family projections for Canada and the Provinces to 2001, Catalogue 91-517, Table A, 199, Table B, 212, Table C, 225; 1986 Census of Canada, summary tabulations, Table DM86A02, July, 1987. Reproduced with permission of the Minister of Supply and Services Canada.

gradual declines that do occur. Among today's elderly, most (85.7 percent of men, 92.2 percent of women in 1981) are not in the paid work force, not even as part-time or intermittent workers (Statistics Canada, 1982). They are at a point in the life cycle when many own the houses they live in outright. Three quarters own single detached two- or three-bedroom houses; 60 percent have fully paid their mortgages, 95 percent of those who are 85 years of age or older. In addition, in 1983, 60 percent owned their own cars (Statistics Canada, 1983). Despite the argument that one requires less money for such things as clothes and transportation when not in the paid work force, many elderly have been described as house rich and cash poor. They may own a house, but they do not have sufficient cash flow for the maintenance of their house and for day-to-day necessities, although some may be affluent enough to be free from such problems.

It is important to remember there are as many differences among the elderly as among younger persons. Housing is one example. At one time there was much debate in gerontology over the benefits of segregated housing, such as retirement communities, for the elderly. It is now recognized that some elderly people prefer such living arrangements. Apartments in downtown areas close to amenities offer many seniors what they believe to be relative security that allows them simultaneously to maintain autonomy and independence (Chappell and Horne, 1987). Still others prefer to remain

Table 10-5   Percentage of Population 65+ by Marital Status and Gender in Canada

		1921*	1931	1941	1951	1961	1971	1981	1986	2001[1]
Females 65+:	Single	10.2	10.9	11.2	10.4	10.2	10.7	9.5	8.6	10.4
	Married	39.8	40.2	41.0	41.6	41.2	39.2	39.9	41.0	32.5
	Widowed	49.9	48.9	47.7	47.9	48.4	49.4	49.0	48.2	57.1
	Divorced	.1	.1	.1	.1	.2	.7	1.5	2.1	
		100.0	100.1	100.0	100.0	100.0	100.0	99.9	99.9	100.0
Males 65+:	Single	8.7	10.5	11.8	11.8	10.8	10.6	8.5	7.5	9.8
	Married	67.4	65.2	64.5	65.7	68.5	71.8	75.5	76.7	69.0
	Widowed	23.8	24.1	23.6	22.3	20.4	16.7	14.1	13.5	
	Divorced	.2	.1	.2	.2	.4	.9	1.8	2.3	21.2
		100.1	99.9	100.1	100.0	100.1	100.1	99.9	100.0	100.0

1. Projection
(see Table 10-4 for footnotes and sources)

Table 10-6 Living Arrangements among the Elderly, 1981

	MALE		FEMALE	
	Number	%	*Number*	%
Population in private households	939 000	93.4	1 202 000	89.6
Nursing homes and other institutions	66 000	6.7	140 000	10.4
	1 005 000	100.1	1 342 000	100.0
Of Those in Private Households:				
Live with family persons (spouse or unmarried children)	725 000	77.2	561 000	46.7
Live with relatives	57 000	6.1	173 000	14.4
Live alone	131 000	13.9	434 000	36.1
Live with others	26 000	2.8	34 000	2.8
	939 000	100.0	1 202 000	100.0

SOURCE: Statistics Canada, *The Elderly in Canada*, Ottawa: Minister of Supply and Services, 1984, Table 3. Reproduced with permission of the Minister of Supply and Services Canada.

in their own homes. It is important that a variety of housing alternatives be available to meet the needs and preferences of a heterogeneous elderly population.

Those who are elderly in Canada today are pioneers of this stage in the life cycle. Never before in history have so many lived so long. It is a new experience for society, which suggests it will take time for appropriate social roles to evolve. What are we supposed to do when we are old? As already noted, most old people do not work for pay, their children have left the household to establish their own families, and they are still in relatively good health and can function well.

The elderly spend much of their time with others, with family members and with friends. Interaction with family members tends to revolve around visits and family get-togethers which include a host of interactional exchanges: emotional support, sharing and exchanging of goods and information, companionship, and assistance. Within the family, intergenerational relations tend to be confined only to two generations—children and grandchildren— although this may change as the demographic shift leads to many three- and four-generation families. While the elderly's interaction with their

Table 10-7 Average Income of Families and Unattached Individuals by Gender and Age Group, 1971–1985

	MALE		FEMALE	
Year	*65–69*	*70+*	*65–69*	*70+*
1971	$ 7 172	$ 5 007	$ 3 987	$ 3 468
1973	8 341	6 475	4 654	4 019
1975	10 995	7 741	5 968	4 837
1979	15 761	12 317	9 194	7 553
1981	21 700	16 131	12 258	10 724
1982	24 220	20 839	13 837	11 273
1985	29 090	23 093	14 898	14 506

SOURCES: All figures come from Statistics Canada, *Income Distribution by Size in Canada.*

1971–Table 38, 61, CS13-207, 1971
1973–Table 41, 74, CS13-207, 1973
1975–Table 41, 76, CS13-207, 1975
1979–Table 45, 88, CS13-207, 1979
1981–Table 45, 96, CS13-207, 1981
1982–Table 45, 94, CS13-207, 1982
1985–Table 45, 98, CS13-207, 1985

Reproduced with permission of the Minister of Supply and Services Canada.

grandchildren tends to be social, with their children it often includes the additional component of assistance. Canadian society does not appear to value "volunteer activity," as is evident in the fact that only 21 percent of adults engaged in such tasks in 1980 (Statistics Canada, 1980). Among the elderly the figure is about the same and these tend to be people who engaged in volunteer work when they were younger.

Interactions with friends (age peers) are as important for the elderly as they are for the young. Most of us desire the company of those having similar experiences, who share common histories, who view the future from a similar standpoint. Age peers share these things with one another.

One of the challenges of understanding life in old age today is doing so from the viewpoint of the elderly themselves. As Roadburg (1985) has noted, the elderly define leisure differently than do those working for pay. Retirees tend to define leisure in terms of enjoyment and relaxation; those working for pay, in terms of free time. Since the elderly consider their days free time, they unsurprisingly cease to associate free time with leisure. Nevertheless, we know that those things in life which contribute to personal happiness, such as good health, good relations with family and friends, and socio-economic means, are common to younger and older persons. Continuity into old age of the life style that prevailed in one's middle years is also considered important.

Contemporary elders in Canada do not usually perform roles which society considers important and functional, but the implications of their decline in status are not really known. Friedmann and Orbach (1974) suggest that most elders adjust well to retirement since it is perceived and accepted as a normal and expected phase in the life cycle. The roles and activities that contribute most to our identity and self-esteem during old age are also not known. Lack of knowledge in these areas stems from a major emphasis in studying role losses (widowhood and retirement, for example) in old age rather than role involvements. Only recently have some researchers started to study the more positive aspects of later life. Clearly health declines in old age, even though for most it is not a period of total handicap. Nevertheless, when deterioration is experienced, elderly people turn to their family and friends, just as younger members of society do.

SUPPORT SYSTEMS IN OLD AGE

As noted at the beginning of this chapter, many studies have found that the isolated nuclear family is not common in Western industrial societies. Similarly, there is little evidence to support the prevalence of the classical extended family in pre-industrial societies. The three-generation family living under one roof, with elders playing important roles, is not widespread in Europe and almost nonexistent in the United States (Laslett, 1976).

Fewer people lived to the age of 65 years in pre-industrial periods and, of those who did, not all lived comfortably. Nevertheless, the family as the centre of intimate relationships has historically provided, as it does now, interpersonal support, warmth, and commitment for people of all ages. Indeed, evidence suggests that support from kin and friends is the primary source of assistance (informal care) for elders in contemporary society. Estimates from the United States suggest that approximately 80 percent of all care (excluding emotional support) is currently provided by close relatives and friends (Biaggi, 1980). Canadian data (Chappell, 1985; Chappell and Havens, 1985) indicate that 94 percent of elders receiving any assistance do so from informal networks. In addition, 80 percent of the 15 percent who receive formal care from, for example, community service agencies and hospitals receive care from family and friends simultaneously.

Assistance refers primarily to instrumental activities of daily living. Elderly persons often have family or friends who help in these matters. While few elderly people are impaired in terms of basic activities of daily living, dysfunctions in any one of them is serious and can lead to long-term institutional care, especially when family and friends cannot provide assistance.

Almost everyone needs companions and intimate confidantes. This is no less true during one's old age than during one's younger years, and almost all elderly people report having both. A recent Winnipeg study (Chappell,

1987) indicates 96 percent of the elderly have companionship and 84 percent have confidante relationships. Among those who are married, men and women are equally likely to consider their spouse a companion. However, men are more likely to name their spouse as a confidante. Women—even those who are married—are more likely to name a daughter or a friend either instead of or in addition to the spouse. Men seem to rely emotionally more exclusively on their spouses than do women; women seem to be more successful at substituting friendship for family ties (Hess and Waring, 1980).

In a complex post-industrial society such as Canada, an individual (regardless of age) confronts the problem of coping with a massive barrage of information. For effective decision-making and efficient use of services, the average person has to develop the capacity to collect relevant information on matters critical for day-to-day living. For example, if a specific service or form of assistance is available to an average Canadian and he or she does not know about it, that person would be deprived of such a service. In this regard, little is known about the "informational needs" of the elderly in Canada. It is imperative that the elderly people know of the various services and forms of assistance available to them so that they can determine those that suit their needs and, having done so, determine the most efficient way of receiving them. Researchers and professionals are concerned with finding appropriate methods of providing the elderly with pertinent information, including suggestions regarding options and their suitability to their needs—for example, which of the latest health fads and exercise programs suit senior citizens in a community.

The quality of supportive relationships frequently depends on who is involved. Relationships with spouses, for example, differ from those with daughters. We turn next to a discussion of the patterns of kin support for the elderly.

Spouses

The spouse plays a vital role in assisting his or her partner all through the marital career, a role that extends into old age and can become critical. Older couples tend to redistribute domestic and other chores when the health of either or both deteriorates. Because women generally marry men older than themselves and have a greater life expectancy, they are more likely than their husbands to assume care-giving roles: as women age, therefore, they shoulder more responsibility and work. Nevertheless, the advantages of the marital relationship are believed to extend beyond the care-giving role to include sustained companionship. Hess and Soldo (1985) note that older couples are more likely than singles of comparable age to live in a household by themselves, to own their own building and, even at the extremes of old age and functional disability, much less likely to be institutionalized. Spouses are more likely than others to provide care for greater disability and illness. The husband and wife unit appears to be well-suited to the provision of care, especially for chronic conditions.

Children

In one's old age, the most frequent caregivers other than the spouse are children, especially daughters. The roles played by daughters and sons are somewhat different and often gender-based. Daughters provide physical and emotional care, sons provide supervision and money, if and when needed. If, however, a daughter is unavailable either because there is none or because of distance, sons do take on the extra roles (Horowitz, 1981; Lipman and Longino, 1983).

The proportion of senior citizens who live with or near a child has remained relatively constant throughout the decade; most live close to at least one child (Hanson and Sauer, 1985; Marshall et al., 1981). Elderly people prefer "intimacy at a distance:" they prefer to maintain their independence as much as possible as well as maintain relations with their children. They prefer not to live with their children.

Some research findings suggest children are the only source of informal care other than the spouse for the elderly. Lopata (1978) studied widows' economic support systems (gifts of food, money, clothing), service support systems (transportation, help in making major decisions, help in child care, shopping), social support systems (movies, visits, sports, and other shared social activities), and emotional support systems (sentiments about themselves and about others). She concluded that most of her subjects (widows in the Chicago area) were very independent and called upon their children for all but economic matters. She concluded that the functionality of any but the parent-child ties in the kinship network had been strongly exaggerated.

Other Relatives

After the spouse and children, other relatives (brother, sisters, grandchildren, nieces, nephews, cousins, in-laws) are believed to be the most frequent source of assistance. Some gerontologists (for example, Cantor, 1979) believe assistance is provided through an orderly, hierarchical selection process determined by the primacy of the relationship between the giver and the recipient. This pattern suggests a preferential order—spouse first, followed by daughters, sons, other relatives, and friends and neighbours. Other gerontologists postulate a task specificity model (Litwak, 1985), where the nature of the task is most important for determining who provides assistance. Spouses are said to be best at providing assistance requiring long-term commitments and a close continued proximity. Other kin are said to provide the best support in areas requiring long-term commitment but no close proximity (such as during prolonged illness). Friends are best suited in instances where mutual affection and similarity of experiences are important; neighbours where proximity but not long-term commitment is necessary, such as emergencies and loans of household items. Which of these explanations (hierarchical selection or task specificity) is correct, if either, is not known.

Despite their differences, both the hierarchical and task specificity models suggest that the elderly turn to the formal care system only when the care is not provided by family or friends. However, research on care provided by kin other than the spouse, children, or friendship groups is scant. To date there are few studies that systematically compare the nature and frequency of assistance provided to the elderly by such informal groups as kin and friends, and the nature and frequency of assistance provided by such formal groups as social and medical service agencies.

The evidence on the importance of "other relatives" is, however, not consistent, particularly in studies of widowhood. Lopata (1978) found that her Chicago-area widows call on their friends as companions only for social activities. Siblings and other relatives were not important contributors to the aspects of life she studied.

However, Canadian data on widows suggest that siblings are important "other kin." Martin Matthews (1987) reported substantial support from siblings, especially sisters. Harvey and Harris (1985), in another Canadian study, reported that the median contact with siblings among widows was two or three times a month. Furthermore, Chappell (1987) found that, among her Canadian respondents, siblings were important sources of support, after the spouse and children. These researchers observed that their respondents in Canada maintained a higher level of residential stability than Lopata's Chicago-area widows. Another difference between the Canadian respondents and Lopata's was the tendency among the Chicago-area widows to live with their children.

Non-Kin

There is little research on the role friends play in the life of elders, although impressionistic evidence indicates that friends constitute an important part in the lives of contemporary Canadians, including senior citizens. Unlike kinship ties, friendship bonds are characterized by voluntary involvement, affective bonds, and consensus. Friends tend to be similar: they have comparable characteristics in terms of age, role, socio-economic status, and they are usually of the same sex. They share common experiences, including the demands of changes in their marital and family careers. However, even though friendships can involve serious commitment and endure, the obligation to friends is believed to be smaller than it is to family.

A recent study in Winnipeg (Chappell, 1987) compared the role of family members with non-family members in their provision of care (basic activities of daily living and instrumental activities of daily living) and emotional support. The elders were asked about the support from the social network they believed was available in times of need, as well as about persons who were currently giving them support. The data confirmed previous findings: the marital or couple relationship is crucial in old age. However, the benefits of such a relationship are not always reciprocal—when one of the spouses, usually the husband, experiences a deterioration in health the wife tends to provide care. Consequently, the husband is effectively removed from the role of potential provider of care for his wife. Virtually all the elderly persons in the study recognized the presence of a large network of individuals that included their own immediate and extended kin and friends.

According to the study, when a spouse was absent, children, particularly daughters, were the most likely providers of care. A substantial proportion of the respondents also named their extended kin and friends. Importantly, the modified extended family as a source of care tended not to be intergenerational beyond children. Elderly individuals tended to step outside their extended-kin network in times of need rather than jump a second generation to their grandchildren. In terms of actual assistance, friends provided care prior to the extended kin but after the spouse, children, and siblings had done so. That is, the modified extended family of actual caregiving extended to spouse, children, and siblings, with non-kin helping out when these kin were overextended, unavailable, or did not provide assistance.

Friends are of similar ages. In old age, they share similar experiences such as retirement, widowhood, and children leaving home. They also share adjustments to declining health, common interests based on similar generational experiences in a rapidly changing society, and the pressure of coping with relative proximity to death. Some gerontologists (for example, Haas-Hawkings, 1978) believe that friendships, because they rest on mutual choice and mutual need, and involve a voluntary exchange of sociability between equals, are especially important in sustaining a person's sense of usefulness and self-esteem.

Loss of friendship through death is inevitable in old age. Nevertheless, new friendships can be established at any age. Lopata (1975) argues that those who develop their social skills earlier in life are the ones who will fare better during old age.

In this section, we have discussed different kin relations (spouse, children, siblings, and so on) and their supportiveness in old age. It should also be noted that relationships have negative as well as positive aspects and some, on balance, are far from completely beneficial for those involved.

Cohler and Lieberman (1980) found much stress involved in "supportive relationships" among three European ethnic groups. Cantor (1983) reports that providers of care who are emotionally close to the recipient experience more stress than those who are less emotionally attached. Hagestad (1981) has drawn our attention to the overload and strain which can accompany the "bridge position" of the middle generation—two generations (their children and aging parents) claim their time, material resources, energy, and emotions.

When family and friends can no longer cope with the provision of care, or if there is no informal network to provide care, the formal care system is established to ensure that the needs of the elderly are met. The next section turns to a discussion of the Canadian health care system.

THE ELDERLY AND THE FORMAL CARE SYSTEM

Estimates suggest that only 20 percent of assistance for the elderly comes from the formal care system (Biaggi, 1980). Nevertheless, concerns over the increasing costs of such a system are expressed, and elderly persons are the greatest adult users of that system. It is important to note, however, that a small proportion of the elderly (about 20 percent) are very heavy users of formal services, while the remainder use no more than the average adult (Roos et al., 1984). Furthermore, while health-care costs are increasing, the rate of increase in Canada is less than that in most industrialized nations. Evans (1984) estimated that we spent over $30 billion in 1982 on national health expenditures (including hospitals, physician services, dental services, prescribed drugs, and personal health care). This represented 8.4 percent of our gross national product.

Institutional Care   Facilities for long-term care (nursing homes, homes for the elderly, personal care homes) are established for those who cannot cope on their own, with or without the help of family and friends. While much was said about long-term institutional care in the 1960s and 1970s, less than 10 percent of the elderly in Canada are in long-term institutional care at any one time. In 1981, only about 6.7 percent of the elderly were in long-term institutions. However, about 33 percent of those aged 85 and over lived in nursing homes in that year (Chappell et al., 1986). That is, while the proportion in institutions at any given time is small, one quarter to one third of elderly persons can expect to spend some time in a long-term care facility before they die.

Physicians and Hospitals   Other aspects of the formal care system are comprised largely of physicians and acute-care hospitals. As has been argued elsewhere (Chappell et al., 1986), Canada's health care system is oriented mainly to medical and institutional care. Evans (1976) pointed out that physicians control approximately 80 percent of insured health-care costs. Only 19 percent of the total health-care expenditures go directly to physicians, who nevertheless control or influence hospital admissions, pre- scriptions, medical tests, and recommendation of return visits. In essence, the physicians, not the patients, make decisions about the use of expensive health services. Patients usually can have access to hospitals only if admitted by a physician. Hospital costs, however, represent about half of total insured expenditures. Unravelling the practices of physicians from hospital utiliza- tion appears impossible: clearly physicians play a major role in the use of these institutions.

Data on utilization confirm that the focus of the current health care system is on the physician and the institution. From 1970 to 1979, 50 percent of insured health-care costs were received by the hospitals and nursing homes (institutional care), 25 percent was for salaries in professional services (in- cluding, but not exclusively, physician services), 10 percent for drugs and medical appliances, and only 15 percent for other costs (Statistics Canada, 1983). In terms of use, the Canada Health Survey (Health and Welfare Canada and Statistics Canada, 1981) reveals one or more visits to a physician by 85 percent of elderly persons in the previous year. Although figures for com- munity care are difficult to obtain, it is estimated that in 1981 0.8 percent of elderly persons received Meals on Wheels or similar services, 3.5 percent, transportation services, 4.3 percent, homemaker or home help services, 4.3 percent, assistance with shopping and banking, and 2.7 percent, nursing or other medical calls at home (Statistics Canada, 1983).

While the hospitals tend to concentrate on short-term acute care of the elders, the illnesses these individuals experience are mainly chronic con- ditions or acute flare-ups of chronic conditions. A major shortcoming of Canada's health-care system is its inability to meet adequately the needs of the chronically ill elderly, especially within the community. In gerontology, the importance of chronic disease, measured as the extent to which one's ability to function is impaired, assumes a broad definition of health. Such a definition includes economic, social, and psychological, as well as medical aspects. All of these aspects can affect functioning.

Community Services   In Canada, not until the 1970s was there a sub- stantial growth in home health-care services. At that time there was rec- ognition that existing resources were most able to meet the needs of the very sick (nursing homes) and the very healthy (housing units), but less able to meet the needs of those in between. Early home care programs offered medical and related services essentially to shorten hospital stays rather than to treat and maintain people who need chronic or long-term care.

In the late 1970s, scholars and other interested persons critically ex-

amined long-term institutional care for the elderly. Dulude (1978), for example, reported that fully 45 percent of the elderly in nursing homes in
1975 were self-sufficient. That is, almost half of these people could have
remained in the community with proper support. Appropriate levels of
community support are considered less expensive than institutional care.
The aging of the population has raised concerns that there will be greater
and more costly demands made on an already expensive medical care
system. This has intensified the search for alternatives.

In 1975, the number and variety of home care programs were growing
but there was little consistency in objectives, eligibility criteria, services
offered, staffing, the use of terms, or funding. At that time, Manitoba was
the only province with a universal home care program that was not dependent on medical authorization. During the mid- to late-1970s, home care
programs emerged which, in turn, led to a comprehensive definition of
services.

Community support services are important not only in the services they
offer elderly people directly but also in the assistance they offer the one
who provides the care. Care-givers do not want to relinquish their role, but
they do want sufficient assistance so that they do not suffer burnout or a
decline in their own health that would curtail their ability to continue. Caregivers, especially those giving total or close to total care, need relief to
conserve their limited resources; they need appropriate information on what
care they should be providing and how they ought to do it; they need
support from others who understand what they are going through.

Health-Care Systems

There is at present little understanding of the interplay between informal
and formal care systems. Some evidence suggests that elders initially turn
to their kin and friends; only after they exhaust these sources do they seek
assistance from professionals. It is now also evident that the use of formal
services is found much less frequently than reliance either exclusively on
the informal network or on both sources (Evans and Northwood, 1979). A
Winnipeg study (Chappell, 1987) found that those elderly who engage in
self-care tend to be the ones who also use formal care services. However,
whether one receives assistance from family and friends is unrelated to
whether one uses self-care or formal services. Given the self-initiated nature
of contact with formal services (especially with physicians), formal care can
be viewed as a type of self-care: by and large, individuals decide by themselves whether to go to a doctor, just as they decide for themselves to take
up an exercise program or to eat certain types of foods. The data further
suggest that individuals within the social network, if they are available, help

elderly individuals in times of short-term incapacity. However, for longer-term conditions they turn to the formal health care system.

POLICY ISSUES

It is important for any social policy to begin from an informed and accurate understanding of the group concern. For too long there has been a focus on the problem of the elderly and the problems for society associated with them. A closer examination of findings in this area suggests that old age is not the period of devastating decline in health as it was believed to be in the past. Rather, decline in health is gradual and individuals generally adjust to it. The health of most aged persons is relatively good. In addition, very few elderly persons are isolated either from family or from friends. Gerontological research has found that the notion of the isolated nuclear family is not applicable to the elderly. Rather, family intimacy at a distance more accurately describes the preference and reality of life styles of the elderly. Elderly people frequently interact and have exchanges with family members, but they prefer to maintain their independence and autonomy and not live with their children.

A major question that still remains to be addressed concerns the role for the elderly in Canadian society: should society consider a directly beneficial role for the elderly? At present, the elderly usually relinquish major social roles, such as paid labour, child rearing, and so on. It is still not clear whether a more actively contributive role will evolve for the elderly, or whether, given the elderly's proximity to death, it would be better for society for no such role to emerge.

Nevertheless, contemporary Canadian elders are pioneers of a new but uncertain society. For the first time in history more people are living longer than ever before. Today's elderly are shaping and defining a role in society for the elderly in the future. They have shown us the strength and importance of family ties even in twentieth-century post-industrial society. It is critical to understand the role played by family and friends: not to do so may lead one to the conclusion that more pressure should be put on families to care for their elderly members. However, evidence clearly shows that this would be counterproductive. Family and friends already shoulder their share of the burdens involved in caring for the elderly. Indeed, they need relief to enable them to continue with their current load.

Existing studies do not support the suggestions by some social policy experts that family members be given financial incentives to care for elderly members. Arling and McAuley (1983) report that major sources of stress or strain among providers of care are not financial. Emotional stress and restraints in time and freedom are the most common complaints. Other studies reported similar results (Sussman, 1976; Noelker and Poulshock, 1982).

Providers of care are not asking for financial incentives. They do not wish to relinquish their role; they do, however, require emotional support and relief in order to continue playing it and to maintain their own health.

Another reason to expand community social services for the elderly is the need for more adequate care for the elderly themselves. The elderly suffer more with chronic conditions than with acute illnesses: for most of their lives they can cope at home with appropriate community supports. However, without these supports, many have no option but to enter long-term institutional care.

The recognition of the importance of community and social services for an aging population is occurring at a time when a powerful, expensive, specialized, and technologically complex medical system is already in place. In Canada and in the United States this system generally has not undergone a major transformation in response to the changing composition of the elderly population. McKeown (1979), Dubos (1963), and McKinlay and McKinlay (1977) have demonstrated that the decline in mortality rates in this century is not primarily due to medical intervention. Maxwell (1975) and Weller and Manga (1982) have shown that the major illnesses experienced by the elderly are chronic rather than acute illnesses, and health-care expenditures have little relationship to health outcome (for example, whether the patient will die). Syme and Berkman (1981) and Grant (1984) have shown, however, that social class and poverty correlate significantly with personal health. The socio-economically disadvantaged in our society are more likely to suffer from various illnesses and to die earlier than the more advantaged. This is not to deny, of course, the important roles physicians play in successfully mending bones, using drugs to stop the spread of infection, or performing important surgery. However, a mere increase in the number of doctors and hospitals and the provision of more and better prescription drugs would not necessarily address the complex needs and demands of an aging society.

CONCLUSION

In this chapter we have provided an overview of the elderly in Canada, arguing that they are a vital part of their families. While there are many differences found among elderly people, as among any age group, specific trends characterize this population: their numbers are increasing and will continue to do so until the baby boom reaches age 65. Moreover, the elderly population is itself aging—we have many more "old" old people in society than we used to, a trend that will continue for some time, and elderly women outnumber elderly men. It is important to note that old age is a different experience for women than it is for men. Women are much more likely than men to experience widowhood. Prior to that, a woman is likely the major provider of care for her husband in his last years. When their own health declines women are much more likely to receive assistance from their children, especially their daughters, from their siblings, and from their friends.

Much of old age is, however, characterized by relatively good health. The elderly spend much of their time socializing with and visiting family members and friends. These interactions are characterized by exchanges of information, of support, and of goods and services. However, when health deteriorates sufficiently and family and friends are no longer available, or are no longer able to provide support, the formal health-care system assumes the responsibility. We argue here that our health-care system, with its emphasis on medical and short-term acute care, is not particularly well suited to an aging society. However, the provision of supportive services from the community that take into account psychological, economic, social, as well as medical well-being, is more likely to meet the needs of an aging society. It is important to recognize that, even when formal services are being received, family members are important. Families who provide care themselves need support from that system, particularly in the form of respite care and informational services. However, even if an elderly member becomes institutionalized, family still plays an important role in visiting that individual, helping to maintain his or her identity, and providing support and information. Gerontological research confirms the overwhelming importance of family ties in old age.

Suggested Readings

Brody, Elaine.
   1981   "Women in the Middle and Family Help to Older People." *The Gerontologist* 13:412-417.

Cantor, Marjorie.
   1979   "Neighbours and Friends: An Overlooked Resource in the Informal Support System." *Research on Aging* 1:434-463.

Chappell, Neena, and Betty Havens.
   1985   "Who Helps the Elderly Person: A Discussion of Informal and Formal Care." In Warren Peterson and Jill Quadagno, eds., *Social Bonds in Later Life*. Beverly Hills, CA: Sage, 211-227.

Chappell, Neena, Laurel Strain, and Audrey Blandford.
   1986   *Aging and Health Care, A Social Perspective*. Toronto: Holt, Rinehart and Winston.

Gee, Ellen.
1987   "Historical Change in the Family Life Course of Canadian Men and Women." In Victor Marshall, ed., *Aging in Canada*. Markham: Fitzhenry & Whiteside, 265-287.

Hanson, Sandra, and William Sauer.
1985   "Children and their Elderly Parents." In William Sauer and Raymond Coward, eds., *Social Support Networks and the Care of the Elderly*. New York: Springer, 41-66.

Hess, Beth, and Beth Soldo.
1985   "Husband and Wife Networks." In William Sauer and Raymond Coward, eds., *Social Support Networks and the Care of the Elderly*. New York: Springer, 67-92.

Hess, Beth, and Joan Waring.
1980   "Changing Patterns of Aging and Family Bonds in Later Life." In Arlene Skolnick and Jerome Skolnick, eds., *Family in Transition*. Boston: Little, Brown.

Matthews, Anne Martin.
1987   "Widowhood as an Expectable Life Event." In Victor Marshall, ed., *Aging in Canada*. Second ed. Markham: Fitzhenry & Whiteside, 343-366.

Roos, Noralou, Evelyn Shapiro, and Leslie Roos.
1984   "Aging and the Demand for Health Services: Which Aged and Whose Demand?" *The Gerontologist* 24:31-36.

11

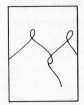

Divorce and Remarriage

John F. Peters

Although most Canadians who marry do not dissolve their marriages, the number of those who do is increasing. Besides the death of a spouse, there are numerous ways in which marriages are terminated, among them desertion (often called "a poor man's divorce"), separation, annulment, and divorce. Divorce is not only a legal termination of marriage but also a termination of emotional and personal commitment between spouses. In this chapter, some salient aspects of divorce in Canada, including changing laws, statistical trends, children of divorced parents, and remarriage, will be discussed. Also included is an account of the major theoretical perspectives on divorce.

Historically, marital dissolutions have always taken place in Canada, as they have elsewhere, although not as frequently or easily as in recent decades. The main reason for fewer divorces in the past was that the stability of marriage was assured by the strong influence of religious and social norms. Separated or divorced persons were socially stigmatized and often seen as unstable, fickle, or sinful. Children in single-parent familes, especially those in which fathers were absent, were pitied. Wives commonly took the blame for not keeping their marriages intact. In a milieu dominated by patriarchal values, women were expected to tolerate and accommodate the failings of their husbands so as to maintain the stability of marriage.

Furthermore, there was a qualitative difference in the nature of marriage. Interpersonal relations between spouses, determined by mutual commitment and love, also fulfilled rigid gender roles. Ideally, a good husband provided for the family, and a good wife looked after the needs of the children and husband. Physical affection between married couples was often confined to the bedroom and possibly dominated by the male. Religious values, especially those of Roman Catholicism, stipulated that excessive romanticism and sexuality were not to be part of marital life: sexual expression was permitted primarily for procreation. Personal affirmation and individual rights were not focal points of concern in marital relationship. However, with the increasing urbanization and industrialization of Canada, new values and aspirations have emerged. Secularism, individualism, and egalitarianism have changed the traditional character of marriage. Marriage, for most contemporary Canadians, has become a personal enterprise directed at the fulfilment of one's social, emotional, and sexual needs. Consequently, there is growing intolerance on the part of Canadians to stay in marriages that fail to meet their needs and this, in part, has led to the increasing number of divorces. Pressured by the changing approach to marriage and by those who seek divorce, the legal system has also changed.

LEGAL ASPECTS OF DIVORCE

To understand the legal aspects of divorce, we should bear in mind that legal codes governing divorce have changed over a period of time in response to social demands. In the last three decades laws pertaining to divorce in North America have moved toward what is called "no-fault divorce." Based on the work of Weitzman and Dixon (1986), the following section traces the changes in divorce laws in North America and then turns to Canadian laws on divorce.

Transition in the Divorce Law

Weitzman and Dixon (1986:338-351) have outlined four fundamental changes in laws which, in turn, have led to "no-fault divorce." First, divorce laws of the 1940s and the 1950s were based on the values and norms that supported the gender-based division of roles and responsibilities in traditional legal marriages. Such norms and values stipulated that the husband would support his wife and their children in a marriage that would last a lifetime. However, should divorce have occurred, the wife, if virtuous, would receive continued support, or alimony. The wife's duty was to raise children, and the husband's to provide economic support.

Second, traditional divorce laws specified grounds for divorce. Unless one of the spouses was declared to have committed a marital offence, divorce could not be obtained. Since marriage was deemed a permanent bond. it could be broken only by a serious marital offense such as adultery, cruelty, or desertion. It was in the state's interest to maintain the stability of marriage regardless of the marital satisfaction of individual couples. The state's interest in marriage and the family was to ensure a proper performance of two key functions: reproduction and socialization, which are assumed to be performed best by the family. As a result, the conditions for divorce were very stringent. Furthermore, the grounds for divorce were often sexist. In New Brunswick, for example, a husband could petition for divorce if his wife committed adultery, but the wife needed to prove her husband's adulterous behaviour in addition to cruelty in order to file for divorce.

Third, traditional legal divorce was based upon adversary proceedings. The success of the applicant depended on his or her ability to prove the other's marital offence. If both were found guilty, then the divorce was less likely to be granted. In general, however, the adversarial system in the courts of establishing the innocence or guilt of either of the spouses led to abuses, collusion, and inequities.

Fourth, "traditional divorce law linked the financial terms of the divorce to the determination of fault" (Weitzman and Dixon, 1986:343). It was the intent of the courts not only to determine the guilt or innocence of the partners in question, but to find the degree of their guilt, and to punish or reward accordingly. The wife found guilty of adultery was usually not awarded alimony while the husband found guilty of cruelty or adultery was asked to pay his wife for the transgression. Thus, matrimonial property was used as a tool to punish the partner who was at fault, and to reward the innocent or offended partner. In practice, the legal system almost always found the husband guilty with the result that the wife was entitled to continued protection after divorce. Weitzman and Dixon argue further that custody awards were also associated with the principle of fault. When proven guilty, the wife was readily identified as an "unfit" mother and, therefore, deprived of the benefit of being preferred custodial parent.

In recent years, however, the "fault principle" governing the divorce laws has given way to "no-fault divorce," an indication of changing attitudes toward marriage and divorce in North America. The phenomenon of no-fault divorce is a legal attempt "to bring divorce legislation in line with the social realities of marital breakdown in contemporary society" (Weitzman and Dixon, 1986:345). It is based on the recognition of conditions where "unreconcilable differences have caused the irremediable breakdown of the marriage." Those who advocate the no-fault divorce have many reasons to do so. Their principal aim, however, is to eliminate the hypocrisy, perjury, and collusion that had become part of the legal proceedings under the traditional fault system (Kay, 1968:1223). Furthermore, the no-fault divorce law helps "to reduce the adversity, acrimony and bitterness surrounding divorce, and to create conditions for more rational and equitable settlements of property and spousal support" (Hogoboom, 1970).

In essence, the no-fault divorce law permits a couple to dissolve their marriage without establishing the fault of either partner. An acknowledgment by either or both that their marriage has broken down is sufficient for the court to issue a decree. Furthermore, no-fault divorce and traditional law have two contrasting perspectives on the marriage contract. In traditional law, violators of the contract were punished and victims were legally protected. The no-fault law, on the other hand, does not use the moral character of the partners or the history of the marriage as criteria in determining rewards. Justice is based instead on the equality of husband and wife, and fairness demands an equal share of property for both parties.

The Canadian Divorce Laws

The history of divorce law in Canada reflects a transition in the legal grounds for divorce: prior to 1968 the grounds were primarily marital offences, and in 1968 marital breakdown was added. Amendments of Canadian divorce law in 1986 moved the grounds closer to no-fault divorce.

Canadian legislation pertaining to divorce is under federal rather than provincial jurisdiction. Therefore, unlike the United States, Canada has one legal standard for divorce throughout the nation, the roots of which are in the English law. Also to be noted is the strong influence that was exercised by the Anglican church in English Canada and by the Roman Catholic church and the agrarian nature of society in Québec. The result was the maintenance of inflexible divorce laws for nearly a century after Confederation. For example, prior to the liberalization of divorce laws, the courts granted divorce in the event of a marital offence, either physical cruelty or adultery. The judicial system sought to punish the offending party. There was a double standard, with greater facility for divorce for the male applicant. In fact, Québec courts did not deal with divorce until 1968. Prior to this date the number of legal divorces in Canada were relatively few. However, as Pike (1975) argues, the low divorce rate before 1968 is not necessarily an indication of marital stability. Given the complex, costly, and time-consuming divorce procedures, many of those who would have divorced in a more liberal context opted for "empty-shell" marriages, marriages with little or no emotional content.

A more liberal approach to divorce emerged when the Québec religious establishment's domination over Canadian divorce laws and morality declined. Besides, there was considerable pressure on the lawmakers to amend the antiquated divorce laws in response to social and cultural changes that Canada had experienced in recent decades. Other western countries had adopted a more modern view at least a decade earlier and it was argued that Canada too should move in this direction. The result was the legislation passed in 1968 expanding the grounds on which one could seek divorce in Canada.

The Divorce Act of 1968   The Divorce Act of 1968 made a distinction between two broad categories of grounds on which divorce could be petitioned: marital offences and marital breakdown. The list of marital offences includes adultery and physical and mental cruelty. The marriage breakdown clause includes addiction to alcohol, separation, and desertion. This category was introduced to reduce blame and guilt and to permit individuals socially and psychologically to live past a marriage which, for all practical purposes, has broken down beyond reconciliation. Separation, as a legal basis for divorce, could only be used after establishing to the court that the couple had lived apart for three years; the period of desertion was set at five years.

Although the 1968 reform of the divorce laws in Canada was significant, the changes were less extensive than earlier developments that occurred in other Western societies. Consequently, demands for further changes were made by various groups. The Canadian Bar Association, the Federal Advisory Council on the Status of Women, and the Law Reform Commission of Canada all petitioned for further reforms. Their two main concerns were (a) the divorce process always had to have a guilty party, and (b) the lengthy three-year wait for what was considered divorce without fault. The main arguments in favour of further changes to the divorce laws were that the traditional approach to marriage was no longer tenable in a society that was undergoing sweeping socio-economic changes, including changes in the status of women both within and outside marriage and the family. Moreover, other Western societies, such as Sweden and a number of the states in the United States, already had in place more flexible divorce laws. In response to such pressures, Canadian lawmakers further amended the divorce laws in 1986 and effectively created the opportunity for couples seeking divorce to opt for no-fault divorce, or at least the Canadian version of it.

The Divorce Act of 1986   The Divorce Act passed on July 3, 1986, retains several characteristics of the older act. For example, the matrimonial offences clause that permits divorce for reasons of adultery and physical and mental cruelty remains intact. However, the petitioner may now seek divorce after one year of separation rather than after three years. A couple may even petition before the completion of one year of separation and be issued a decree of divorce by the time the full year of separation has ended; should both parties agree to divorce the decree absolute could theoretically be granted the day after application, or as soon as a judge holds the hearing.

These developments seem to give Canadians a version of no-fault divorce, a type of marriage dissolution enacted and agreed to by the two principal parties who initiated the union in the first place. As in the past, couples may attempt to reconcile by living together for up to 90 days at one time within the one-year separation period. Such co-residence does not invalidate the one-year separation clause. Cases which are contested, or cases involving physical or mental cruelty involve more complex legal procedures.

The amended law clearly stipulates that no collusion, condonation, or connivance can take place in the divorce courts. Collusion refers to conspiracy to fabricate or suppress evidence, to deceive the administration of justice in the courts. Condonation has reference to the accused party's approval of actions deemed eligible for divorce (for example, condoning adultery or physical abuse). Connivance occurs when one party lies to incriminate the other, for instance, implying one of the grounds for divorce has taken place when in fact it has not. Should the court find these impediments, the case is dismissed.

The Divorce Act of 1986 is subtitled, "An Act respecting divorce and corollary relief." Although custody and the division of matrimonial assets are under provincial jurisdiction, the Act has some relevant statements regarding these family matters, and merits some discussion.

The new law has at least three provisions which are aimed at the preservation of the institution of the family in Canada. The first pertains to reconciliation. The legal advisor must by law inform the spouse that the legal process has the intent or wish of reconciliation and thus must inform the client of marriage counselling or guidance. Furthermore, the legal advisor must inform the spouse of mediation services. The courts must satisfy themselves that there is no possibility of reconciliation of the spouses. Should reconciliation seem possible, the court is ordered by law to adjourn.

The second provision addresses child custody. The child(ren)'s "best interest" is of prime importance to the courts. Unless there is some justifiable reason to the contrary, *both* parents must have access to the child. The non-custodial parent must have knowledge of the child's "health, education and welfare." In the event of a change of residence the non-custodial parent must be informed a month in advance. Both parents "have joint financial obligation to maintain the child." Nevertheless, it should be kept in mind that although the new law, for the first time in Canadian history, recognizes the possibility of joint custody, the courts still retain considerable discretion in awarding it. This leaves room for rancour if a judge assigns the custody of the child to either of the parents.

The third provision concerns judgments relating to property or children. The adulterous person is not to be disfavoured, nor is the virtuous or innocent party to be rewarded for past behaviour.

The new law will not, however, satisfy all Canadians and it is subject to enormous discretion on the part of the judges. For example, some judges may lean toward a financial settlement which favours the principal wage earner, a value deeply rooted in the capitalistic way of life and which will often be propitious for the husband. Judges as well as some members of the public prefer mothers to gain custody of children. Some traditionalists still feel it is unfair that the adulterer or neglectful parent should go through divorce unpenalized.

Within the new law is the desire that divorced women's ability to enter the labour force and prosper be equal to that of men. Given the social handicaps women experience owing to their gender, few social scientists consider this facet of the law practical, at least for the immediate future. Men and women who began their career in the 1970s have a distinct advantage over women who entered careers in the late 1980s, especially those in middle age. Nonetheless, it should be recognized that the implementation of no-fault divorce is a step toward eventual socio-economic equality between men and women.

Fundamentally, three elements in the traditional divorce law have been altered by the recent Divorce Act. First, it allows the applicants to choose grounds for divorce other than those included in the marital offences provision. Should the plaintiff accept the one-year separation, he or she need not testify against the other for such marital offences as adultery, cruelty, or desertion. The "irreconcilable differences" are now not explained in the Divorce Act, an example of the legal process being neutral rather than condemnatory. The recent Divorce Act precludes the adversary process for those who choose to dissolve their marriages with a one-year separation, the intention being that much of the trauma involved in proceedings employing "fault" as grounds for divorce will be eliminated and psychological damage to the parties and families involved will be reduced.

Second, the financial aspects of the divorce are now based ideally on equity, equality, and economic need, not on fault or gender-based role assignments. Financial settlements take into consideration the economic situations rather than weight of the partner's guilt or innocence. Men and women in divorce are not burdened with the responsibility of traditional gender roles. The new norms, evident in the modern social reality, are the bases for certain aspects of the new Act. The intent of certain sections of the new legislation is to facilitate adjustment in the post-divorce period. The traditional assumption that a husband had to continue to support his wife, possibly for life, is becoming a thing of the past. Hofstadter and Levittan (1967:55) state that the traditional divorce laws created a "host of physically and mentally competent young women into an army of alimony drones." Canadian law also holds both parents responsible for child support.

Third, no-fault divorce establishes, in principle at least, equality between sexes. The husband is not viewed as the head of the family, nor the wife the sole caretaker of children: she is responsible for her own economic support and in most provinces property is divided equally.

In sum, the 1986 Divorce Act has moved a step closer to no-fault divorce. The Act has retained offences such as adultery and cruelty as fault grounds for an immediate divorce, but has simultaneously reduced the no-fault waiting period from three years to one year. Also important in the new Act is the scrapping of a judicial hearing for uncontested cases. No law could address the needs of all persons and the revised Divorce Act certainly does not, yet it now provides means for those who wish to eliminate ruinous legal costs, interpersonal rancour, the use of child custody as a bargaining chip, and the pain and trauma associated with divorce: a couple can now conceivably opt for one-year separation (essentially, no-fault) and seek divorce without a judicial hearing. From this point of view, the Act is humane and responds to the demands of couples in conflict.

DIVORCE RATES IN CANADA

Divorce Rates

Statistical assessments of the incidence of divorce are usually made annually and reported as crude and refined divorce rates. The crude divorce rate is calculated on the basis of the number of divorces granted each year per 100 000 population. It is labelled "crude" because the referent population of 100 000 includes every Canadian regardless of age or marital status. Nevertheless, this is the most common method of measuring the incidence of divorce in most societies. Table 11-1 presents the data on the incidence of divorce in Canada in terms of frequencies and the crude rate. It is evident that, following the 1968 reform in the divorce law, the rates gradually increased, reaching their peak in 1982, and since then they appear to have stabilized. Although the increasing divorce rate in Canada has alarmed many people, compared to that of other industrial societies it is rather low. For example, among the Western nations, the United States has the highest rate; rates in Canada, Sweden, and Australia are comparatively low.

Because the crude divorce rate overlooks several important demographic factors, demographers and sociologists prefer to use what is termed the refined divorce rate. The refined rates are calculated in terms of the number of divorces granted annually per 100 000 married women aged 15 years or

Table 11-1   Frequency and Crude Divorce Rates for Canada for Selected Years (per 100 000 population)

Year	Frequency	Rate	Year	Frequency	Rate
1921	558	6.4	1976	54 207	235.8
1931	700	6.8	1978	57 155	243.4
1941	2 462	21.4	1979	59 474	251.3
1951	5 270	37.6	1980	62 019	259.1
1961	6 563	36.0	1981	67 671	278.0
1968	11 343	54.8	1982	70 436	285.9
1969	26 093	124.2	1983	68 567	275.5
1970	29 775	139.8	1984	65 172	259.4
1971	29 685	137.6	1985	61 980	244.4

SOURCE: Statistics Canada, *Marriage and Divorces, Vital Statistics*, vol. II, 1970–1985. Reproduced with permission of the Minister of Supply and Services Canada.

Table 11-2   Divorce Rates for 100 000 Females of Age 15+ for
Selected Years

Year	Rate	Percent change	Year	Rate	Percent change
1970	621.0	11.6	1978	1016.1	2.2
1971	607.2	-2.2	1979	1050.4	3.4
1972	649.9	7.0	1980	1084.8	3.3
1973	716.4	10.2	1981	1129.2	4.2
1974	860.1	19.5	1982	1164.4	3.1
1975	942.4	9.6	1983	1125.2	-3.4
1976	985.6	4.6	1984	1061.9	-5.6
1977	994.2	0.9	1985	1003.5	-5.5

SOURCE: Statistics Canada, *Vital Statistics, 1976–85*, Ottawa. Reproduced with permission of the Minister of Supply and Services Canada.

older. In Table 11-2, the refined rates for the period between 1969 and 1985 are given. The dramatic change in rate occurred in 1969, a year after the reformed divorce laws came into effect. It is apparent that those who were waiting for the amended laws made use of them to dissolve their marriages. If we ignore the incidence of divorce for that year, we note a gradual increase up to 1982 and then a slow decline. There are few sociological or demographic explanations for the declining trend. It may be hypothesized that declining marriage rates, the rise in the average age at marriage, the increasing number of singles and the voluntarily childless, and the increasing number of those who live together without legal marriage have all contributed to fewer marriages which, in turn, have led to a slight decline in divorce.

A measurement the popular press frequently uses is a comparison of the number of divorces with the number of marriages in any given year. According to this method of calculation, the number of divorces per 1000 marriages in Canada for the years 1982 to 1985 were 374, 371, 351, and 367. If this method is taken seriously, as some journalists and social commentators do, one out of three marriages in 1985 ended in divorce. However, this measurement is not sociologically valid. The error lies in the fact that the number of divorces comes from a population not just of those who married in a given year but also of those who married in previous years.

Provincial Variation

The data in Table 11-3 on crude and refined divorce rates of provinces suggests three general patterns. First, with the exception of Nova Scotia, the Atlantic provinces register lower divorce rates than most other provinces.

Table 11-3   Crude and Refined Divorce Rates by Province for Selected Years

PROVINCE	1971		1976		1981		1985	
	C.D.R.	*R.D.R.*	*C.D.R.*	*R.D.R.*	*C.D.R.*	*R.D.R.*	*C.D.R.*	*R.D.R.*
Newfoundland	28.7	145.1	76.0	355.7	100.2	447.2	96.6	430.9
P.E.I.	54.7	265.2	98.1	442.7	152.6	660.3	167.6	722.0
Nova Scotia	91.6	418.8	211.6	920.7	269.6	1132.7	265.4	1122.5
New Brunswick	76.1	359.5	138.5	605.6	191.6	805.8	189.1	809.1
Québec	86.3	400.5	243.6	1040.8	298.1	1237.1	240.3	1035.1
Ontario	158.5	669.2	224.9	914.4	251.4	995.5	230.0	909.7
Manitoba	140.1	611.7	190.0	799.4	233.8	959.4	216.3	897.6
Saskatchewan	88.1	391.5	131.0	554.4	199.5	821.7	189.0	784.0
Alberta	224.6	993.5	309.9	1317.2	376.2	1555.7	344.9	1431.4
B.C.	225.6	948.7	333.7	1346.9	347.4	1361.6	288.0	1134.4
Yukon/N.W.T.	332.5	711.1	194.1	976.6	204.7	984.0	228.0	1120.0

SOURCE: Statistics Canada, 1975–1985, *Marriages and Divorces, Vital Statistics*, Ottawa. Reproduced with permission of the Minister of Supply and Services Canada.

Second, Ontario, Manitoba, and Saskatchewan tend to maintain moderate rates, placing them in the middle of the two extreme positions. Third, Alberta, British Columbia, and the Yukon and Northwest Territories have consistently shown higher rates than most Canadian provinces. The rates in Québec have been low until recently because of the influence of Catholicism. However, in recent years the influence of the Roman Catholic church has considerably declined with the result that divorce rates have risen.

Increases and declines in provincial rates should be considered over a long period of time in order to draw an accurate picture. Québec registered 13 899 divorces in 1980 and 19 193 in 1981. This is an increase of 38 percent in one year. Divorces consistently dropped annually for the following three years. Such statistics call for further careful analysis. In this case the time necessary for legal processing and the drop in the number of marriages in the province of Québec influenced the changes in the divorce rates.

Age at Divorce

The median age at divorce in 1985 was 36.7 for the male and 34.1 for the female. The majority of divorcing women and men are between the ages of 25 and 34, and 30 and 39 respectively. In terms of the duration of marriage in Canada, the popular myth is that the seventh year is critical for the survival of a marriage. Nevertheless, the average duration of marriage for divorced

Table 11-4   Divorces by Duration of Marriage for Selected Years

Duration	1971 Number (%)	1976 Number (%)	1981 Number (%)	1982 Number (%)	1985 Number (%)
Under 1 year	75(0.3)	153(0.3)	163(0.2)	195(0.3)	177(0.3)
1–4 years	4 299(14.4)	8 885(16.4)	1 182(1.7)	11 907(16.9)	9 676(15.6)
5–9 years	7 482(25.2)	16 002(29.5)	21 987(32.5)	22 573(32.0)	18 312(29.5)
10 + years*	17 382(59.4)	25 040(46.2)	44 340(65.6)	34 675(49.2)	28 165(45.4)
Total	29 238(100)	54 207(100)	67 671(100)	70 436(100)	61 980(100)

* Includes those who have not stated the duration of their marriage.
Source: Statistics Canada, 1971–1985, *Marriages and Divorces, Vital Statistics*,
   Ottawa. Reproduced by permission of the Minister of Supply and
   Services.

persons in Canada was 12.5 years in 1985. Obviously this average is influenced by marriages that last 25 or 30 years. As the data in Table 11-4 point out, the highest frequency of divorces occurs between three and nine years of marriage, a trend that has remained fairly consistent in the last decade and a half.

THEORETICAL PERSPECTIVES

The aforementioned empirical details pertaining to divorce in Canada should be understood in the context of theoretical perspectives that are attempts to explain why divorces occur and what contributes to marital stability in any society. In this section, a brief overview of the sociological perspectives related to divorce is presented. This overview is somewhat selective, since an exhaustive treatment would require more space than this chapter permits.

One way of explaining the incidence of divorce is to examine the background characteristics of the spouses so as to determine their proneness to divorce (Goode, 1976:538-39). Characteristics such as an urban background, marriage at a young age, short duration of acquaintanceship, a short period of engagement, parents with an unhappy marriage, religious commitment measured in terms of church-attendance, kin disapproval of marriage, dissimilar backgrounds, and disagreement over husband and wife role obligations are all indicators of proneness to divorce. Most findings suggest that the relationship between these background characteristics and marital instability is valid.

Another approach to unstable marriages is to focus upon the nature of interpersonal relationships (Nye and Berardo, 1973:497-500). Crucial in this respect are three forms of relationships: the aborted marriage, the mediocre functioning family, and the interrupted functioning family.

Troubles in the aborted marriage are evident very early in the relationship. In some cases normal sexual relations are not prevalent or the husband is continuously unemployed. In other cases, the couple is not prepared to take on adult work roles and responsibilities normally involved in marriage. Also, a spouse may, soon after marriage, realize that he or she has made a wrong choice and, therefore, desires to terminate the relationship. The aborted marriage may be termed a non-marriage: a marriage in the sociological sense never did exist, and normal relationships between spouses necessary for a permanent marriage were not established.

The second type of marriage is the mediocre functioning family. Familial roles and family functioning are present but only minimally so. The level of material well-being is often marginal. The home is not attractive to spouses, their emotional needs are rarely met, and there is constant bickering and quarrelling between them. For them, marriage is unrewarding and does not yield an intense positive emotional effect. The marriage may last for several years and, should divorce occur, emotional disruption is minimal.

The third type of marriage, according to Nye and Berardo, is the interrupted functioning marriage. In this relationship, the family initially functions very well and is characterized by strong positive effects. The marriage satisfies both spouses until it is interrupted, probably because of the strong attachment of one spouse to a third person, because of alcoholism, or because of a priority of work over family.

Farber suggests for contemporary society a permanent availability model, in which a potential mate, whether single, divorced, widowed, or married, is theoretically available to any individual of the opposite sex (Farber, 1964:109-112). This model may seem appropriate in a society where divorce is on the increase and remarriage is common.

A marriage is a voluntary association. When the commitment becomes greater to a person of the opposite sex other than the spouse, a new association may be established. Thus there is a sense of being permanently available. "All members of a society face a constant pressure to be highly competent in interpersonal relations if they wish to maintain their current marriage and remain in a favourable competitive position in the perennial marriage market" (Farber, 1964:478). From this perspective, it appears that divorce is functional and remains an inevitable part of the western marriage process.

According to Levinger, one may look at divorce as the final step in a process of estrangement (1976). Levinger analyzes divorce in terms of exchange theory, in which a relationship is viewed as an exchange of costs and rewards. Rewards would include love, material goods, services, status, and comfort. Costs include discomfort, irritation, insults, and decreasing status. Relationships cost time, money, and physical and mental energies. A relationship becomes strengthened as the rewards exceed or are weighed close to the costs. When costs exceed the rewards fragmented or strained relationships result.

Levinger's theory is based upon three concepts; forces of attraction, forces of barrier, and alternative attractions. These forces and alternatives have a bearing on whether one actually chooses marital dissolution, and they combine psychological and economic variables.

Forces of attraction are those factors which give an individual second thoughts about severing the marital relationship. These attractions include the level of family income, home ownership, occupational status (usually that of the husband), the ability to communicate with one's spouse, sexual enjoyment, companionship, and esteem. Forces of barrier are those that discourage the severing of the existing relationship. These forces are numerous and include the expenses of a divorce, separate living costs, obligation to the marital bond, religious constraint, pressures from the primary group and community, and responsibility to one's children. When forces of barrier are weak, alternatives which appear attractive will be investigated.

Alternative attractions are other options that draw the individual away from marriage. These may include independence and a greater opportunity for the fulfilment of one's potential. For some they may mean alternate affectional rewards in a companion, possibly eventual remarriage.

The analysis of the status of women from the perspective of feminism has added a new dimension to our understanding of the marital stress that leads to dissolution. Although these analyses do not always focus on the dissolution of marriage as Ambert's work does (1980), they nonetheless draw our attention to the implications of the inequality of women in Canadian law (Eichler, 1982) and in employment (Armstrong and Armstrong, 1978; Luxton, 1980; Wilson, 1982). Gender inequality, women's increasing awareness of their socially oppressed position, and their drive to seek improvement in their status in domestic and economic sectors of society tend to alter the nature of marital and family relationships. The stress generated in the process would quite possibly predispose some men and women to dissolve their unions.

In the last two decades research on divorce has focused increasingly on the process of separation and divorce which tends to occur in identifiable phases. For example, Bohannan (1970) identifies the six stations of divorce which characterize, in varying degrees, each divorce. In the emotional divorce, the trust between husband and wife disappears. "Two people . . . grate on each other because each is disappointed." In the legal divorce and economic divorce, the concern is the process of seeking the divorce decree and then the satisfactory settlement of financial matters. Of course each involves the division of property. Coparental divorce constitutes about half of North American divorces: in these cases, issues relating to child custody, parental responsibilities, and visitation rights are of prime importance. The

Table 11-5   Alleged Grounds for Divorce by Offence/Breakdown

Grounds	1973 (N = 48, 945)	1976 (N = 73, 013)	1981 (N = 90, 678)	1985 (N = 79, 433)
Marital Offences				
Adultery	30.3	30.4	31.1	28.5
Cruelty[1]	29.3	34.2	36.6	36.2
Other	0.3	0.3	0.2	0.2
Marriage Breakdown				
Separation	33.1	31.0	28.7	32.7
Other[2]	7.0	6.1	3.4	2.4

1. includes physical and mental cruelty.
2. includes addiction to alcohol, desertion, and other grounds.

SOURCE: Statistics Canada, 1974–1985, *Marriages and Divorces, Vital Statistics*, Ottawa. Reproduced with permission of the Minister of Supply and Services Canada.

community divorce refers to changes that occur in friends and in the neighbourhood of the divorced individual because of his or her change of status from married to single. The psychic divorce concerns the divorced person's regaining a sense of individual identity because of being "uncoupled." In the modern era individuals who have established their own identity during marriage, or during the deteriorating years of the marriage will find the psychic divorce less traumatic.

With the exception of those in the feminist tradition, the aforementioned theoretical explanations have generally been derived from the experiences in the United States. In fact, few Canadian studies have systematically examined the causes of divorce and, therefore, the relevance of the theoretical perspectives noted above is subject to their verification by Canadian data.

An examination of the grounds individuals use when petitioning for divorce might provide some insights into the reasons for divorce in Canada (Table 11-5). Some caution is necessary, however, in interpreting the data because the grounds on which couples legally seek divorce do not necessarily reflect the real reason for divorce. For example, those who desire immediate dissolution of their marriage can get it on the grounds of adultery. However, in order to establish this premise one has to include a corespondent, that is, the person with whom a spouse has developed a sexual or conjugal relationship. The development of such an extramarital relationship is in itself a demonstration of the distance between legally married spouses. Likewise, separation demonstrates a deteriorated interpersonal relationship, but a couple may have decided not to use the fault principle and instead have chosen to wait the obligatory three years before seeking a legal dissolution of their marriage.

Furthermore, the data in Table 11-5 show that about two thirds of Canadians who have sought divorce in the last twelve years have chosen to do so on the grounds of marital offences. This does not necessarily imply that these individuals preferred to use fault as grounds for divorce. Quite likely, many in this category simply did not wish to wait for three years. It would be interesting to compare these data with that of divorces that will occur in the next few years, as the near no-fault provision will have been in effect for several years.

CHILDREN AND DIVORCE

With an increase in the number of divorces it is expected that the number of children affected by divorce will also increase. More than 50 percent of all divorces include at least one dependent child, as shown in Table 11-6. Divorcing parents with one or two children contribute 85 percent of about 56 000 children annually affected directly by divorce. The number of children with divorced parents is steadily increasing in Canada, and it is evident now that most childcare centres and school classrooms contain some children from divorced homes. In some classrooms children of single parents outnumber children from two-parent homes. Until the mid-1960s it was commonly held that homes characterized by continuing tension between spouses should remain intact for the sake of the children. This is no longer the view, at least among those who have sought divorce in recent years.

At a time when the idea of individual satisfaction supersedes personal sacrifice for the group, few continue to believe in family togetherness at all

Table 11-6 Divorces by Number and Percentages of Dependent Children, 1985

Number of Children	Number of Divorces	Percent of Divorces	Total Number of Children
0	30 076	48.5	0
1	13 719	22.1	14 756
2	13 548	21.9	27 096
3	3 732	6.0	11 196
4	715	1.2	2 860
5 or more	190	.3	950 +
	61 980	100.0	55 821 +

SOURCE: Statistics Canada, *Marriages and Divorces, Vital Statistics*, vol. II, 28, Ottawa. Reproduced with permission of the Minister of Supply and Services.

costs. Children are affected by a constantly strife-ridden environment just as they are affected by a family unit severed by divorce. Which is worse has become a moot question: the issue is not whether children are harmed by their parents' divorce, but in what way they are adversely affected by the structural changes inherent in divorce. Findings from the research are not conclusive, although this problem has attracted considerable public and scholarly attention. When discussing the children of divorced parents, one must consider the age of the child, the number and sex of siblings, the relationship between the father and mother, relations of the children with their parents, the impact of the parent's dissension, the family's socio-economic status, and the emotional, social, and economic resources available in the post-separation period.

Previous research suggests that the time just before the divorce and the year following the divorce are the most disruptive and stressful to children (Wallerstein and Kelly, 1976). The disorganization of their family life threatens children much more than the conflicting parents would ever realize. Initially, children desire a reconciliation between their parents. Often, children of divorced parents feel guilty because they tend to think they are the cause of their parents' separation or divorce. They frequently confront troubling questions: "Where will I live?" "With whom will I live?" "Will I still get to see Daddy (or Mommy, or my sister or brother)?" In other words, children are anxious about their own future, the effects of which are seen in their school performance as well as in their social deportment.

The Wallerstein and Kelly study showed that a year after the divorce, 50 percent of the children had returned to a normal developmental pattern. Their psychological problems had eased. On the other hand, 25 percent became progressively more troubled after their parents' separation; "their sadness lingered, their self-esteem dropped, and their relationships with other people were shallow and unrewarding" (Wallerstein and Kelly, 1976).

Adolescent children more readily accept their parents' divorce: they know that the relationship was not wholesome and did not nurture family members anyway. A child's self-esteem is strongly affected when their parents' marriage is ridden with chronic conflict and hostility (Raschke and Raschke, 1979). One study concludes that some children of divorce are more cooperative and empathetic and they manifest greater independence than children from intact families (Hetherington, Cox and Cox, 1978). Children mature and become more responsible because of the demands of their new home situations. Many custodial parents nurture a close, almost adult relationship with their children. One researcher concludes that "there is little evidence suggesting that divorce is directly related to negative developmental consequences for children" (Marotz-Baden et al., 1978:8). However, another study shows the adolescent's reaction to include "anger, sadness, a sense of loss and betrayal, as well as feelings of shame and embarrassment" (Bell, 1983:533).

A major area of adjustment for children is the loss of one of the parents. Contacts with their biological parents may be sporadic, or only at regular weekly intervals, and these tend to be qualitatively different from those in intact familes. Interaction also may be brief, awkward, and superficial. At times, the child may be caught in a conflict of loyalty and emotional commitment between the separated parents. Research also shows that a child's continued association with grandparents is directly related to the frequency of contact with the respective parent.

THE SINGLE-PARENT FAMILY

The single-parent family or lone-parent household refers to a home with one parent and one or more dependent children, most often the natural parent and child(ren). In 1981, there were 714 000 lone-parent households in Canada. This is 11.3 percent of all families, or a rise of 1.5 percent in five years. The majority of single-parent families are results of divorce or separation: of the single-parents in 1981, 31 percent are separated, 26 percent divorced, 33 percent widowed, and ten percent have never married. About 83 percent of these families are headed by females. Children under 25 years of age living with lone parents now number over one million, or 13 percent of all children (Statistics Canada, 1985).

Furthermore, lone parents who are widows tend not only to be older than single parents but also tend to have more children who are older than those in single-parent families that have resulted from divorce or separation. Nevertheless, lone-parent families tend to be smaller than two-parent families. In 1981 54 percent had one child while 29 percent had two children. While only 7 percent of the single never-married lone parents are male, 22 percent of the separated and 17 percent of divorced lone parents are male. The higher percentage of fathers among separated than among divorced lone parents raises several interesting questions. Does this signal a new trend in which an increasing number of mothers are prepared to terminate their marriage even if they do not gain custody of the child? Are fathers in this decade more interested and persistent in caring for their child(ren)? Then again, the separation period may be a "temporary" period when the father experiments to see whether child care is feasible for him, and when he later realizes the time and energy necessary to care for children, he may consent to the mother's gaining custody. Second, the courts may be biased in favour of awarding custody to mothers, thus causing some fathers to lose the custody of their children.

The increasing acceptance of cohabitation (see Chapter Five) may result in many children of single parents gaining the company of another adult who may have a quasi-parent status in the household. In cases where such an adult stays for a short period of time, there is little chance of any significant relationship developing between children and their parent's live-in friend. If this occurs many times, children will likely experience stress. Only in those situations where the stay is permanent (with or without marriage) may meaningful relationships emerge.

There are some indications of what the future of lone parents will be. As the divorce rate is not likely to decline significantly in the next decade, the number of lone-parent families will likely remain high. The trend in Canada is towards smaller families and a shorter duration of marriage before a divorce takes place. Consequently, the average size of lone-parent families will be smaller. The recent changes in the divorce law may decrease the number of separated lone-parent families and correspondingly the number of divorced lone-parent families will increase.

The number of never-married lone parents is not likely to shift dramatically. There are two groups among never-married lone parents: those who became a parent unintentionally, and those females who sought pregnancy with no inclination to marriage or cohabitation. The latter group comprises women between 25 and 35 years of age, many of whom are neither affluent nor working class.

Two Canadian researchers note that income is the key difference between the lone-parent and the two-parent family. Davids (1985) shows that the income of the average female lone parent is less than half the income of two-parent families. Male lone parents fall about midway between. Ambert's (1985) study indicates that fathers generally fare better as parents because they have more economic resources, receive community support, and their efforts are appreciated. Such a positive social context has an influence on the children. In contrast, mothers have fewer and more sporadic economic resources, are stigmatized within the community, have less self-esteem, and their efforts are taken for granted. Such personal conditions of struggle and strain negatively influence her children.

Single-parent families encounter a number of economic problems. Financial support from a former spouse may be irregular in amount and frequency. For many, housing is a problem. The dwellings of single-parent families need more repair than other dwellings, primarily because of neglect and insufficient resources (Davids, 1985:6). Parents have less time to spend with the children because of their dual role as parent and breadwinner. Hetherington (1979) calls this the "double loss."

The family is likely to be stereotyped and stigmatized by the community. The contact with the former spouse is maintained for a while after separation often only because of property settlements and visitation rights. The pattern of friendships also changes. As friends tend to align with one or other of the partners, divorced couples are unlikely to maintain the level and quality of interaction which existed prior to their marital dissolution. Many women also experience a drop in self-esteem or confusion in their senses of identity (Nelson, 1985).

It should be noted further that the terms single parent, lone parent or solo parent are rather inadequate (Hanson and Sporakowski, 1986), since they suggest that either a father or mother raises the child single-handedly. Often this is not the case. The non-custodial parent is often involved with the child financially and emotionally. The non-custodial parent may act as a role model and a relevant significant other, and may also give counsel to the child.

REMARRIAGE

The annual proportion of people who marry for the first time is declining. More persons in their late teens and early twenties are delaying marriage and, therefore, reducing the chances of their ever marrying. Cohabitation has become more socially acceptable. Further, remarriages are no longer stigmatized. In 1967, 12.3 percent of all marriages involved either one or two partners who had experienced divorce. By 1985, the figure had risen to 28.7 percent (Statistics Canada, 1985).

There is a distinct pattern of courtship and partnership among the divorced. Males are somewhat more likely to remarry. The younger the age at divorce, the greater the likelihood of remarriage. Young divorced women without children often are more desirable mates in the remarriage market than those who are older and have children. Over 50 percent of the divorced who remarry marry a partner who is also divorced. Remarrying couples are also more heterogeneous in terms of age, race and religion than those who marry for the first time. The age difference between the partners is much larger than commonly found among first married. The wedding ceremony is likely to be civil rather than religious, and attended by fewer persons than a first marriage.

Women in the upper economic strata or men in the lower strata are the least likely to remarry. Women in the professions are economically self-sufficient and generally do not wish to rush into another marriage unless non-economic reasons persuade them to do so. Also, many men may have reservations about marrying a successful women, especially if their own socio-economic status is lower than that of successful divorced women. Lower-class men find it hard to remarry because their limited economic resources bring little in practical terms to a woman seeking economic stability.

Some people contend that the remarried will experience marital stability because of lessons learned in the first relationship. Though fewer than 50 percent of remarriages end in divorce, this percentage is higher than the figure for the once-married population. There are several contributing factors which make the two groups difficult to compare. First, a significant difference lies in the fact that often one of the remarried partners has children from the previous marriage and therefore enters remarriage with family obligations. Approximately half of all remarriages include dependent children, each of whom comes with his or her own history, and unique personality. New methods of raising and disciplining children become necessary for the reconstructed family. There are marital wounds that are either healing or in need of healing. The presence of the new stepparent, the non-custodial parent, and stepsiblings calls for redefinition and re-adjustment of family relations and causes stress. Evidence suggests that divorce is more likely to occur in a remarriage if children from a previous marriage are present than when children are born in the remarriage (Gullotta, Adams, and Alexander, 1986:260). Furthermore, strong emotions often accompany financial support that the non-custodial parent is forced by the courts to pay the ex-spouse. The non-custodial parent, for instance, may not believe these monies are used solely for the children's needs.

Second, the higher probability of divorce in remarriage stems from personal factors. The partners in remarriage are likely to bring unresolved personal problems from their first marriage. The entry into remarriage may have been too sudden as the courtship process preceding remarriages is usually shorter than in first marriages. Some marry for reasons which do not really contribute to a healthy marriage—the children's sake, the fear that there will be no subsequent chance to remarry, or coercion by the courting partner (often the male). Goode (1956) observes that the norm-lessness of the status of "divorced" in our society places a pressure upon individuals to marry again.

Finally, the remarried have been divorced before: they have already experienced social stigma, the complexity of the legal system, and the reactions of parents, kin, friends and acquaintances. They may be less reluctant to seek divorce a second time.

THE BLENDED FAMILY

The blended family is also referred to as the reconstituted family. When a single parent marries a partner who is not the biological parent of the child, it is generally the mother who brings children into the second marriage since, for example, in 82 percent of divorces in 1984 the custody of children was awarded to the mother (Statistics Canada, 1985:26). Other types of the blended family occur when the father brings children into the marriage and the mother does not, or both parents bring one or several children to their remarriages. Over time, other children may be born to the remarried spouses.

Blended family members are under pressure to make a number of adjustments. For example, the behavioural patterns of a single-parent family with visits from the non-custodial parent must be changed to a new set of relations which now include a step-parent. The non-custodial parent may feel competition from the step-parent for the attention, affection, loyalty, interest, and time of his children. The role of step-parent is not clearly defined in either domestic or legal contexts. Step-parents often try too hard or move too fast to gain the children's affection and acceptance (Vischer and Vischer, 1979). Duberman's (1973) study points out that the role of step-mother is particularly difficult because of the societal belief that the natural mother-child bond is peculiarly intimate. Step-parents play the parental role while the natural parent seeks to maintain some continuity to earlier parenting.

In some cases, children welcome a new parent, especially if there has been little contact with the non-custodial parent. Most children and parents respond well to the new challenge of the blended family, though considerable adjustment is necessary. Invariably, all members in a blended family face a restructuring of their family relations. Step-siblings often share a room, possessions, and parental time. They are introduced to step-kin but these relationships seldom become as meaningful as consanguinal kin. Messinger (1984:161) found that children in his study frequently remarked that "We are not a family . . ., we are a bunch of people living together. We live in a house, not a home."

The number of parents in Canada who have raised one or more step-children is relatively small. The proportion is higher for males (4.4 percent) than for females (2.1 percent) (Burch, 1985:17). This difference reflects the fact that women are more often awarded custody after divorce.

Not all step-parents officially adopt the child(ren) in the blended family. Some preliminary Canadian research indicates that only 16 percent of the males and two percent of the females legally adopt their stepchildren (Burch, 1985:19-20). The reason for this action is not clear. Many non-custodial fathers may not wish to relinquish their parental right. At the same time some step-fathers may be reluctant to accept the full legal responsibility.

With respect to children, Gross (1985) identifies four types of remarriage families. In the retention family the children perceptually retain both biological parents, even though one of them does not live in the same home. These children do not accept the new spouse of their custodial parent. In the substitution family the children replace one biological parent with a step-parent. In the reduction family the child has rejected the non-custodial parent and has not accepted the step-parent as parent. In the augmentation family children accept both biological parents as well as one of the step-parents as a member of the family.

CONCLUSION

We have seen that the number of divorces has increased considerably in Canada over the past quarter-century. Laws have become more liberal— some would say, more progressive. These changes mark a shift from a collective moralistic interpretation to an individualistic, private, and much less condemnatory interpretation of divorce. Society and individuals have become much more tolerant of divorce, remarriage, and the blended family.

There are several helpful sociological approaches to the subject of divorce. Exchange theory, based upon rewards and costs, appropriately addresses the decision-making process. Symbolic interaction is relevant with regard to marriage, commitment, and family, as well as to the marriage partner, through the dynamic process of social change. This sociological framework is also useful in our recognizing the process of redefining self-identity through the separation and post-divorce experience. The structural functional approach illuminates the stability of the family maintained despite the disruption of separation and divorce. Family members adapt and accommodate; most adults remarry; a semblance of equilibrium is once again achieved.

The function of the extended-family members for a divorcing family has changed. Kin play less of an emotional and supportive role. Professionals in the helping agencies, whether within government or private agencies, provide counsel and economic resources. Governmental funds, however, almost always appear limited. At times, clients become impatient with the ever-expanding bureaucracy, or with the slow process of their own development. The public, the government, and particularly the families under stress, seek means to address the hurts created by institutions and individuals within society.

Suggested Readings

Ambert, Anne-Marie.
   1980   *Divorce in Canada*. Toronto: Academic Press.

Capaldi, Fredrick, and McRae, Barbara.
   1979   *Step-families*. New York: New Viewpoints/Vision Books.

Eichler, Margrit.
   1988   *Families in Canada Today* (Chapter 9). Second ed. Toronto: Gage.

Irving, Howard H.
   1980   *Divorce Mediation*. Toronto: Personal Library Publishers.

McKie, D.C., Prentice, B., and Reed, P.
   1983   *Divorce: Law and the Family in Canada*. Ottawa: Minister of Supply and Services.

Wallerstein, Judith S., and Kelly, Berlin Joan.
  1980   *Surviving the Breakup: How Children and Parents Cope with Divorce.*
         New York: Basic.
Weiss, Robert S.
  1975   *Marital Separation.* New York: Basic.

12

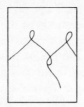

THE FAMILY, LAW, AND SOCIAL POLICY

Joseph C. Ryant

Social policy comprises the laws, administrative arrangements, and entitlements made in response to societal perceptions of problems, needs, and aspirations. Instituted through processes which are ostensibly political, although not always governmental, and it is influenced in significant ways by differences in ideology, economic interest, political party platforms, public opinion, and community mores, to the extent that the content of a given social policy is likely to be constantly changing, now an advance, then a retreat, and then again an improvement of yet another sort. Consequently, the making of social policy is both evolutionary and incremental, factors that make it difficult for the content of policy to be either comprehensive or internally consistent.

This is certainly the case with respect to the collection of social policies which bear upon Canadian families. Not even the federal government would claim that Canada has a "family policy,"despite the fact that there are myriad laws, programs, and administrative regulations and provisions which directly and indirectly affect families in extremely important ways. These formulations are made at different times, in different parts of the decision-making apparatus, and for different reasons. Sometimes they contradict one another. They reflect opposing ideological trends and differ in the inclusiveness of their application. Nevertheless, Canada does have a family policy—the sum of all the seperate decisions made with reference to family life—and there are important threads of consistency that indirectly bind that policy together. There are two explanations for this consistency; both take an economically deterministic position. Wilensky and Lebreaux (1958), in an essentially liberal argument, have described two ways in which the development of social policy is a response to the imperatives of capitalistic growth. First, residual policies are made to correct the damage to family life and individual well-being caused by excessive demands of the industrial revolution. Then, as capitalism matures and individuals serve more routinely as delegates for the family in the workplace and the marketplace, institutional policies are made to replace some of the lost functions of absent family members and to protect the family from the ebbs and flows of the economy as a whole. On the other hand, Ian Gough (1979), a neo-Marxist, sees social policy concerned with the family socializing the costs of reproducing the labour force; it thereby assists capital accumulation, and legitimizes the capitalist state (see also Djao, 1983).

Whether the liberal or Marxist view is adopted, there is little doubt that family social policy mediates between family and the economy, in property relations, in labour force participation, and in participation in the market for goods and services. Owing to this mediating function, a more comprehensive perspective on family policy is emerging, even though the policy elements themselves are achieved piecemeal. Four main factors have influenced the convergence of disparate policies. First, basic demographic changes in Canada, noted in Chapter Five, have created pressures for change in old and initiation of new policies. Second, direct and indirect political influence of feminist ideologies on policy-makers is growing. Third, welfare state planners design income transfer programs with increasing sophistication and these programs redefine in many ways the economic importance of family roles and functions. Finally, the family has received greater attention in the design and provision of personal social services.

DEMOGRAPHIC CHANGES IN CANADA

Four major areas of demographic change have instigated the need for revisions of social policy. First, changes in the composition of the labour force, particularly the rising participation of women, have created obvious needs for action by the state. Second, there have been changes in family formation—marriage, divorce and remarriage, and the higher incidence of common-law unions. Third, there have been significant changes in Canadian society in the population distribution by sex and age, and the next fifty years presage an aging population (see Chapter Ten). Finally, the birth rate in Canada is well below that required for population replacement; whether we will continue to rely only upon immigration or whether we will introduce pro-natalist policies is an important issue. These four demographic trends are linked and many policy decisions have been made in response.

Labour Force Composition

Canada, in common with all advanced economies, has experienced high mobility of labour. Rural areas have become greatly depopulated in response both to the demand for non-agricultural labour and to the surplus of agricultural labour caused by technological development. Resource industries have been opened in the west and the north. Some regions experience periods of boom, attracting workers from other parts of the country, only to discard them during the economic recession that often follows. At every level of employment, occupational success depends in part upon a readiness to pull up stakes and relocate.

A major consequence of this trend is the unlikelihood that adult children will live in the same locale as their parents. The significant decrease in the residential propinquity of close kin, especially parents and married children has occasioned major changes in the nature of mutual assistance among kin in times of need: couples with young children are less able to have the immediate assistance of their parents; similarly older parents are less able to call upon their adult children (Land and Parker, 1978; Moroney, 1986; see also Chapter Eight).

The composition and size of the labour force have also changed due to the massive increases in the participation of women. Even within a short span of ten years (1977-1986), the number of female workers has increased by 38 percent from 3.62 million to 4.98 million (Statistics Canada, reported in *The Financial Post*, "Outlook '87," Winter, 1986-87:101). The nature of female labour-force participation has also changed. The participation of married women has increased from 3.5 percent to about 65 percent in the years between 1931 and 1984 (see Chapter Five). Increases in the labour force participation of female single parents have occurred probably because work yields higher levels of income than those available through government transfer payments such as provincial or municipal social assistance.

There are, as well, fewer permanent withdrawals of women from paid labour for purposes of childbearing. More women are choosing not to have children and, for those that do, the average number of births per woman has fallen from 3.8 in 1961 to 1.7 in 1984 (see Chapter Five and Beaujot, 1986:15). Absences from the labour force due to children, when they do occur, tend to be of considerably shorter duration as growing numbers of couples and female lone parents make arrangements for the care of their preschool children. In many families, the working woman contributes substantially to family income, about 30 percent of family income on average (Chapter Five). While the position of the family as a consumption unit may have improved, the needs of the family for child-related services have increased greatly as a consequence, a problem as yet unresolved in Canadian social policy. The ability of working women to provide assistance to others in the extended family has also been considerably reduced.

Although women workers used to experience rates of unemployment higher than those of men, changes in the economy have tended to equalize this risk. In 1985, the male unemployment rate was 10.3 percent, the rate for females 10.7 percent (*The Financial Post*, "Outlook '87":5). In periods of high unemployment, or where employment is seasonal, it is not unusual for a woman to be able either to find new work or to continue working at the very time her husband is unemployed. Nevertheless, within each occupational category, women's average earnings are approximately two thirds of men's average earnings. Women are also still found in low-paying jobs, particularly in the service, clerical, and non-unionized manufacturing sectors. These factors put stresses on family life because income levels, even in intact families, may not cover the purchase of services that is made necessary by the nonavailability of female domestic work.

Marriage, Divorce and Remarriage

The extent of marital breakdown in Canada, as it has in other Western industrial nations, has increased since 1950. Marriages are more likely to end in failure than ever before. The average duration of marriages that end in divorce is shorter: not only are more couples terminating their marriage, they are not waiting as long to do so as they did prior to 1968. Reform of divorce laws in that year made it possible for many of those couples long separated to become legally divorced under terms more personally acceptable than those formerly available. Further reform has reduced from three years to one year the waiting period for divorces on the grounds of marriage breakdown (see Chapter Eleven).

There is still a high rate of remarriage, although it is higher for men than for women. One or both partners may already have children from a previous marriage and have some form of custody over them, from which emerges several complicated family forms. The term "blended family" is used to describe these units, which form as a result of either legal marriage or common-law union. However, the term masks the wide variety of possible arrangements. The characteristics of each case depend on the child custody status of each partner and on whether or not the new couple produces children.

Separation and divorce raise important issues—the division of property, support for the spouse, child custody, child maintenance, visiting rights— that require legal or personal resolution. Much of the legal framework encompassing these matters is built upon the presumed need to provide protection for all the parties to a divorce action. Whether the legal system does this adequately, or fairly, is arguable.

Common-law unions exist for long durations and frequently involve children. Many partners in common-law unions have been previously married and bring children from these marriages into the new union. The extent to which, and the ways in which, policies made for the legally married protect the parties to failed common-law relationships is an important area of family policy. While the law treats the spouses in a dissolved common-law union as if they had been married in some respects—division of assets acquired while together, child support—in other areas, such as custody of children and visiting rights, the treatment is not identical.

There is a notable increase in the number of unmarried women, especially those who are very young, who bear children. Of Canadian women between 15 and 19 years old who gave birth in 1984, 68 percent were unmarried (Statistics Canada, 1985). The majority of their children are raised by the young mothers, either in legal or common-law unions with the fathers, or with the help of grandparents while still in the grandparental home, or even on their own. A student of social work conducting research on adolescent pregnancy has estimated that of 6963 children born to 15- to 19-year-old Manitoba females in 1984, 2085 are being raised by their single parent. Of the 1256 mothers in this group who married the fathers of their children, an estimated half will have separated within four years, adding another 626 single parents to the over 2000 already noted (McCrie, 1986).

Some sociologists (see, for example, Beaujot, 1986, and Chapter Five) believe these changes reflect the growing tendency of individuals to focus more on personal fulfilment than social expectations or group interests. Many of Canada's more recent social policies, such as changes in the Divorce Act and the extinction of illegitimacy as a legal status, have tended to support the free exercise of individual choice, even when it is contrary to more traditional family values. Increasingly, however, the exercise of individual choices, such as getting divorced, young unmarried women bearing children, both parents of preschool children working full time, has worked only because the state intervenes with programs and services to solve the family problems that result. Even though state action tends to be far less than what is required, family policy has become a battleground for conflicting ideologies. There is considerable public debate over whether the state ought to be involved in such matters: the conservative sections of the population argue against the weakening of traditional aspects of the family.

Age and Sex Composition

Social policy has always responded, though not always appropriately, to major changes in population characteristics. The baby boom that followed the end of the Second World War was associated with a number of benefits directed primarily at families with young children. One example is the massive increase in public expenditure for all levels of education, which would assist the baby-boom generation's move from the family to the labour force. Similar increases in public spending for health care and for protection of the income of the elderly have been due in part to Canada's aging population (see Chapter Ten).

A significant demographic event of recent decades in Canada is the declining birth rate. "Baby boomers" are evidently not as fecund as their own parents. The average size of a family has decreased: as noted in Chapter Five, one- and two-child families have become more prevalent, and more than ever before families are making the decision to be childless. Statistics Canada projects that the fertility rate will continue to fall, moving from 1.7 in 1986 to 1.4 by 1996, and remain stable thereafter. It is further estimated that the 0 to 17 year age group will progressively decline as a proportion of the total population, moving from 28.1 percent in 1981 to 14.9 percent in 2031, a dramatic reduction of almost 100 percent in just 50 years (Statistics Canada, 1986).

Concomitantly, Canada's population of the elderly is increasing even more rapidly, both in absolute numbers and as a proportion of the total population. In 1981, those aged 65 and over numbered 2.4 million persons or 9.7 percent of the population (Statistics Canada, 1986). Life expectancy at birth of those classified in 1981 as elderly (born before 1917) was 72.2 years for males, 78.8 years for females. In 1981, men who were already 65 could expect to live an average of 14.9 years longer; women who were 65 in 1981 could expect another 19 years on average (Statistics Canada, 1984). There is little doubt that there has been a dramatic extension of longevity over the last half century.

Population projections for the next 50 years suggest an acceleration of the aging trend. Life expectancy is estimated to reach 74.9 years for males and 81.6 years for females by 1996. An almost 300 percent increase in the numbers of the elderly is projected over the 50 years from 1981. It is estimated that by 2031 there will be 7.1 million persons 65 years or over: the elderly are expected by then to constitute 26.6 percent of the population (Statistics Canada, 1986; see also Chapter Ten).

Spending on social policy already demonstrates this shift, at least in the case of income security programs. In 1986, when there were 2.33 persons 17 years or younger for every person 65 or older (Statistics Canada, *Population Projections for Canada, Provinces and Territories, 1984-2006*), federal and provincial social security transfers to each group were in an approximately equal inverse ratio. That is, an estimated eight billion dollars were directed to families with children while 17.3 billion dollars were transferred to the elderly (computed from data provided by the Canadian Council on Social Development, 1986). As the ratio of elderly to young reverses and becomes 1.78 elderly persons to every youth by 2031, the transfer of public dollars will be aimed even more at the elderly.

The greater demand on social spending by the elderly is not the only function of their growth in numbers: there are also great differences between the numbers of men and women over the age of 65. In 1981, there were 109 females for every 100 males in the 65 to 79-year-old age group. For those 80 years and older, the ratio was 125 women for every 100 men (Statistics Canada, 1984). These differences will become more pronounced over the next 50 years because of the differences between the longevity of women and men. Of equal importance is the fact that elderly women are far less likely than men to be living in family units. In 1981, approximately three quarters of men over the age of 65 were married whereas approximately 60 percent of elderly women were either never married, or widowed or divorced (Canada, 1981 Census). Finally, elderly women are much more likely than men to receive low incomes.

Population Replacement

The projections noted above estimate that the proportion of the population between 18 and 64 years of age will remain fairly stable over the next 50 years (assuming a constant permitted immigration of 50 000 persons per year). To the extent that social policy expenditure is affected by the size of tax revenues, projections suggest that government's ability to raise the revenues will not be reduced. However, the composition of the dependent population (aged 17 and under and 65 and over) will shift increasingly from youth to the elderly.

At the same time, the predicted levels of fertility are insufficient to maintain population size. As Beaujot (1986) suggests, the desirability of maintaining, or even increasing, population size is a political question: the research evidence is not the only important determining factor nor is it conclusive. However, should we decide as a nation to attempt to maintain a stable population of about 25 million, without changing current levels of fertility, the internal composition of the population would shift increasingly to those born abroad. Henripin, cited in Beaujot (1986), estimates proportions of those born abroad ranging from 25 percent at a rate of 1.7 births per woman in Canada to 50 percent should fertility fall as low as 1.2 children per woman.

Hence the choices are fairly clear. If present trends continue as predicted, doing nothing means undergoing a decline in population size. Increasing the reliance on immigration results in a different population mix and political consequences that are unknown. To adopt a pro-natalist policy probably entails attempting to reduce the labour force participation of women and to increase the public support of child care for those women who still wish to work. While the present Canadian government has made an undetailed commitment to funding daycare, it has not made it in the context of population policy. Indeed, one wonders if government has yet been apprised of the issue. Population replacement will likely emerge as a major issue in public policy; the choice will probably favour an increase in the fertility rate rather than reliance solely on immigration.

THE INFLUENCE OF FEMINIST ANALYSIS

Deeply entrenched customs, traditions, and legal codes have caused women to experience a lower status in Canada. Notwithstanding the improvements in their position over the last 20 years, women, both within and outside the family, are still at a disadvantage compared to men. The politically active feminist movement that appeared early in the 1960s has sought to achieve equal status for women wherever they choose to participate. In this regard, feminist analysis has made a major contribution to contemporary social policy debates: its impact on family policy, for instance, has been important (Eichler, 1973, 1983a; Wilson, 1977; see also Chapter Two).

The feminist influence on family policy is complex. Much attention has been paid to the position of women within the family, attention that is not always recognized by the opponents of feminist ideology. Feminist analysis is better known for its support of women's ability genuinely to choose roles in the workplace and outside the family, generally. As the exercise of such choices requires increased and easier access to family services that are substitutes for those traditionally provided by wives and mothers, opponents to these changes accuse feminists of recommending policies that threaten traditional family life.

In Canada, the issue of women pursuing interests outside the family is highly contentious. It contradicts patriarchal values, which support the restricted participation of women in a male-dominated society and the retention of women in what are regarded as crucial domestic roles. Feminist analysis challenges the validity of values that support the domestic segregation of women. These challenges do not necessarily lead to an articulation of either explicit or coherent family policy. Nevertheless, advocates for particular feminist positions do appear to recognize that the "traditional" family of the mother at home, the father as sole breadwinner, and two children, occurs in a minority of cases. Therefore, they see the need to address some of the weaknesses associated with a contemporary family life that departs so substantially from traditional assumptions, and to argue for specific policies to address major problems.

Changes Sought within the Family

The feminist critique of the woman's "place" within the family has contributed to several important reforms that are for the most part recent and still incomplete. Most of the provinces have now revised, or will soon revise, legislation on the division of marital property. These changes aim to provide women with an equal share after their divorce of the assets accumulated over the course of the marriage. Divorce laws have been amended twice since 1968 to include "no-fault" as grounds for divorce and to reduce the compulsory period of separation from three years to one year as a condition for legal dissolution of marriage (see Chapter Eleven). Provinces have shown a greater readiness to enforce court orders on alimony and child support; however, problems of enforcement continue, especially when a former spouse moves to another province. While child custody and access can still be a problem in contested cases, several provinces have introduced new courts which are less adversarial in procedure. Provinces may provide access to mediation services as well. Although it is still not the norm, children who are the subjects of custody disputes are increasingly being granted the right to separate legal counsel to protect their interests, which may be different from those of the parents.

Feminists have also been in the forefront of lobbying for policies which protect women and their children from domestic violence. The Criminal Code has been amended to recognize as an offence sexual assault of a woman by her husband. Previously, laws on rape specifically excluded marital sexual assault. Wife battering has also received increased official attention. In several provinces, the attorney general has required the police to lay a charge against the offender instead of relying upon the victim to do so. There has been partial success, more in urban than rural areas, in establishing crisis shelters where battered women, and their children, may take refuge from their husbands. Female victims of marital violence who have low incomes are also eligible for legal aid in most provinces.

In making the general public and the makers of social policy more aware of family violence, feminist lobbyists have also helped to focus concern upon abuse of children, sexual or otherwise. Most victims of child sexual abuse are female and most perpetrators are male. There have been large increases in the number of reported cases, partly because the law compels reporting suspected incidents and partly because much greater public attention is now paid to the crime. Many experts also believe the prevalence of the crime itself has increased. Social services have been introduced to provide the victims with protection and treatment. At present, perpetrators are more likely to be dealt with by the legal system than to receive counselling or psychological treatment.

Finally, feminist groups have assisted in focusing attention upon the economic vulnerability of wives and mothers. Of major concern has been the issue of pensions (Dulude, 1981; Eichler, 1983b), particularly for those married women who have insignificant labour-force attachment, or none at all, and are as a result eligible only to share the pension or survivor benefits of their spouses. The divorce law now entitles a woman to half of her husband's Canada/Québec Pension Plan credits earned during the marriage.

Provinces have jurisdiction over most private employment-related pension plans. To date, most plans do not require that the male employee choose a pension payout option that takes into account the declared interests of the wife. Now on the policy agenda are partially formulated proposals that would give pensions to women who work without pay in the home; however, it is not certain whether a proposal of this nature is likely to become law.

Other Changes

In its demands for equality in the workplace, feminist analysis has supported policies which, where adopted, have become part of the collection of decisions, programs and services called family policy (Wilson, 1977). The issues are highly controversial because they involve different views of the role of women within the family. That some policies have moved somewhat toward the feminist position is the probable result of political and legal pressure for greater equality, which has been made more effective by the increased participation of women in the labour force. Economic imperatives have created opportunities for the emancipation of women from full-time domestic labour. These opportunities have fuelled calls for the public provision of substitutes for women's services to families (Land and Parker, 1977). However, as services such as daycare become available, even in limited amounts, those who espouse the more traditional role for wives and mothers (see Boyd, 1984, cited in Chapter Five) find support for their position in the evidence of increasing family breakdown, juvenile crime, neglect and abuse of children and significant departures from the norm of legal marriage. A dialectical process of the making of family policy has thus been set in motion.

The previous paragraph suggests that it is more likely for the state to substitute for women's services than it is to call upon men to redefine their share of domestic labour. The feminist position has been to support public policy which emancipates women from some family roles; the call for men to take on a greater share of the work has been a minor theme by comparison. Even where there is a view of family policy which admits of the state sharing responsibility for the care of dependent family members with wives, mothers, and daughters, there are sharp disagreements on the funtions for which each has responsibility and the terms and conditions of the sharing. The three areas of care most often involved in the policy arena are related to dependent children, ill or disabled family members, and the elderly.

For example, publicly provided child care has been a major issue in women's political activity for more than four decades. In Western European, Scandinavian, and Eastern Bloc nations, daycare has long been an entrenched occupational benefit. In North America, the provision of quality care to the children of working women is only conditional, a fact attributable to traditional values concerning the roles of mothers and to a lack of agreement over who should provide the care, where it should be provided, and who should pay for it. In Canada, where the state has assisted in the provision of free or subsidized daycare, only families on low incomes by whom the benefit is used to aid the pursuit of work, education, or training are eligible. The expansion of this program until now has been constrained by spending cuts in the public sector. Announced government intentions to provide more state support to daycare will provoke strong opposition from those who adhere to more traditional views of the role of women.

Feminist analysis has been only somewhat less vocal about the assumption that female relatives should provide the bulk of the care to ill or disabled family members. It is clear that the major burden falls on the shoulders of the mother, in the case of a child, or the wife or adult daughter in the case of a spouse or parent. The increase in female labour-force participation has moderated the degree of these expectations and has led to the introduction of services to substitute for those usually rendered by mothers, wives, and daughters. These services are highly rationed: eligibility most often depends both on low income and on the work-related unavailability of those who would normally provide family care.

A new tendency in social policy threatens to tip the scales once more toward the expectation that women family members will provide most of the care of the ill and disabled (Armstrong, 1984). De-institutionalization, often called community care, has become a popular approach in state-provided services to the chronically ill and the disabled, both because it is alleged to avoid the negative effects of residency in long-term care facilities and because it is thought to provide the ill and disabled with a more "normal" life. It is sometimes also claimed to be less costly. In fact, the saving of public dollars depends almost entirely on whether the alternative care is provided by family members. If adequate support and developmental services were to be established in the community as a supplement to family work, imagined economies disappear. A worse choice exists—placing the mentally ill in communities without adequate support services—and the growing numbers of street people who forage in the community is evidence of its use. In the main, however, much of the effort to send home the physically and developmentally disabled, the chronically ill, and those who have suffered from mental disorders, will depend on the ability of women based in the home to assume these responsibilities.

Within limits, the same dilemma over women staying at home or going into the labour force exists with respect to care for the elderly (Cohen, 1984). The availability of a healthy spouse or adult children, especially daughters, is a major determinant of the ability of a frail or poor elderly person to maintain a separate residence in the community. Provision of care within the home is available only to the extent that family help is unavailable. However, there are limits to the expectation that the elderly should receive assistance primarily within the family. Adults often do not live in the same communities as their parents. The elderly themselves have some political influence in the area of state-provided services, particularly where their needs can be met in ways less expensive than acute care or extended hospitalization. Furthermore, as the population continues to age, the sons and daughters of the elderly are themselves more likely to be among the elderly and less able to provide care.

Undoubtedly, the availability of abortion is politically the most contentious family issue with which feminist organizations are involved. The issue of free choice and a woman's right to determine what happens to her own body is challenged not only on religious grounds but as a major affront to the sanctity of the traditional family. In 1988, the Supreme Court of Canada struck down Criminal Code provisions about abortion. This decision has left the federal government with the politically dangerous task of formulating new abortion legislation at a time when opinions are almost completely polarized. It has also permitted the provinces to make abortion policy "by the back door" by regulating medical insurance payments for abortion. Some provinces have defined the issue as resting between a woman and her doctor. Other provinces have insisted upon approval of applications by the same hospital committee system that was ruled invalid by the Supreme Court. Still others, notably British Columbia, have attempted (thus far unsuccessfully) to restrict payment for abortion to cases of urgent medical necessity only. No better example is currently available of the politicization of the making of social policy and how issues on which there are obvious deep divisions are dealt with in a pluralist model of political decision-making.

THE DESIGN OF THE INCOME TRANSFER PROGRAM

The primary aim of social security is to protect the purchasing power of individuals subject to low income. Income transfer also redistributes income for reasons other than need, for example, in the case of tax preferences for particular types of investment behaviour. Although most income transfers are made with no reference to the family, significant programs either select the family as a beneficiary, or they are instituted on the basis of certain assumptions about the family.

Most income security programs are instituted with the family in mind. Only with respect to the elderly is there tolerance of supporting individuals in the same way as income support is provided to family units. Recognition of the integrity of the family unit was slow to emerge in the official public reaction to "indigency" or "pauperism." Men were separated from their dependents, children from their parents. Indeed, separate workhouses for the children of those who could not support them were part of the English Poor Law tradition. In less official reactions to family poverty, the poor were encouraged to place their children in apprenticeship, into "service," or worst of all, in orphanages. Even late in the nineteenth century, well-meaning English charitable organizations, such as Dr. Barnardo's, were exporting "street arabs"—runaway children of the very poor—to Canada, Australia, and New Zealand, to provide farm and house labour in exchange for the foster care of rural families.

The Family and Techniques of Social Security

Over the course of the twentieth century, there has been increasing respect for the right of a family, even if very poor, to remain intact. Dennis Guest's (1980) excellent history of the growth of social security in Canada chronicles this development. Pensions for war widows and their children and disability allowances for the families of veterans were the building blocks upon which other programs directed at the family were developed. Even early forms of last-resort programs whose candidates were subject to means tests—social assistance and municipal welfare—recognized the right of the unemployed but still employable father to remain part of the family unit without threatening the subsistence needs of the wife and children. These programs subsequently went further, supporting the right of single mothers to stay at home to raise their children. These rights of eligibility remain, notwithstanding the entry into the labour force of other women with children still at home. Indeed, only with respect to the young, single, able-bodied unemployed have social assistance entitlements been reduced in amount and made more difficult to obtain.

The importance of child rearing was recognized by the state through the introduction of family allowance, a universal payment paid on behalf of children to their mothers. Its original status as part of a postwar pro-natalist policy is revealed by its popular name, "baby bonus." Even with modifications over the years, the program continues to this day as the only unconditional transfer payment in Canada for families who have and care for children.

The Canadian government has introduced another major social security program for families with dependent children living on low income. Administered through the income tax system, an efficient and non-stigmatizing method, a refundable child tax credit program has been introduced to augment the income of families earning no more than approximately 90 percent of Canadian median income. The amounts of the credit have recently been increased, but the range of eligibility has been narrowed so that the upper stratum of the poor is now excluded from full benefits. A number of Canadian provinces have introduced similar but much smaller subsidy programs to support the ability of families on low incomes to raise their children.

While social security measures have met some of the costs of raising children and have, on that account, been directed at the nuclear family, the system has taken a different approach with respect to the elderly. The state has recognized that economic growth depends upon mobility of labour, which increases the risk of geographically or socially separating adult children from their aging parents. A variety of social security programs was introduced to support the independence of the retired elderly. The cornerstone is the universal grant program, Old Age Security, with Guaranteed Income Supplement attached for those elderly who have no, or very little, other income. For those who have worked, there is also the Canada/Québec Pension Plan, which offers a small pension based on contributions up to the level of the average industrial wage. These programs offer only modest levels of support, but they do permit the elderly to live independently if they so desire or if they must. Tax-deferred investment programs have been introduced which permit contributors to build up retirement nest eggs while still in their prime years of earning. The value of such programs will redound primarily to people in the middle to high-income range. Social security for the elderly has acted as a response to, and a reinforcement of the reality that the two-generation family is the norm in Canadian society.

A number of important social insurance programs, designed to protect families from the risk of income loss or major expense, have been introduced. The Canada/Québec Pension Plan has already been mentioned. Unemployment Insurance is available under terms and conditions determined as much according to political as to technical design considerations. The benefits vary with the amount earned while employed and their duration depends upon the number of weeks worked prior to unemployment. Workers' Compensation reimburses workers for the costs of work-related accidents or illness and provides income to those who cannot work for either of these reasons. While these programs cover the entire working population of Canada, they are especially important for families on low income. Under Medicare, all families are protected from the potentially staggering costs of health care through the provision of insured physician and hospital services.

Adequacy and Equity

While programs to protect the economic stability of families appear to be well established as part of the design of Canadian social policy, the issue of adequacy of support also has to be addressed. The debate centres on two questions. Do families have enough economic support? Is the system fair to those on low incomes?

The issue of adequacy has to be viewed in the context of Canadian social policy, which uses a relative, not absolute, definition of poverty. With few exceptions, the subsistence needs of poor families are assured but only at a meagre level. Average transfer-payment income in Canada is roughly half the Statistics Canada "low income cut-off" (a technical term used by Statistics Canada to identify family units that spend as much as 58 percent of their income on food, shelter and clothing) for families in urban areas, about a quarter of the median family income for families of three or more. That poor families are having serious difficulty in making ends meet is evident in the proliferation of food banks, a 1980s version of Depression-era soup kitchens. While government pronouncements indicate the intention of selectively directing higher benefits to the very poor, these programs are designed to cut benefits off at income levels so low as to exclude the upper strata of the poor. Even more vexing is the fact that most of the costs of programs designed to help the poor are borne by the poor themselves (National Council of Welfare, 1985; Canadian Council on Social Development, 1986).

This raises the question of equity. Do social security transfer payments to families on low incomes have a redistributive effect? Do those persons at higher levels of income carry their fair share of the cost? It would appear that massive amounts of money are directed to the poor. Almost 24 billion dollars of Canadian social security in 1984-85 was directed either to the poor or to income protection. An additional 16 billion dollars was spent on programs, such as Family Allowance and Old Age Security, directed at all members of certain demographic groups, and to those who receive Canada/Québec Pension Plan. Much of this money ended up in the hands of families on low incomes. Do these transfers put a greater proportion of total family income in the hands of poor families? Sadly, they do not. Since 1931, notwithstanding the massive growth of social security transfer, the proportion of total family income received by the bottom 20 percent of Canadian families remained on average at slightly over four percent. Income policy is ultimately not redistributive. The income share of the second lowest quintile has successively declined from 11.2 percent in 1951 to 10.3 percent in 1984. A similar decrease, 18 percent to 17.1 percent is noted for the middle quintile. The fourth quintile has increased its share from 23.3 percent to 25 percent, a 20 percent greater share of income than its proportion of the population. Moreover, not only has the highest quintile received 43 percent of total family income—more than twice its proportion of the population—it has maintained approximately that share since 1931. Despite the huge transfer payments, poor families do no better and wealthy families do no worse (all figures from Canadian Council on Social Development, 1986).

The Family and the Income Tax System

At this writing, the Canadian government has introduced a White Paper on Tax Reform. It proposes major changes to the income tax system, many of which are said to be of great benefit to families on lower incomes. These claims are vigorously disputed by social policy advocacy organizations such as the National Council on Welfare, and the Canadian Council on Social Development. It is unclear at this time what changes will actually be legislated at the end of the consultation period established by the government. For these reasons, we will discuss the income tax system as it was prior to June 1986, the pre-White Paper era.

Earlier, an apparent anomaly was raised in relation to income transfer and income distribution. It is explained partially by recognizing that the income tax system is an important method of income transfer. The tax system has many characteristics which permit earners of high income, particularly from non-salary sources, to shelter much of that income from taxation. Many of the means by which this is done have nothing to do with the family. However, most features that implicate families tend to favour the affluent over the poor.

The personal income tax system permits deductions from taxable income for a number of family characteristics. The cost of supporting a spouse who earns little or no income is recognized. Some feminists oppose this feature of the spousal exemption: they feel it demeans women and it insufficiently recognizes the real value of work in the home (Eichler, 1983a). The support of dependent children, and even of children above the age of majority, not receiving an income, still in the parental home, and full-time students, is recognized by tax exemption. The tax system recognizes the support given to aged or infirm family members by permitting other deductions from taxable income. Deductions are also permitted for actual childcare expenses, with a limit placed both on the amount deductible per child and on the total amount permitted per family. These tax exemptions are available only to those with the highest income who file family tax, usually the male. To his income must also be added the amount received by the mother in family allowances. The family-status tax exemptions are based on the assumption that families with dependent members have higher expenses and less disposable income and that this should be taken into account in the calculation of taxable income.

At various times, subject to the vagaries of the federal budget affecting a particular taxation year, a number of discretionary exemptions are available that depend upon economic behaviour of the family. A taxpayer, with a high income, usually the male, can contribute to his spouse's registered retirement savings plan and have the amount of the contribution deducted from his taxable income. He may also make an interest-free loan to his spouse or his children, which permits them to make investments that are substantially free of taxation. Unused tax benefits available to one spouse can be transferred to the other. All these and other arrangements have recently been available to families with high income as a way to minimize their tax burden. The advantages accrue disproportionately to families with high income for two reasons. The first is that they are more likely to have the disposable income that permits the discretionary economic behaviour the tax system rewards. In addition, the after-tax dollar value of deductions from taxable income is greater for the taxpayer with a high income because his or her tax rate increases the saving realized on every dollar sheltered from taxation (National Council of Welfare, 1985). For example, in 1984, the value per child of the child tax exemption to a one-earner two-child family in Ontario was $0, $203, $246, and $320 at the income levels of $10 000, $20 000, $30 000, and $45 000 respectively (Canadian Council on Social Development, 1985). This same general difference is experienced for virtually every family-related item rewarded by exemption in the tax system: the benefits are regressive.

Tax credits, on the other hand are progressive in their impact since they are reductions from tax payable rather than from taxable income. A $100 tax credit represents a greater proportional saving to someone earning $5000 than to someone earning $50 000. Therefore, tax credits are preferred by designers of social security programs when the avowed intention is to benefit those on low incomes. A further advantage of the child tax credit to families on low incomes is its refundability. This relatively new invention in the social security field permits families at levels of income so low that they do not pay taxes to receive full payment from the tax system of the tax credit for which they are eligible. Should there ever be a time when a guaranteed annual income is accepted as part of Canadian social policy, it will likely be delivered by means of a refundable tax credit.

PERSONAL SOCIAL SERVICES AND THE FAMILY

Three major developments in personal social services have had an impact on the services and entitlements we call family policy. Since 1967, the child welfare program has responded to its critics by increasing the efforts of its agencies to keep intact families that would otherwise be rent asunder by the apprehension of one or more of the children. The second development has been the increased concern over family violence, primarily that directed at girls and women. This concern has not yet resulted in the corresponding growth of the services provided to victims. Finally, there has been a great surge of interest in the field of marital and family therapy, with concomitant increases both in the demand for and supply of these services.

Child Welfare

In the area of child welfare, many evaluations have confirmed (see, for example, Ryant et al., 1985) that the traditional practice of removing a neglected child from the family has not led to appreciably better conditions for the children than had they not been apprehended. Child welfare agencies aquired a reputation for providing services which weakened family life or of doing little to assist in the resolution of the family problems that created the need to protect children. In response to these criticisms, Canadian child welfare systems—which are within provincial jurisdiction—have embraced goals and objectives that generally stress services, focused on the family, and which encourage the removal of children only as a last resort. Since the mid-1970s, most provinces have revised child welfare laws to stress the critical role of child and family services. In some provinces, actual changes have been made in the organization of such services. Indeed, a dispassionate evaluation of the legislative and organization changes might lead one to conclude that child welfare practice has become more concerned with helping children in the context of their families by working more with the families as the unit of attention.

In general, that this is not the case is due to the failure of funding and of helping techniques. The redefinition of child welfare coincided with the rising political concern with deficit spending and the size of public debt. Monetarist economic thinking, which tends to blame social policy spending for large budget deficits, has become dominant in policy-making at both the federal and the provincial level. Allocation of public funds to those who deliver child welfare services falls well short of what is required to meet the new objectives. Underfunded services inevitably tend to be services of last resort: removal of children from their families and their placement with either foster parents or in group foster homes are the most expedient choices. However, the task of child welfare would not be easily accomplished even with larger budget allocations. The techniques of successful intervention into highly disorganized families, the traditional targets of the system, are not fully developed. Services will improve only with more experience in conceiving and testing new helping techniques, with the retraining and reorientation of workers in the field, and with the education of new workers who have relevant and well-developed skills to achieve family improvement. While all such measures are expensive, it is as much on a more successful system of practice as on funding that the intended family orientation of child welfare depends.

Family Violence

Public awareness of family violence is at a higher level than ever before and the issue is on the leading edge of family policy development. Opinion is divided as to whether its actual incidence has increased or whether, always a feature of family life, it has come more into the open now that it is publicly condemned. That children are both physically and sexually abused (a major concern for child welfare services) has become all too clear (*Report of the Committee on Sexual Offences Against Children and Youth*, 1984). Cases of wife-battering are now publicly reported more often and there is a greater likelihood that the perpetrator will be criminally charged. The attention now given to family violence has elicited new social policy responses.

The services are designed to protect the victims and to repair, if possible, the psychological damage they have suffered. Like all social services in the 1980s, where they are available they are insufficiently supplied and under-funded. There are more services for urban than for rural women. This is a serious problem, particularly for abused farm women who are too far from their closest neighbours to be assisted when in difficulty.

This relatively recent awareness of and sensitivity to family violence is important for policy because it implicitly redefines family relationships. The family members who are physically abused no longer need to suffer in silence. To this extent, at least, women and children are no longer to be treated as the chattels of their husbands and fathers; however, a variety of legal and social service problems remain to be solved.

The New Popularity of Marital and Family Therapy

Psychiatry, clinical psychology and social work have all made marital and family therapy a major new subfield of their practices. In the United States, it is emerging as a separate field; the first generation of practitioners, drawn from other professions, are educating and training people whose first and only training will be in the field. Many different approaches are used in marital and family therapy. For example, some attempt to alter communication patterns within the family, others focus on patterns brought into the family from the spouses' respective families of origin, and still others deal with the strength and permeability of boundaries in the relationships between family members. What seems to be common to marital and family therapy is the view of the family as a small social system with its own structure and process and that the family as system, not individual family members, is the target of intervention.

In Canada, marital and family therapy is not yet, and may never become, fully a part of the array of publicly provided services. The reasons for this are identical to those associated with the rationing of all personal social services: the coincidental effects of fiscal restraint and the attitude that public social services exist only for the poor rather than for the entire community. Notwithstanding these limitations the emergence of the field as such may have a salutary effect on social policy. That the family as a unit has become the focus of increased attention and is to be treated as a unit in which problems are solved, even when the symptoms appear to be attached only to individual family members, are important perspectives to account for when developing personal social services. Perhaps in small ways such as these, policies for families move closer to becoming a coherent family policy.

CONCLUSION

In Canada, as in most Western industrial nations, family life has been determined by the nature of the economy. As it has adapted to opportunities or reacted to stress, the family has taken on plural forms and different identities. State action has been necessary to assist the family in its function of mediating between individual family members and society as a whole. This action, diverse and disparate as it is, forms the content of what we call family policy. It is not deliberately or explicitly plotted out. It is neither comprehensive nor even internally consistent. Nevertheless, it does evolve and, however imperfectly, it reflects a temporary consensus about what families are perceived to need at a particular time. Given the nature of the policy-making process, these conditions will continue to prevail.

Suggested Readings

Canada.
  1987   *Basic Facts on Social Security Programs.* Ottawa: Department of Health and Welfare.
Eichler, Margrit.
  1988   *Families in Canada Today.* Second ed. Toronto: Gage.
Gabarino, James.
  1982   *Children and Families in the Social Environment.* New York: Aldine
Gough, Ian.
  1979   *The Political Economy of the Welfare State.* London: Macmillan.
Kamerman, Shiela B., and Alfred Kahn, eds.
  1978   *Family Policy: Government and Families in Fourteen Countries.* New York: Columbia University Press.

Moscovitch, Allan, and Jim Albert, eds.
1987   *The Benevolent State: The Growth of Welfare in Canada.* Toronto: Garamond.

Moroney, Robert M.
1986   *Shared Responsibility: Families and Social Policy.* New York: Aldine.

Wilson, Elizabeth.
1977   *Women and the Welfare State.* London: Tavistock.

13

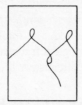

ALTERNATIVE LIFE STYLES: TWO DECADES OF CHANGE

Robert N. Whitehurst

Following the Second World War, the United States of America emerged as the leader of the industrialized societies. Although it militarily assisted the allied nations, it did not experience the destruction that Germany and other European countries did. Instead, the war enabled Americans to build a strong capitalist economy within a democratic framework. Such a development led to a belief among many Americans (certainly among the conservative political elite) that their economic system and political philosophy are second to none and, therefore, they should not only preserve it but promote it as well wherever and whenever they choose to do so. There were blatant expressions of intolerance toward communism, and military intervention to eradicate its influence was perceived as the responsibility of the United States. However, in the mid-1960s, this belief came under intense scrutiny by the majority of the baby-boom generation. It not only challenged the fundamental political and economic assumptions of the previous generation but also engaged in formulating alternative life styles in matters of marriage, family, and living patterns. Such formulations were only the beginning for movements aimed at the achievement of increased equality for women, greater sexual freedom, rights for homosexuals, and other progressive trends in political, economic, and personal life. Sociologists became interested in these life styles, as they appeared to be organized reactions against the dominant establishment.

Young people, especially those in larger metropolitan areas and in universities, were involved or became involved, in movements concerned with free speech, war, poverty, and women's rights. Some "gurus" of the time advocated sexual freedom and the use of drugs as a means of reacting to the conventional society. Almost a quarter century has passed since the emergence of these so-called alternative life styles. Many have since disappeared, others have gone underground, still others have been somewhat integrated into our institutional life. The main purpose of this chapter is to examine briefly within a sociological framework the factors that led to the emergence and decline of the alternative life styles.

HISTORICAL FACTORS IN SOCIAL CHANGE DURING THE 1950s AND 1960s

Although most of the research on counterculture or alternative life styles has been conducted in the United States, there are some differences to distinguish the Canadian case. When we raise the issue as to what these differences were and how they affected Canadians, we find that we lack definitive comparative data to demonstrate significant differences (Spencer, 1985). Canadians tend to be more law-abiding and to trust officials more than Americans do; at the same time they adhere to a more pluralistic set of norms, which allows for variations in life styles. In general, the Canadian alternatives of the 1960s and 1970s followed the same lines as movements in the United States, although, as usually occurs, some activities developed and diffused somewhat after they had become popular in the United States. Few major differences, however, can be confirmed by data.

Many of the factors that led to movements that affected youth were part of the "beat" culture of the late 1950s. Very small groups of dropouts in certain urban areas had formed and developed anti-establishment ideologies, anti-work and pro-drug subcultures. Being a "beatnik" in the late 1950s or early 1960s meant being unclean, without direction, without ambition or aspirations, and in favor of drugs. In some ways, this period was historic in that it set the stage for a variety of changes in marital and family life, some of which led to what later came to be seen as alternative life styles. We will discuss some important factors that contributed to changes during the 1960s and 1970s.

Anti-Communism: The McCarthy Era

North American society was passing through the late phases of the so-called McCarthy era (after U.S. Senator Joseph P. McCarthy, a fanatical opponent of communism). Political oppression in the U.S. was aimed at all forces even vaguely suspected of being to the left of the dominant centre of American politics. Anti-communist sentiment emerged from the cold-war period during which there was deep suspicion of anything associated with Russia or communism. This trend was one of the early political influences that polarized groups in America. The young, educated, and liberal took a stand against activities such as those fomented by the House Un-American Activities Committee. This committee was either hated and feared as blatantly paranoid, or supported as the saviour of America—keeping the communists out of North America. While McCarthyism did not have a direct impact on the Canadian political process, the consequences of the opposition to tactics adopted by McCarthy and his followers did cross the border in the form of liberal values and tolerance to opposing political ideologies.

Economic Affluence

Increasing economic affluence characterized the times with a psychology of plenty. North America in general had not suffered the destruction caused by the Second World War that Germany or other European nations had. One result was the early building of an industrial base, making America the supreme productive power of the time. Consequently, postwar North America experienced unprecedented affluence. Except for the few, it was not a time of shortages or hard times. Although the postwar re-adjustment period was essentially over by the 1960s, high demands for consumer goods created easily available jobs, as did the military buildup when the United States began its serious entrance into the Vietnam war. The myth of an invincible America was left mostly undisturbed, notwithstanding cold-war fears and, of course, experiences in Vietnam and Cambodia. It was commonly believed that anyone who wanted employment could find it. This was, of course, not entirely true: poverty was still rife among some groups. The belief that individuals and groups could accomplish whatever they aspired to dominated the collective thinking of North Americans. What was neglected was the increasing inequality experienced by blacks, women, and the poor classes in both urban and rural North America.

The War Against Poverty

In both Canada and the United States during the early 1960s, poverty and structured inequality, in the midst of the general affluence, became the focus of attention and reform. This could be attributed, in part, to a number of events dramatized by the mass media and to changes in the political system. The period can be described as a new awakening on many fronts. Poverty and discrimination were recognized as critical social problems: it was relatively easy to get a minimum consensus among the activists on the need to eradicate them. Even though a "war against poverty" was declared by liberal politicians, it was in fact not very effective because it polarized the conservatives, especially those who persisted in advocating Social Darwinism (or those who were subtly racist) and liberals. In Canada as well, various groups pressured governments, both provincial and federal, to examine and develop policies to ameliorate poverty. This led to the institution of a Royal Commission by the Senate in the 1970s.

Racial and Ethnic Discrimination

Although racial and ethnic prejudices and discrimination in Canada have existed historically, they have surfaced only recently as social issues calling for redress. By contrast, racial prejudice and discrimination have been part of the history of the United States and remain as yet unresolved problems. In Canada, native peoples had essentially stayed on reservations; other visible minorities in urban enclaves. With the liberalization of immigration policies, however, an increased number of non-white groups entered Canada and concentrated in specific neighbourhoods of selected cities (for example, in Toronto and Vancouver). This altered the racial composition of Canadian society, which had historically been white. This has been one of the factors for the emergence of ethnic and racial prejudice and discrimination as a social problem in Canada just as it had been in the United States.

Television, Education, and Religion   Another development that contributed to change in the 1960s was the growth of television. This new medium brought images of an affluent, happy, and patriotic America. Images of an America characterized by equality and freedom were of course contradicted by real life in the racial ghettos of large cities. As television became increasingly common in lower-class homes and in the ghettos, it unwittingly provided a new impetus for social change. The sections of American society that had suffered centuries of poverty (historically blacks, and now Chicanos and other minority groups) realized that the new affluence was mainly enjoyed by the white groups and they were left with few opportunities to share it. This realization led to many violent riots in the 1960s. These riots, followed by the demands from black and liberal white leaders, resulted in the creation of many programs to increase educational and occupational opportunities for the poor black and other racial and ethnic minorities. Although such reforms helped a number of individuals, the problem of poverty remains for many of these groups.

As more students were urged to enter universities in larger numbers, the realities of the system created more conflicts and discontinuity than ever before. The generation of idealistic students of the 1960s was exposed to conflicting messages from differing sources in ways no other generation had experienced. Television, modern liberal education, and declining religious influence added to a great probability of young people's altering their perceptions about the way the real world operated. In addition, after the Second World War, the influence of Eastern religions and philosophies began to be felt in America as many Asian religious leaders came to American cities to share their views of the ways in which self and society are related. For example, Maharishi Mahesh Yogi and Maharishi Rajnish from India as well as Reverend Sueng Moon from Korea have had significant followings both in Canada and the United States. Courses in some colleges offered by gurus such as Allen Watts in the 1960s added a new dimension to the search for meaning in life. The postwar generation of Americans and Canadians learned from these sources that much of the world perceives life in terms other than the Protestant ethic of norms and goals focusing on achievement.

Childhood Socialization

The strong pro-family and pro-natalist norms that continued into the postwar era gave rise to new approaches to child rearing. Children were no longer seen as economically valuable: their value and significance was seen to be in the pride that individuals derive from raising them well. The extent of a child's middle-class manners, social skills, and, above all, intellectual achievement reflected the quality of the parents. Children were often described as the new status symbols of the late 1950s. Child-rearing experts advised parents to "ease up"—to be less rigorous and compulsive in following routines and discipline. The traditional approach, "spare the rod and spoil the child," was set aside in the more liberal and affluent era.

Some observers called the new style "permissive," a term never well defined, except that people usually used it pejoratively. When children did not behave in a manner considered to be properly adjusted, they were said to be products of permissive child rearing, or "spoiled." It is unlikely that many parents followed an extremely permissive set of guidelines, but the term was convenient as a simple device to aid in the understanding of a complex problem. The term also conveyed the image that many children and young people shared the new affluence their parents experienced. As with all stereotypes, there is some truth to the image of more permissive times. When we combine the expectations of mature behaviour imposed on children with the permissive or more liberal norms, we can better understand the reasons for the sexual revolution. Driving youngsters into more mature intellectual and social activities also created a new potential for the expression of sexual interests at earlier ages. Cultural forces seemed to lead youth into mature sexual behaviour, but there was little understanding as to why they were more sexually active than their predecessors. The youngsters of the 1960s began to dress like adults and many cultivated adult sexual behaviour. They were conscious of the need to be attractive and sensual more than were previous generations of their age group. This was encouraged partly by the new awareness of the economic potential of youth culture: the availability of contraceptives, distinctive clothing, music, cosmetics, language, cars, and illegal drugs all distanced in some ways the middle- and upper-class North American youth from their elders. The time was propitious for young people to feel more powerful and more rebellious than any previous generation. Demographically, their large numbers created market conditions favourable to such a development and allowed them to form coalitions, potential power blocs aimed at change.

As postwar families tended to measure the attainment of the good life according to economic security and consumerism, children of middle-class parents often felt a combination of forces that encouraged rebellious tendencies. Children were often viewed as new status symbols, precious to their families insofar as they exhibited good behaviour and achievement. The pressure to achieve high intellectual, cultural, and educational standards was a heavy burden for many children of the 1950s and 1960s (Seeley et al. 1956). Although they experienced a level of affluence and health that no generation had previously experienced, their often negative reactions to the Vietnam war and other social issues disturbed many elders. Education and affluence left many of them with searching questions about some basic issues: family, marriage, sex, and equality. In their concern for maintaining a good living for their families, many parents failed to understand the emotional needs of their children. Sharing money instead of time with children became the norm for many families.

Many of these children grew up with mixed feelings about their parents and their success, since they tended to feel as young adults that something was missing from their lives. It may not have been inevitable that this attitude would result in rebelliousness—unconventional sexuality, uncleanliness, and radical leanings. Nevertheless, these characteristics are all commonly attributed to this period. The messages of the flower children of the 1960s included a rejection of some of the dominant values of their parents. Parents, on the other hand, were not primarily concerned about what the youth felt were the real problems of their age: inequality, war, racism, poverty, and, later, sexism. It would be incorrect, however, to assume that all flower children were very young; some leaders were older. Nevertheless, there was a dominant norm among counterculture groups not to trust anyone over the age of thirty. Such tendencies were generally shaped by the mass media, particularly by television. The portrayal of the counterculture groups in relation to their ideals and practices validated an already existing dividing line between the so-called establishment and the counterculture groups.

It should also be noted that at times there occurred a kind of reverse socialization effect: young people sometimes convinced their parents of the rightness of their causes and values. At times it was also embarrassing for the children of parents who acted like hippies. Some parents and older persons took on the appearance and values of hippies, often with skepticism or bemused acceptance.

The Sexual Revolution and Sexual Equality

A consequence of the social trends of the 1960s was the polarization of ideological positions, creating conflicts between many parents and children, most of which could not be easily resolved. In this social, economic, and political setting, alternatives to marriage and traditional family structures arose in a variety of experimental forms. The late 1950s witnessed the end of one phase of the battle of the sexes. After their return from the Second World War, men reasserted their dominance and leadership in families and their authority over females; this included efforts to coerce women to avoid working outside the home (Skolnick, 1983). However, in order to maintain the desired standard of living, families had to generate higher incomes. Many men took additional jobs, a practice which reduced the opportunity for family togetherness. The end of this period saw an increase in the number of mothers seeking paid employment. As noted in Chapter Five, the increased participation of married women with or without children in the labour force was followed by a decline in the size of the family in Canada, and the United States as well. The availability and acceptance of the pill and other contraceptives facilitated such trends. While families are gradually adapting to such changes, there are many problems that remain to be resolved (see Chapter Seven).

An important development of the 1960s was ideologically supported and organized opposition to sexual inequality both outside and within marriage and the family. However, sexism did not become a very pressing issue until the later years of the 1960s and the early 1970s. Although there were a few feminists championing women's causes, they were considered by most to be an eccentric left-wing minority not to be taken seriously. Not until Betty Friedan's *Feminine Mystique* (1963) had been in print for about five years were there signs of massive organization of feminist and activist women (Leslie and Korman, 1985).

Sex and Self-awareness

Part of the so-called sexual revolution of the 1960s was the changes in attitudes and behaviour concerning sexuality. In California, the Free Speech movement gained popularity. Consequently, talk about sex was inevitable as we moved into more liberal times. Outrageous publications offending conventional morality began to appear. *Screw* magazine, the Berkeley *Barb*, and the Sexual Freedom League's publications provided their readers with something beyond the pale of what was considered at the time normal. Negative reactions by the so-called establishment to such activities no doubt increased the interest of many young people in talk about sex, thus indirectly encouraging sexual activities. Further liberalization of sexual behaviour was encouraged by the Human Potential movement, Gestalt groups, and various sorts of encounter groups (for example, The Sexual Freedom League in California in the 1960s). These groups seemed to hold the promise of growth: they allowed contacts with other liberal-minded, if not permissive, people, insights into the self, and ways to get along better with others.

Life Styles that have not Survived

Many of the open alternatives of the 1960s allowed for experimentation with forms of sex that were touted as promoting sexual freedom and personal growth. A general normative context of exploration of self through expanding interpersonal relationships emerged, primarily in and around large cities. In some groups, fear of involvement or refusal to participate in some of these activities such as group sex and homosexuality were considered neurotic "hang-ups." People willing to exlore the new boundaries of sexual, social and political meanings were provided with a variety of new experiences. Nude and encounter therapy, meditation, and a variety of other experiences dramatically opened up possibilities for self-examination and relationships with others. The high turnover and dropout rates associated with alternatives of the time, however, can be partially explained by discrepancies individuals found between their fantasies and the realities found in these alternatives. By the mid-1970s there were indications of a shifting emphasis from group activities to more personal means of insight and awareness.

Three alternatives of the times that did not survive, at least in any major form were hippies, communes, and swinging, all of which were most prevalent in the 1970s. To be a hippie, or a communard, or to swing did not necessarily signify rejection of all normal family values, but rather, they involved adding on to or rejecting parts of dominant family values (such as restrained or monogamous sexuality, cleanliness, individualism, hard work, achievement, and money. The term "family" often took on meanings broader than that of common kin. The failures of family perceived by members of the counterculture were often seen to be corrected by new forms that rejected some values and actions or added values and actions approved by the new groups as more appropriate. Marriage, when it was valued by the counterculture, did not contain many of the older established meanings as the era of "open marriages" progressed. Most persons practising sexually open marriages accepted many parts of conventional life styles. Likewise, many hippies were committed to the counterculture on weekends and holidays only.

Hippies   The hippie movement of the 1960s is often explained in terms of a rejection of American values and the work ethic by a generation raised by parents who were products of these values. The hippies rejected the more conventional norms of achievement, consumerism, and the accumulation of wealth. Consequently, they dropped out of the mainstream society and chose to live in communes or wherever they could find shelter and food, whether in urban core areas or in rural settings. They also tended to appropriate land or vacant buildings for their use until they were driven out by the legal owners of the property.

At the time, the hippie movement was seen as making a political and social comment on American social and economic institutions mainly because it rejected many items esteemed by conventional society. However, lacking strong organization, leadership, discipline, and a coherent philosophy, as well as commitment to its own professed values and norms, the movement disintegrated within a few years.

Communes   Communes are not new to North American society. Historically, many religious and utopian communes have been instituted in both Canada and the United States. However, the communes that arose in the 1960s were not based on religion or well-formed ideologies but on a strong opposition to the North American way of life, including marriage and the family, (Libby and Whitehurst, 1977). Many kinds of communes emphasized many different forms of interpersonal relationships. For example, the Sandstone commune near Los Angeles, more than other groups, stressed sexual freedom as a basis for its organization.

The Sandstone commune offered "swinging" weekends with free sex (after an entry fee was paid) and an opportunity to join a community whose goal was no less than to make the world a more humane and habitable place (Talese, 1980). Nevertheless, the utopian goals of the community were not realized. The sincere utopians who organized the commune felt that once persons could get beyond the sexual inhibitions which our society imposed in early socialization, participants would undertake the task of building a community. This did not occur in practice. A small core of utopians were able to maintain the community for a few years, but most persons went to Sandstone simply for sexual encounters.

There were other types of anarchist communes as well, in California and other western regions of North America. For example, the anarchistic communes of California in the 1960s briefly persisted on a strong anti-organization theme of "do your own thing." Since that meant smoking dope, writing poetry, making love, and meditating (and allowing children similar privileges), the work needed for the survival of the commune often did not get done. It was in this period that some serious questions about the persistence of gender roles arose, because women continued to cook, wash dishes, and care for the households or children in the communes. The assumption was that if one gave freely what one could and shared resources, the group would survive happily. This obviously proved to be erroneous on both counts: they were not especially happy places because too many members did not contribute and, since the groups were unstable, they did not persist. Furthermore, practices such as giving young children access to drugs and sex may have led to dissolution of a particular commune earlier than might otherwise have happened. This does not mean that members of a given commune perceived breakups as negative experiences. They deemed rather that the particular place was not meeting their needs. A flexibility of interpretation arose as to what each separate experience meant and most often members did not see as failures much that the conventional society would label as failures.

Some observers note that the 1960s provided a positive context in which to interpret new experiences. Although new experiences of any variety may be limited in their potential benefits for anyone, participants could define all experience as adding to their potential for growth, their knowledge, and their fund of experience, all of which effects may be defined as positive.

Swinging   The easiest and least painful mode of violating a norm like monogamy is still found in clandestine affairs. Other kinds of extramarital sex are too costly and painful for most people. The best examples can be found in the attempts to maintain sexually open marriages or relationship contracts which allow many sexual partners. Conflict theorists note that the power exercised by the establishment must be considered critical in determining the degree of deviance. The "sexual underground" has always comprised activities and supporters that varied from the conventional modes of relationship prevailing at the time. What also seems true is that relatively affluent times encourage the growth of the sexual underground, (Whitehurst and Booth, 1980).

Currently in North America a large federation of swinging clubs holds annual conventions and regional meetings for its thousands of members, an unknown proportion of which are either ephemeral or relatively inactive members. Swingers are generally of middle- and upper-class backgrounds, although it is not uncommon for some from the working class to participate as well (Bartell, 1971; Gilmartin, 1977). They find themselves in continuing conflict with local authorities in many places in Canada and the U.S. over the operaton of their clubs; nevertheless, they have managed to sustain several clubs, as well as publications. In a less pluralistic society, they would be seriously repressed and not survive. It is difficult to assess the proportion of North Americans who engage in swinging activities either occasionally or regularly. However, various estimates suggest that it is about 2 percent of the adult population in North America (Hunt, 1974; Macklin, 1980:910). Many who try swinging as a life style find it not entirely to their liking and soon drop out. It ought to be noted also that, in this period, what came to be defined as the "sexual revolution" more often affected liberalized female than male behaviours. It is still a matter of contention if in fact "revolution" is the correct term to describe sexual changes occurring at the time. Only in our very recent history has the amount of extramarital sex apparently waned as a popular activity of adults: this seems more due to the continued threat of AIDS than to a revival of traditional morality.

Whether these three movements achieved their goals even marginally is still a matter of debate. At the time, however, they made a strong impression and today we can still find vestiges of some of these activities. Perhaps the most important result of alternative sexual practices is the relative ease today with which many North Americans approach sexual matters. The movements of this period can be held at least partly responsible for permissive sexual attitudes and behaviour. It is also logical to assume that if people can discuss sexual matters more freely and hold liberal views on the matter, they will be less reluctant to engage in sexual activities contrary to traditional expectations.

There is virtually no sphere of human activity that has not been affected in some ways by the sexual revolution. Whether or not we agree a genuine revolution has occurred is less important than looking at some of the present consequences of these changes.

CHANGE AND STABILITY IN ALTERNATIVE LIFE STYLES

Although some alternative life styles created in the 1960s disappeared after a short time, many left an indelible mark. Some of these practices are of no more than passing historic interest today, but many of the values and beliefs engendered in them persist in some modified ways (Kanter, 1985). An important consequence of the experiments with alternatives characteristic of the 1960s is the contemporary tendency to view many forms of marriage and the family simply as variants of the traditional patterns. Thus, single parents, childless couples, cohabiting couples, even marriages in which there were elements of role-reversal in households which in the 1960s were all subject to various negative labels are now simply tolerated as alternatives tailored to the needs of individuals or couples.

Alternatives, according to our definition, include any lifestyle (often including, but not necessarily, at least one intimate partner) which is at variance with approved nuclear family structure, whether it is voluntary or involuntary. When we examine why many of these alternatives changed, were co-opted by the mainstream population, or vanished, we recognize several factors, some of which we will focus on here.

Sources of Change

There is no uniform explanation as to what caused changes in relationships between males and females in the period between 1960 and 1980. The vast majority of such explanations fall within what is now described as feminist tradition (for a review, see Eichler, 1986; Chapter Two in this volume). Nevertheless, some clear trends can be discerned, even though there is little consensus on causal connections. Economic factors are critical in analysis of these changes. The psychology of plenty slowly dissipated after the 1960s. Recession, inflation, impending shortages, unemployment, and the decline of the dominance of the American economy in the early 1970s led to growing dissatisfaction among the young. Many of those who dropped out of the system returned to its fold with the determination to change it while being part of it. This was often due to their disappointment with various movements of the 1960s and the fear of not getting a job as they became more scarce. Furthermore, in a rapidly changing society, the mass media's interest in swinging, hippies, communes, and group marriage quickly waned: these patterns, no longer interesting news items, were replaced by such issues as oil shortages, venereal diseases (herpes and, later, AIDS), and terrorism. Lacking in purpose, resources, commitment, and public attention, many of the alternatives with sexual activities as their focus receded to the background in the 1980s.

People in positions of power frequently refused employment to persons who appeared, in dress and manners, to be hippies. To complicate matters, the norms of acceptance of persons with beards, for example, were broadened; some counterculture norms became part of the dominant culture. Other effects can be traced to the fact that many persons were marginal in the counterculture. Many who clung to the edges of that counterculture were committed to its liberal or radical ideals only in superficial or ambivalent ways. As more persons became "weekend hippies" and donned the costumes of the counterculture simply to idle around Yorkville in Toronto or other urban centres, the purpose of the counterculture was lost, trivialized, or marginalized. Some formerly benign urban areas became areas of hard-core drug use and thus lost their general appeal. People often found aspects of the counterculture to their liking, but also wanted to maintain a more conventional identity and keep their jobs. Strains were evident in many people who tried to participate selectively in both cultures. This crossover effect between two cultures was in part responsible for elements of the counterculture adapting to the normal day-to-day behavioural patterns. Permissive sexual attitudes and dress habits, less compulsive work orientations, marijuana, and, in general, being "laid-back" became normative for the mainly young persons who had passed through "the scene" in the 1960s. As jobs became scarce with the economic recession of the early

1970s, however, large numbers of young people moving from one end of the country to the other (where things were rumored to be better) slowed to a trickle. Whereas in the period from 1969 through 1971 young persons sometimes spent a week at some stopover points headed toward Vancouver trying to get rides, by the mid-1970s, hitchhiking essentially disappeared as a mass phenomenon.

Furthermore, in hard economic times, parents are reluctant to support children who do not pursue clearly defined educational and occupational goals. In addition, alternative life styles based on utopian ideals were frequently found wanting and subsequently disappeared (Whitehurst, 1971). Besides the problems engendered by the naive hope that like-minded persons could form communities and survive because of assumptions of hippie brotherhood, many other problems prevail for the survival of alternatives.

Since many of these alternative forms are considered deviant and perhaps threats to the establishment, negative reactions to alternatives occurred at many levels of society. Some persons who chose to cohabit found themselves at odds with landlords, letter carriers, and parents. Since the 1970s, however, we must note that virtually none of these negative responses affect cohabitants today. Nevertheless the point remains that many of the alternatives were not positively or benignly accepted by the conventional community. Were sanctions still activated against unmarried couples living together, cohabitation would not have become so popular. Cohabitation does not really threaten our dominant institutions as it is commonly seen as a premarital interlude or a temporary arrangement. Some of the sanctions against lifestyle deviants were effective however; some were successful in bringing about the dissolution of some alternative life styles. Changes in the economy and lack of institutional support are critical to the failures of some alternatives.

Alternative Life Styles: A Conceptualization

Most of the alternatives that required persons to set aside well socialized normative practices of monogamy, or that demanded a high level of community consciousness and sharing, were likely doomed to failure from the start. North American family socialization is simply oriented too much toward the self, too privatized and individualistic, to allow easy transition to such utopian life styles.

On the one hand, the existence of many of the alternatives of the time led to the liberalization of attitudes and practices concerning sexuality, marriage, and the family. On the other hand, hardened resistance to any activity that deviated from conventional family life became organized and has persisted until today. Although sociologists often make an assumption that we live in a liberal pluralistic society today (and this is partly true), large sections of our population do not easily tolerate pluralism of family forms. We are thus caught in a period in which many sub-groups compete for loyalty and support in diverse ideological contexts. This condition may be considered the converse of Durkheim's concept of anomie (1951). In Durkheim's explanation, free choice in one's work and one's life would prevent the problem of anomie or the feeling of living without norms or structural constraints. The notion of polynomia (overchoice) might help us understand the current society. We live in an era of multiple choices which may complicate our existence because of conflicting norms and because of demands made on all of us. This problem has also been defined by Berger, who points out that "modern man finds himself confronted not only by multiple options of possible courses of action but also by multiple options of possible ways of thinking about the world" (1979:17). He suggests that we may now choose such disparate items in our lives as our automobiles, sexual life style and religious preference. Never before have so many had so many choices and normative preferences offered them in such a short space of time.

If we ask why such a small proportion of the total population actually became involved in alternatives, we might seek one explanation in the concept of the "mainstream hypothesis." This notion informs us that, on the basis of probabilities, most people will not stray too far from the mainstream of normatively approved actions. All sociology is predicated on such a premise, that people will predictably respond in such a mainstream fashion most of the time in most of their activities. Swinging entails high moral, social, and personal costs for all except the most daring and adventuresome; affairs cost less, and monogamy costs least of all in this framework since it is the most highly approved sexual behaviour.

Perceived sanctions carry great weight in our decision-making processes. Many people confront difficult questions: What will our reference groups and significant others think if they find out? How would this hurt my primary relationship? What risks, such as discovery, disease, or disappointment, are involved? It is easier by far to stay in the mainstream as most of us are not innovators willing to take the risks and pay the prices implied in these questions. The current fear of AIDS has also provided a definitive pull away from exploration of alternatives. Many persons involved in the sexual revolution reached the conclusion that fantasies are often best left unfulfilled in reality: they found that their fantasies of free sex and multiple partners or sharing of partners simply did not produce as many of the desired results as anticipated.

To counterbalance the centripetal force compelling most persons to act in accordance with mainstream norms, there is always a minority of moral entrepreneurs and a variety of persons on the fringes who for a number of reasons like to live on the edge of what is normatively approved. A concept that helps us understand the centrifugal pulls related to fringe, deviant, or borderline behaviours is the "principle of limits." Although the major moral force in society tends to pull most persons toward that mainstream normative order, there are a number of conditions that push others outward, away from that central normative context. Some persons are risk-takers: they tempt fate by living on the thin normative edge of society and find the challenge of beating the system invigorating. Others genuinely feel that some of the rules are antiquated, irrational, or repressive: they refuse to play by the rules, recognizing the weight of sanctions that can be applied, and take their chances. For whatever reasons (and the leaders in such activities are generally males), many persons are persuaded that their own actions are justified. They therefore will push back normative boundaries by testing them, sometimes changing them, for themselves and their own groups, if not for everyone.

These opposing forces are always at work—the pull toward the mainstream against more or less organized resistance to the boundaries which is in turn met by counter-resistance that strives to maintain the status quo. Thus, conflict theorists, who recognize struggle as basic to society and insist on comprehending the dialectical processes of challenge and of give-and-take in conflict, rivalry, and competition, need to be heard and understood, for they have much to teach us.

Some insights into counterculture life styles can be gained in a brief examination of the following factors as they affected alternative life styles:

Resources Most counterculture groups or movements had few real resources that would have contributed to their long-term survival.

Commitment Most of the adherents to alternative life styles were only partially committed to long-term survival of the counterculture.

Mass-support potential The possibility of widespread support was strictly limited, except in cases such as cohabitation, where the behaviour in question was not considered a threat to marriage or as serious deviance.

Ideological position The distance of the alternatives from the mainstream was at times too great for them to expect support on a large scale. This was less so for cohabitation, which helped it to survive and become somewhat integrated as less stigmatized behaviour than other counterculture activities.

Leadership Both the longevity of the counterculture and the quality of its leadership proved in most instances too thin for the survival of alternatives. In a sense, however, it should be recognized that any kind of organization was anathema to many young persons of the time, making longevity of organization difficult or impossible.

Previous experience Although counterculture forms have a long history in North America, they have often suffered from both internal and external problems. The basic difference in the last two decades is the massive appeal and large-scale willingness (likely generated by increased affluence, freedom, and education) to risk an attempt at a different life style. This does not mean, however, that any of these forms can be expected to become dominant or to change basic institutions.

Social change Economics, technology, education, and liberalization in urbanized America in the 1960s and 1970s all created a context for experimentation and changes in values. The times were right for the experiments that occurred in these decades.

CONCLUSION

Changes that affect various life styles emanate from many sources. They must be understood as part of a continuous process of fluctuation and tensions: the dialectical processes work both for and against change. How stable any new form will be and whether it remains more or less permanent depend on economic conditions, the changes in social values and norms that accompany new technology, and the abilities of adherents to the form to define and promote change as a positive or desirable goal. Since there are always counter-trends and conservative forces that promote stability, change will be problematic in a democratic and pluralistic setting. We cannot accurately predict social responses to change. The general societal trend in North America has been toward personal freedom of choice, within limits. The choice of a variant life style has always entailed costs and benefits to the practitioner. Since most people prefer to adhere to mainstream norms, we can confidently predict greater stability than change in future. At the same time, it must be understood that the principle of limits also pulls a number of risk-takers to the edge of normative behaviour and to more rapid change than many would like. Excluded from this prediction is any sudden social upheaval caused by natural or revolutionary forces. Severe shortages, wars, depressions, or other catastrophes could dramatically alter our current social stability.

Cohabitation was pointed out in this chapter as one example of relative institutionalization of an alternative form. Other alternatives remain in the society because of tolerance inherent in the pluralistic ideology. Of course, when some groups in society perceive that certain forms of behaviour threaten established family or social practices, they may choose to abandon passive approaches and mobilize public opinion and organize resistance movements against the threatening life style (for example, movements against abortion and pornography).

Most persons in our society do not fully recognize the ways in which the behavioural patterns of the 1960s and 1970s have become part of contemporary social life. The broader acceptance of different styles of dress, freedom of language, permissive sex, and more liberal attitudes toward work may be seen as residual parts of the counterculture that remain, albeit in subdued forms. Conservative voices have had only moderate success in challenging many of the liberal changes that occurred during the period in question. By critically evaluating the nature of these changes and their limitations and meanings for today and the future, we can contribute to the sociological construction of reliable conceptual approaches to help us understand and deal with change more effectively.

Suggested Readings

Berger, Peter L.
  1979 *The Heretical Imperative*. New York: Anchor/Doubleday.

Kanter, Rosabeth Moss.
  1985 "The New Utopian Vision." In L. Cargan, ed., *Marriage and the Family: Coping With Change*. Belmont, CA: Wadsworth, 347-354.

Leslie, G.R., and S. Korman.
  1985 *The Family in Social Context*. Toronto: Oxford University Press.

Libby, Roger W., and R.N. Whitehurst, eds.
  1977 *Marriage and Alternatives*. Glenview, IL: Scott-Foresman Co.

Seeley, J.R., R.A. Sim and E.W. Loosley.
  1956 *Crestwood Heights*. New York: Basic.

Skolnick, Arlene.
  1983 *The Intimate Environment*. Third ed. Boston: Little, Brown.

Spencer, Metta.
  1985 *Foundations of Modern Sociology*. Canadian fourth ed. Scarborough: Prentice Hall.

Talese, Gay.
  1980 *Thy Neighbor's Wife*. Garden City, NY: Doubleday.

Whitehurst, R.N.
  1971 "Back to the Land: The Search for Freedom and Utopia in Ontario." Unpublished, available from the author, University of Windsor, Windsor, Ont. N9B 3P4.

Whitehurst, R.N., and G.V. Booth.
  1980 *The Sexes: Changing Relationships in a Pluralistic Society*. Agincourt: Gage.

BIBLIOGRAPHY

Acheson, Ann W.
1980 "The Kutchin Family: Past and Present." In K. Ishwaran, ed., *Canadian Families: Ethnic Variations*. Toronto: McGraw-Hill Ryerson.

Adams, Bert N.
1968 *Kinship in an Urban Setting*. Chicago: Markham.

Alzate, Heli.
1984 "Sexual Behavior of Unmarried Columbia University Students: A Five Year Follow-Up." *Archives of Sexual Behavior* 13:121-132.

Ambert, Anne-Marie.
1980 *Divorce in Canada*. Toronto: Academic Press.

———.
1985 "Custodial Parents: Review and a Longitudinal Study." In B. Schlesinger, ed., *The One Parent Family in the 1980s*. Toronto: University of Toronto Press.

Ambert, Anne-Marie, and Maureen Baker.
1984 "Marriage Dissolution: Structural and Ideological Changes." In M. Baker, ed., *The Family*. Toronto: McGraw-Hill Ryerson, 85-103.

Anderson, Alan, and L. Driedger.
1980 "The Mennonite Family: Culture and Kin in Rural Saskatchewan." In K. Ishwaran, ed., *Canadian Families: Ethnic Variations*. Toronto: McGraw-Hill Ryerson.

Aries, Philippe.
1962 *Centuries of Childhood: A Social History of Family Life*. New York: Vintage.

Arling, Greg, and William McAuley.
1983 "The Feasibility of Public Payments for Family Caregiving." *The Gerontologist* 23:300-306.

Armitage, Andrew.
1978 "Canada." In Sheila B. Kamerman and Alfred J. Kahn, eds., *Family Policy: Government and Families in Fourteen Countries*. New York: Columbia University Press, 367-399.

Armstrong, Pat.
1984 *Labour Pains: Women's Work in Crisis*. Toronto: Women's Educational Press.

Armstrong, Pat, and Hugh Armstrong.
1978 *The Double Ghetto: Canadian Women and their Segregated Work*. Toronto: McClelland and Stewart (Second ed. 1984).

———
1979 *A Working Majority: What Women Must Do for Pay*. Ottawa: Canadian Advisory Council on the Status of Women.

271

Armstrong, Pat, and Hugh Armstrong.
1983   'Beyond Sexless Class and Classless Sex: Towards Feminist Marxism."
        Studies in Political Economy 10(Winter):7-43. Reprinted in Pat Armstrong,
        Hugh Armstrong, Patricia Connelly, and Angela Miles, *Feminist Marxism
        or Marxist Feminism*. Toronto: Garamond, 1985.

————.
1985   "Theorizing Women's Work." Paper prepared for Conference "Labour,
        Women and Technology." August 1985. Inter-University Center for Post-
        Graduate Studies, Dubrovnik, Yugoslavia.

————.
1986   "More for the Money: Redefining and Intensifying Work in Canada." Paper
        prepared for Conference "Work and Politics: The Feminization of the
        Labour Force." March 1986. Center for European Studies, Harvard University.

Baker, Maureen.
1984   "His and Her Divorce Research: New Theoretical Directions in Canadian
        and American Research." *Journal of Comparative Family Studies* 15:17-
        28.

Baker, Maureen.
1985   *What Will Tomorrow Bring? . . . A Study of the Aspirations of Adolescent
        Women*. Ottawa: Canadian Advisory Council on the Status of Women.

Balakrishnan, T.R.
1986   "Changing Nuptiality Pattern and Its Fertility Implications in Canada."
        Paper presented at the Conference "Family Crisis." November 28-29, 1986.
        University of Ottawa.

Bank, Stephen P., and Michael D. Kahn.
1982   *The Sibling Bond*. New York: Basic.

Barber, John.
1987   "Sex in the Eighties." *Maclean's* 100 (2).

Barr, Howard M.
1976   "The Kinship Role." In F. Ivan Nye, ed., *Role Structure and the Analysis
        of the Family*. Beverly Hills, CA: Sage.

Barrett, F.M.
1980   "Sexual Experience, Birth Control Use and Sex Education of Unmarried
        Canadian University Students." *Archives of Sexual Behaviour* 9:367-390.

Barrett, Michele.
1980   *Women's Oppression Today*. London: Verso.

Barrett, Michele, and Mary McIntosh.
1982   *The Anti-social Family*. London: Verso.

Bartell, Gilbert D.
1971   *Group Sex*. New York: Peter H. Wyden.

Bayer, Alan E.
1977   "Sexual Permissiveness and Correlates as Determined through Interaction
        Analyses." *Journal of Marriage and the Family* 39:29-40.

Beaujot, Roderic.
1986 "Dwindling Families: Making the Case for Policies to Sustain or Raise the Birth Rate in Canada." *Policy Options* 7.

Becker, Gary S.
1981 *A Treatise on the Family*. Cambridge, MA: Harvard University Press.

Beland, François.
1984 "The Family and Adults 65 Years of Age and Over." *Canadian Review of Sociology and Anthropology* 21:302-317.

Bell, Robert R.
1983 *Marriage and Family Interaction*. Homewood, IL: Dorsey.

Bell, Robert R., and Jay B. Chaskes.
1970 "Premarital Sexual Experience Among Coeds, 1958 and 1968." *Journal of Marriage and the Family* 32(February):81-84.

Bem, Sandra L.
1974 "The Measurement of Psychological Androgyny." *Journal of Consulting and Clinical Psychology* 42:155-162.

Bengtson, Vern, James Dowd, David Smith, and Alex Inkeles.
1975 "Modernization, Modernity, and Perceptions of Aging: A Cross-Cultural Study." *Journal of Gerontology* 30:688-695.

Berger, Brigitte, and Peter L. Berger.
1984 *The War Over the Family*. Garden City, NY: Doubleday Anchor.

Berger, Peter L.
1979 *The Heretical Imperative*. Garden City, NY: Doubleday Anchor.

Berger, Peter L., and Thomas Luckmann.
1966 *The Social Construction of Reality*. Garden City, NY: Doubleday Anchor.

Bernard, Jessie.
1972 *The Future of Marriage*. New York: Bantam.

Best, Raphaela.
1983 *We've All Got Scars*. Bloomington, IN: Indiana University Press.

Biaggi, Mario.
1980 Testimony before the Select Comittee on Aging, House of Representatives, 96th Congress, Washington, DC.

Bibby, Reginald W., and Donald C. Posterski.
1985 *The Emerging Generation: An Inside Look at Canada's Teenagers*. Toronto: Irwin.

Bierstedt, R.
1963 *The Social Order*. Second ed. New York: McGraw-Hill.

Bohannan, P.
1970 *Divorce and After*. Garden City, NY: Doubleday.

Boissevain, Jeremy.
1976 "Family and Kinship Among Italians in Montreal." In K. Ishwaran, ed., *The Canadian Family*. Revised ed. Toronto: Holt, Rinehart and Winston.

Bone, M.
  1986   "Trends in Single Women's Sexual Behaviour in Scotland." *Population Trends* 43:7-14.

Bott, Elizabeth.
  1957   *Family and Social Network.* London: Tavistock.

Boulet, Jac-Andre, and Laval Lavalle.
  1984   *The Changing Economic Status of Women.* Ottawa: Economic Council of Canada.

Boyd, Monica.
  1977   "The Forgotten Minority: The Socioeconomic Status of Divorced and Separated Women." In Patricia Marchak, ed., *The Working Sexes.* Vancouver: University of British Columbia, 47-71.

———.
  1984   *Canadian Attitudes Toward Women: Thirty Years of Change.* Ottawa: Labour Canada.

Brake, Michael.
  1985   *Comparative Youth Culture: The Sociology of Youth Cultures and Youth Subcultures in America, Britain and Canada.* London: Routledge and Kegan Paul.

Branch, Laurence, and Alan Jette.
  1981   "Elders' Use of Informal Long-Term Care Assistance." Paper presented at the annual meeting of the Gerontological Society of America, Toronto.

Breton, Raymond.
  1984   "The Production and Allocation of Symbolic Resources: An Analysis of the Linguistic and Ethnocultural Fields in Canada." *The Canadian Review of Sociology and Anthropology* 21:123-144.

Briggs, Jean L.
  1970   *Never in Anger: Portrait of an Eskimo Family.* Cambridge, MA: Harvard University Press.

Brim, Orville, G., Jr.
  1966   "Socialization through the Life Cycle." In O.G. Brim, Jr. and Stanton Wheeler, *Socialization After Childhood: Two Essays.* New York: Wiley.

Brim, Orville G., Jr., and Jerome Kagan, eds.
  1980   *Constancy and Change in Human Development.* Cambridge, MA: Harvard University Press.

Brinkerhoff, Merlin, and Eugen Lupri.
  1983   "Conjugal Power and Family Relationships: Some Theoretical and Methodological Issues." In K. Ishwaran, ed., *The Canadian Family.* Toronto: Gage.

Brody, Elaine.
  1981   "Women in the Middle and Family Help to Older People." *The Gerontologist* 13:412-417.

Buchignani, Norman, Doreen M. Indra, and Ram Srivatsava.
1985   *Continuous Journey: A Social History of South Asians in Canada.* Toronto: McClelland and Stewart.

Burch, T.K.
1985   *Family History Survey—Preliminary Findings.* Ottawa: Minister of Supply and Services.

Burch, Thomas K., and Ashok K. Madan.
1986   *Union Formation and Dissolution: Results from the 1984 Family History Survey.* Ottawa: Minister of Supply and Services.

Burgess, E.W., Harvey Locke, and Mary Thomes.
1971   *The Family: From Traditional to Companionship.* New York: Van Nostrand and Reinhold.

Burnet, Jean.
1984   "Myths and Multiculturalism." In Ronald J. Samuda, John W. Berry, and Michel Laferriere, eds., *Multiculturalism in Canada.* Toronto: Allyn and Bacon, 18-29.

Burr, Wesley, Reuben Hill, F. Ivan Nye, and Ira Reiss, eds.
1979   *Contemporary Theories About the Family.* 2 vols. New York: The Free Press.

Burstein, M., N. Tienhaara, P. Hewson, and B. Warrander.
1984   "Canadian Work Values." In Graham S. Lowe and Harvey J. Krahn, eds., *Working Canadians.* Toronto: Methuen, 3-14.

Burstyn, Varda.
1985   "Masculine Dominance and the State." In Varda Burstyn and Dorothy Smith, *Women, Class, Family and the State.* Toronto: Garamond, 45-89.

Caine, Lynn.
1985   *What Did I Do Wrong? Mothers, Children, Guilt.* Toronto: PaperJacks.

Campbell, Douglas F., and David C. Neice.
1979   *The Ties that Bind—Structure and Marriage in Nova Scotia.* Port Credit: The Scribbler's Press.

Campbell, Douglas F., and Madeline A. Richard.
1979   "The Differential Effects of Ethnicity and Cultural Setting on Religious Intermarriages in Toronto and Montreal, 1971." Paper presented at the Canadian Population Society Meetings. Saskatoon.

Canada.
1981   *Census.* Ottawa: Minister of Supply and Services.

Canada.
1984   *1981 Census Update.* Ottawa: Minister of Supply and Services.

Canada.
1984   *Report of the Committee on Sexual Offences Against Children and Youth.* Vols. 1 & 2. Ottawa: Minister of Supply and Services.

Canada.
1986   *Bill C-47.* Ottawa: The Minister of Justice, 1-14.

Canada.
  1987 *Basic Facts on Social Security Programs.* Ottawa: Department of Health and Welfare.

Canadian Council on Social Development.
  1985 *Child and Elderly Benefits: Consultation Paper.* Ottawa.

———.
  1986 "Work and Income in the Nineties." Ottawa.

Canadian Ethnic Studies.
  Bulletin of the Research Center for Canadian Studies. Calgary: University of Calgary, n.d.

Cantor, Marjorie.
  1979 "Neighbours and Friends: An Overlooked Resource in the Informal Support System." *Research on Aging* 1:434-463.

———.
  1983 "Strain among Caregivers: A Study of Experience in the United States." *The Gerontologist* 23:597-604.

Capaldi, Fredrick, and Barbara McRae.
  1979 *Step-families.* New York: New Viewpoints/Vision Books.

Carisse, Collette.
  1964 *Planification des Naissances en Milieu Canadien-Français.* Montréal: Presses de l'Université de Montréal.

———.
  1976a "Cultural Orientations in Marriage between French and English Canadians." In Lyle E. Larsen, ed., *The Canadian Family in Comparative Perspective.* Scarborough: Prentice-Hall.

———.
  1976b "Life Plans of Innovative Women: A Strategy for Living Feminine Role." In Lyle E. Larsen, ed., *The Canadian Family in Comparative Perspective.* Scarborough: Prentice-Hall.

Casler, L.
  1969 "This Thing Called Love is Pathological," *Psychology Today* 3:18-76.

Catton, W.R.
  1964 "A Comparison of Mathematical Models for the Effect of Residential Propinquity of Mate Selection." *American Sociological Review* 29.

Census Canada.
  1987 *Summary Tabulations.* Ottawa: Minister of Supply and Services.

Chappell, Neena.
  1985 "Social Support and the Receipt of Home Care Services." *The Gerontologist* 25:47-54.

———.
  1987 "The Interface Between Three Systems of Care: Self, Informal, and Formal." In Russell Ward and Sheldon Tobin, eds., *Health in Aging: Sociological Issues and Policy Directions.* New York: Springer.

Chappell, Neena, and Betty Havens.
1985   "Who Helps the Elderly Person: A Discussion of Informal and Formal Care." In Warren Peterson and Jill Quadagno, eds., *Social Bonds in Later Life*. Beverly Hills, CA: Sage, 211-227.

Chappell, Neena, and John Horne.
1987   "Housing and Supportive Services for Elderly Persons in Manitoba—Final Report." Winnipeg: Centre on Aging, University of Manitoba.

Chappell, Neena, Laurel Strain, and Audrey Blandford.
1986   *Aging and Health Care, A Social Perspective*. Toronto: Holt, Rinehart and Winston.

Cheal, David.
1988   *The Gift Economy*. London: Tavistock.

———.
1984   "Transactions and Transformational Models." In Norman K. Denzin, ed., *Studies in Symbolic Interaction*. Vol. 5. Greenwich, CT: JAI Press.

———.
1986   "The Social Dimensions of Gift Behaviour." *Journal of Social and Personal Relationships* 3:423-439.

———.
1987a   " 'Showing Them You Love Them': Gift Giving and the Dialectic of Intimacy." *Sociological Review* 35:150-169.

———.
1987b   "Intergenerational Transfers." In Alan Bryman and Bill Bytheway, eds., *Rethinking the Life Cycle*. London: Macmillan.

Cherlin, Andrew.
1978   "Remarriage as an Incomplete Institution." *American Journal of Sociology* 84:634-650.

Chimbos, Peter D.
1971   "Immigrants' Attitudes Toward Their Children's Interethnic Marriages in a Canadian Community." *International Migration Review* 5:5-7.

———.
1980   "The Greek-Canadian Family: Tradition and Change." In K. Ishwaran, ed., *Canadian Families: Ethnic Variations*. Toronto: McGraw-Hill Ryerson.

Christensen, Harold T., and Christina F. Gregg.
1970   "Changing Sex Norms in America and Scandinavia." *Journal of Marriage and the Family* 32:616-627.

Clark, Susan, and Andrew S. Harvey.
1976   "The Sexual Division of Labour: The Use of Time." *Atlantis* 2(Fall):46-65.

Clayton, Richard R.
1972   "Premarital Sexual Intercourse: A Substantive Test of the Contingent Consistency Model." *Journal of Marriage and the Family* 34(May):273-281.

Clement, Wallace.
1975   *The Canadian Corporate Elite*. Toronto: McClelland and Stewart.

Cohen, Leah.
1984   *Small Expectations: Society's Betrayal of Older Women*. Toronto: McClelland and Stewart.

Cohen, Marjorie Griffin.
1987   *Free Trade and the Future of Women's Work*. Toronto: Garamond.

Cohler, Bertram, and Morton Lieberman.
1980   "Social Relations and Mental Health: Middle-Aged and Older Men and Women from Three European Ethnic Groups." *Research on Aging* 2:445-469.

Colling, R.
1975   *Conflict Sociology*. New York: Academic Press.

Condry, John C., and Douglas Keith.
1983   "Educational and Recreational Uses of Computer Technology." *Youth & Society* 15:87-112.

Connelly, M. Patricia, and Martha MacDonald.
1983   "Women's Work: Domestic and Wage Labour in a Nova Scotia Community." *Studies in Political Economy* 10:45-72.

Cooper, David.
1964   *The Death of the Family*. London: Pelican.

Corelli, Rae.
1987   "AIDS and Sex," *Maclean's*. Vol. 100 (5).

Cowgill, Donald, and Lowell Holmes.
1972   *Aging and Modernization*. New York: Appleton-Century-Crofts.

Cruikshank, Julie.
1971   "Matrifocal Families in the Canadian North." In K. Ishwaran, ed., *The Canadian Family*. Toronto: Holt, Rinehart and Winston.

Cumming, Elaine, and William Henry.
1961   *Growing Old: The Process of Disengagement*. New York: Basic.

Damas, David.
1971   "The Problem of the Eskimo Family." In K. Ishwaran, ed., *The Canadian Family*. Toronto: Holt, Rinehart and Winston.

Danziger, Kurt.
1971   *The Socialization of Immigrant Children*. Toronto: Institute of Behavioural Research, York University.

————.
1976a   "Differences in Acculturation and Patterns of Socialization Among Italian Immigrant Families." In Robert M. Pike and Elia Zureik, eds., *Socialization and Values in Canadian Society*. Vol. 2. Toronto: The Carleton Library, Macmillan.

————.
1976b   "The Acculturation of Italian Immigrant Girls." In K. Ishwaran, ed., *The Canadian Family*. Revised ed. Toronto: Holt, Rinehart and Winston.

Darling, C.A., D.T. Kallen, and J. Vandusen.
1984 "Sex in Transition, 1900-1980." *Journal of Youth and Adolescence* 13:385-399.

Davids, Leo.
1985 "The Lone-Parent Family in Canada: The Quantitative 1985 Backgrounds." In B. Schlesinger, ed., *The One Parent Family in the 1980s*. Toronto: University of Toronto Press.

Davidson, J. Kenneth, Sr., and Gerald R. Leslie.
1977 "Premarital Sexual Intercourse: An Application of Axiomatic Theory Construction." *Journal of Marriage and the Family* 39:15-25.

Davies, Mark, and Denise B. Kandel.
1981 "Parental and Peer Influences On Adolescents' Educational Plans: Some Further Evidence." *American Journal of Sociology* 87:363-387.

De Lamater, J., and P. MacCorquodale.
1979 *Premarital Sexuality*. Madison: WI: University of Wisconsin Press.

Denton, Margaret, and Alfred A. Hunter.
1982 "Economic Sectors and Gender Discrimination in Canada: A Critique and Text of Block and Walker . . . And Some New Evidence." Women's Bureau Series A (*Equality in the Workplace*): No. 6. Ottawa: Labour Canada.

Dickinson, James, and Bob Russell.
1986 "Introduction: The Structure of Reproduction in Capitalist Society." In James Dickinson and Bob Russell, eds., *Family, Economy and State*. Toronto: Garamond, 1-20.

DiRenzo, Gordon J.
1977 "Socialization, Personality, and Social Systems," *Annual Review of Sociology* 3.

Djao, A.W.
1983 *Inequality and Social Policy: The Sociology of Welfare*. Toronto: John Wiley & Sons.

Donnelly, F.K.
1986 "The Kinship Network of West Isles Parish." In F.K. Donnelly, ed., *Family and Household in Mid-Nineteenth Century New Brunswick*. St. John: University of New Brunswick.

Doten, Dana.
1938 *The Art of Bundling*. New York: Holt, Rinehart and Winston.

Dowd, James.
1980 "Industrialization and the Decline of the Aged." Paper presented at the annual meeting of the American Sociological Association. New York.

Driedger, Leo.
1983 "Ethnic Intermarriages: Student Dating and Mating." In K. Ishwaran, ed., *Marriage and Divorce in Canada*. Toronto:Methuen.

Duberman, L.
1973 "Step-Kin Relationship." *Journal of Marriage and the Family* 35:283-292.

Dubinsky, Karen.
1985 "Lament For a 'Patriarchy Lost'?: Anti-Feminism, Anti-Abortion and R.E.A.L. Women in Canada." Ottawa: Canadian Research Institute for the Advancement of Women.

Dubos, Rene.
1963 "Infection into Disease." In Dwight Ingle, ed., *Life and Disease*. New York: Basic.

Dulude, Louise.
1978 *Women and Aging: A Report on the Rest of Our Lives*. Ottawa: Canadian Advisory Council on the Status of Women.

———.
1981 *Pension Reform with Women in Mind*. Ottawa: National Action Committee on the Status of Women.

———.
1984 *Love, Marriage and Money... An Analysis of Financial Arrangements Between the Spouses*. Ottawa: Canadian Advisory Council on the Status of Women.

———.
1985 "Fringe Benefits and the Female Workforce." In Economic Council of Canada, ed., *Towards Equity: Proceedings of a Colloquium on the Economic Status of Women in the Labour Market. November 1984*. Ottawa: Minister of Supply and Services, 71-78.

Dumas, Jean.
1985 *Report on the Current Demographic Situation in Canada*. Ottawa: Minister of Supply and Services.

Duncan, Barry L., Mary Ann Kraus, and M. Bernadine Parks.
1986 "Children's Fears and Nuclear War: Systems Strategy for Change." *Youth & Society* 18:28-44.

Dunning, R.W.
1971 "Changes in Marriage and the Family among the Northern Ojibwa." In K. Ishwaran, ed., *The Canadian Family*. Toronto: Holt, Rinehart and Winston.

Durkheim, Emile.
1951 *Suicide*. New York: The Free Press.

Duvall, Evelyn, and Brent Miller.
1985 *Marriage and Family Development*. New York: Harper and Row.

Eastman, William F.
1971 "First Intercourse." *Sexual Behavior* 2 (January):22-27.

Ehrenreich, Barbara.
1984 *Hearts of Men: American Dreams and the Flight from Commitment*. New York: Anchor.

Ehrenreich, Barbara, and Deirdre English.
1978 *For Her Own Good*. Garden City, NY: Doubleday Anchor.

Eichler, Margrit.
1973   "Women as Personal Dependents." In Marylee Stephenson, ed., *Women in Canada*. Toronto: New Press, 36-55.

_____.
1980   *The Double Standard*. New York. St. Martin's Press.

_____.
1981a   "The Inadequacy of the Monolithic Model of the Family." *Canadian Journal of Sociology* 6:367-388.

_____.
1981a   "Power, Dependency, Love and the Sexual Division of Labour." *Women's Studies International Quarterly* 4:201-219.

_____.
1983a   "The Industrialization of Housework." In Eugen Lupri, ed., *The Changing Position of Women in Family and Society*. Leiden: E.J. Brill, 430-443.

_____.
1983b   *Families in Canada: Recent Changes and Policy Consequences*. Toronto: Gage.

_____.
1983c   "Women, Families and the State." In Joan Turner and Lois Emery, eds., *Perspectives on Women in the 1980's*. Winnipeg: University of Manitoba Press.

_____.
1985a   "The Connection between Paid and Unpaid Labour." In Paula Bourne, ed., *Women's Paid and Unpaid Work*. Toronto: New Hogtown Press, 61-78.

_____.
1985b   "And the Work Never Ends: Feminist Contributions." *Canadian Review of Sociology and Anthropology* 22:619-644.

_____.
1988   *Families in Canada Today*. Second ed. Toronto: Gage.

Elder, Glen H., Jr., and Jeffrey K. Liker.
1982   "Hard Times in Women's Lives: Historical Influences across Forty Years." *American Journal of Sociology* 88:241-269.

Elkin, Frederick.
1964   *The Family in Canada*. Ottawa: Vanier Institute of the Family.

_____.
1983   "Family, Socialization, and Ethnic Identity." In K. Ishwaran, ed., *The Canadian Family*. Toronto: Gage, 145-158.

_____.
1985   "The English Canadian Family." In Stuart A. Queen, Robert W. Habenstein, and Jill S. Quadango, eds., *The Family in Various Cultures*. Fifth ed. New York: Harper and Row, 335-345.

Elkin, Frederick, and Gerald Handel.
1984   *The Child and Society: The Process of Socialization.* Fourth ed. New York: Random House.

Ellis, Godfrey J.
1983   "Youth in the Electronic Environment." *Youth & Society* 15:3-12.

Engels, Friedrich.
1942   *The Origin of the Family, Private Property and the State.* New York: International.

Evans, Robert.
1976   "Does Canada Have Too Many Doctors? Why Nobody Loves an Immigrant Physician." *Canadian Public Policy II,* 147-160.

————.
1984   *Strained Mercy: The Economics of Canadian Health Care.* Toronto: Butterworths.

Evans, Ron, and Lawrence Northwood.
1979   "The Utility of Natural Help Relationships." *Social Science and Medicine* 13A:789-795.

Farber, Bernard.
1964   *Family: Organization and Interaction.* San Francisco: Chandler.

Fels, Lynn.
1981   *Living Together: Unmarried Couples in Canada.* Toronto: Personal Library.

Ferrell, Mary Z., William L. Tolone, and Robert H. Walsh.
1977   "Maturational and Societal Changes in the Sexual Double-Standard: A Panel Analysis." *Journal of Marriage and the Family* 39: 255-271.

Firestone, Melvin M.
1978   "Socialization and Interaction in a Newfoundland Outport." *Urban Life* 7:91-110.

Firth, Raymond.
1956   *Two Studies of Kinship in London.* London: Athlone.

Forcese, Dennis.
1975   *The Canadian Class Structure.* Toronto: McGraw-Hill Ryerson.

Fox, Bonnie, ed.
1980   *Hidden in the Household.* Toronto: The Women's Press.

Fox, Bonnie J., and John Fox.
1986   "Women in the Labour Market 1931-81: Exclusion and Competition." *The Canadian Review of Sociology and Anthropology* 23 (February):1-21.

Francis, E.K.
1955   *In Search of Utopia: The Mennonites in Manitoba.* Altona, Man.: D.W. Friesen.

Frappier, J.
1983   "Evaluation of a Sex Education Program in High School." Unpublished manuscript. Montreal: University of Montreal.

Frayser, Suzanne G.
1985   *Varieties of Sexual Experience.* New Haven, CT: HRAF Press.

Frideres, James, Jay Goldstein, and R. Gilbert.
1971   "The Impact of Jewish-Gentile Intermarriages in Canada: An Alternative View." *Journal of Comparative Family Studies* 2:268-275.

Friedan, Betty.
1963   *The Feminine Mystique.* New York: Dell.

Friedmann, Eugene, and Harold Orbach.
1974   "Adjustment to Retirement." In Silvano Arieti, ed., *American Handbook of Psychiatry.* Second ed. New York: Basic, 609-645.

Friesen, Bruce K.
1986   "Labelling Youth Cultures Deviant: Traditional Gender Roles in Heavy Metal." Unpublished master's thesis. Calgary: University of Calgary.

Furstenberg, F., Jr.
1975   "Unplanned Parenthood: The Social Consequences of Teenage Child-bearing." Unpublished manuscript. Philadelphia: University of Pennsylvania.

Furstenberg, F., Jr., et al.
1983   "The Life Course of Children of Divorce: Marital Disruption·and Parental Contact," *American Sociological Review* 48.

Garbarino, James.
1982   *Children and Families in the Social Environment.* New York: Aldine.

Garigue, Philippe.
1962   *La Vie Familiale des Canadiens Français.* Montreal: Presses de l'Université de Montréal.

――――.
1968   "The French Canadian Family." In Bernard R. Blishen, et al., eds., *Canadian Society.* Toronto: Macmillan.

――――.
1976   "French Canadian Kinship and Urban Life." In K. Ishwaran, ed., *The Canadian Family.* Revised ed. Toronto: Holt, Rinehart and Winston. (First published in *American Anthropologist* 58 (December 1956)): 1090-1100.

Gavigan, Shelley.
1987   "Women and Abortion in Canada: What's Law Got to Do with it?" In Heather Maroney and Meg Luxton, eds., *Feminism and Political Economy.* Toronto: Methuen, 263-282.

Gecas, Viktor.
1979   "The Influence of Social Class on Socialization." In W.R. Burr et al., eds., *Contemporary Theories About the Family.* Vol. 1. New York: The Free Press.

――――.
1981   "Contexts of Socialization." In Morris Rosenberg and Ralph H. Turner, eds., *Social Psychology: Sociological Perspectives.* New York: Basic, 165-199.

Gee, Ellen Thomas.
1982 "Marriage in Nineteenth-Century Canada," *Canadian Review of Anthropology and Sociology* 19.

Gee, Ellen.
1987 "Historical Change in the Family Life Course of Canadian Men and Women." In Victor Marshall, ed., *Aging in Canada*. Markham: Fitzhenry & Whiteside, 265-287.

Gerner, Goody T.
1987 "Growing Pains," *Maclean's* 100 (September 7)

Gerson, Mary-Joan, Judith L. Alpert, and Mary Sue Richardson.
1984 "Mothering: the View from Psychological Research." *Signs* 9:434-453.

Gibbins, Roger, J.R. Ponting, and G.L. Symons.
1978 "Attitudes and Ideology: Correlates of Liberal Attitudes towards the Role of Women." *Journal of Comparative Studies* 9.

Gibson, J.
1972 "Kin Family Network: Overheralded Structure in Past Conceptualization of Family Functioning." *Journal of Marriage and the Family* 34.

Gilmartin, Brian G.
1977 "Swinging: Who Gets Involved and How?" In Roger Libby and Robert N. Whitehurst, eds., *Marriage and Alternatives: Exploring Intimate Relationships*. Glenview, IL: Scot, Foresman, 161-185.

Glass, Jennifer, Vern L. Bengston, and C. Dunham.
1986 "Attitudes Similarity in Three-Generation Families: Socialization, Status Inheritance or Reciprocal Influence?" *American Sociological Review* 51.

Goetting, Ann.
1982 "The Six Stations of Remarriage: Developmental Tasks of Remarriage After Divorce." *Family Relations* 31 (April): 213-222.

Goode, William J.
1959 "The Theoretical Importance of Love." *American Sociological Review* 24.

———.
1963 *World Revolution and Family Patterns*. Glenco, IL: The Free Press.

———.
1966 "Family and Mobility." In R. Bendix and S.M. Lipsett, eds., *Status and Power: Social Stratification in Comparative Perspective*. New York: The Free Press.

———.
1956 *Women in Divorce*. New York: The Free Press.

———.
1982 *The Family*. Second ed. Englewood Cliffs, NJ: Prentice-Hall.

Gordon, Michael.
1972 "Exploding the High Divorce Rate Myth." *Family Circle*. December:18-21.

Gordon, Michael.
1981   "Was Waller Ever Right? The Rating and Dating Complex Reconsidered."
        Journal of Marriage and the Family 43:67-76.

Gordon, Milton M.
1964   *Assimilation in American Life*. New York: Oxford University Press.

Gough, Ian.
1979   *The Political Economy of the Welfare State*. London: Macmillan.

Grant, A.J.
1931   *A History of Europe from 1494 to 1610*. New York: Methuen.

Grant, Karen.
1984   "The Inverse Care Law in the Context of Universal Free Health Insurance
        in Canada: Toward Meeting Health Needs Through Social Policy." *Soci-
        ological Focus* 17:137-155.

Green, Maureen.
1976   *Fathering*. New York: McGraw-Hill.

Greenfield, Sydney M.
1965   "Love and Marriage in Modern America: A Functional Analysis." *The
        Sociological Quarterly* 6:361-377.

Greer, Germaine.
1984   *Sex and Destiny*. New York: Harper and Row.

Gregorovich, Andrew, ed.
1972   *Canadian Ethnic Groups Bibliography*. Toronto: Ontario Department of
        the Provincial Secretary and Citizenship.

Gross, Penny.
1985   "Kinship Structures in Remarriage Families." Unpublished Ph.D. Thesis.
        Toronto: University of Toronto.

Guberman, Connie, and Margie Wolfe, eds.
1985   *No Safe Place: Violence Against Women and Children*. Toronto: The
        Women's Press.

Guest, Dennis.
1980   *The Emergence of Social Security in Canada*. Vancouver: University of
        British Columbia Press.

Gullotta, T., G. Adams, and S. Alexander.
1986   *Today's Marriages and Families*. Belmont, CA: Brooks/Cole Publishing.

Gunderson, Morley.
1976   "Work Patterns." In Gail Cook, ed., *Opportunity for Choice*. Ottawa:
        Information Canada, 93-142.

Guppy, Neil, Paulina D. Mikicich, and Ravi Pendakur.
1984   "Changing Patterns of Educational Inequality in Canada." *Canadian Jour-
        nal of Sociology* 9:319-331.

Haas-Hawkings, Gwen.
1978   "Intimacy as a Moderating Influence on the Stress of Loneliness in
        Widowhood." *Essence* 2:249-258.

Hagestad, Gunhild.
1981 "Problems and Promises in the Social Psychology of Intergenerational Relations." In Robert Fogel, E. Hatfield, Sara Kiesler, and Ethel Shanas, eds., *Aging: Stability and Change in the Family*. New York: Academic Press, 11-46.

Hanson, Sandra, and William Sauer.
1985 "Children and their Elderly Parents." In William Sauer and Raymond Coward, eds., *Social Support Networks and the Care of the Elderly*. New York: Springer, 41-66.

Hanson, Shirley, and M.J. Sporakowski.
1986 "Single Parent Families." *Family Relations* 35(1):3-8.

Harding, Deborah, and Emily Nett.
1984 "Women and Rock Music." *Atlantis* 10:60-76.

Hardy, Kenneth R.
1964 "An Appetitional Theory of Sexual Motivation." *Psychological Review* 71:1-18.

Harvey, Carol, and Maureen Harris.
1985 "Decision-Making During Widowhood: The Beginning Years." Paper presented at the Beatrice Paolucci Symposium. July, 1985. Ann Arbor, MI: Michigan State University.

Havighurst, Robert, and Ruth Albrecht.
1953 *Older People*. New York: Longmans Green.

Health and Welfare Canada and Statistics Canada
1981 *Canada Health Survey*. Ottawa: Minister of Supply and Services.

Heer, David.
1962 "The Trend of Interfaith Marriages in Canada." *American Sociological Review* 27:245-50.

Heer, David, and Charles A. Hubey.
1975 "The Trend of Interfaith Marriages in Canada: 1922 to 1972." In S. Parveez Wakil, ed., *Marriage, Family, and Society*. Toronto: Butterworths.

Heller, Anita Fochs.
1986 *Health and Home: Women as Health Guardians*. Ottawa: Canadian Advisory Council on the Status of Women.

Hernandez, Donald J.
1986 "Childhood in a Sociodemographic Perspective." *Annual Review of Sociology* 12:159-180.

Herold, E.S., and L. Way.
1983 "Oral-Genital Behavior in a Sample of University Females." *Journal of Sex Research* 19:327-338.

Herold, Edward S.
1984 *Sexual Behaviour of Canadian Young People*. Markham: Fitzhenry & Whiteside.

Hess, Beth, and Beth Soldo.
1985 "Husband and Wife Networks." In William Sauer and Raymond Coward, eds., *Social Support Networks and the Care of the Elderly*. New York: Springer, 67-92.

Hess, Beth, and Joan Waring.
1980 "Changing Patterns of Aging and Family Bonds in Later Life." In Arlene Skolnick and Jerome Skolnick, eds., *Family in Transition*. Boston: Little, Brown.

Hetherington, E.M., M. Cox, and R. Cox.
1978 "The Aftermath of Divorce." In J.H. Stevens and M. Mathews, eds., *Mother-Child, Father-Child Relations*. Washington, DC: National Association for the Education of Young Children, 149-179.

———.
1979 "Family Interaction and Social, Emotional and Cognitive Development of Children Following Divorce." In V. Vaughn and B. Barzelton, eds., *The Family: Setting Priorities*. New York: Science and Medicine.

Hill, Reuben.
1949 *Families Under Stress*. New York: Harper.

———.
1970 *Family Development in Three Generations*. Cambridge, MA: Schenkman.

———.
1971 "Modern Systems Theory and the Family." *Social Science Information* 10:7-26.

Hill, Reuben, and Roy Rodgers.
1964 "The Developmental Approach." In Harold Christensen, ed., *Handbook of Marriage and the Family*. Chicago: Rand McNally, 171-211.

Hiller, Harry.
1986 *Canadian Society: A Macro Analysis*. Scarborough: Prentice-Hall.

Himelfarb, Alexander, and James C. Richardson.
1982 *Sociology for Canadians*. Toronto: McGraw-Hill Ryerson.

Hitchman, and Gladys Symons.
1976 "The Effects of Graduate Education on the Sexual Division of Labour in the Canadian Family." A Paper presented at the Western Association of Sociology and Anthropology Annual Meetings. Mimeo.

Hobart, Charles W.
1966 *Italian Immigrants in Edmonton: Adjustment and Integration*. Ottawa: Information Canada.

———.
1972a "Orientations to Marriage Among Young Canadians." *Journal of Comparative Family Studies* 3:171-193.

———.
1972b "Sexual Permissiveness in Young English and French Canadians." *Journal of Marriage and the Family* 34(2):292-303.

Hobart, Charles W.
1976   "The Changing Family Patterns Among Ukrainian-Canadians in Alberta."
        In Lyle E. Larson, ed., *The Canadian Family in Comparative Perspective*.
        Scarborough: Prentice-Hall.

————.
1974   "The Social Context of Morality Standards Among Anglophone Canadian
        Students." *Journal of Comparative Family Studies* 5:26-40.

————.
1979   "Courtship Process: Premarital Sex." In G.N. Ramu, ed., *Courtship, Mar-
        riage and the Family in Canada*. Toronto: Macmillan, 37-58.

————.
1984   "Changing Profession and Practice of Sexual Standards: A Study of Young
        Anglophone and Francophone Canadians." *Journal of Comparative Fam-
        ily Studies* 15:231-256.

Hofstadter, Samuel H., and Shirley R. Levittan.
1967   "Alimony—A Reformulation." *Journal of Family Law* 7:51-60.

Hogoboom, William P.
1971   "The California Family Law Act of 1970: 18 Months' Experience." *Journal
        of Missouri Bar*, 584-589.

Homer, Clark.
1968   *Domestic Relations*. St. Paul, MN: West.

Horna, Jarmila, and Eugen Lupri.
1987   "Fathers' Participation in Work, Family Life and Leisure: A Canadian Ex-
        perience." In Charles Lewis and Margeret O'Brien, eds., *Problems in
        Fatherhood*. London: Sage.

Hornick, J.
1978   "Premarital Sexual Attitudes and Behavior." *Sociological Quarterly* 19:534-
        544.

Horowitz, Amy.
1981   "Sons and Daughters as Caregivers to Older Parents: Differences in Role
        Performance and Consequences." Paper presented at the annual meeting
        of the Gerontological Society of America, Toronto.

Hostetler, John A., and Gertrude E. Huntington.
1967   *The Hutterites in North America*. New York: Holt, Rinehart and Winston.

Hoult, Thomas F., Laura Henze, and John Hudson.
1978   *Courtship and Marriage in America*. Boston: Little, Brown.

Hum, Derek.
1983   *Federalism and the Poor: A Review of the Canada Assistance Plan*. Toronto:
        Ontario Economic Council.

Hunt, Morton.
1974   *Sexual Behavior in the Seventies*. New York: Dell.

Hunter, A.A.
1981   *Class Tells: On Social Inequality in Canada*. Toronto: Butterworths.

Inkeles, Alex.
1968 "Society, Social Structure, and Child Socialization." In John A. Clausen, ed., *Socialization and Society*. Boston: Little, Brown, 73-129.

Irving, Howard.
1972 *The Family Myth: A Study of Relationships between Married Couples and their Parents*. Toronto: Copp Clark.

Irving, Howard H.
1980 *Divorce Mediation*. Toronto: Personal Library.

Ishwaran, K.
1977 *Family, Kinship, and Community: A Study of Dutch-Canadians*. Toronto: McGraw-Hill Ryerson.

———.
1971 "The Canadian Family." In K. Ishwaran, ed., *The Canadian Family*. Toronto: Holt, Rinehart and Winston, 3-20.

———.
1983 "Introduction: Perspectives on Marriage and Divorce." In K. Ishwaran, ed., *Marriage and Divorce in Canada*. Toronto: Methuen, 1-41.

Ishwaran, K., ed.
1980 *Canadian Families: Ethnic Variations*. Toronto: McGraw-Hill Ryerson.

Jansen, Clifford J.
1971 "The Italian Community in Toronto." In John L. Elliot, ed., *Immigrant Groups*. Vol. 2. Scarborough: Prentice-Hall.

Jarmulowski, Vicki.
1985 "The Blended Family: Who are They?" *Ms.* 13 (February):33-34.

Jenks, Chris, ed.
1982 *The Sociology of Childhood*. London: Batsford.

Johnson, Laura C., and Rona Abramovitch.
1986 *Between Jobs: Paternal Unemployment and Family Life*. Toronto: Social Planning Council of Metropolitan Toronto.

Kaats, Gilbert, and Keith E. Davis.
1970 "The Dynamics of Sexual Behavior of College Students." *Journal of Marriage and the Family* 32:390-399.

Kagan, Jerome.
1984 *The Nature of the Child*. New York: Basic.

Kalbach, Warren E.
1970 *The Impact of Immigration on Canada's Population*. Ottawa: Dominion Bureau of Statistics.

———.
1974 "Propensities for Intermarriage in Canada as Reflected in the Ethnic Origins of Native-Born Husbands and their Wives: 1961 and 1971." Paper presented at the Annual Meeting of the Canadian Sociology and Anthropology Association. August, 1974. Toronto.

Kalbach, Warren E.
1983   "Propensities for Intermarriage in Canada as Reflected in Ethnic Origins of Husbands and their Wives 1961-1971." In K. Ishwaran, ed., *Marriage and Divorce in Canada*. Toronto: Methuen.

Kalbach, Warren E., and Wayne McVey.
1979   *The Demographic Bases of Canadian Society*. Second ed. Toronto: Macmillan.

Kalbach, Warren E., and Madeline A. Richard.
1986   "Ethnic Intermarriage and the Changing Canadian Family." Paper presented at the Federation of Canadian Demographers' Colloquium, "The Family in Crisis: A Population Crisis?" Ottawa: University of Ottawa.

Kallen, Evelyn.
1976   "Family Life Styles and Jewish Culture." In K. Ishwaran, ed., *The Canadian Family*. Revised ed. Toronto: Holt, Rinehart and Winston.

Kamerman, Sheila B., and Alfred Kahn, eds.
1978   *Family Policy: Government and Families in Fourteen Countries*. New York: Columbia University Press.

Kanter, Rosabeth Moss.
1985   "The New Utopian Vision." In L. Cargan, ed., *Marriage and the Family: Coping With Change*. Belmont, CA: 347-354.

Katz, Sidney.
1986   "Blame Mother." *Chatelaine* 59(July):59, 110-112.

Kay, Herma Hill.
1970   "A Family Court: 'The California Proposal.'" In P. Bohannan, ed., *Divorce and After*. Garden City, NY: Doubleday.

Keller, J., S.S. Elliott, and E. Gunberg.
1982   "Premarital Sexual Intercourse Among Single College Students." *Sex Roles* 8:21-32.

Kennedy, Leslie W., and Dennis W. Stokes.
1982   "Extended Family Support and the High Cost of Renting." *Journal of Marriage and the Family* 44.

Kinsey, Alfred C., and Paul Gebhard.
1953   *Sexual Behavior in the Human Female*. Philadelphia: W.B. Saunders.

Kinsey, Alfred C., Wardell Pomeroy, and Clyde E. Martin.
1948   *Sexual Behavior in the Human Male*. Philadelphia: W.B. Saunders.

Kirk, H. David.
1985   *Adoptive Kinship*. Brentwood Bay, BC: Ben-Simon Publishers.

Kirkendall, Lester A.
1961   *Premarital Intercourse and Interpersonal Relationships*. New York: The Julian Press.

Kome, Penney.
1982   *Somebody Has To Do It: Whose Work is Housework*. Toronto: McClelland and Stewart.

Kome, Penney.
1983 *The Taking of Twenty-Eight: Women Challenge the Constitution*. Toronto: The Women's Press.

Kralt, John.
1977 *Ethnic Origins of Canadians*. Ottawa: Census of Canada, Profile Studies, Demographic Characteristics. Bulletin 5. Catalogue 99-790:1-9.

Kurokawa, Minako.
1971 "Mennonite Children in Waterloo County." In John L. Elliot, ed., *Immigrant Groups*. Vol. 2. Scarborough: Prentice-Hall.

Kuypers, Joseph, and Vern Bengtson.
1973 "Social Breakdown and Competence: A Model of Normal Aging." *Human Development* 16:181-201.

Labour Canada.
1986 *When I Grow Up: Career Expectations and Aspirations of Canadian Schoolchildren*. Ottawa: Women's Bureau.

Labour Canada.
1986 *Women in the Labour Force*. 1985-1986 Edition. Ottawa: Minister of Supply and Services.

Lachapelle R., and J. Henripin.
1982 *The Demolinguistic Situation in Canada: Past Trends and Future Prospects*. Montreal: The Institute for Research and Public Policy.

Laing, R.D.
1971 *The Politics of the Family and Other Essays*. New York: Pantheon Books.

Laing, R.D. and A. Esterson.
1964 *Sanity, Madness and the Family*. London: Tavistock.

Lambert, Ronald D.
1971 *Sex Role Imagery in Children: Social Origins of Mind*. Royal Commission on the Status of Women in Canada. Study 6. Ottawa: Information Canada.

Lambert, Wallace E.
1981 "Social Influences on the Child's Development of an Identity." In Robert C. Gardner and Rudolf Kalin, eds., *A Canadian Social Psychology of Ethnic Relations*. Toronto: Methuen, 57-75.

Lambert, Wallace E., Josiane F. Hamers, and Nancy Frasure-Smith.
1980 *Child-Rearing Values: A Cross-National Study*. New York: Praeger.

Land, Hilary, and Roy Parker.
1978 "United Kingdom." In Sheila B. Kamerman and Alfred J. Kahn, eds., *Family Policy: Government and Families in Fourteen Countries*. New York: Columbia University Press, 331-366.

Landsberg, Michele.
1982 *Women and Children First*. Markham: Penguin.

Larson, Lyle E.
1976 *The Canadian Family in Comparative Perspective*. Scarborough: Prentice-Hall.

Lasch, Christopher.
1977   *Haven in a Heartless World: The Family Besieged.* New York: Basic.

Laslett, Peter.
1976   "Societal Development and Aging." In Robert Binstock and Ethel Shanas, eds., *Handbook on Aging and the Social Sciences.* New York: Van Nostrand Reinhold, 87-116.

Latowsky (Kallen), Evelyn.
1971   "The Family Life Styles and Jewish Culture." In K. Ishwaran, ed., *The Canadian Family.* Toronto: Holt, Rinehart and Winston.

Lauer, Jeanette, and Robert Lauer.
1985   "Marriages Made to Last." *Psychology Today.* June:22-26.

Laws, Judith Long.
1971   "A Feminist Review of the Marital Adjustment Literature." *Journal of Marriage and the Family* 33:483-516.

Lee, John.
1973   *The Colours of Love.* Toronto: New Press.

———.
1975   "The Romantic Heresy." *Canadian Review of Anthropology and Sociology* 12(4):514-528.

LeMasters, E.E., and John DeFrain.
1983   *Parents in Contemporary America.* Homewood, IL: Dorsey Press.

Leslie, G.R., and Korman S.
1985   *The Family in Social Context.* Toronto: Oxford University Press.

Levinger, George.
1976   "A Social Psychological Perspective on Marital Dissolution." *Journal of Social Issues* 32(1):21-47.

Lewin, Bo.
1982   "The Adolescent Boy and Girl: First and Other Early Experience with Intercourse from a Representative Sample of Swedish School Adolescents." *Archives of Sexual Behavior* 11:417-428.

Lewis, Robert A., and Marvin B. Sussman, eds.
1986   *Men's Changing Roles in the Family.* New York: Haworth.

Libby, R.W.
1977   "Creative Singlehood as a Sexual Life Style: Beyond Marriage as a Rite of Passage." In R.W. Libby and R.N. Whitehurst, eds., *Marriage and Alternatives: Exploring Intimate Relationships.* Glenview, IL: Scot, Foresman.

Lindemann, C.
1974   *Birth Control and Unmarried Women.* New York: Springer.

Lipman, Aaron, and Charles Longino.
1983   "Mother is Alone Now: Sons and Daughters of Married and Widowed Mothers." Paper presented at the annual meeting of the Gerontological Society of America. San Francisco.

Lipman-Blumen, Jean.
1984 *Gender Roles and Power.* Englewood Cliffs, NJ: Prentice-Hall.

Little, Jean.
1984 *Mama's Going to Buy You a Mockingbird.* Markham: Penguin.

Litwak, Eugene.
1960a "Geographic Mobility and Extended Family Cohesion." *American Sociological Review* 25:385-394.

———.
1960b "Occupational Mobility and Extended Family Cohesion." *American Sociological Review* 29.

———.
1960c "Use of Extended Family Group in Achievement of Social Goals: Some Policy Implications." *Social Problems* 7.

———.
1985 *Helping the Elderly: The Complementary Roles of Informal Networks and Formal Systems.* New York: The Guilford Press.

Lopata, Helena.
1975 "Support Systems of Elderly Urbanites: Chicago of the 1970's." *The Gerontologist* 15:35-41.

———.
1978 "Contributions of Extended Families to the Support Systems of Metropolitan Area Widows: Limitations of the Modified Kin Network." *Journal of Marriage and the Family* 40(2):355-364.

Lowe, Graham.
1986 "Women, Work and the Office: The Feminization of Clerical Occupations in Canada, 1901-1931." In Veronica Strong-Boag and Anita Clair Fellman, eds., *Rethinking Canada.* Toronto: Copp Clark Pitman.

Lupri, Eugen, and Donald L. Mills.
1983 "The Changing Roles of Canadian Women in Family and Work: An Overview." In Eugen Lupri, ed., *The Changing Roles of Women in Family and Society: A Cross-Cultural Comparison.* Leiden, The Netherlands: E.J. Brill, 43-77.

———.
1987 "The Household Division of Labour in Young Dual-Earner Couples: The Case of Canada." *International Review of Sociology* 23.

Lupri, Eugen, and James Frideres.
1981 "The Quality of Marriage and the Passage of Time." *Canadian Journal of Sociology* 6:283-305.

Luxton, Meg.
1980 *More Than a Labour of Love: Three Generations of Women's Work in the Home.* Toronto: The Women's Press.

———.
1983 "Two Hands for the Clock: Changing Patterns in the Gendered Division of Labour in the Home." *Studies in Political Economy* 12(Fall):27-44.

Mackie, Marlene.
1983 *Exploring Gender Relations.* Toronto: Butterworths.

———.
1986 "Socialization." In Robert Hagedorn, ed., *Sociology.* Third ed. Toronto: Holt, Rinehart and Winston, 63-97.

———.
1987 *Constructing Women and Men: Gender Socialization.* Toronto: Holt, Rinehart and Winston.

Mackie, Marlene, and Merlin B. Brinkerhoff.
1986 "A Crack in the Looking Glass: The Enigma of Female Self-Esteem." Unpublished manuscript. Calgary: University of Calgary.

Macklin, Eleanor.
1980 "Non-Traditional Family Forms: A Decade of Research." *Journal of Marriage and the Family* 42 (4):905-922.

MacLeod, Linda.
1980 *Wife Battering in Canada: The Vicious Circle.* Ottawa: Minister of Supply and Services for the Canadian Advisory Council on the Status of Women.

Mann, W.E.
1967 "Canadian Trends in Premarital Behavior." Bulletin 198. Ottawa: The Council for Social Service.

———.
1968 "Non-Conformist Sexual Behavior on the Canadian Campus." In W.E. Mann, ed., *Deviant Behavior in Canada.* Toronto: Social Science Publishers, 300-309.

———.
1970 "Sex at York University." In W.E. Mann, ed., *The Underside of Toronto.* Toronto: McClelland and Stewart, 158-174.

Mannheim, Karl.
1952 "The Sociological Problem of Generations." *Essays on the Sociology of Knowledge.* London: Routledge and Kegan Paul.

Maranell, Gary M., Richard A. Dodder, and David F. Mitchell.
1970 "Social Class and Premarital Permissiveness: A Subsequent Test." *Journal of Marriage and the Family* 32 (February):85-88.

Marchak, Patricia.
1985 "Canadian Political Economy." *Canadian Review of Sociology and Anthropology* 22:673-709.

Maroney, Heather, and Meg Luxton.
1987 "From Feminism and Political Economy to Feminist Political Economy." In Heather Maroney and Meg Luxton, eds., *Feminist and Political Economy.* Toronto: Methuen, 5-28.

Marotz-Baden, R., G.R. Adams, N. Beuche, B. Munro, and G. Munro.
1979 "Family Form or Family Process? Reconsidering the Deficit Family Model Approach," *Family Coordinator* 28:5-14.

Marshall, Victor, Carolyn Rosenthal, and Jane Synge.
1981   "The Family as a Health Organization for the Elderly." Paper presented at the annual meeting of the Society for the Study of Social Problems, Toronto.

Masters, William H., and Virginia E. Johnson.
1966   *Human Sexual Response.* Boston: Little, Brown.

————.
1970   *Human Sexual Inadequacy.* Boston: Little, Brown.

Masters, W., V. Johnson, and R.C. Kolodny.
1985   *Sex and Human Loving.* Boston: Little, Brown.

Mathews, Ralph, and Ann-Martin Matthews.
1986   "Infertility and Involuntary Childlessness: The Transition to Non-Parenthood." *Journal of Marriage and the Family* 48.

Matthews, Anne Martin.
1987   "Widowhood as an Expectable Life Event." In Victor Marshall, ed., *Aging in Canada.* Second ed. Markham: Fitzhenry & Whiteside, 343-366.

Matthiasson, John S.
1980   "The Inuit Family: Past, Present, and Future." In K. Ishwaran, ed., *Canadian Families: Ethnic Variations.* Toronto: McGraw-Hill Ryerson.

Maxwell, Robert.
1975   *Health Care: The Growing Dilemma.* New York: McKinsey & Co.

Maykovich, Minako Kurokawa.
1975   "Ethnic Variation in Success Value." In Robert M. Pike and Elizabeth Zureik, eds., *Socialization and Values in Canadian Society,* vol. 2. Toronto: Macmillan, The Carleton Library.

————.
1976   "Alienation and Mental Health of Mennonites in Waterloo County." In K. Ishwaran, ed., *The Canadian Family.* Revised ed. Toronto: Holt, Rinehart and Winston.

Maynard, Fredelle.
1985   *The Child Care Crisis.* Markham: Penguin.

Maynard, Rona.
1984   "Divorced Dads: How Can We Make Them Pay Child Support?" *Chatelaine* 57 (May):65, 154, 156, 158, 160-162, 166.

McCrie, Iris.
1986   "The Poverty of Children who Bear Children." Winnipeg: unpublished paper.

McFarlane, Bruce A.
1975   "Married Life and Adaptations to a Professional Role: Married Women Dentists in Canada." In S.P. Wakil, ed., *Marriage, Family and Society.* Toronto: Butterworths, 359-366.

McKeown, Thomas.
1979   *The Role of Medicine.* Princeton, NJ: Princeton University Press.

McKie, D.C., B. Prentice, and P. Reed.
1983 *Divorce: Law and the Family in Canada.* Ottawa: Minister of Supply and Services.

McKinlay, John, and Sonja McKinlay.
1977 "The Questionable Contribution of Medical Measures to the Decline of Mortality in the United States in the Twentieth Century." *Milbank Memorial Fund Quarterly.* Summer.

McLanahan, Sara, and Julia Adams.
1987 "Parenthood and Psychological Well-being." *Annual Review of Sociology* 13.

McLaren, Arlene T.
1983 "Holier than Whom? Problems and Progress in Research on Women and the Family in Northern Resource Communities." Paper presented to the Canadian Research Institute for the Advancement of Women, Vancouver.

McPherson, Barry.
1983 *Aging as a Social Process.* Toronto: Butterworths.

McRoberts, Hugh A.
1985 "Mobility and Attainment in Canada: The Effects of Origin." In Monica Boyd et al., *Ascription and Achievement: Studies in Mobility and Status Attainment in Canada.* Ottawa: Carleton University Press, 67-100.

McVey, Wayne, and Barrie W. Robinson.
1981 "Separation in Canada: New insights Concerning Marital Dissolution." *Canadian Journal of Sociology* 6:353-366.

Meissner, Martin, Elizabeth W. Humphreys, Scott M. Meis, and William J. Scheu.
1975 "No Exit for Wives: Sexual Division of Labour and the Culmination of Household Demands." *The Canadian Review of Sociology and Anthropology* 12(4):424-39.

Messinger, Lillian.
1984 *Remarriage: A Family Affair.* New York: Plenum Press.

Miall, Charlene E.
1985 "Perceptions of Informal Sanctioning and the Stigma of Involuntary Childlessness." *Deviant Behavior* 6:383-403.

Michelson, William.
1985 *From Sun to Sun: Daily Obligations and Community Structure in the Lives of Employed Women and their Families.* Totawa, NJ: Rowman and Allanheld.

Middendorp, C.P., W. Brinkman, and W. Koomen.
1970 "Determinants of Premarital Sexual Permissiveness: A Secondary Analysis." *Journal of Marriage and the Family* 32 (August):369-379.

Miles, Angela.
1985 "Economism and Feminism: Hidden in the Household. A Comment on the Domestic Labour Debate." In Pat Armstrong, Hugh Armstrong, Patricia Connelly and Angela Miles, *Feminist Marxism or Marxist Feminism.* Toronto: Garamond, 39-51.

Mindel, Charles H., and Robert W. Habenstein.
1976   *Ethnic Families in America: Patterns and Variations.* New York: Elsevier.

Mirande, Alfred M.
1968   "Reference Group Theory and Adolescent Sexual Behavior." *Journal of Marriage and the Family* 30:572-577.

Montreal Health Press.
1980   *A Book About Birth Control.* Montreal: Author.

Moreux, Colette.
1973   "The French Canadian Family." In M. Stephenson, ed., *Women in Canada.* Toronto: General.

Morgan, D.H.J.
1975   *Social Theory and the Family.* London: Routledge and Kegan Paul.

Moroney, Robert M.
1986   *Shared Responsibility: Families and Social Policy.* New York: Aldine.

Moscovitch, Allan, and Jim Albert, eds.
1987   *The Benevolent State: The Growth of Welfare in Canada.* Toronto: Garamond.

Mullins, Nicholas.
1973   *Theories and Theory Groups in Contemporary American Sociology.* New York: Harper.

Murdock, George P.
1949   *Social Structure.* New York: The Free Press.

Nakamura, Alice, and Masao Nakamura.
1985   "A Survey of Research on the Work Behaviour of Canadian Women." In W. Craig Riddell, ed., *Work and Pay: The Canadian Labour Market.* Toronto: University of Toronto Press in cooperation with the Royal Commission on the Economic Union and Development Prospects for Canada, 171-218.

Nass, G.D., and G.W. McDonald.
1982   *Marriage and the Family.* Don Mills: Addison-Wesley.

National Centre for Health Statistics.
1986   "Births, Marriages, Divorces, and Deaths for March 1986." *NCHS Monthly Vital Statistics Report* 35 (3):1.

National Council of Welfare
1985   *Giving and Taking: The May 1985 Budget and the Poor.* Ottawa.

Nelsen, Randle W.
1985   "The End of Childhood: Technological Change, Parenting and the School." *Canadian Review of Sociology and Anthropology* 22.

Nelson, Geoff.
1985   "Family Adaptation Following Marital Separation/Divorce: A Literature Review." In B. Schlesinger, ed., *The One-parent Family in the 1980s.* Toronto: University of Toronto Press.

Nett, Emily.
1978 "A Research Note: On Reviewing the Canadian Literature on Marital Interaction, 1967-1977." *Journal of Comparative Family Studies* 9:373-383.

———.
1981 "Canadian Families in Social-Historical Perspective." *Canadian Journal of Sociology* 6:239-260.

———.
1986 "The Family." In Robert Hagedorn, ed., *Sociology*. Third ed. Toronto: Holt, Rinehart and Winston, 343-379.

Noelker, Linda, and S. Walter Poulshock.
1982 *The Effects on Families of Caring for Impaired Elderly in Residence*. Final Report. Washington, DC: U.S. Department of Health and Human Services, Administration on Aging.

Norris, Joan.
1987 "Psychological Processes in the Development of Late-Life Social Identity." In Victor Marshall, ed., *Aging in Canada*. Markham: Fitzhenry & Whiteside.

Northcott, Herbert C.
1983 "Who Stays Home? Working Parents and Sick Children." *International Journal of Women's Studies* 6:387-394.

Nye, Ivan F., and Felix M. Berardo.
1981 *Emerging Conceptual Frameworks in Family Analysis*. New York: Praeger.

O'Brien, Mary.
1979 "Reproducing Marxist Man." In Lorenne Clark and Lynda Lange, eds., *The Sexism of Social and Political Theory*. Toronto: University of Toronto Press, 99-116.

———.
1981 *The Politics of Reproduction*. Boston: Routledge and Kegan Paul.

O'Bryan, K.G., J.G. Reitz, and O.M. Kuplowska.
1976 *Non-Official Languages: A Study of Canadian Multiculturalism*. Ottawa: Minister of Supply and Services.

Oakley, Ann.
1974 *The Sociology of Housework*. London: Martin Robertson.

Ornstein, Michael.
1983 *Accounting for Gender Differentials in Job Income in Canada: Results from a 1981 Survey*. Series A (*Equality in the Workplace*): No. 2. Ottawa: Labour Canada.

Osterreich, Helgi.
1976 "Geographic Mobility and Kinship: A Canadian Example." In K. Ishwaran, ed., *The Canadian Family*. Toronto: Holt, Rinehart and Winston (first published in 1966).

Palmore, Erdman, and Kenneth Manton.
1973 "Ageism Compared to Racism and Sexism." *Journal of Gerontology* 28:363-369.

Papper, Ann.
1983 "The One and Only." *Quest* (December):38-42.

Park, Robert.
1928 "Human Migration and Marginal Man." *American Journal of Sociology* 33.

Parr, Joy, ed.
1982 *Childhood and Family in Canadian History.* Toronto: McClelland and Stewart.

Parsons, Talcott.
1943 "The Kinship System of the Contemporary United States." *American Anthropologist* 45.

Perlman, D.
1973 "The Sexual Standards of Canadian University Students." In D. Koulack and D. Perlman, eds., *Readings in Social Psychology: Focus on Canada.* Toronto: Wiley, 139-159.

Peter, Karl.
1987 *The Dynamics of Hutterite Society: An Analytical Approach.* Edmonton: University of Alberta Press.

Peters, John.
1984 "Cultural Variations in Family Structure." In Maureen Baker, ed., *The Family: Changing Trends in Canada.* Toronto: McGraw-Hill Ryerson, 63-84.

Piddington, Ralph.
1971 "A Study of French Canadian Kinship." In K. Ishwaran, ed., *The Canadian Family.* Toronto: Holt, Rinehart and Winston.

———.
1973 "Kinship Network among the French-Canadians." In G.L. Gold and Marc Adelard Tremblay, eds., *Communities and Culture in French-Canada.* Toronto: Holt, Rinehart and Winston.

Pike, R.
1975 "Legal Access and the Incidence of Divorce in Canada: A Sociohistorical Analysis." *Canadian Review of Sociology and Anthropology* 12:115-133.

Pineo, Peter C.
1976 "The Extended Family in Working Class Areas in Hamilton." In K. Ishwaran, ed., *The Canadian Family.* Toronto: Holt, Rinehart and Winston.

Pineo, Peter C., and E. Dianne Looker.
1983 "Class and Conformity in the Canadian Setting." *Canadian Journal of Sociology* 8:293-317.

Pogrebin, Letty C.
1983 "Do Americans Hate Children?" *Ms.* 12 (November):47-50, 126-127.

Ponting, J. Rick.
1986 "Canadian Gender Role Attitudes." Unpublished.

Pool, Ian, and Maureen Moore.
1986 *Lone Parenthood: Characteristics and Determinants.* Ottawa: Minister of Supply and Services.

Porter, John.
1965   *The Vertical Mosaic: An Analysis of Social Class and Power in Canada.*
        Toronto: University of Toronto Press.

Postman, Neil.
1982   *The Disappearance of Childhood.* New York: Dell.

Price, John A.
1985   "Canadian Ethnic Families." In K. Ishwaran, ed., *The Canadian Family.*
        Toronto: Holt, Rinehart and Winston.

Pryor, Edward T.
1984   "Canadian Husband-Wife Families: Labour Force Participation and Income
        Trends 1971-1981." *The Labour Force,* May 1984 (Cat. no. 71-001):93-109.

Queen, Stuart A., and Robert W. Habenstein.
1974   *The Family in Various Cultures.* New York: J.B. Lippincott.

Quindlen, Anna.
1987   "Baby Craving." *Life* 10 (June).

Radecki, Henry.
1970   *Polish-Canadian, Canadian-Polish, or Canadian?* Toronto: York Univer-
        sity, Mimeograph.

_____.
1976   *Polish Groups in Canada.* Toronto: McClelland and Stewart.

_____.
1980   "The Polish-Canadian Family: A Study in Historical and Contemporary
        Perspectives." In K. Ishwaran, ed., *Canadian Families: Ethnic Variations.*
        Toronto: McGraw-Hill Ryerson, 41-64.

Ramu, G.N.
1976   "Marriage and the Family in Canada." In G.N. Ramu and Stuart D. Johnson,
        eds., *Introduction to Canadian Society: Sociological Analysis.* Toronto:
        Macmillan Canada.

_____.
1977   *Family and Caste in Urban India.* Delhi: Vikas.

_____.
1983   "Courtship and Marriage." In K. Ishwaran, ed., *The Canadian Family.*
        Toronto: Gage.

_____.
1984   "Family Background and Perceived Marital Happiness: A Comparison of
        Voluntary Childless and Parental Couples." *Canadian Journal of Soci-
        ology* 9.

_____.
1985   "Voluntarily Childless and Parental Couples: A Comparison of their Life
        Styles." *Life Styles: A Journal of Changing Patterns* 7.

Ramu, G.N., and Nicholas Tavuchis.
1983   "Family in Canada or the Canadian family?" In K. Ishwaran, ed., *The Ca-
        nadian Family.* Toronto: Gage, 57-69.

Ramu, G.N., and Nicholas Tavuchis.
1986 "The Value of Children and Parenthood Among Voluntarily Childless and Parental Couples." *Journal of Comparative Family Studies* 17.

Raschke, H., and Raschke, V.J.
1979 "Family Conflict and Children's Self-concepts: A Comparison of Intact and Single-Parent Families." *Journal of Marriage and the Family* 41:367-374.

Rashid, A.
1985 *The Muslim Canadians: A Profile*. Ottawa: Minister of Supply and Services.

Reiss, Ira L.
1966 "The Sexual Renaissance in America: A Summary and Analysis." *The Journal of Social Issues* 22:123-137.

———.
1967 *The Social Context of Premarital Sexual Experience*. New York: Holt, Rinehart and Winston.

———.
1980 *Family Systems in America*. New York: Holt, Rinehart and Winston.

Reiss, Ira L., and Brent C. Miller.
1974 "A Theoretical Analysis of Heterosexual Permissiveness." Technical Report II. Minneapolis, MN: The Minnesota Family Study Center.

Reiss, Paul J.
1962 "Extended Kinship System: Correlates and Attitudes on Frequency of Interaction." *Marriage and Family Living* 24.

Richer, Stephen.
1979 "Sex-role Socialization and Early Schooling." *The Canadian Review of Sociology and Anthropology* 16:195-205.

———.
1984 "Sexual Inequality and Children's Play." *The Canadian Review of Sociology and Anthropology* 21:16-180.

Richmond, Anthony H.
1967 *Immigrant and Ethnic Groups in Metropolitan Toronto*. Toronto: Institute for Behavioral Research, York University.

Riddell, Craig W.
1985 *Work and Pay: The Canadian Labour Market*. Toronto: University of Toronto Press in cooperation with the Royal Commission on the Economic Union and Development Prospects for Canada and the Canadian Government Publishing Centre, Supply and Services Canada.

Roadburg, Alan.
1985 *Aging: Retirement, Leisure and Work in Canada*. Toronto: Methuen.

Robinson, Bryan E., and Robert L. Barret.
1986 *The Developing Father*. New York: Guilford Press.

Robinson, Patricia.
1987 *Women's Work Interruptions: Results from the 1984 Family History Survey*. Ottawa: Minister of Supply and Services.

Rodman, Hyman, Susan A. Lewis, and Baralyn B. Griffith.
1984   *The Sexual Rights of Adolescents.* New York: Columbia University Press.

Rogers, Judy.
1986   *Attitudes Towards Alternative Work Arrangements—A Qualitative Assessment Among Employers in Metropolitan Toronto.* Toronto: Social Planning Council of Metropolitan Toronto.

Romanuic, A.
1984   *Current Demographic Analysis. Fertility in Canada: From Baby Boom to Baby Bust.* Ottawa: Minister of Supply and Services. Cat. no. 91-524E.

Roos, Noralou, Evelyn Shapiro, and Leslie Roos.
1984   "Aging and the Demand for Health Services: Which Aged and Whose Demand?" *The Gerontologist* 24:31-36.

Rose, Arnold.
1968   "The Subculture of Aging: A Framework for Research in Social Gerontology." In Bernice Neugarten, ed., *Middle Age and Aging.* Chicago: University of Chicago Press, 29-34.

Rosenthal, Carolyn.
1985   "Kinkeeping in the Family Division of Labour." *Journal of Marriage and the Family* 47.

————.
1987   "Aging and Intergenerational Relations in Canada." In Victor Marshall, ed., *Aging in Canada.* Markham: Fitzhenry & Whiteside, 311-342.

Rosenthal, Carolyn J., and Victor W. Marshall.
1986   "The Head of the Family: Social Meaning and Structural Variability." *The Canadian Journal of Sociology* 11:183-198.

Ryant , Joseph C., et al.
1975   *A Review of Child Welfare Policies, Programs, and Services in Manitoba.* Winnipeg: The Queen's Printer.

Schlesinger, Benjamin.
1971   "Remarriage as Family Reorganization for Divorced Persons." In K. Ishwaran, ed., *The Canadian Family.* Toronto: Holt, Rinehart and Winston, 377-395.

————.
1979   *Families: Canada.* Montreal: McGraw-Hill Ryerson.

————.
1983   "Living in One-Parent Families: The Children's Perspective." In K. Ishwaran, ed., *The Canadian Family.* Toronto: Gage, 331-339.

————.
1985   "The Single Teen-age Canadian Mother in the 1980s: A Review." In Benjamin Schlesinger, ed., *The One-Parent Family in the 1980s.* Toronto: University of Toronto Press, 35-56.

Schnaiberg, Allan, and Shelley Goldenberg.
1986   "From Empty Nest to Crowded Nest: Some Contradictions in the Return-

ing-Young-Adult Syndrome." Paper presented to the American Sociological Association, New York.

Schneider, David M.
1968 *American Kinship: A Cultural Account.* Englewood Cliffs, NJ: Prentice-Hall.

Seccombe, Wally.
1974 "The Housewife and her Labour under Capitalism." *New Left Review* 83:3-24.

————.
1980 "Domestic Labour and the Working-Class Household." In Bonnie Fox, ed., *Hidden in the Household.* Toronto: The Women's Press, 25-99.

————.
1986a "Marxism and Demography: Household Forms and Fertility Regimes in the Western European Transition." In James Dickinson and Bob Russell, eds., *Family, Economy and State.* Toronto: Garamond, 23-55.

————.
1986b "Reflections on the Domestic Labour Debate and Prospects for Marxist-Feminist Synthesis." In Roberta Hamilton and Michele Barrett, eds., *The Politics of Diversity.* London: Verso, 192-207.

Seeley, John, E.A. Sim, and E.W. Loosley.
1956 *Crestwood Heights: A Study of the Culture of Suburban Life.* New York: John Wiley.

Shanas, Ethel, and Gordon Streib.
1965 *Social Structure and the Family.* Englewood Cliffs, NJ: Prentice-Hall.

Shevky, E., and W. Bell.
1955 *Social Area Analysis: Theory Illustrative Application Procedures.* Stanford, CA: Stanford University Press.

Shibutani, Tamotsu, and Kian M. Kwan.
1965 *Ethnic Stratification: A Comparative Approach.* New York: Macmillan.

Shkilnyk, Anastasia M.
1985 *A Poison Stronger Than Love: The Destruction of an Ojibwa Community.* New Haven, CT: Yale University Press.

Simmel, George.
1950 *The Sociology of George Simmel.* New York: The Free Press.

Singer, Benjamin D.
1986 *Advertising & Society.* Don Mills: Addison-Wesley.

Skipper, James K., Jr., and Gilbert Nass.
1966 "Dating Behaviour: A Framework for Analysis and Illustration." *Journal of Marriage and the Family* 28:412-420.

Skolnick, Arlene.
1983 *The Intimate Environment.* Third ed. Boston: Little, Brown.

Smigel, E.O., and R. Seidon.
1968 "Decline and Fall of the Double Standard." *Annals of the American Academy of Political and Social Science,* 6-17.

Smith, C.W.
1985 "Uncle Dad." *Esquire* 103 (March):73-85.

Smith, D.S. and M.S. Hindus.
1975 "Premarital Pregnancy in America 1640-1971: An Overview and Interpretation." *Journal of Interdisciplinary History* 4:537-570.

Smith, Dorothy E.
1973 "Women, the Family and Corporate Capitalism." In Marylee Stephenson, ed., *Women in Canada*. Toronto: New Press, 2-35.

———.
1981 "Women's Inequality and the Family." In Allan Moscovitch and Glenn Drover, eds., *Inequality*. Toronto: University of Toronto Press, 156-195.

———.
1984 "The Renaissance of Women." In Ursula Martius Franklin et al., *Knowledge Reconsidered: A Feminist Overview*. Ottawa: Canadian Research Institute for the Advancement of Women, 1-14.

———.
1985 "Women, Class and Family." In Varda Burstyn and Dorothy Smith, *Women, Class, Family and the State*. Toronto: Garamond, 1-44.

Spencer, Metta.
1985 *Foundations of Modern Sociology*. Canadian fourth ed., Scarborough: Prentice-Hall.

Spiro, Melford.
1956 *Kibbutz: A Venture in Utopia*. New York: Shocken.

Statistics Canada.
1979 *Canada's Families*. Ottawa: Minister of Supply and Services.

———.
1980 *Survey of Volunteer Workers*. Ottawa: Minister of Supply and Services.

———.
1982 *1981 Census of Canada*. Ottawa: Minister of Supply and Services.

———.
1982 "Initial Results from the 1981 Survey of Child Care Arrangements." *Labour Force Survey Research Paper Number 31*. Ottawa: Minister of Supply and Services.

———.
1983 *Fact Book on Aging in Canada*. Ottawa: Minister of Supply and Services.

———.
1983 *Historical Statistics of Canada*. Ottawa: Minister of Supply and Services. Cat. no. CS11-516E.

———.
1984 *The Elderly in Canada*. Ottawa: Minister of Supply and Services.

———.
1984 *Canada's One-Parent Families*. Ottawa: Minister of Supply and Services.

Statistics Canada.
1984 *Women in the Work World*. Ottawa: Minister of Supply and Services.

———.
1984 *Living Alone*. Ottawa: Minister of Supply and Services.

———.
1984 *Canada's Immigrants*. Ottawa: Minister of Supply and Services.

———.
1985 *Births and Deaths, 1983 and 1984*. Ottawa: Minister of Supply and Services.

———.
1985 *Family Expenditures in Canada*. Ottawa: Minister of Supply and Services.

———.
1985 *Women in Canada: A Statistical Report*. Ottawa: Minister of Supply and Services.

———.
1985 "Marriages and Divorces." *Vital Statistics*, vol. II. Ottawa: Minister of Supply and Services.

———.
1985 *Informat* (March 2). Ottawa: Minister of Supply and Services.

———.
1985 *The Labour Force*. Ottawa: Minister of Supply and Services. January. Cat. no. 71-001.

———.
1986 *Population Projections for Canada, Provinces and Territories, 1984-2006*. Ottawa: Minister of Supply and Services.

———.
1986 *Marriage and Divorce, Vital Statistics, Vol. II, 1985* Ottawa: Minister of Supply and Services.

———.
1987 "Report on the Demographic Situation in Canada, 1986." *Current Demographic Analysis*, vol. 2. Ottawa: Minister of Supply and Services.

Status of Women Canada.
1986 *Report of the Task Force on Child Care*. Ottawa: Minister of Supply and Services. Cat. no. SW41-1/1986E.

Stein, Maurice R.
1964 *The Eclipse of Community*. New York: Harper and Row.

Stephens, William N.
1963 *The Family in Cross-Cultural Perspective*. New York: Holt, Rinehart and Winston.

Stone, Lawrence.
1979 *The Family, Sex, and Marriage in England 1500-1800*. New York: Harper and Row.

Strasser, Susan.
1982 *Never Done*. New York: Pantheon.

Stratton, J.R., and S.P. Spitzer.
1967 "Sexual Permissiveness and Self-Evaluation: A Question of Substance and a Question of Method." *Journal of Marriage and the Family* 29:434-441.

Strong-Boag, Veronica.
1982 "Intruders in the Nursery: Child Care Professionals Reshape the Years One to Five, 1920-1940." In Joy Parr, ed., *Childhood and Family in Canadian History*. Toronto: McClelland and Stewart, 160-178.

———.
1985 "Discovering the Home: The Last 150 Years of Domestic Work in Canada." In Paula Bourne, ed., *Women's Paid and Unpaid Work*. Toronto: New Hogtown Press, 35-60.

Sturino, Franc.
1980 "Family and Kin Cohesion Among Southern Italian Immigrants." In K. Ishwaran, ed., *Canadian Families: Ethnic Variations*. Toronto: McGraw-Hill Ryerson.

Sullivan, Teresa A.
1983 "Family Morality and Family Mortality: Speculation on the Demographic Transition." In William V. D'Antonio and Joan Aldous, eds., *Families and Religions*. Beverly Hills, CA: Sage, 49-66.

Suransky, Valerie P.
1982 *The Erosion of Childhood*. Chicago: University of Chicago Press.

Sussman, Marvin B.
1976 "The Family Life of Old People." In Robert Binstock and Ethel Shanas, eds., *Handbook of Aging and the Social Sciences*. New York: Van Nostrand Reinhold, 218-243.

———.
1953 "The Help Pattern in the Middle Class Family." *American Sociological Review* 18.

———.
1959 "Isolated Nuclear Family: Fact or Fiction." *Social Problems* 6.

———.
1965 "Relationships of Adult Children with their Parents in the United States." In E. Shanas and Gordon Streib, eds., *Social Structure and the Family*. Englewood Cliffs, NJ: Prentice-Hall.

Sussman, Marvin B., and Lee Burchinal.
1962 "Parental Aid to Married Children: Implications for Family Functions," *Marriage and Family Living* 24.

Syme, S. Leonard, and Lisa Berkman.
1981 "Social Class, Susceptibility and Sickness." In Peter Conrad and Rochelle Kern, eds., *The Sociology of Health and Illness: Critical Perspectives*. New York: St. Martin's Press, 35-44.

Synnott, Anthony.
1983 "Little Angels, Little Devils: A Sociology of Children." *The Canadian Review of Sociology and Anthropology* 20:79-95.

Talese, Gay.
1980   *Thy Neighbor's Wife*, Garden City, NY: Doubleday.

Tausig, Christine.
1984   "Class of 84: They Don't Have Dreams." *University Affairs* (March):2-3.

Tavuchis, Nicholas.
1972   *Family and Mobility Among Greek Americans*. Athens: National Center of Research.

_____.
1976   "Mobility and Family: Problems and Prospects." *Cornell Journal of Social Relations* 11.

Taylor, G. Rattray.
1959   *Sex in History*. London: Thames and Hudson.

Teevan, James J., Jr.
1972   "Reference Groups and Premarital Sexual Behavior." *Journal of Marriage and the Family* 34:283-291.

Thorne, Barrie.
1982   "Feminist Rethinking of the Family." In Barrie Thorne and Marilyn Yalom, eds., *Rethinking the Family*. New York: Longman, 1-24.

Tomasson, Richard F.
1970   *Sweden: Prototype of Modern Society*. New York: Random House.

Townson, Monica.
1983   *Equality in the Workplace: A National System of Fully-Paid Parental Leave for Canada. Policy Choices, Costs and Funding Mechanisms*. Ottawa: Supply and Services for Labour Canada.

Tremblay, Marc-Adelard, and Marc Laplante.
1971   *Famille et Parente en Acadie*. Ottawa: Musée National du Canada.

_____.
1973   "Authority Models in the French-Canadian Family." In Gerald L. Gold and Marc-Adelard Tremblay, eds., *Communities and Culture in French Canada*. Toronto: Holt, Rinehart and Winston.

Trost, Jan.
1977   "The Family Life Cycle: A Problematic Concept." In Jean Cuisenier, ed., *The Family Life Cycle in European Societies*. The Hague: Mouton, 467-481.

Trovato, Frank.
1986   "Change in the Marriage Rate Among Canadian Women, 1921-25 to 1981-85." Paper presented at the conference on "Family Crisis." Ottawa: University of Ottawa, November 28-29.

Turkle, Sherry.
1984   *The Second Self: Computers and the Human Spirit*. New York: Simon and Schuster.

U.S. Bureau of the Census.
1984a   "Marital Status and Living Arrangements: March 1983." Washington, DC: U.S. Government Printing Office, Series P-20, No. 389, 6.

U.S. Bureau of the Census.
1984b   "Births, Deaths, Marriages, Divorces—Fertility Rate." *Statistical Abstracts of the United States 1985*. Washington, DC: U.S. Government Printing Office, 57.

Udry, J. Richards.
1974   *The Social Context of Marriage*. Toronto: J.B. Lippincott.

Ursel, E. Jane.
1984   "Toward a Theory of Reproduction." *Contemporary Crises* 8:265-292.

———.
1986   "The State and the Maintenance of Patriarchy: A Case Study of Family, Labour and Welfare Legislation in Canada." In James Dickinson and Bob Russell, eds., *Family, Economy and State*. Toronto: Garamond, 150-191.

Valle, Frank G.
1971   "Kinship, the Family and Marriage in the Central Keewatin." In K. Ishwaran, ed., *The Canadian Family*. Toronto: Holt, Rinehart, and Winston.

Veevers, Jean.
1980   *Childless by Choice*. Toronto: Butterworths.

Vischer, E.G., and J.S. Vischer.
1979   *Step-families: A Guide to Working with Stepparents and Stepchildren*. New York: Bruner/Mazel.

Wakil, Parveez, C.M. Siddique, and F.A. Wakil.
1981   "Between Two Cultures: A Study in Socialization of Children of Immigrants." *Journal of Marriage and the Family* 43.

Wakil, S.P., and F.A. Wakil.
1975   "Campus Dating: An Exploratory Study." In S.P. Wakil, ed., *Marriage, Family and Society*. Toronto: Butterworths.

Waller, Willard.
1937   "The Rating and Dating Complex." *American Sociological Review* 2:727-735.

———.
1938   *The Family: A Dynamic Interpretation*. New York: The Dryden Press.

Wallerstein, Judith S., and Kelly, Berlin Joan.
1980   *Surviving the Breakup: How Children and Parents Cope with Divorce*. New York: Basic.

Wańkowicz, Melchior.
1973   *Three Generations*. Trans. K. Cękalska. Toronto: Canadian-Polish Research Institute in Canada.

Watson, Roy E.
1981   "The Effects of Premarital Cohabitation on Subsequent Marital Adjustment." A paper presented at the Canadian Sociology and Anthropology Annual Meetings, Halifax.

Wayne, Jack.
1986   "The Function of Social Welfare in a Capitalist Economy." In James Dick-

inson and Bob Russell, eds., *Family, Economy and State*. Toronto: Garamond, 56-84.

Weinfeld, Morton, and John J. Sigal.
1986 "The Effects of the Holocaust on Selected Socio-Political Attitudes of Adult Children of Survivors." *The Canadian Review of Sociology and Anthropology* 23:365-382.

Weiss, Robert S.
1975 *Marital Separation*. New York: Basic.

Weitzman, L.S., and R.B. Dixon
1986 "The Transformation of Legal Marriage Through No-Fault Divorce." In A. Skolnick and J. Skolnick, eds., *Family in Transition*. Fifth ed. Toronto: Little, Brown, 338-351.

Weller, Geoffrey, and Pran Manga.
1982 "The Reprivatization of Hospital and Medical Care Services: A Comparative Analysis of Canada, Britain and the United States." Revision of paper presented at the 10th World Congress of Sociology, Mexico City.

White, Julie.
1980 *Women and Unions*. Ottawa: Supply and Services for the Canadian Advisory Council on the Status of Women.

Whitehurst, R.N.
1971 "Back to the Land: The Search for Freedom and Utopia in Ontario." Unpublished. Available from the author, University of Windsor, Windsor, Ont. N9B 3P4.

Whitehurst, Robert N.
1984 "The Future of Marriage and the Nuclear Family." In Maureen Baker, ed., *The Family: Changing Trends in Canada*. Toronto: McGraw-Hill Ryerson.

Whitehurst, R.N., and G.V. Booth.
1980 *The Sexes: Changing Relationships in a Pluralistic Society*. Agincourt: Gage.

Whitehurst, Robert N. and G.R. Frisch
1974 "Sex Differences in Dating Orientations: Some Comparisons and Recent Observations." *International Journal of the Sociology of The Family* 4.

Wiebe, Paul D. and G.N. Ramu.
1971 "Marriage in India: A Content Analysis of Matrimonial Advertisements." *Man in India* 51:111-120.

Wilensky, Harold, and Charles N. Lebreaux.
1958 *Industrial Society and Social Welfare*. New York: Russell Sage Foundation.

Wilkins, Russ, and Owen Adams.
1983 *Healthfulness of Life*. Montreal: The Institute for Research on Public Policy.

Williams, John E., and Deborah L. Best.
1982 *Measuring Sex Stereotypes: A Thirty-Nation Study*. Beverly Hills, CA: Sage.

Williams, Tannis MacBeth, ed.
1986 *The Impact of Television: A Natural Experiment in Three Communities*. Orlando, FL: Academic Press.

Wilson, Elizabeth.
1977   *Women and the Welfare State*. London: Tavistock.

Wilson, G., and M. Cook, eds.
1979   *Love and Attraction*. New York: Pergamon Press.

Wilson, S.J.
1982   *Women, the Family and the Economy*. Toronto: McGraw-Hill Ryerson.

Winch, Robert.
1977   *Familial Organization*. New York: The Free Press.

Winn, Marie.
1983   *Children Without Childhood*. Markham: Penguin.

Wirth, Louis.
1938   "Urbanism as a Way of Life." *American Journal of Sociology* 44.

Young, Michael, and Peter Willmott.
1957   *Family and Kinship in East London*. New York: Penguin.

Zaretsky, Eli.
1976   *Capitalism, the Family, and Personal Life*. New York: Harper & Row.

Zelizer, Viviana A.
1981   "The Price and Value of Children: The Case of Children's Insurance."
       American Journal of Sociology 86:1036-1056.

Zureik, Elia T., and Robert M. Pike.
1975   "Preface." In Elia T. Zureik and Robert M. Pike. eds., *Socialization and
       Values in Canadian Society*. Vol. 1. Toronto: McClelland and Stewart.

Zwarun, Suzanne.
1985   "Singles Who Choose Motherhood." *Chatelaine* 58 (August):62, 92, 94-95.

AUTHOR INDEX

SUBJECT INDEX